HISTORY
and
FUTURE
of MASS
MEDIA

THE HAMPTON PRESS COMMUNICATION SERIES
Mass Communication and Journalism
Lee B. Becker, supervisory editor

forthcoming

HISTORY
and
FUTURE
of MASS
MEDIA

An Integrated
Perspective

DAVID DEMERS
Washington State University

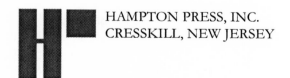

HAMPTON PRESS, INC.
CRESSKILL, NEW JERSEY

All photographs and illustrations in this book are in the public domain. The author thanks the following institutions for making them available:

The Perry-Castañeda Library at the University of Texas at Austin
Wikipedia Foundation Inc., operators of Wikipedia.com
The American Memory Collection at the Library of Congress

Cover illustration by Alexander Zhilyaev, courtesy of Fotolia.com

Other Books by the Same Author

An Interpretive Introduction to Mass Communication (Allyn & Bacon/Pearson Education, 2004)
Global Media: Menace or Messiah? (Hampton Press, 2002, revised edition)
Global Media News Reader (Marquette Books, 2003, edited)
Mass Media, Social Control and Social Change: A Macrosocial Perspective (Iowa State University Press, 1999, edited with K. Viswanath)
The Media Essays: From Local to Global (Marquette Books, 2003)
The Menace of the Corporate Newspaper: Fact or Fiction? (Iowa State University Press, 1996)
Precision Journalism: A Practical Guide (Sage Publications, 1987)
Terrorism, Globalization and Mass Communication (Marquette Books, 2003, edited)

Library of Congress Cataloging-in-Publication Data

Demers, David, 1953-
    History and future of mass media : an integrated perspective / David Demers.
        p. cm.
    Includes bibliographical references and index.
    ISBN 978-1-57273-806-5 (hardcover : alk. paper) -- ISBN 978-1-57273-807-2 (pbk. : alk. paper)
    1. Mass media--History. I. Title.
    P90.D46 2007
    302.23--dc22

                                                        2007032274

Hampton Press Inc.
23 Broadway
Cresskill, NJ 07626
www.hamptonpress.com

To scholars, professionals and citizens who
proactively defend the First Amendment and the
principles of freedom of speech and of the press

Contents

PREFACE

This monograph was written to appeal to three different types of readers.[1]

The first is social science scholars, particularly mass communication researchers and historians who are interested in seeing how social structural theory can be used to explain the past as well as predict the future of mass media. Most history books emphasize discrete events and actions rather than structural trends. They do a good job describing past events, but they are often short on explanation and rarely attempt to predict future trends. This is not surprising as most historians take their intellectual inspiration more from the humanities than the social sciences. In contrast, most of my theoretical training is in sociology, in which historical trends such as structural differentiation, rationalization, industrialization and urbanization play a central role in many theories of media and society.

This book provides a more integrated perspective. In terms of historical events, it has, by design, far less detail than one would find in a historical book.[2] However, in terms of explanatory and predictive content, this book is much more detailed, and it contains both original and secondary historical and empirical research. It employs Media System Theory to explain past trends and to make some general predictions about the future of mass media (see the "Introduction" for more details).[3] In the language of that hackneyed aphorism about the forest and trees, this book gives scholars a look at the contours of the

---

[1]A monograph is a book or work that focuses on a single subject and employs a particular theoretical perspective (i.e., in this case, a structural model of social change). A textbook, in contrast, is written specifically for a high school or college course and usually examines a wide range of perspectives or theories in a field of knowledge.

[2]I still use a traditional history textbook in my course, but the students read each chapter in this book first before reading the details in the other book.

[3]The second part of this book, which examines the future of mass media, updates and extends arguments made in my earlier book, *Global Media: Menace or Messiah* (Cresskill, NJ: Hampton Press, 1999). However, the *Global Media* book had only a very brief chapter on history of mass media, which is examined in depth in this book.

forest and ground view of the trees while traditional history books give them a closeup look at the bark, limbs and leaves.

In addition to scholars, this book was written to appeal to public policy makers, who no doubt will be most interested in the seven predictions in the last chapter. Most scholars in the social sciences — especially critical and cultural theorists and neo-Marxists — believe corporate mass media are incapable of producing information and knowledge that contribute either to democratic ideals or to decentralization of political power. They believe corporate media place profits ahead of all other goals. This book, which examines the historical and empirical evidence, shows that this position is mostly wrong.

Corporate organizations did not invent greed. And although corporate media can be criticized in absolute terms for failing to produce content that opposes power elites in favor of disadvantaged groups and peoples, empirical research and structural theory clearly show that in relative terms corporate media produce content that is more critical of the power structure and the status quo. This finding helps explain the stability and durability of capitalism itself as a social and economic institution.

The third type of reader to which this book is targeted is students in the social sciences, especially in the fields of history, mass communication, sociology and political science. This book is useful in a wide variety of upper level undergraduate and graduate-level courses, including American history, history of mass communication, seminars in mass media and society, media management courses, and political science and sociology courses.

This book is divided into three major sections. Part I examines the history of print mass media. Part II looks at the history electronic mass media. These histories, by design, are not comprehensive. They focus mainly on key changes affecting media institutions. Both agency (or individual decision making) and social structure are used to explain these changes (see "Introduction" for elaboration of this integrated approach). Part III of the book begins by presenting the neo-Marxist view of the future of mass media in capitalism. The subsequent chapters critique this model and present an alternative model for explaining the role and function of media in society. The final chapter concludes with seven predictions or trends for the future of mass media.

I am grateful to Theresa and Lee Ann, my spouse and daughter, for their patience and support during this and other book projects. I also thank Heath Campo, one of my students who caught some errors and oversights; Lee B. Becker of the University of Georgia, who has provided support for this and other projects I have developed through the years; Barbara Bernstein, publisher of Hampton Press, who, unlike other publishers in the field, is willing to publish monographs, not just textbooks; Matthew Hudelson, associate professor of mathematics at Washington State University, for assistance in developing the quadratic equation (see "Introduction") that is the foundation for the argument that structurally complex media are more vigorous editorially than their entrepreneurial counterparts; and professors Doug Underwood (University of Washington) and Douglas Blanks Hindman (Washington State University), who read the book and provided valuable feedback. I alone accept responsibility for errors or omissions.

David Demers
Associate Professor of Communication
Washington State University

INTRODUCTION

The sociohistorical theory presented in this book can be summarized in seven propositions:

1. The origins and development of mass media are largely a "by-product" of increasing industrialization and urbanization, or what sociologists often call *structural differentiation*.[1] Structural differentiation creates problems of communication and control, and mass media and other formal means of communication emerged in part to help resolve some of these problems.

2. One unintended consequence of the rise of mass media is that political power, in relative terms, generally has become less centralized in Western countries and the United States. Books, newspapers and, later, other forms of mass media helped facilitate citizen input into the political system, as well as the development of representative democracies.

3. Although mass media have helped decentralize political power, political power remains highly centralized in all societies, and mass media continue to reinforce the powerful groups and organizations in those societies. Media content supports and reinforces dominant values and institutions, and that content generally does more to

[1]This concept is also sometimes called *social differentiation* or *structural pluralism*. Structural differentiation can be defined as the process through which an institutional activity divides and becomes more specialized. The division of labor is a good example. As a business grows, the owners or managers usually create new and more specialized roles and tasks. Structural differentiation generally leads to increased interdependence among social actors, which means they depend more upon each other to achieve their goals. More information about how I define this and other terms in this book can be found in David Demers, *Dictionary of Mass Communication and Media Research: A Guide for Students, Scholars and Professionals* (Spokane, WA: Marquette Books, 2005).

advance the interests of elites than it does the masses and alternative or nonmainstream groups that have little or no power.

4. Like schools, churches, the police and other social institutions, mass media play a key role in maintaining social order — they are, so to speak, "agents" of social control.[2] But mass media also can produce content that facilitates social change — change that can, at times, benefit disadvantaged and challenging groups.[3] In fact, content that is critical of dominant institutions and values often "cools down" critics and helps explain the persistence and stability of modern capitalism, an economic system that has shown a great capacity to adapt and change under a wide range of social, political and economic conditions.

5. Contrary to popular and scholarly wisdom, large-scale corporate mass media organizations do not produce content that is less critical of dominant elites and institutions than their entrepreneurial counterparts (e.g., structurally less complex, family owned and managed media). Instead, the bulk of the empirical research shows that corporate media produce content that is more critical of the power structure and its elites. Corporate media are not radical agents of change, to be sure, but they produce content that is more critical of the status quo because they are more insulated from parochial political and economic pressures.[4] The managerial revolution, which removes owners from the decision-making process and elevates

---

[2]*Social control* is defined here as attempts, whether intentional or not, by the state or by social institutions — including mass media — to regulate or encourage conformity to a set of values or norms through socialization or through the threat of coercion, or both. The *state* is a political entity legally permitted to use force within a particular territory. A *social institution* is a group or organization composed of people working to achieve goals that are sanctioned by the larger society. The goals are guided by values, norms and roles. A *value* is an abstract idea that people in a society or group consider desirable, good or bad. A *dominant value* is one that most people consider desirable. *Norms* are rules that guide behavior. *Socialization* is the process by which people learn to conform to social norms and values. *Roles* are social positions with certain rights and obligations and they link individuals to organizations. *Coercion* is a type of social interaction in which the individual or group is compelled to behave in certain ways either by force or threat of force. A *law* is a formal norm that has been approved, sanctioned or implemented by a state or political entity (e.g., legislature or head of state).

[3]*Social change* is the difference between current and antecedent conditions in culture or social structure.

[4]A formal definition of the corporate form of organization is provided in Chapter 4.

professionalism as a structural feature of the organization, is largely responsible for this phenomenon.

6.   Although traditional mass media have helped decentralize political power during the past four centuries, those media are themselves now losing some of their power[5] to mediate information and knowledge in society. The Internet is largely responsible for this loss in power. It has given individuals and organizations the ability to circumvent traditional mass media when it comes to news, information and entertainment content. This may be interpreted as being part of the general trend toward decentralization of political power inadvertently initiated by the printing press nearly six centuries ago.

7.   Mass media in the 21st century will continue to grow and become more complex and specialized in absolute terms, but those media (and global media in particular) generally will lose market share and power in relative terms. Metaphorically, the media "pie" will get larger in absolute terms but each slice will get proportionately smaller. Increasing competition, brought on in part by the rise of indigenous media around the world, and access to information on the Internet largely are responsible for the loss of power in relative terms.

The purpose of this book is to illustrate and back up these propositions, which are part of a more general theory I call "Media System Theory" (MST).[6] Although this may seem like a routine approach to scholarship, there actually are very few historians who develop formal theories of history and very few social scientists who do historical research. Many historians are uncomfortable with the idea of generating nomothetic theories that transcend time and place, and many social scientists are uncomfortable using ideographic historical evidence to test or support contemporary theories of the press.

Part of the discomfort stems from the different philosophical assumptions that have undergirded each of these approaches. History as a discipline has more strongly associated itself with the humanities than with the social sciences. The "humanist" approach tends to see human beings (or social actors[7])

---

[5]*Power* is defined here as the ability to influence or control the actions of other social actors, either through coercion, authority or both.

[6]For more details about Media System Theory, see Chapter 4 in David Demers, *The Menace of the Corporate Newspaper: Fact or Fiction?* (Ames: Iowa State University Press, 1996).

[7]*Social actor* is defined here as a goal-oriented individual or institution.

as "agents" who actively create and make the social world, exercising free will and choice. Historical events, humanists argue, are unique and are best explained by the actions, goals and desires of human beings. People construct "society" and make history.

In contrast, the social science model has tended to view human beings as having a more limited capacity to act and change the social world. Instead, they argue that pre-existing or emerging political, economic and social conditions, "forces" or trends are the prime movers of history. Individuals, in contrast, play a supporting rather than a lead role , because their roles are defined largely by the social system and its needs as opposed to free will or choice. In other words, social actors are viewed as "victims" of culture and social structure. To explain human behavior and human history, the "social science perspective" holds that one must place primacy on social, political and economic "forces" or events.[8]

From the 1950s to the 1980s, debates over which model — the humanist or social scientist — better fit reality were often disputatious. Scholars on both sides were indignant and even dogmatic. The humanists argued that social scientists had taken humanity out of human history, while social scientists argued that humanists were failing to generate knowledge because their observations were too particularistic and too relative.[9] In sociology, this debate began to wane in the 1960s as a new theory of social action began to take hold — one that could incorporate both perspectives without sacrificing elements of either.

The accommodating position held that agency and structure are both "at work"[10] in the social world. People have the capacity to choose between

---

[8]The debate over the primacy of structure versus agency is thousands of years old, and rooted in the philosophical debate over determinism versus free will (or volunteerism). See Rudolf Carnap, *An Introduction to the Philosophy of Science* (New York: Basic Books, 1966); Keith Lehrer (ed.), *Freedom and Determinism* (Atlantic Highlands, NJ: Humanities Press, 1966); and Bernard Berofsky (ed.), *Free Will and Determinism* (New York: Harper & Row, 1966). In mass communication research, the debate is sometimes framed as "passive" versus "active" audiences or consumers.

[9]Dennis Wrong, "The Oversocialized Conception of Man in Modern Sociology," *American Sociological Review, 26*:183-93 (1961).

[10]Sociologist Robert K. Merton is said to the be first social scientist to articulate the idea that there is no necessary conflict between an agency and structure. "The core process that Merton conceives as central to social structure," Arthur L. Stinchcombe writes, "is the choice between socially structured alternatives" ("Merton's Theory of Social Structure," pp. 11-33 in Lewis Coser [ed.], *The Idea of Social Structure: Papers in Honor of Robert K. Merton* [New York: Harcourt Brace, 1975], p. 12). Since then, debates about micro versus macro and free will and determinism have diminished significantly in the field of sociology (see Jeffrey Alexander, "The New Theoretical Movement," pp.

alternative courses of action, but those choices are shaped and constrained by social structure and culture,[11] as well as by psychological, organic and physiological phenomena. Thus, each generation is born into a social world that they, themselves, did not create, but upon which they shape and mold for future generations to come (e.g., creating, changing or eliminating various forms of social organization, rules, laws, values or practices). The accommodating position thus strikes a balance between agency and structure (or free will and determinism in philosophy).

The university setting provides a simple example to illustrate the interaction between agency and structure. Several times a week professors and students come together in a classroom for instruction. This behavior forms a pattern, or a structure, even though the pattern varies from day to day and is never completely duplicated in either a physical, psychological or social sense.[12] Individuals are linked to social structures (or social systems[13]) through roles, which are often fairly well defined. Professors, for example, are expected to teach and do research, and students are expected to study and learn. These roles and the values that accompany them comprise part of the university culture, and, of course, are learned long before students and faculty come together in the university setting.

The First Amendment (a cultural or structural feature of the larger social system) gives professors a great deal of freedom when it comes to the content of their lectures. But this freedom is not absolute. University rules and procedures set boundaries. Faculty lectures are expected to focus on course content. Faculty who stray too often from that topic can be punished. At the same time, students have the ability to question ideas presented in class; but they, too, can be punished if they disrupt class. Thus, individual choice and action are shaped or constrained by the structure of a social system (its rules and values). Faculty and students have the capacity (free will) to violate the rules, but few do so because there are punishments for doing that (e.g., failing

---

77-101 in Neil J. Smelser [ed.], *Handbook of Sociology* [Newbury Park, CA; Sage, 1988]). However, some scholars in the fields of mass communication and communication studies still see agency and structure as operating independent of each other.

[11]*Social structure* is defined here as enduring patterns of relationships within a society or organization. *Culture* is defined as the ideas, values, beliefs and norms that people hold as well as the products they produce (e.g., a newspaper).

[12]Some sociologists refer to this as *structuration*, or the "structuring of social relations across time and space." The point is that "structure" in the social world is fluid, in contrast to the static nature of, say, the structure of a building. See Anthony Giddens, *The Constitution of Society* (Cambridge: Polity Press, 1984).

[13]A social system is usually defined as two or more individuals who depend upon each other to achieve their goals.

a course or getting fired from one's job) and rewards for following them (e.g., getting a good grade or getting a promotion). In short, structure and culture impose constraints on choice and action, and structure and culture are themselves often changed and modified by social actors over time (e.g., students have more power today to evaluate professors' teaching performance than they did in the past).

This model of human behavior, which I call the *probabilistic theory of social action*, means that one cannot predict or explain all aspects of human behavior. There is always an element of unpredictability in social action, because social actors always have the capacity to reject or violate systems rules and values. Predicting individual behavior is often difficult or impossible, as criminologists have learned.[14] However, knowing something about the structure or culture of a society (e.g., knowledge about the rules and the rewards and punishments for engaging in certain kinds of behaviors) gives historians and social scientists the power to make many predictions about institutional and individual behavior in general terms.[15]

To illustrate, let's say you supervise the work of two people. They generally get along, but sometimes they have interpersonal conflict. With two subordinates, you have one potential case of conflict to deal with at any one point in time. Now let's add one more subordinate to the setting. How many potential cases of one-on-one conflict do you have now? Three, because you have three pairs of relationships. Now add a fourth subordinate. How many

---

[14]Almost all historians talk about social structure when studying history. But most still take an individualistic, or psychological, approach when explaining social phenomena. They usually focus on the decisions of powerful political leaders and elites. Some scholars refer to this as the "great person" theoretical approach. Great person theories are important and worthwhile, for human history involves individual choice or volition. But great person theories fail to provide a full accounting of social phenomena. They cannot, for example, explain why most mass media today are highly complex organizations, characterized by lots of written rules and procedures. The founders and subsequent owners and managers of those media organizations did not consciously set out to create a big company or one with lots of rules and regulations — in fact, many of them didn't even like rules (who does?). But changes in the structure of their organizations (i.e., increasing numbers of employees) over time often "drove" them to create more formal rules to solve problems of communication and control (e.g., standardizing procedures, coordinating the work of employees, codes of ethics).

[15]The impact of structure on choice should not be underestimated. A good lesson comes from one university, where I witnessed a group of agency-oriented, anti-bureaucratic faculty begin adding more rules and layers of bureaucracy to the department after coming to power.

potential cases of conflict do you have now? Six. Add a fifth subordinate, and you get 10. Add a sixth and you get 15, etc.[16]

The upshot is that conflict between pairs of people increases quadratically (i.e., at a faster pace) as you add more subordinates.[17] Without even knowing anything about the psychology of the people involved, you can predict that the potential for one-on-one conflict will be much greater as the number of subordinates in an organization increases. In fact, doubling the number of subordinates from three to six actually quintuples the potential for one-to-one conflict (from 3 to 15).[18]

In short, all things being equal, a large-scale organization will have more internal conflict than a smaller one — in absolute as well as relative terms. In the parlance of the sociologist, there are more "structural opportunities" for people to come into conflict with each other. (By the way, that's why larger academic departments tend to have more conflict among faculty than smaller ones.) The "quadratic theory of social conflict" explains in part why larger organizations often get a bad rap. In relative terms, they may actually have less interpersonal conflict than a smaller organization, but they are perceived to have more conflict because they usually have more absolute cases of it.[19] When applied to society as a whole, the theory also means that social conflict will increase as societies become more structurally complex. This, in turn, has consequences for social institutions like the mass media.

Thus, one of the more useful aspects of a sociohistorical approach to the study of history is that one can make generalizations or predictions about how people and organizations or society will act or change without even knowing anything about how the social actors themselves think (although that is important to study as well, because structure cannot explain or understand

---

[16]See Chapter 13 for a graph and elaboration on this quadratic model.

[17]The mathematical equation for this model is [n x (n-1)]/2, where n equals the number of social actors. For example, if one has nine social actors in an organization, the potential for social conflict is [9 x (9-1)]/2, or 72 divided by 2, which equals 36. I am grateful to Matthew Hudelson, associate professor of mathematics at Washington State University, for assistance in developing this quadratic equation.

[18]And note that we actually have underestimated conflict, because we haven't even taken into account group conflict — that is, groups of subordinates matched with other groups of subordinates. There is, by the way, a practical consequence to this illustration: If upper-level executives in your organization evaluate you in terms of the amount of conflict among your subordinates, you would be wise to explain the "principle of quadratic conflict" to them if you supervise a large number of employees.

[19]Because larger organizations have more conflict, they also tend to have more formalized means of dealing with conflict (e.g., administrative appeal processes, grievance boards, complaint procedures).

everything). Of course, these predictions are not without boundaries. One of the most important (and this applies to the seven trends listed in the last chapter of this book) is that they tend to be general; that is, one can make broad generalizations about social actors or institutions, but predicting the action of any individual social actor is difficult or impossible.[20] Social actors can and do make choices that reject or violate system rules and values. Nevertheless, a sociohistorical perspective that combines a traditional, agency-based historiography with a structural approach gives scholars a powerful tool for understanding not only the past and present but the future as well, as this book shall illustrate.

---

[20]For example, criminologists can predict with great accuracy that about one-tenth of juveniles arrested for a crime will be chronic offenders who commit a disproportionate amount of crimes, but they have not been able to accurately identify those offenders.

Part I

A Brief History of Print Mass Media

Chapter 1

THE PRINTING PRESS AND THE INFORMATION REVOLUTION

 Y ou couldn't call Johannes Gutenberg a revolutionary. He didn't even care much for politics. He was an entrepreneur who spent most of his time working on his secret invention — a printing press.
But that's what started all the trouble.

When Gutenberg perfected his press about 1450, ordinary people had few rights and little power. Emperors, kings, nobles, lords, religious leaders and tribal chiefs ruled in most areas of the world — some with an iron fist. Most of them monopolized the production and dissemination of knowledge and ideas, which helped them maintain power over people.

Johannes Gutenberg

But Gutenberg's printing press made it much more difficult for elites to control the production and distribution of knowledge and ideas. In fact, the printing press enabled people who were critical of those in power to easily and cheaply produce and distribute their ideas.

Gutenberg is often remembered for inventing the first printing press. But this is not true. As noted in the this chapter, the Chinese invented wood block printing nearly a thousand years earlier. What Gutenberg invented was a new type of printing press, one which used movable type. He also invented more advanced forms of ink.

But his real legacy lies not in the inventions. It lies in the "information revolution" that his printing press started — a revolution that in many areas of the world helped lessen the power of political and religious rulers and set the stage for representative democratic government.

Tragically, Gutenberg did not live long enough to see this shift in power, nor did he fully enjoy the fruits of his labor. An investor sued him a few years after he set up the press, and he lost control of his printing shop. He died a decade later.

11

CHAPTER OVERVIEW

This chapter examines the origins of human communication and the impact of the printing press. It contains four major themes.

The first is that complex social organization (or basically large societies) would not have been possible without written communication. Interpersonal communication works well in small groups and societies, but it cannot solve problems that emerge as organizations or societies grow and become more complex. Mass media are not necessary for societies to exist, but they are necessary for highly complex ones.

The second theme is that, throughout history, political and religious elites have restricted access to information and knowledge, partly because it helped them maintain control over people. Knowledge is power, but control of knowledge is also power. Elites have long recognized these axioms, and prior to the printing press ordinary people in most places in the world were illiterate and depended heavily upon elites for understanding the world.[1]

The third theme is that political power generally has become less centralized since the time of Gutenberg. And the fourth major theme is that the printing press and mass media are primarily responsible for this shift in political power. That's because the spread of knowledge and information has made it much more difficult for elites to maintain control.

THE ORIGINS OF HUMAN COMMUNICATION

When did humans first communicate?

This is not really a fair question, because it assumes that the evolutionary origins of the human species (Homo sapiens) can be identified and that communication was not a characteristic of pre-human ancestors. Evolution is a continual process, and many nonhuman animals and creatures also

---

[1]This historical review was synthesized from a number of sources, including David Crowley and Paul Heyer (eds.), *Communication in History: Technology, Culture, Society*, 2nd ed. (White Plains, NY: Longman, 1995); Warren Chappell, *A Short History of the Printed Word* (Boston: Nonpareil Books, 1970); Melvin DeFleur and Sandra Ball-Rokeach, *Theories of Mass Communication*, 5th ed. (New York: Longman, 1989); Michael Emery and Edwin Emery, *The Press in America*, 6th ed. (Englewood Cliffs, NJ: Prentice-Hall, 1988); Robert S. Fortner, *International Communication: History, Conflict, and Control of the Global Metropolis* (Belmont, CA: Wadsworth, 1993); David Sloan (ed.), *The Media in America: A History*, 5th ed. (Northport, AL: Vision Press, 2002); and Anthony Smith, *The Newspaper: An International History* (London: Thames and Hudson, 1979).

communicate. If evolutionary theory is correct,[2] then many pre-human ancestral forms also communicated with their own kind.

Indeed, the archeological evidence supports this proposition. Some of our early ancestors — such as the Australopithecus and homo erectus — were using stone tools as early as 2.5 million years ago. The development and use of such tools would not have been possible without some level of interpersonal communication. Analysis of fossils indicates that these ancestors could utter some sounds, even though their vocal chords were not highly developed. As such, scholars believe they relied heavily on gesture as a form of communication and that they had limited use of symbols.[3]

For a long time scholars argued that humans were the only species to use symbols as well as tools. But animal researchers have dispelled these anthropocentric assumptions. Chimpanzees and other highly evolved animals use tools, communicate with sounds and gestures, and even solve simple math problems. The significance of these findings cannot be understated: They illustrate that the study of humans and culture cannot be divorced from the rest of nature — that humans are a part of and not separate from or "above" the natural world per se.

But even though other creatures use symbols and tools, humans today are clearly unique in at least one important respect: *Much of their communication takes place in the absence of geographic proximity*. In fact, humans in many parts of the world today rely heavily on technology and the mass media — such as the telephone, radio, television and the Internet — to achieve their personal and professional goals. Humans can communicate with each other even when separated by space, time or both. No other creatures on earth can do this; it is made possible because of symbols, language and technology.

---

[2]This author does not believe evolutionism and creationism are incompatible. If a god created the world, then that god also could have created the laws of evolution. But a distinction should be made between two approaches. Evolutionism is a scientific theory, because it can be tested through empirical observation. Archeological evidence provides overwhelming support to the theory of evolution. Creationism, on the other hand, is not a scientific theory, because it cannot be empirically verified. Creationism is a philosophical doctrine and, thus, the belief in creationism is an act of faith. This does not mean that creationism isn't true; it just means that creationism cannot be empirically verified using scientific methods.

[3]A symbol is something that stands for or represents another object or thing. A skull and crossbones, for example, has come to symbolize poison, danger, or pirates, depending upon the context. Language and words are also symbols. They represent certain objects and ideas

BEFORE THE WRITTEN WORD

No one will ever know the origins of symbols, because many symbolic artifacts have been lost or destroyed. But Neanderthalers were using non-tool symbols at least 45,000 years ago and probably much earlier.[4]

Neanderthalers

Neanderthalers, who appeared about 150,000 years ago, didn't look like modern humans, and anthropologists disagree about whether modern humans are descended from them. They may simply be a long-lost cousin. The species disappeared about 25,000 B.C.

But for a time they thrived in Europe, Palestine, South Africa and even Java. They made fires, hunted using chipped stones as weapons, lived in temporary shelters and caves, and buried their dead. Artifacts found in graves also suggest that they believed in life after death. In other words, they had "culture."

Reconstruction of a Neanderthal child at the University of Zürich.

Like earlier human ancestors, Neanderthalers had a limited vocal chord structure and, consequently, probably relied heavily on gestures to communicate. Theirs was an oral culture. Knowledge about the world and how to survive in it was primarily passed along from generation to generation through word of mouth and gesture. The invention of an alphabet and written language would not come until about 5000 B.C.

But Neanderthalers were no simpletons. They had highly developed tools. They carved images on stones. And they made small trinkets and ornaments. In other words, they made and used symbolic objects.

The oldest known artifact is a small oval plaque that had been carved from a woolly mammoth tusk about 45,000 years ago. When scholar Alexander Marshack examined the plaque under a microscope, he found that its edges had been polished and worn by repeated handling. In other words, the object wasn't

---

[4]Alexander Marshack, "The Art and Symbols of Ice Age Man," pp. 10-20 in David Crowley and Paul Heyer (eds.), *Communication in History: Technology, Culture Society,* 2nd ed. (White Plains, NY: Longman, 1995).

a tool but was a symbolic artifact. It might have been used in religious ceremonies, but its actual purpose remains a mystery.[5]

The Cro-Magnons

Some scholars believe the Neanderthalers were displaced by the Cro-Magnons, whose skeletal remains began showing up about 75,000 years ago. Other popular culture theories contend that some Neanderthalers survived, and they are the reclusive "abominable snowmen." Although there is no evidence to confirm this theory, their disappearance remains a mystery.

The Cro-Magnons looked a lot like modern humans, and their art, oral language and tools were much more sophisticated than the Neanderthalers. A 30,000-year-old bone plaque discovered in France, for example, is engraved with 29 marks, which appear to record the phases of the moon. Cro-Magnon cave paintings also are very sophisticated and full of vitality. And their vocal chord structure was also more developed, enabling them to articulate a greater number of sounds and words.

But the Cro-Magnons had no written language. They, too, were an oral culture. And in such cultures, older people (35 years of age would be "old age" in those times) typically garnered a lot of respect because they carried with them knowledge of the past. They were, in other words, "walking encyclopedias."

Mathematics, which is a symbolic system, also began to emerge around this time. About 17,000 years ago, the ancient Incas in Peru developed a system of counting that used knots and colored strings, which they used to keep tabs on food inventories, population and gold production.

A short time later the Chinese began using a more sophisticated symbolic system — one which used cuneiform, or little wedge-shaped marks, to represents objects and ideas. The ancient Egyptians, Persians, Babylonians, Akkadians, and Assyrians also were using cuneiform or hieroglyphic characters. But *pictographic-ideographic* systems, as they are now called, were cumbersome and were not very effective for communicating complex ideas on a day-to-day basis.

EARLY HISTORY OF WRITING

Written languages in the form of words and sentences did not appear until about 3000 B.C. — a mere 5,000 years ago. A consonant alphabet was invented

---

[5]Ibid.

in the Middle East and was carried by the Phoenicians, who lived near modern-day Lebanon, to the Greeks, who added vowel sounds to it. The advantage of the alphabet and script writing was that an infinite number of words and ideas could be created using a small number of characters.

Scrolls and Scribes

The ancient Mesopotamians developed writing on clay tablets. But the tablets were heavy and not very transportable.

The Egyptians solved this problem with the invention of a light-weight paper-like writing material made from *papyrus,* a tall reed. The leaves would be interlocked like a woven basket and then hammered until they fused together. The final product was a scroll, which was unrolled as it was read. Some scrolls were 30 feet in length. Papyrus made it possible to store and transmit knowledge and information easily over space and through time, which in turn made it easier for elites to rule from distant places.

Most early scrolls and manuscripts were created for political and religious purposes. They contained prayers, rituals, laws, incantations, and government records. But some were produced for commercial or educational purposes.

In 600 B.C., scribes copied poems, speeches and orations by hand and sold them. In Latin, the word "scribe" means "to write." Scribes were usually monks or government officials. In addition to hand-copying books, scribes also were often editors and interpreters of the religious as well as governmental laws. During the Egyptian empire, the government employed thousands of scribes, who became a privileged class. They did not have to do manual labor or pay taxes. In the 5th century B.C., students of the famous philosopher Plato also sold or rented transcripts of his lectures.

Literacy Limited

But despite the development of the alphabet and written language, most people in most places around the world were illiterate and remained so until the 20th century. Literacy was not essential to survive in ancient times. Experience was usually the best teacher, and interpersonal communication was more than sufficient to get through everyday life. In fact, with the exception of democratic Greece,[6] no one even thought ordinary people needed to be informed about political matters. In most places it was illegal for ordinary

---

[6]Male citizens could participate in political decision making in Athens but the concept of democracy excluded women and slaves.

people to learn to read and write. That privilege was reserved for political and religious elites and some philosopher-scholars.

Needless to say, under these conditions people's knowledge of the world was quite limited. What they did know was obtained primarily from government officials, travelers, the local pub and the local church. Yet, it was still difficult for them to get accurate information about events. Memories were not always very good, and stories would often change as they were passed from person to person. Rumors spread easily. And news took a long time, often months or years, to make its way across continents.

Nevertheless, as history approached the birth of Jesus Christ, the demand for knowledge and information was growing. Agricultural methods were improving, people were less nomadic, and more towns and cities were springing up. Written communication enabled organizations and rulers to coordinate more effectively the actions of their subordinates at a distance. The division of labor also expanded; in other words, work became more specialized. This also meant that people, especially in the towns and cities, became more *interdependent*. In other words, to achieve their goals, such as finding food and shelter, they (city dwellers) needed to rely more heavily on other people (farmers).

News in the Roman Empire

In ancient Rome, interest in news about the world was growing. Although most people couldn't read, people of means could pay professional speakers a coin called a "gazet" to speak the news. That's why some modern newspapers still call themselves "Gazette." Between 59 B.C. and A.D. 222, the Roman authorities published a hand-lettered "daily gazette" that was posted in city squares.

The Romans also refined book reproduction to the point that several hundred hand-written copies of the same work could be made in a short time. Most were produced on papyrus. The Greeks, meanwhile, began producing *vellum*, or *parchment* — a writing material made from the skins of animals, such as goats, sheep or calves. Books were made from "pages" of vellum bound together and protected by a pair of wooden boards. The Chinese also were creating books from strips of bamboo and were printing on silk.

Although papyrus, parchment and silk were light and portable, they were expensive to produce and often difficult to obtain. The Chinese solved these problems in about A.D. 105 with the invention of paper, which was made from a mixture of bark and hemp.

But the Europeans didn't begin using paper until after the 12th century, when the Moors[7] introduced paper-making processes to the Spanish. The Romans used papyrus until about the 4th century, when vellum became the preferred writing material. By the time of Gutenberg's printing press, however, paper mills had been established in every major European city and parchment was being used less and less. Paper was much cheaper and lighter than parchment, even though it would not last as long.

MIDDLE AGES

During the Middle Ages (A.D. 500 to 1450), monks in the Roman Catholic Church spent a great deal of their time copying books. Bookmaking was also stimulated by the growth of universities in Paris and Bologna during the 12th century.

After the 12th century, as the volume of material for copying began to grow, private scripting houses began opening up and literate citizens were paid to do the work. But the modern printing press basically ran the scribe out of business in the 15th and 16th centuries.[8]

Block Printing

The concept of a printing press can be credited to the Chinese. During the 6th century A.D., they invented and refined block printing. Basically, this involved carving images on wood and dipping the image into ink and pressing it onto paper or some other surface.

Block printing greatly facilitated the distribution of Confucian texts, which extolled the values of devotion to parents, family and friends, ancestor worship, justice and peace. By the year A.D. 1000, the Chinese were publishing weekly reports called Tching-pao. Crude forms of newspapers made from wood blocks also began to appear in Europe.[9]

But in the Middle Ages (A.D. 500 to 1450) news still traveled very slowly — generally no faster than the speed of a horse or a sailboat. In 1431, for example, it took 18 months for news of Joan of Arc's death to reach

---

[7]Muslims who lived in northern Africa and who conquered Spain in the 8th century.

[8]Elizabeth Eisenstein, "The Rise of the Reading Public," pp. 105-113 in David Crowley and Paul Heyer (eds.), *Communication in History: Technology, Culture, Society*, 2nd ed. (White Plains, NY: Longman, 1995).

[9]T. F. Carter, "Paper and Block Printing — From China to Europe," pp. 94-104 in David Crowley and Paul Heyer (eds.), *Communication in History: Technology, Culture, Society*, 2nd ed. (White Plains, NY: Longman, 1995).

Constantinople. Not until the invention of the telegraph in the 19th century would communication become separated from transportation.[10]

For the time being, most people got their news from the local church or from travelers. A church service often included brief reports about happenings in the local community as well as the world beyond. Traveling entertainers, musicians and poets also brought news of the outside world. They recited poems and songs, which were more easily memorized if performed in rhyme. Storytelling became an art form.

Interestingly, many people didn't trust written documents, because many — possibly up to a third — were forged. A living person was the ultimate source of truth. That's one reason why courts of law today place so much emphasis on eyewitness testimony.

The Value of Older People

One consequence of the dependence upon oral communication was that older people were highly valued. They were, so to speak, vessels of knowledge.

According to historian and BBC television personality James Burke: "In an age when experience was what counted most, power was in the hands of the elders. They approved local customs and practice, and in matters of legal dispute they were the judges. They resisted change: Things were done because the elders confirmed that they had always been done so."[11]

But getting accurate information was still very difficult during these times. A dialect spoken in one community was often incomprehensible 50 miles away. Rumors also were abundant and often resulted in tragic consequences. There are many instances in history when violent mobs acted on the basis of inaccurate information.

Scholasticism

Moreover, political and religious rulers exacerbated these problems. They hoarded books. The written word was for god's eyes and his chosen priests, not for common people. In fact, during the Middle Ages, many political and

---

[10]James Carey, "Time, Space and the Telegraph," pp. 154-159 in David Crowley and Paul Heyer, *Communication in History: Technology, Culture Society,* 2nd ed. (White Plains, NY: Longman, 1995).

[11]James Burke, "Communication in the Middle Ages," pp. 80-89 in David Crowley and Paul Heyer (eds.), *Communication in History: Technology, Culture, Society,* 2nd ed. (White Plains, NY: Longman, 1995), p. 80.

religious elites discouraged the spread of ideas and knowledge, especially ideas critical of rulers or the church.

This practice was reinforced by scholasticism, a philosophical system based on religious revelation and classical Greek writings. Scientific experiments and real-world observation were discouraged. Roman Catholic authorities preached that truth and knowledge could be found only in studying the Bible and classical scholars like Aristotle.

Control of Knowledge Is Power

Needless to say, scholasticism reinforced the near-absolute power and authority of religious leaders, even when they were wrong. One of the best examples of the how this power was abused involved the debate over whether the earth revolved around the sun.

The Roman Catholic church maintained that the sun and planets revolved around the earth, which was the center of the universe. The *Ptolemaic System*, as this was called, had to be correct, the church argued, because God created the universe and made humans the center of attraction.

In the 16th century, Nicholas Copernicus introduced his *heliocentric theory* of planetary motion, which placed the sun at the center of the solar system. The earth and other planets revolved around the sun. Copernicus died in 1543, the same year the final version of his theory was published. The church condemned his theory.

Less than a century later, Galileo Galilei invented a telescope and proved Copernicus' theory. But this was heresy. In 1633 the infamous *Inquisition* sentenced Galileo to life in prison for violating a 1616 decree forbidding him to discuss Copernicus's theory. Galileo's sentence was commuted to house arrest after he recanted his theories.

Galileo

The church eventually stopped persecuting scholars. But the church did not apologize for persecuting Galileo until 1992 — three centuries later.[12] The story of Galileo illustrates that knowledge is power.

---

[12]Interestingly, in the year 2000, Pope John Paul II apologized for all past wrongs the church committed against Jews, woman and minorities — the first time a Pontiff has done that.

But even more important, it also shows that control of knowledge is power.[13] For many centuries, political and religious leaders controlled the development and distribution of knowledge, and they used that "knowledge" to control people. But the modern printing press would soon shake up the status quo.

EARLY HISTORY OF PRINT MASS MEDIA

Almost every school child learns something about Gutenberg and his printing press. Yet many details about his life are still a mystery, including his birth date.

Johannes Gänsfleisch zur Laden zum Gutenberg was born about 1400, perhaps as early as 1394, in the German City of Mainz. His father was an aristocrat. Gutenberg was trained as a goldsmith, which gave him experience in working with metals. In 1438, he and a partner began experiments in printing, but little is known about his work after 1444 because he kept it a secret.

Nevertheless, by 1450 it appears that Gutenberg had perfected his invention. In that same year he borrowed money Johann Fust, a wealthy investor, for the purpose of publishing in Latin a Bible that contained 42 lines of text per page. The project was completed sometime between 1453 and 1455.

Many historians argue that the *Gutenberg Bible* should have generated a substantial profit for the printing business. Presumably, Gutenberg could have paid Fust back. But for reasons that are unclear, Fust filed a lawsuit against Gutenberg in 1455 to recover his investment and he forced Gutenberg out of the business.

Traditional historiography suggests that this ruined Gutenberg. But more recent research indicates that Gutenberg was able to set up another printing

The Gutenberg Bible

shop, which he may have operated into the 1460s. He never became rich from his invention. He died in relative obscurity in 1468.

---

[13]George A. Donohue, Phillip J. Tichenor and Clarice N. Olien, "Mass Media Functions, Knowledge and Social Control," *Journalism Quarterly*, 50:652-9 (1973).

Printing Spreads

But Gutenberg's invention survived him and, in fact, spread very quickly.

The Italians set up their first printing press in 1469. England had one in 1476. By the close of the 15th century, more than 1,000 printers were doing business in nearly 250 European cities. They printed more than 6,000 separate books and pamphlets. Thus, the first mass medium — book and pamphlet publishing — was born.

The first printers, who also served as editors, sold their books directly to readers and employed agents to sell their books at universities. One publisher in 1470s Germany had 16 shops and agents in almost every major city in the Christian world. The cost of these books was far less than the hand-written counterparts, and they were much more accurate.

The first press in the Western Hemisphere was set up in Mexico City in the 1530s. Historians estimate that this and eight other printing presses in Mexico City published 204 books by the end of the century, nearly all of them religious (Catholic).[14] The second printing press arrived in Lima, Peru, in the 1580s. And the first printing press in North America was established in Cambridge, Massachusetts, in 1639.

In northern Europe, the first printing presses were primarily used to publish government and religious documents and books. But in Italy the presses mostly turned out secular works, including classical Greek and Roman literature. In fact, one publisher in Venice, Aldus Manutius, became famous for printing and distributing Greek poetry and philosophy to much of the Western world. Some printing houses were publishing content that was critical of traditional authorities. The Protestant Reformation, in fact, would not have been possible without the printing press.

Printing and the Protestant Reformation

In the early 1500s, many Europeans were becoming disenchanted with the Roman Catholic Church, which was the dominant religion. The Church exercised a great deal of power over its subjects, partly because it viewed the role of the church as an intermediary between God and the individual.

In contrast, critics emphasized the idea of a personal relationship between God and the individual. One of the dissidents was Martin Luther, a German priest who in 1517 allegedly affixed to the door of a church his "Ninety-five

---

[14]Cited in John Tebbel, *A History of Book Publishing in the United States: Volume I, The Creation of an Industry 1630-1865* (New York: R.R. Bowker, 1972), p. 3.

Theses," which questioned or challenged some of the practices of the Catholic church. This event might have gone unnoticed, except that copies of the theses were printed and widely circulated. Eventually, the church excommunicated Luther.

Luther's ideas and the ideas of other religious reformers spread quickly across Europe because of the printing press. Among other things, these ideas helped fuel the Peasant War of 1524-1526. Although sympathetic to the peasants, Luther withdrew his support when they used violence. Then, after the war, he was critical of the nobles who brutally put down

Martin Luther

the uprising. But the Reformation movement could not be stopped, and the number of Protestants grew dramatically in Europe and eventually England.

The social impact of Gutenberg's printing press has not been lost on Catholic authorities. Interestingly, in 1910 the *Catholic Encyclopedia* wrote about Gutenberg with a mixture of admiration and reservation:

> The invention of Gutenberg should be classed with the greatest events in the history of the world. ... Culture and knowledge, until then considered aristocratic privileges peculiar to certain classes, were popularized by typography, although in the process *it unfortunately brought about an internal revolution in the intellectual world in the direction of what is profane* [secular] *and free from restraint* [church control]. [brackets and emphasis added][15]

In other words, the printing press stole some power from the Catholic church.

Printing and Traditional Authority

But the social impact of the printing press went far beyond religion.

Historian Elizabeth L. Eisenstein points out that printed materials enabled university students to challenge traditional authority structures and ways of thinking.

---

[15]Heinrich Wilhelm Wallau, "Johann Gutenberg" in *The Catholic Encyclopedia, Volume VII* (New York: Robert Appleton Company, 1910; online edition copyright 1999 by Kevin Knight).

Previous relations between masters and disciples were altered. Students who took advantage of technical texts which served as silent instructors were less likely to defer to traditional authority and more receptive to innovating trends. Young minds provided with updated editions, especially of mathematical texts, began to surpass not only their own elders but the wisdom of the ancients as well.[16]

Indeed, one might even argue that the "age of experience" was coming to an end. Older people were losing their "knowledge value." The printing press allowed knowledge and ideas to transcend experience. They could now be stored easily and cheaply in books and other printed materials.

Increased availability of secular material also contributed to the so-called *Renaissance*, which began in the 14th century or so and ended in the 17th century. During this time there was increasing emphasis on the worth of the individual and humanism. Art and literature also dealt with subjects other than religion and aristocratic life.

The spirit of the Renaissance is reflected in the artistic works of Michelangelo and the literary works of Miguel de Cervantes, who wrote *Don Quixote*, which is considered to be one of the world's first major novels. Other Renaissance thinkers like Francis Bacon and John Locke argued that knowledge came from reason and real-world experience or empirical observation. This perspective stood in direct contrast to religious doctrines, which held the world was mostly unchangeable and everyone had their place.

The Authorities Respond

But political systems did not change much during the Renaissance. In fact, the Church and state in many places became even more powerful. Not until the 18th century and the "Age of Enlightenment" did significant political reforms come about. And change was hampered in many places because authorities were worried about an unregulated press.

In 1529, Henry VIII, the monarch who beheaded Ann Boleyn and other ex-wives, issued the first list of prohibited books. He also began licensing printers. Henry's goal was to stop the growing Protestant movement, which challenged his Church of England. But these controls and many arrests were not always successful. A black market press flourished, and Protestantism grew during Henry's reign.

---

[16]Elizabeth L. Eisenstein, *The Printing Revolution in Early Modern Europe* (Cambridge: Cambridge University Press, 1983), p. 259. Also see Elizabeth L. Eisenstein, *The Printing Press as an Agent of Change* (Cambridge: Cambridge University Press, 1980).

English monarchs tried other methods to control the press. In 1557 Queen Mary established the *Stationers Company*, which exercised a monopoly over printed material. The term stationer was applied to people who published or distributed books, to distinguish them from printers. The Stationers Company would conduct weekly searches of London printing houses. This approach worked for a time.

Another relatively effective control was the Star Chamber court, which imposed severe penalties on those who criticized the authorities. In 1584, William Carter was hanged for printing pamphlets favorable to the Catholic cause. However, this infuriated the Puritans, who in the mid-1600s overthrew the monarchy and ruled Great Britain for a short time.

Led by Oliver Cromwell, the Puritans abolished the Star Chamber in 1641. This led to more calls for freedom of expression. In 1644, Englishman John Milton wrote *Areopagitica,* which is perhaps the single most widely cited work in defense of a free press. Its most famous phrase is:

[T]hough all the winds of doctrine were let loose to play upon the earth, so truth be in the field, we do injuriously by licensing and prohibiting to misdoubt her strength. Let her [truth] and falsehood grapple; who ever knew truth put to the worse, in a free and open encounter?

In other words, Milton was arguing that truth will conquer falsehood in a free and open encounter.[17]

But by 1649, Cromwell turned out to be no more tolerant than the English monarchs he overthrew. And, ironically, Milton served as his

John Milton

chief censor. After the restoration of the monarchy in 1660, the authorities continued to license printers. But the age of *prior restraint* — in which authorities could prevent publication in advance — was waning.

---

[17]In theory, Milton's idea seems sound. But in practice, the public often cannot distinguish truth from falsehood in the mass media, because it doesn't have access to enough information. The ethic of objectivity (see Chapter 16) also contributes to the confusion, because under many conditions it requires reporters to quote sources who the reporters know are lying. Reporters are required to report all sides to a story, even those that are untruthful. Good reporters also present the truthful side, but there are no guarantees the public will be able to distinguish between the two.

In 1679 and 1694, the English Parliament allowed two licensing acts to expire. This didn't end suppression of speech, to be sure. But it did end licensing and prior restraints. Afterward, authorities used laws of treason and seditious libel to prosecute people. *Seditious libel* is the act of writing or publishing material that either stirs up rebellion or is critical of the authorities.

Ultimately, however, the demise of prior restraint was probably less a function of increasing tolerance than it was of the difficulty of controlling a rapidly growing publication industry. In fact, the demand for news and information was growing so fast that irregularly published pamphlets could no longer meet the needs. Politicians, government officials, merchants, manufacturers and other elites needed regular updates of politics and events. The newspaper emerged to help satisfied this need.

THE ORIGINS OF NEWS

The idea of news is not new. Ancient empires and tribal societies used messengers to transmit news of treaties, deaths and council decisions. As noted earlier, the Chinese and Roman empires also published handwritten news reports.

In 1415 northern European wood block printers were publishing *flysheets*, which contained news reports on a small, one-sided, untitled piece of paper. A larger version called *broadside* or *broadsheet* came into existence after Gutenberg's printing press. In England, the broadsides were often published before public executions and were sold to spectators.

The oldest known preserved report of a news event printed on a moveable-type printing press is a story about a 1541 storm and earthquake in Guatemala.[18] Interestingly, that report is preceded by a statement that adroitly illustrates the social control functions[19] of the press as a tool for religious authorities: "It [the disaster] is an event of great astonishment and great example so that *we all repent from our sins and so that we will be ready when God calls us*" [italics added].

But the first *newspapers* — which are usually defined as news sheets that contain a title and are published at least once a week — did not appear until 1609 in Germany. They dispensed *tydings*, or what we today commonly call news. According to historians Michael Emery and Edwin Emery, the term news

---

[18]Michael Emery and Edwin Emery, *The Press in America: An Interpretive History of the Mass Media*, 6th ed. (Englewood Cliffs, NJ: Prentice Hall, 1988), p. 4.

[19]*Social control* is defined here as attempts, whether intentional or not, by the state or by social institutions, including mass media, to regulate or encourage conformity to a set of values or norms through socialization or through the threat of coercion, or both.

(from the four winds, north-east-west-south) was coined to distinguish between casual dissemination of information and the deliberate attempt to gather it.[20]

The *Weekly News* (1622-41) was the first continuously published newspaper in England. The newspaper contained mostly foreign news, but after 1628 it included debates from the English Parliament. By the 1630s, printing houses in Austria, Belgium, France, Germany and the Netherlands were publishing newspapers. Books, newsletters and crude newspapers were becoming widely available to ordinary citizens. In London alone from 1640-1660, which was during the Puritan Revolution, more than 30,000 news publications and pamphlets were printed.

The earliest magazine — which is usually defined as a printed collection of essays, stories, articles and poems published less frequently than a newspaper (usually once a month) — appeared in 1663 in Germany. Others appeared in France, England and Italy before the end of the 17th century. They primarily contained essays on political and social thought.

The first continuously published newspaper in the United States began publishing in 1704. The first English-language magazine also appeared in London in that year. The first newspaper in Latin America, the *Gaceta de México*, a monthly, began publishing in 1722 in Mexico City. In 1750, London had five daily newspapers, six tri-weeklies, five weeklies and several other publications, for a combined circulation of 100,000.

---

[20]Emery and Emery, *The Press in America*, p. 7.

Chapter 2

EARLY HISTORY OF
NORTH AMERICAN PRINTING

In 1638, The Reverend Jose Glover set sail from England to set up the first
printing press in North America. His goal was to publish works that spread the
ideas of the Puritan faith. But he never lived to see that happen. He died from
a fever on the voyage over.

The printing press he had purchased would eventually be put into use in
Cambridge, Massachusetts. But the *Cambridge Press*, as it would be called, was
used for more than just religious documents.

From 1630 to 1670, Cambridge Press published 157 books and pamphlets.
Of those, 63 were religious, four were poetry, eight were historical or
biographical, and the rest were schoolbooks, officials publications, Harvard
(College) theses, and almanacs.[1]

The first document printed was the *Freeman's Oath*, to which every
householder in the colonies had to subscribe before becoming a citizen of the
colony. The oath, of course, was an instrument of social control — a way of
ensuring obedience to the Crown. In 1640, the first book, titled the *Bay Psalm
Book*, was published.[2] It, too, promoted conformity to religious doctrine.

Cambridge Press was the only print shop in the colonies for 37 years. It
closed in 1692, after which printing presses were set up in Boston, Philadelphia
and New York.

CHAPTER OVERVIEW

This chapter, which examines the early history of the press in America,
continues the theme that the printing press and newspapers helped decentralize
political power. The press gave ordinary people opportunities to challenge the

---

[1]John Tebbel, *A History of Book Publishing in the United States: Volume I, The Creation
of an Industry 1630-1865* (New York: R.R. Bowker, 1972), p. 15.
[2]Tebbel, *A History of Book Publishing in the United States, Vol. I*, pp. 8-12.

status quo, although in the main most content that came off the press helped those in power achieve their goals.

This chapter also argues that the actions or decisions of individuals alone cannot fully explain the origins of newspapers. Rather, six "environmental" factors — population growth, improved transportation and postal services, improved economic conditions, literacy, increasing tolerance of the press, and financial support — played a key role in the growth and development of early American newspapers.

Also included in this chapter are brief personality profiles of two great men in the history of communication, Benjamin Franklin and Voltaire. Their stories attest to the power that individual social actors can have on the history of mass communication.

THE COMPLIANT PRESS

As a rule of thumb, colonial authorities generally had few problems earning the loyalty of most early American printers. After all, writes magazine historian John Tebbel,

> a printer who opposed either ... [the church or state] would find himself cut off from the printing of sermons, or from publishing the business of the Assembly, a lucrative contract in itself. One who aspired, later, to publish a newspaper could not do so without a license. Freedom of the press, in short, was not a belief of the colonies' founding fathers; control and manipulation were the means to an authoritarian end.[3]

Indeed, some colonial authorities even despised the press. In 1671, Sir William Berkeley, governor of Virginia, wrote that he was grateful his colony did not have a printing press:

> But I thank God, there are no free schools nor printing, and I hope we shall not have these ... for learning has brought disobedience, and heresy, and sects into the world, and printing has divulged them, and libels against the best government. God keep us from both.[4]

But even though most printers were submissive to government authority, the Crown, to be on the safe side, gave colonial authorities the right to regulate the printing. After King James II ascended the throne in 1685, he instructed the

---

[3]Tebbel, *A History of Book Publishing in the United States,* Vol. I, p. 5.
[4]Quoted in Tebbel, *A History of Book Publishing in the United States*, Vol. I, p. 1.

governor of the New York colony "to provide by all necessary orders that no person keep any press for printing, nor that any book, pamphlet or other matters whatsoever be printed without your special leave & license first obtained."[5] This instruction was part of the royal orders given to colonial governors for 40 years. And it was enforced on two separate occasions in the late 1600s.

PUBLISHING WITHOUT AUTHORITY

The first time came in 1689, when William Bradford, who had operated a printing press since 1685, published a copy of the colony's charter without permission of the local authorities. He was ordered not to do any more printing without a license. He then helped set up a paper mill. Bradford got into trouble again in 1692 and the authorities seized his press, but he was not punished. In fact, Bradford eventually was appointed the Royal Printer to New York, a post he held for nearly a half century.

The second time authorities imposed prior restraint occurred in 1690, when Benjamin Harris published the first machine-printed newspaper in the American colonies. *Publick Occurrences, Both Forreign and Domestick* appeared in Boston on September 25, 1690. It was three pages long and contained stories about Indians who kidnaped several children, a small-pox epidemic, a fire in Boston a week before, the possible bribery of the friendly Mohawk Indians by someone who had caused them to turn against the colonists, and a scandal involving the French king and his daughter-in-law. The last two items angered colonial authorities, who banned it. Harris, originally from London, went back to running a coffee house and selling books.[6]

Although Harris is given credit for publishing the first machine-printed news account in the colonies, the first continuously published newspaper was the *Boston News-Letter*, which appeared April 24, 1704. The publisher was John Campbell, the local postmaster who previously had been issuing hand-written newsletters to colonial authorities. Unlike Harris, Campbell made a special effort to please authorities. This helped the weekly survive for nearly two decades.[7]

But James Franklin, the older brother of famous Benjamin, broke ranks in 1721 and refused to publish his *New England Courant* "with authority." His

[5]Tebbel, *A History of Book Publishing in the United States*, Vol. I, p. 2.

[6]Sidney Kobre, "The First American Newspaper: A Product of Environment," *Journalism Quarterly*, 17:335-45 (1940), p. 335.

[7]Jean Folkerts and Dwight L. Teeter, Jr., *Voices of a Nation: A History of Mass Media in the United States*, 2nd ed. (New York: Macmillan, 1994), pp. 20-23.

newspaper, which was the third one founded in the colonies, frequently criticized religious and political leaders. James was jailed and forbidden to publish any more. But he got around this by naming his brother, Ben, the publisher. Ben eventually ran away and went on to became one of the most respected and admired journalists and Americans in history (more on Ben to come).

The Zenger Trial

The most prominent case involving freedom of the press in the 1700s was the trial of John Peter Zenger. In 1734, a group of wealthy New York merchants and landowners who wanted more control of colonial affairs asked Zenger, who had just opened up his own printing shop, if he would publish a paper supporting their views. He agreed.

The first issue of Zenger's *New York Weekly Journal* appeared on November 5, 1733. A month later the newspaper criticized Colonial Governor Sir William Cosby for allegedly permitting French warships to spy on lower bay defenses. The newspaper also published a commentary that accused the British colonial bureaucracy of incompetence for its role in a dispute between Cosby and some colonists. The colonists were amused but not the governor. Cosby charged Zenger with seditious libel, a crime that normally allowed authorities to punish people who criticized the government even if the criticism was true.

Andrew Hamilton

Andrew Hamilton, a famous 80-year-old Philadelphia lawyer, represented Zenger when the trial began on August 4, 1735. To the surprise of almost everyone, Hamilton immediately conceded that Zenger had published the stories critical of the governor. Needless to say, the prosecutor was very pleased with this admission, because normally this would have meant a conviction. Truth was not recognized as a defense for seditious libel.

But Hamilton insisted that the words must be false for a conviction to stand. "The falsehood makes the scandal, and both the libel," he said, adding that he will "prove these very papers that are called libel to be true."

During closing arguments, Hamilton asked the jurors to follow their own consciences without fear of official reprisals. He added:

> Men who injure and oppress the people under their administration provoke them to cry out and complain; and then make that very complaint the foundation for new oppressions and prosecutions. ... But ... the

question before the court and you gentlemen of the jury, is not of small nor private concern. ... It is the best cause. It is the cause of liberty.[8]

The Verdict

The jury found Zenger innocent of the charges. Zenger and Hamilton were heros to the colonists. Interestingly, though, the Zenger case had no immediate impact on libel law. In fact, after the Revolutionary War a number of American newspapers editors were jailed for seditious libel.

But the major principle of the Zenger case — that truth is a defense for libel — was eventually codified into law. Today, a libel plaintiff must prove that the material was false. Cases like Zenger also helped legitimize the press as a Fourth Estate — that is, as an institution that has the right to draw attention to abuses of power in the various branches of government (more on the Fourth Estate later).

Early American Publishing

Early newspapers like Campbell's, Franklin's and Zenger's were small-scale productions. Circulations usually were less than 1,000 and rarely exceeded 2,000. As a consequence, the owner usually wore many hats, including that of editor, reporter, printer, advertising salesperson, and circulation manager. Many were also the local postmaster. Role specialization was not highly developed.

Most of the news published in colonial newspapers was about national or international affairs. The accounts were usually lifted from English or other colonial newspapers. Local news stories, when they appeared, were often taken from other colonial newspapers, private letters, correspondence and personal conversations with governmental officials.

Some newspapers published novels, including Daniel Defoe's *Robinson Crusoe*, in serial form. But rarely did publishers seek out news. News reporting as an institution did not emerge with regularity until the early 1800s, when newspapers began covering Congress and the White House.

The first American magazines appeared in 1741. They included Benjamin Franklin's *The General Magazine* and Andrew (son of William) Bradford's *American Magazine*. The magazines contained essays, poems, book reviews, sermons and news. By the end of the 1700s, more than 100 magazines had been

---

[8]Michael Emery and Edwin Emery, *The Press in America: An Interpretive History of the Mass Media*, 6th ed. (Englewood Cliffs, NJ: Prentice Hall, 1988), pp. 38-44.

published, although none of them survived. Even Franklin could not turn a profit from his magazine. But this would change in the 19th century, and Franklin did make money at newspaper journalism.

BEN FRANKLIN: "THE GRAND OLD MAN OF THE PRESS"

Benjamin Franklin

When Benjamin Franklin arrived in Philadelphia in 1723, he was tired, unkempt, hungry, and almost broke.[9] He purchased three loaves of bread for three cents. He put a loaf under each arm and ate the third as he walked down the street in search of work and lodging. People grinned at the sight of this plainly clothed 17-year-old who had spare shirts sticking out of his pockets.

But seven years later they were no longer laughing. That's because Franklin had become one of the most successful printers, writers and publishers in Philadelphia. He would go on to claim a number of other titles, including that of diplomat, inventor, politician, scientist, educator and business leader. He was, without question, one of the great "Renaissance" men, and many argue one of the last.

He proved lightning was electricity. He secured money and arms for the colonists during the Revolutionary War. He was a member of the Constitutional Convention of 1787. He wrote witty aphorisms, such as: "Early to bed and early to rise make a man healthy, wealthy and wise." He invented a stove that to this day heats many cabins and some homes across the country (the "Franklin Stove") and refused to patent the invention so that it could be widely copied and distributed. He was admired for his compassion, wit, sensitivity and intelligence. And he was a good listener.

But one of Franklin's most important contributions is often overlooked: He made American journalism respectable and profitable. Other publishers and writers before him were dull and often had many financial problems. Few could turn a profit from their newspapers.

---

[9]Sources for this brief biography include Benjamin Franklin, *The Autobiography of Benjamin Franklin* (Boston: Bedford Books of St. Martin's Press, 1993); Benjamin Franklin, *The Papers of Benjamin Franklin,* edited by Leonard W. Labaree and Whitfield J. Bell, Jr. (New Haven: Yale University Press, 1959); Car Van Doren, *Benjamin Franklin* (New York: The Viking Press, 1938); and Michael Emery and Edwin Emery, *The Press in America: An Interpretive History of the Mass Media,* 6th ed. (Englewood Cliffs, NJ: Prentice Hall, 1988).

But, as Michael Emery and Edwin Emery point out,

Franklin showed that a good journalist and business person could make money in the publishing field. ... When intelligent and industrious youths saw the possibilities of journalism, as developed by the grand old man of the press, they began to turn more often to this calling. Getting this improved type of personnel into the craft was the best possible tonic for American journalism.

Franklin was born January 17, 1706, in Boston, Massachusetts. He was the 15th child and the 10th son of 17 children. He was the youngest son of a long line of youngest sons dating back to his great grandfather. His father, a soapmaker and candlemaker, thought he was special because of that.

Franklin learned to read early and devoured every book he could get his hands on. But his formal education ended at age 10. He was at age 12 apprenticed to his older brother, James, a printer. James was very strict with Ben. He worked him 14 hours a day and boxed his ears if he misbehaved.

In 1721, James founded a weekly newspaper called the *New-England Courant* and he asked readers to contribute articles. Ben typeset these articles and knew he could write as well. So in 1722 he wrote 14 essays that satirized the Boston authorities and society. He anonymously signed them "Silence Dogood," a fictitious Boston widow. The articles were immensely popular. But when James found out Ben was the author, he put an end to them.

In late 1722, James was imprisoned for publishing articles critical of the authorities. He was released a short time later and forbidden to publish a newspaper. So, to get around this rule, he made Ben the publisher. Unbeknownst to the authorities, however, James had Ben sign papers that allowed James to retain ownership and control of the newspaper. Several months later, Ben had an argument with James and ran away from home. Ben could not find work in New York City so he went on to Philadelphia, which became his home for the rest of his life.

As Ben walked down the street that day, one of the people chuckling at him was his future common law wife, Deborah Read. Franklin ended up as a lodger at the Reads' home. Deborah and Ben never formally married. They began living together in 1730. Their common-law marriage lasted 44 years, until her death in 1774. They raised three children, one of whom was Ben's son from a previous relationship.

In 1725, Franklin spent a year in London, where he impressed everyone with his keen intellect and his superb swimming abilities. In 1726, he returned to Philadelphia and to the printing business. In 1729, he purchased the *Pennsylvania Gazette* and turned it into the best newspaper in the colonies. The popularity of the newspaper brought in advertising revenue, and Franklin excelled as a printer, writer, and advertising copywriter. More than half of his income came from the newspaper, the rest from his printing business.

From 1732 to 1757 he published *Poor Richard's Almanack*, a rich source of prudent and witty aphorisms on the value of thrift, hard work, and the simple life, such as "God helps those who help themselves." In 1748, at age 42, Franklin retired to live comfortably on his income. But his life was anything but leisurely.

He helped other printers set up newspaper in other colonies. He also was deputy postmaster general of the colonies. He helped found an insurance company, a hospital and a college that later became the University of Pennsylvania. When he invented the free-standing "Franklin stove" in 1740, he refused to take out a patent on it because he didn't feel it was right to benefit personally from such inventions. He wanted everyone to benefit. He invented lightning rods, which saved many buildings around the world. Of course, he also invented the bifocal lenses that are helping this author write the text you are now reading.

Franklin was elected to the Pennsylvania Assembly in 1751 and spent the next 40 years as a public official in one capacity or another. He signed the Declaration of Independence in 1776 at the age of 70.

But his most important political contribution was serving as the colonial diplomatic representative to France, where he secured money and resources to help the colonists fight the war against Britain. Most historians argue that without the assistance of France, the colonists would have lost the war. He returned home in 1785 and served as president of Pennsylvania for three years and attended the Constitutional Convention of 1787. He died on April 17, 1790, at the age of 83.

COLONIAL PRESS READERS

From 1639 to 1799, at least 86,000 separate books, pamphlets, broadsides, newspapers and magazines were published in the United States.[10] Despite this growth, printed media during this era still were directed largely to elite audiences — to government officials, politicians, business people and educated elites. Most ordinary citizens could not read or afford a newspaper or magazine, nor was reading important to them in their everyday lives. All they needed to know they learned through experience and interpersonal communication.

---

[10]Tebbel, *A History of Book Publishing in the United States,* Vol. I, p. 14.

But things were changing. Literacy rates were rising. By the end of the 18th century, more than 6 out of 10 men in the New England colonies were literate. At the same time, the church and state were losing their monopolies over information and knowledge. Only about a third of the material printed was religious in nature and less than a fifth was governmental. More than a fifth was secular literature.

Perhaps more importantly, the state could not contain news that was critical of the crown and British authorities. And the American Revolution seemed to confirm Virginia Governor Sir William Berkeley's fears that printing could bring "disobedience."

THE REVOLUTIONARY WAR PRESS

Before the Revolutionary War (1776-83), the colonies had fewer than 40 newspapers. Most of them published content that served the interests of — or at least didn't upset — the British authorities. Even Isaiah Thomas, who became the most important Patriot editor, took a moderate stance before the war. Under the name plate of his *Massachusetts Spy* were the words, "A Weekly Political and Commercial paper — Open to All Parties, but Influenced by None."

But political dissent was growing. More and more colonists were becoming disenchanted with British control, and their concerns were not unique in the Western world.

Age of Enlightenment

During the 17th century, much of Europe was also under the influence of the *Age of Enlightenment*, sometimes called the "Age of Reason." Enlightenment thinkers like Jeremy Bentham in England, Jean-Jacques Rousseau in France, and Thomas Jefferson, Benjamin Franklin and Thomas Paine in America wrote books and articles that embraced reason and scientific knowledge and disputed ideas based upon traditional authority, dogma and religious speculation. Other Enlightenment thinkers believed ordinary people should have a greater role in governing their communities. They opposed tyranny and oppression and believed humans could, through scientific research, solve social problems and make the world a better place.

One of the most influential Enlightenment writers was France's Voltaire, who wrote *Candide*, a powerful attack on organized religion. Voltaire, who is often called the father of the French Revolution, also coined the famous phrase:

"I detest what you write, but I would give my life to make it possible for you to continue to write."[11]

Voltaire: "The Defender of Free Speech"

The English mob surrounded the Frenchman and shouted: "Hang him. Hang the Frenchman." This was the 1720s, a time when no love was lost between the English and the French. But the angry mob was no match for this man. "Men of England, you wish to kill me because I am a Frenchman," he replied. "Am I not punished enough in not being born an Englishman?" This response pleased the crowd so much that they cheered him and offered him an escort back to his lodgings.[12]

Voltaire

Wit was only one of the many talents of François Marie Arouet, who is better known today by his pen name, Voltaire. He was a prolific writer and philosopher; the first leader of the Enlightenment; the father of the French Revolution; and a source of inspiration for many American revolutionaries and journalists. He was, even during his lifetime, one of the most admired and famous people in the world. And he continues to inspire, because he fought for freedom, justice and equality, and he opposed intolerance, superstition and tyranny.

Voltaire was born in 1694 to a middle-class Parisian family. His mother died when he was 7, but he was never close to his father. Rather, he became attached to his godfather, a freethinker and epicurean, or one who enjoys the pleasures of life in moderation.

Voltaire acquired a love for literature, the theater and social life while attending a Jesuit college. But he was skeptical of religious instruction, and became even more critical of institutionalized religion after Louis XIV tried to

---

[11]Quote is from a letter Voltaire wrote to M. le Riche, February 6, 1770. The popular version of the quote reads: "I disapprove of what you say, but I will defend to the death your right to say it." But this alteration was written by one of Voltaire's biographers (S. G. Talentyre [a.k.a. E. Beatrice Hall], *The Friends of Voltaire* [London: Smith Elder, 1906]), who wrote to an attorney in 1935 that it was a description of Voltaire's attitude.

[12]Sources for this brief biography of Voltaire include Wayne Andrews, *Voltaire* (New York: New Directions, 1981); Mary Margaret Harrison Barr, *A Century of Voltaire Study: A Bibliography of Writings on Voltaire, 1825-1925* (New York: B. Franklin, 1972); and Voltaire, François Marie Arouet de, *The Portable Voltaire* (New York: Penguin, 1977).

purge Catholic France of its Protestant subjects. Authorities destroyed Protestant churches; denied Protestants access to some professions; and, in some cases, took Protestant children away from their parents and raised them as Roman Catholics.

After college, Voltaire worked as a secretary for the French embassy in The Hague (Netherlands), and after the death of Louis XIV in 1715 Voltaire became well known in Parisian society for his witty epigrams. Once, when the philosopher Montesquieu fell asleep while reading a speech, Voltaire commented: "Wake him up. He seems to imagine that he's in the audience." On another occasion a noblewoman who returned to court after an absence complained that, "The things they say about me are incredible! They even say I retired to the country in order to give birth to twins." Voltaire responded: "Don't be disturbed ... I only believe half of what I hear in court."

His wit, though, was also a curse. In 1717, he was imprisoned for a year in the infamous Bastille for mocking a nobleman. After release, he wrote *Oedipe*, the first of his theatrical tragedies, which immediately made him the leading playwright of his time.

Voltaire became increasingly critical of despotic authority and the Catholic church. He believed in the primacy of reason over dogma and superstition. He became a deist, or one who believes that reason rather than revelation and authority can prove the existence of God and that God assumed no control in the world after creating it.

After a dispute with a leading French family in 1726, he was beaten up and given a choice between exile or prison. He chose the former, and spent two years in London, where he learned English and studied the writings of political philosopher John Locke and the scientist Isaac Newton. He also enjoyed Shakespearean plays.

What he most admired, though, was the greater level of tolerance the English had for freedom of speech and the press. Although radicals were still punished for treason and seditious libel, England by this time was no longer licensing publishers or engaging in prior restraint. Voltaire made many friends in high literary circles.

When he returned to France, he sought to spread the ideas he learned. He had now accumulated enough money to live comfortably and independently. He wrote a number of plays, only one of which was very successful.

But he also turned to writing history, and in 1734 he wrote *Lettres Philosophiques*, which was designed to illustrate the benign effects of religious toleration. The book extolled the virtues science, reason and empiricism over religion, arm-chair theorizing and religious dogma.

Voltaire also argued that the purpose of life is not to reach heaven through penitence but to assure happiness to all humans through progress in the sciences and arts. The book defined the essence of the Enlightenment and the modern mind.

But French authorities were not amused. A warrant was issued for his arrest in 1734. He escaped and began living with a young woman, Mme. du Châtelet, who shared his intellectual interests and was imbued with a yearning for knowledge. He wrote a number of other successful works, but was often on the move to avoid being arrested by authorities. In 1749, Mme. du Chatelet died giving birth to another man's baby. Her death sent him into a depression.

Voltaire never married. He had affairs with a number of women, but he also had some limits. He once participated in an orgy with a group of liberal friends. When they asked him to come back the following night, he replied: "Ah, no, my friends. Once a philosopher. Twice a pervert."

Voltaire wrote a number of other historical and theatrical works after 1749, but his masterpiece was *Candide*, a book written in 1758 that has been compared to the slapstick humor on "Saturday Night Live." The book attacked religious fanaticism and the injustices of class status and war. The story is about Candide, a naive young disciple of Doctor Pangloss who preaches that this is "the best of all possible worlds." Pangloss, which means "wind bag," represents established religion, which holds that people should accept all forms of suffering and evil and always look for the silver lining. Candide suffers many indignities and becomes disillusioned with the world. He concludes that the best approach is "cultivating his own garden" — in other words, to reject utopian dreams and live within one's capabilities.

Voltaire settled in Ferney, France, in 1758 and lived there until 1778, when he moved to Paris and died at the age of 83.

The Press Takes Sides

In the colonies, the ideas of Voltaire and the Enlightenment were reflected in documents such as Thomas Paine's *Common Sense*, which argued that the colonies received no advantage from being governed by Great Britain. The pamphlet sold an incredible 120,000 copies in 1776, six months before the signing of the Declaration of Independence. *Common Sense* called for the establishment of an independent government and played a key role in mobilizing the colonists against the British. In a matter of weeks, almost every colonist was familiar with its content.

During the war, about half of the newspapers supported the Patriot cause and half the British. Both sides recognized the important role that news and information played during wartime. Both sides also printed content that tried to convince colonists their cause was the more noble one.

Only 20 of the 37 newspapers at the beginning of the war survived, but 33 new papers were established during the war. Most of them supported the Patriots. In fact, the British press was eradicated by the end of the war.

Samuel Adams was the best example of a Patriot editor. He edited the Boston *Gazette*, which became a center for the radicals. Adams also was a member of the Sons of Liberty, the group which staged the famous Boston Tea Party and terrorized the British (see Chapter 15 for a discussion of objectivity, terrorism and the Sons of Liberty).

A number of factors have been cited to explain the origins of the Revolutionary War. One of the most frequently cited is the *Stamp Act of 1765*, which imposed heavy duties on legal documents and paper used in publishing newspapers. This alienated two important colonial groups: lawyers and journalists. When the British pointed out that the colonists themselves had imposed local stamp taxes in Massachusetts and New York, the colonists responded that it wasn't the tax per se, it was the fact that they didn't have representation in Parliament ("taxation without representation").[13]

However, most historians argue that the press, not events like the Stamp Act, played a bigger role in motivating the colonists to fight the war.[14] Historian Arthur M. Schlesinger writes that when colonials "began to feel the tightening grip of imperial control after 1763, they naturally resorted to the printing press to disseminate their views and consolidate a favorable public support."[15] As the war progressed, the colonists became increasingly intolerant of the Tory (British) press, in some cases running publishers out of town.[16]

The U.S. Constitution and Bill of Rights, which were ratified in 1791, also embody the ideas of the Enlightenment. In particular, the First Amendment holds that "Congress shall make no law ... abridging the freedom of speech, or of the press ... ."

---

[13]Ironically, though, no taxes were ever collected and the Stamp Act was repealed.

[14]Only one historian has challenged this perspective, according to Carol Sue Humphrey, "The Revolutionary Press, 1765-1783," pp. 51-68 in Wm. David Sloan (ed.), *The Media in America: A History*, 5th ed. (Northport, AL: Vision Press, 2002), p. 64. Carl Berger argues that propagandists' arguments were less effective than events and that the greatest impact on public opinion came from news, not opinion. See Carl Berger, *Broadsides and Bayonets: The Propaganda War of the American Revolution* (Philadelphia: University of Pennsylvania Press, 1961).

[15]Arthur M. Schlesinger, "The Colonial Newspapers and the Stamp Act," *New England Quarterly*, 8 (1935):63-83.

[16]See Humphrey, "The Revolutionary Press," pp. 65-71. Contemporary public opinion poll research also suggests that people are no more tolerant today. They support freedom of speech and the press in the abstract, but most oppose the idea of allowing communists or others with extreme views to air them in their neighborhoods.

Although U.S. citizens enjoy a degree of freedom of expression that is unmatched around the world, it is important to point out that this doesn't mean freedom of speech and the press are absolute. There are many constraints on expression. Cultural values, for example, limit and shape what speech is considered appropriate, and groups and individuals self-censor all the time. Moreover, groups that violate dominant values, such as neo-Nazis and communists, rarely get positive coverage in mainstream media.[17]

FACTORS INFLUENCING THE FIRST NEWSPAPERS

In explaining the origins of the first newspapers in the United States, historian Sidney Kobre points out that Benjamin Harris probably got the idea for his newspaper from a number of broadsides that were published in Boston in the late 1680s, some of which discussed a conflict over a new British policy that sought to gain tighter control over Massachusetts.

"There were strong indications of the growing interest in printed news and the discussion of current events," Kobre writes.[18] However, Kobre argues, a complete and adequate explanation of the emergence of this newspaper as well as the *Boston News-Letter* — the first regularly published newspaper in the Colonies, which appeared April 24, 1704 — must take into account factors other than the individual actions of the publisher.

> *Public Occurrences, Both Foreign and Domestick* did not spring up by chance. The first American newspapers grew out of the peculiar conditions in the colonial environment, out of the desire for political and commercial news, foreign and domestic, and the need for an advertising medium.[19]

More specifically, Kobre contends that five "environmental" factors account for the emergence of the first newspapers in Boston.

---

[17]Some dissidents argue that the mainstream bias in the media is a conspiracy. But journalists rarely conspire with elites. Rather, the mainstream bias stems from the ethic of objectivity and the structural linkages that news media have with dominant power groups. The ethic of objectivity encourages journalists to seek information from credible, bureaucratic sources, institutions and major political parties (e.g., mainstream sources), and news organizations create beats to cover those sources on a continuing basis. The interesting thing is that journalists themselves are rarely aware of how the stories they write helps support and maintain the status quo. See Chapter 16 for more details.

[18]Kobre, "The First American Newspaper," p. 344.

[19]Ibid.

Population Growth

The first was population growth. By the year 1700, the population in the colonies had grown to about 250,000. Massachusetts had 45,000 settlers, and Boston was the largest city in the colonies.

Although Kobre does not say so, he implies that interpersonal communication alone is an inefficient or ineffective method for communicating many matters of general concern in large social systems.

Improved Transportation and Postal Services

The second factor affecting the development of the first newspapers, according to Kobre, was improved transportation and postal services.

Until the late 1600s, news from other communities or countries was difficult to obtain, which alone would have made it difficult to publish a newspaper. Intercolonial trade and mail service was poor. Travel was chiefly by boats, which were slow and unpredictable. But by 1692, a road system was being developed and the first weekly mail service between Boston and New York had been established.

Improved Economic Conditions

The third factor contributing to the emergence of the first newspapers was improved economic conditions.

Agriculture, manufacturing, trade and commerce increased substantially during the 17th century. Dutch and English farmers, following the Hudson River Valley, raised crops that were shipped to markets in Europe. The colonies also exported cattle, tobacco, lumber, and textile products, and developed their own shipbuilding industries. By 1699, the balance of trade strongly favored the colonies, which exported goods valued at nearly twice the amount they imported.[20] All of the this activity, Kobre writes,

> meant that commercial news was of value. A newspaper man could gather news about local and foreign business from these farmers, shipbuilders, shippers, ship captains. He could print this information in a newspaper and sell it. Many colonists along the seaboard wanted to know what was happening in the political and commercial life of England, the West Indies and other colonies, since they had begun to trade with these places so extensively. Commercial intelligence, or news, was needed for carrying on

---

[20]Kobre, "The First American Newspaper," p. 337.

a profitable business. ... With services and merchandise to sell, shippers needed an advertising medium to tell prospective customers about their cargoes and to advertise their next port of call for anyone who wished to ship freight.[21]

Literacy

The fourth factor influencing the development of the first newspapers was literacy. Economic development and increased productivity freed many people from long work days, giving them more leisure time which, in turn, increased interest in cultural affairs. Libraries, schools and colleges appeared in many communities. In some areas, compulsory education was instituted as early as 1647.

Increasing Tolerance of the Press

The fifth major factor affecting the emergence of the first newspapers was increasing tolerance of the press. During the 17th century, many religious and governmental elites opposed a free press.

But the growth of democratic ideals in England, which was reflected in the English parliament's right to unlicensed publication in 1695, led to the institutionalization of the press in England and drew attention to the fact that the press could be an effective weapon for influencing public opinion in favor of the government's position.[22]

Financial Support

Population growth, transportation, economic development, literacy, and increased tolerance from the government were necessary conditions for the emergence of the press. But they were not sufficient. A sixth factor was financial support.[23]

---

[21]Kobre, "The First American Newspaper," pp. 338-9.

[22]Kobre, "The First American Newspaper," p. 344.

[23]See, e.g., Clarence S. Brigham, *History and Bibliography of American Newspapers 1690-1820* (Worcester, MA.: American Antiquarian Society, 1947); Willard Grosvenor Bleyer, *Main Currents in the History of Journalism* (Cambridge: The Riverside Press, 1927); Emery and Emery, *The Press and America*; Frederick Hudson, *Journalism in the United States: 1690 to 1872* (New York: Harper & Brothers, Publishers, 1873); Sidney Kobre, *Development of American Journalism* (Dubuque, IA: Wm. C. Brown Company Publishers, 1969); and Frank Luther Mott, *American Journalism: A History 1690-1960*, 3rd ed. (New York: The Macmillan Company, 1962).

Many newspapers, especially before the Revolutionary War, depended on a source of income other than advertising or subscriptions for survival. For example, John Campbell, publisher of the *Boston News-Letter*, never had enough subscribers to turn a profit. A government subsidy saved him twice from bankruptcy.

Financial problems like this were not unusual. More than half of the 2,120 newspapers founded between 1690 and 1820 folded before they were two years old; only one in four survived longer than five years.[24] One of the major problems facing newspapers at that time was limited demand for advertising. The industrial revolution, with its consumer-based economy and dependence on markets, was only in its infancy. The newspaper publisher often had to seek financial support elsewhere, including political parties, religious groups, business leaders, or the government. The publisher also was often the local postmaster.

---

[24]Brigham, *History and Bibliography of American Newspapers*, p. xii.

Chapter 3

THE PARTISAN AND
PENNY PRESSES

W atergate. Irangate. Whitewater.

The American public is accustomed to reading or watching news reports that portray its leaders in a less than flattering light. In fact, today the public rarely questions the right of the news media to act as an "adversary of government" — one that writes about or broadcasts news stories that criticize elites or expose corruption. In other words, the power of the news media to act as a "Fourth Estate" has become institutionalized.[1]

But it wasn't always this way.

In 1638, the term Fourth Estate was used to refer to the British Army. The other three were the three estates of Parliament: one representing the nobility, another the clergy and the third the House of Commons. How the term came to be associated with the news media isn't entirely clear.

Nineteenth-century writer Thomas Carlyle gives credit to Edmund Burke, an 18th century British statesman and political philosopher. Burke once commented that in addition to the three estates there was the Reporters' Gallery in Parliament, "a fourth estate more important than they all. It is not a figure of speech or witty saying; it is a literal fact, very momentous to us in these times."

Some historians, however, doubt this report. The first reliable citation is an essay by Thomas Bington Macaulay in 1828, who wrote that "the gallery in which the reporters sit has become a fourth estate of the realm."

---

[1]Sources for this discussion on the Fourth Estate include Thomas Carlyle, *Heroes: Hero-Worship and the Heroic in History* (New York: Cas. Scribner and Sons, 1841), p. 164; Dominic F. Manno, "The 'Fourth Estate': Who Used the Term First?" pp. 24-25 in Hiley H. Ward, *Mainstream of American Media History: A Narrative and Intellectual History* (Boston: Allyn and Bacon, 1997); and George A. Donohue, Clarice N. Olien and Phillip J. Tichenor, "A Guard Dog Conception of Mass Media," paper presented at the annual meeting of the Association for Education in Journalism and Mass Communication, San Antonio, Texas (August 1987), pp. 2-3.

Whatever the origins, the concept plays an important role in the ideology of contemporary journalism and is closely allied with the watchdog concept — or the idea that the press should actively search for abuses of authority and power.

More formally, the assumption behind the Fourth Estate concept, according to mass communication researchers George A. Donohue, Clarice N. Olien and Phillip J. Tichenor, is that the press acts "as a checking mechanism, constantly reminding the government groups about where ultimate sovereignty resides [with the people] and ensuring that the obligations of the social contract are observed." In this country, these ideas are often traced to Thomas Jefferson, the third U.S. president.

Thomas Macaulay

Jefferson believed that even though individuals may make mistakes, the majority of the populace could make sound decisions if given access to accurate and truthful information. He advocated education and argued that the press was an essential source of information and guidance and should be free from governmental control. In addition to educating the individual, the press should serve as a check on the government, to prevent it from infringing on the rights of the individual.[2]

Although the Fourth Estate and watchdog concepts are widely recognized in journalism, historical and scholarly research suggests that the news media in Western countries perform more like a "guard dog" than a watchdog. In other words, the content of the press does more to help elites than masses when it comes to achieving goals. We'll address this issue in more depth later.

CHAPTER OVERVIEW

Three major themes are embedded in this chapter.

The first is that, during the partisan press (or party press) period, the press emerged as a social institution that not only mediated much of the information and knowledge available in American politics and social life, it also emerged

---

[2]Jefferson wrote: "No experiment can be more interesting than that we are now trying, and which we trust will end in establishing the fact, that man may be governed by reason and truth. Our first object should therefore be, to leave open to him all the avenues to truth. The most effectual hitherto found, is the freedom of the press." See Andrew A. Lipscomb (ed.), *The Writings of Thomas Jefferson*, Volume 11 (Washington, DC: Thomas Jefferson Memorial Association, 1904), pp. 32-34.

as an institution that was expected to serve as a check on the other three branches of government (the presidential, congressional and judicial branches). It became, in other words, the *Fourth Estate*.

The second major theme is that the press reflects the power structure of the society or community it serves. After the Revolutionary War, elites aligned themselves into two major political groups (federalists and anti-federalists) and fought each other for power. It is important to point out that the partisan press did not necessarily reflect the concerns of ordinary citizens. Indeed, as this book will argue in many places, the press always reflects the interests and concerns of elites over the masses.

And the third theme is that the penny press hastened the process of decentralization of power begun with the modern printing press. The penny press helped to broaden citizen input into the political system.

THE POST-WAR PRESS

After the Revolutionary War, newspapers entered a period of rapid expansion that coincided with the growth of urban populations. Before the war, the Colonies had 37 newspapers; in 1835, the United States had 1,258.[3] Total urban population increased nine-fold from 1790 to 1840, going from 202,000 to 1.8 million. Total population nearly quadrupled, from about 4 million to 15 million.[4]

More newspapers were established in cities west of Philadelphia, including Cincinnati, St. Louis and Detroit. Yet, despite this growth, newspaper circulation remained limited, even in large urban areas. Subscription fees were high — $6 to $10 a year in advance — an amount that was more than most skilled workers earned in a week and well beyond the means of the less well to do.[5]

Newspapers were more lively and refined after the war, but they were still highly political and commercial in content and oriented toward national and international events.[6] For example, in the 1820s the *Inquisitor Cincinnati Advertiser* devoted the overwhelming majority of its news hole to international,

---

[3]Frederick Hudson, *Journalism in the United States: 1690 to 1872* (New York: Harper & Brothers, Publishers, 1873), p. 770.

[4]U.S. Bureau of the Census, *Statistical Abstract of the United States: 1989* (Washington, DC: U.S. Government Printing Office, 1989).

[5]Michael Emery and Edwin Emery, *The Press in America: An Interpretive History of the Mass Media,* 6th ed. (Englewood Cliffs, NJ: Prentice Hall, 1988), pp. 115-6.

[6]Ibid.

national and state political and business news. Local news, including city council minutes, typically filled less than six inches of the 144-inch news hole.[7]

In 1784, Mathew Carey, an Irish immigrant, began publishing the debates of the Pennsylvania House of Assembly from notes he took himself. First-hand reporting of politics was still a novel idea, and Carey's paper, the *Pennsylvania Herald*, was very successful as a result. Carey's paper supported the Constitutionals, who wanted a strong central government[8] (see Chapter 8 for more on Carey as a book publisher).

Reflecting changes in the political power structure, newspapers also aligned themselves with one or more of the new political parties. This time period is often referred to as the age of the partisan press. Newspapers published a great deal of political content supporting or condemning various political parties and leaders. Political parties also provided financial support for newspapers.

THE TWO PARTY PRESS

After the American Revolutionary War, Alexander Hamilton became the leader of the conservative Federalists. He sponsored and supported the *Gazette of the United States*, a paper edited by John Fenno. The Federalists argued, among other things, for a responsible government.

In contrast, Thomas Jefferson, who was the leader of the anti-Federalists (or "Republicans," which ironically became the Democratic Party in the 19th century) and the third U.S. president, argued for a responsive government — one that met the needs of the people. The anti-Federalists' views were represented in the *National Gazette*, which was edited by Philip Freneau.

These two political parties and their newspapers lashed out against one another in numerous debates, essays and columns. This may not seem all that noteworthy today. But back then the world had never seen anything like it. The

Thomas Jefferson

---

[7]Eight months of issues (August 1819 to March 1820) for the *Inquisitor Cincinnati Advertiser* were content analyzed, and other issues throughout the 1820s were skimmed.

[8]J. E. Hagerty, "Mathew Carey," in *The Catholic Encyclopedia, Vol. III* (New York: Robert Appleton Co., 1908; Online Edition, 1999, Kevin Knight).

United States had become the testing ground for "freedom of the press."

But the new nation soon learned that tolerance only went so far. The content was often inaccurate, scandalous, and libelous. Even Jefferson, who was an adamant supporter of a free press, wrote in 1813 after years of being criticized by Federalist newspapers: "The newspapers of our country by their abandoned spirit of falsehood, have more effectually destroyed the utility of the press than all the shackles devised by Bonaparte."[9]

In 1798, the Federalist-controlled Congress passed the Alien and Sedition Acts, part of which was designed to muzzle anti-Federalist editors. Editors who wrote stories containing "false, scandalous or malicious" comments about the Federalists could be fined $2,000 and imprisoned for two years.

Emery and Emery point out that the law only punished those who wrote false statements, not truthful ones. But it was a step back for freedom of the press. Ten editors and publishers were convicted, and the laws created such a furor that the Federalists were unable to renew it. After Jefferson became president in 1800, he pardoned all those in jail and canceled remaining trials.

Characteristics of the Partisan Press

Mass media historian Wm. David Sloan says the mandate of editors during the partisan press age was to present news and opinion and to win adherents to a paper's political cause. Objectivity or nonpartisanship was not a goal. In fact, "Editors frowned on impartiality," Sloan writes. After 1800, "They proclaimed that to be impartial was to do the country an injustice. ... Even to consider impartiality, some editors argued, was a dereliction of duty."[10]

But there was no balance of opinion in these papers. Only one side was presented. Federalist papers viciously attacked anti-Federalists (later called Republicans), and vice versa. During the War of 1812, most newspapers, regardless of party, supported the war effort. However, some radical Federalist newspapers continued to oppose the war (Republican James Madison was president) and found themselves the victims of attacks from Republican mobs. In one incident, two lives were lost and many people were injured.[11] This incident illustrates that at some times in history, especially during war, some

---

[9]Saul K. Padover, *Thomas Jefferson on Democracy* (New York: Penguin, 1939), pp. 92-92. Thomas Jefferson also wrote in 1787 that "were it left to me to decide whether we should have a government without newspapers, or newspapers without a government, I should not hesitate a moment to prefer the latter."

[10]Wm. David Sloan, "The Party Press: 1783-1833," pp. 69-94 in Wm. David Sloan (ed.), *The Media in America: A History*, 5th ed. (Northport, AL: Vision Press, 2002), p. 75.

[11]Ibid, p. 84.

people place more value on controlling ideas than on protecting the free speech rights of others.

After the demise of the Federalist Party in about 1815, the Republicans (formerly known as the anti-Federalists) held power but unity disappeared by 1824, and two new parties emerged: the Whigs (made up of conservative Republicans and former Federalists) and the Jacksonian Democrats. All three parties organized and published newspapers attacking each other. The Democrats didn't have as many papers as the Whigs, but the election of Andrew Jackson to President in 1828 bolstered the influence of these papers.

During the partisan press era, a typical newspaper was a small-scale operation by today's standards. Circulations usually were less than 1,000 and rarely exceeded 2,000 (the largest was 6,000, in New York City). As a consequence, the owner usually wore many hats, including that of editor, reporter, printer, advertising salesperson, and circulation manager. Only the largest newspapers could afford to hire reporters, and general assignment reporting did not emerge as a significant organizational activity until the early 1800s. Most newspapers depended heavily on other secondary sources of information to fill their pages.

Then as now, most of the news published in newspapers originated in political and commercial centers of power.[12] Unlike today, however, the vast majority of content in early newspapers involved national or international affairs. The accounts were usually lifted from English or other colonial newspapers.

Local news stories, when they appeared, were often gleaned from other colonial newspapers, private letters, correspondence and occasionally personal contacts with governmental officials. Newspapers were directed largely to elite audiences: government officials, politicians and business people. Most ordinary citizens could not read or afford a newspaper, nor was a newspaper important for them in their everyday lives.

---

[12]A great deal of empirical research supports the finding that news media depend heavily on elites for news and information. See, e.g., Mark Fishman, *Manufacturing the News* (Austin, Texas: University of Texas Press, 1980); Todd Gitlin, *The Whole World is Watching: Mass Media in the Making and Unmaking of the New Left* (Berkeley, CA: University of California Press, 1980); Clarice N. Olien, Phillip J. Tichenor and George A. Donohue, "Media Coverage and Social Movements," pp. 139-63 in Charles T. Salmon (ed.), *Information Campaigns: Balancing Social Values and Social Change* (Newbury Park, CA: Sage, 1989); David L. Paletz and Robert M. Entman, *Media Power Politics* (New York: The Free Press, 1981); and Gaye Tuchman, *Making News* (New York: Free Press, 1978).

Thus, one might argue that newspapers at this time didn't really fit the contemporary definition of a "mass medium." That wouldn't come until the 1830s, when the first penny press emerged in New York City.

A BRIEF HISTORY OF THE PENNY PRESS

Twenty-three-year-old Benjamin Day was desperate. For two years he struggled to make a profit from his New York City printing business. But in the early 1830s, competition was stiff, and a plague in 1832, which cut into the city's prosperity, didn't help.

Nevertheless, Day was determined. He believed he could turn his business around if he could publish a newspaper and sell it for one cent. This was a lot cheaper than the six cents most other newspapers cost. For some people, that was a whole day's wage. As such, only political and business elites could afford those newspapers. But Day believed working- and middle-class citizens should have access to news as well.

So, on September 3, 1833, he launched the *New York Sun*, and sold it for 1 cent. It was a big hit. Within six months, the *Sun* had a circulation of 8,000, twice as large as the next nearest rival in the city. And with a big circulation, the advertising poured in. Eventually, subscriptions were no longer the main source of income. Advertising was.[13]

An important part of Day's success formula was an emphasis on local and crime news. Media historian Frank M. O'Brien says Day "wanted a reporter to do the police-court work, for he saw, from the first day of the paper, that was the kind of stuff that his readers devoured."[14] Day hired George Wisner, a former Bow Street reporter in London, to cover the court beat, and his reports soon took up two full columns in the newspaper.[15]

Another factor that appears to have contributed to the commercial success of the *Sun* was its moderate editorial stance. Unlike other newspapers, which vigorously supported one of the various political parties and were often funded by them, Day insisted on keeping his newspaper "neutral." He wrote few editorials on controversial subjects. This approach offended fewer readers and advertisers and probably helped boost circulation.

---

[13]Emery and Emery, *The Press in America*, p. 117.

[14]Frank M. O'Brien, *The Story of the Sun* (New York: George H. Doran Company, 1918), p. 38.

[15]Willard Grosvenor Bleyer, *Main Currents in the History of Journalism* (Cambridge: The Riverside Press, 1927), p. 160.

Day sold the paper in the late 1830s, a decision he later regretted. But his printing and publishing businesses flourished and he died a very wealthy man in 1889.

Local News, Profits and Objectivity

The penny papers, unlike the older press, placed a great deal of emphasis on local news.[16] They covered the police, courts, churches, clubs and special interest groups, and routinized coverage of many social institutions, including Wall Street, the courts, police and government. As media historian Michael Schudson puts it:

> For the first time the American newspaper made it a regular practice to print political news, not just foreign but domestic, and not just national but local; for the first time it printed reports from the police, from the courts, from the streets, and from private households. One might say that, for the first time, the newspaper reflected not just commerce or politics but social life.[17]

But the key factor that distinguished the one-cent alternatives from their more expensive counterparts, according to media historian Dan Schiller, was that the penny papers took business success as their most fundamental goal.[18] The party press served the interests and goals of the political party. Making a profit was desired but not necessary.

The penny papers, in contrast, were specifically created to make a profit. They sought to make money primarily through advertising revenues, not subscription fees, and to do this they needed to increase circulation. Crime news played an important role in boosting circulation of the penny papers. But this was not the only factor. The penny press appealed to a broader audience because it avoided erudite political commentary and was less partisan in content. The penny papers covered church events, accidents, disasters, social news and local government.

---

[16]A readable and even-handed summary of the penny press period can be found in Susan Thompson, *The Penny Press: The Origins of Modern News Media, 1833-1861* (Northport, AL: Vision Press, 2004).

[17]Michael Schudson, *Discovering the News* (New York: Basic Books, 1978), p. 22.

[18]Dan Schiller, "An Historical Approach to Objectivity and Professionalism in American News Reporting," *Journal of Communication*, 29(4):46-57 (1979).

The penny papers did not eliminate political commentary and opinions, but they did de-emphasize them.[19] The party papers, in contrast, appealed to limited segments of the population — usually segments that shared the political and economic views of the newspapers. Their primary function was to promote the political and ideological interests of the parties they served.

Schiller argues that the penny press invented the concept of objectivity. Although the concept was not part of journalism's lexicon until the 20th century, Schiller writes:

> Objectivity developed in tandem with the commercial newspapers' appropriation of a crucial political function — the surveillance of the public good. By means of periodic exposures of violations and infringements of public good — most notably in crime news, a blossoming genre — the newspaper at this juncture presumed to speak as "the public voice." In one jump the newspaper moved from the self-interested concerns of partisan political warfare to the apparently omniscient status of protecting the people as the whole.[20]

The Penny Press Expands

The newspaper industry grew dramatically during the penny press era. From 1830 to 1840 alone, the number of newspapers doubled and yearly circulation tripled, going from about 68 million copies to 196 million copies.[21] On the eve of the Civil War, many metropolitan dailies were exhibiting the characteristics of large-scale organization, including a complex division of labor and a hierarchy of authority.

After Day founded the *New York Sun*, dozens of other penny papers were established in New York City, Albany, Boston, Philadelphia, Baltimore and New Orleans, many of which were growing rapidly.[22] But the success of the penny papers was not welcomed by all. Many of the older papers criticized the coverage of crime news, arguing that it was harmful to the community.[23] Yet

[19]Schudson, *Discovering the News.*

[20]Schiller, "An Historical Approach," p. 47.

[21]Frank M. O'Brien, *The Story of the Sun* (New York: George H. Doran Company, 1918).

[22]David Pearce Demers, "Crime News and the Rise of the Modern Police Department," paper presented to the Midwest Association for Journalism and Mass Communication Historians (Evanston, IL, April 1990).

[23]Bleyer, *Main Currents*, p. 157. Also see Demers, "Crime News and the Rise of the Modern Police Department."

this criticism was short-lived. Competition from the penny papers forced many of the older papers to change their ways. As police historian Roger Lane notes:

> Both the numbers and the circulation of these (penny) papers climbed steadily, with the *Boston Times*, reportedly selling twelve thousand copies a day, leading even the established journals by 1836. All of the "pennies" left state and national politics to their older rivals, in order to concentrate on the local news which these had ignored, especially on violent and exciting incidents. Such stories could be gathered most easily each morning in court, and the popularity of this police court reportage led the more conservative press to adopt it.[24]

Many of established penny papers also did not welcome the arrival of new competitors. In large urban areas, especially New York City, the papers began fighting each other for readership and advertising dollars. The battle reached a high mark in 1840, when James Gordon Bennett's rivals started a movement to boycott the *New York Herald*, which had nearly 40,000 circulation — more than one paper for every 10 residents.[25] The competitors enlisted the help of the leading clergy and accused Bennett of blasphemy. Bennett's racy style of reporting the news spilled over into its coverage of religious news, but Emery and Emery argue that the real cause of the "moral war" was resentment over Bennett's success.[26]

In contrast to the older papers, which were oriented toward business and governmental elites, the penny papers were directed toward the working and middle classes — two groups that were a product of an increasingly urbanized and industrialized society.

From 1820 to 1860, total urban population in the United States increased 10-fold, going from 693,000 to 6.2 million.[27] After the War of 1812, economic investment shifted from shipping to manufacturing and transportation. Factories were producing leather products, clothes, shoes and farm machinery. Fewer and fewer goods and services were made at home for home use. For health care, people turned from homemade remedies to patent medicines and

---

[24]Roger Lane, "Policing the City: Boston 1822-1885," in Jerome Skolnick and Thomas C. Gray (eds.), *Police in America* (Boston: Little, Brown & Co., 1975).

[25]Total population in New York City was about 350,000 in 1840. See Demers, "Crime News and the Rise of the Modern Police Department."

[26]Emery and Emery, *The Press in America*, p. 121.

[27]U.S. Bureau of Census, quoted in *The World Almanac* (New York: Pharos Books, 1988), p. 531

doctors. From 1830 to 1850, the number of miles of railroad increased from less than 100 to nearly 9,000.[28]

Decentralizing Knowledge

The penny papers forever changed the distribution of knowledge in society. No longer was a newspaper for just the elites.

Now the masses had access, and politics would never be the same. The newspaper helped inform a new electorate. When the country was founded four decades earlier, voting rights were reserved for land-holding males. But by the 1830s most states and the federal government permitted all free men the right to vote.

It would be a mistake to argue that the penny newspapers were radical agents of social change. The content they produced played an important role in reinforcing dominant values and social institutions. Crime news, for example, helped define the boundaries of acceptable behavior and legitimate the role of the police and the courts in catching and punishing law breakers. Business news and political news helped people run their businesses and make voting decisions. And the penny papers helped manufacturers sell products to consumers. Advertising was an efficient way to reach potential customers.

But the penny press did broaden citizen input into the political process, while at the same time helping to institutionalize capitalism, industrialism and consumerism.

Factors Facilitating Development of the Penny Press

Increased emphasis on social news and decreased emphasis on partisan commentary boosted circulation, but it does not explain the origins of the penny press, because social news had been part of the newspaper business back to the days of John Campbell.[29]

Some credit certainly goes to Benjamin Day, who borrowed the idea from other publishers who had tried it in other cities but failed. Nevertheless, Day could never have succeeded had it not been for three other social structural factors: technology, education and literacy, and an expanding capitalist economy.

Until the 1820s, the fastest printing presses were capable of producing only about 1,100 papers per hour. By 1830 steam power was adapted to the press

---

[28]Schudson, *Discovering the News*, pp. 43-50.
[29]Demers, "Crime News and the Rise of the Modern Police Department."

which more than tripled the speed of printing.[30] These changes also were accompanied by advancements in paper-making,[31] both of which reduced per-copy costs substantially.

The second factor contributing to the rise of the penny press was literacy and education. Public education emerged in the early 1800s as an important social and economic issue that was backed up by public funding for schools and colleges. By the 1830s, a majority of adults could read, and by 1870 only 20 percent of the population over 10 years of age was illiterate.[32]

Technology and education were necessary conditions for the rise of a mass press, but they were not sufficient. More important than either of these, according to Schudson, was the development of a "democratic market society." He writes:

> A democratization of economic life was in progress. By this I mean simply that more people were entering into a cash (and credit) nexus by becoming investors and by consuming goods produced outside the household and that their attitudes and ambitions were increasingly conditioned by this fact."[33]

The emergence of the penny press reflected a fundamental shift of power in the social system — a shift from the established mercantile and financial leaders to the entrepreneurial capitalists. These new businesses needed a way of promoting their goods and services to consumers, and the penny press provided them that outlet.

Schudson also argues that the penny papers contributed to the development of a market economy in two ways. First, through advertising, the penny papers enlarged the potential market for manufactured goods. Second, the penny papers transformed the newspaper from something that was read at the club or library to a product consumed in the home. The penny papers, Schudson concludes,

> were spokesmen for egalitarianism ideals in politics, economic life, and social life through their organization of sales, their solicitation of

---

[30]Emery and Emery, *The Press in America*, pp. 112-3.

[31]Schudson, *Discovering the News*, pp. 31-5

[32]Mary Beth Norton, David M. Katzman, Paul D. Escott, Howard P. Chudacoff, Thomas G. Paterson and William M. Tuttle, Jr., *A People and A Nation: A History of the United States* (Boston: Houghton Mifflin, 1982), p. 543.

[33]Schudson, *Discovering the News*, p. 45.

advertising, their emphasis on news, their catering to large audiences, and their decreasing concern with the editorial.[34]

In short, the penny press became the first mass medium for delivering consumers to producers.[35] It helped usher in modern capitalism.

AFRICAN AMERICAN NEWSPAPERS

The first newspaper directed at African American readers, the *Freedom's Journal*, was founded in 1827 in New York City after black leaders were refused an opportunity respond to anti-black editorials that appeared in several white-owned newspapers.

The first editor was Samuel Cornish, a white Presbyterian minister who was staunchly opposed to slavery and the idea of establishing colonies for ex-slaves in Cuba and Africa. However, the half-black proprietor, John B. Russwurm eventually reversed the anti-colonization policy and advocated colonization of Liberia. This position was not popular among his readers, and he closed it down in 1829.

About 40 black newspapers were founded before the Civil War. Mass media historian Bernell Elizabeth Tripp points out that most of these newspapers were founded not to oppose slavery per se, "but the fact that blacks were denied access to the established press to voice their opinions on slavery, as well as other concerns, such as education, employment, and moral development."[36]

---

[34]Schudson, *Discovering the News*, pp. 12-60.

[35]George A. Donohue, Clarice N. Olien and Phillip J. Tichenor, "Reporting Conflict by Pluralism, Newspaper Type and Ownership," *Journalism Quarterly*, 62:489-99,507 (1985), p. 491.

[36]Bernell Elizabeth Tripp, "The Antebellum Press: 1820-1861," pp. 141-158 in Wm.

Most of the black newspapers didn't survive longer than two years. Funding was always a problem.

One exception was *The North Star*, which was founded in Rochester, New York, in 1847 by Frederick Douglass, the best-known black man in the United States. Douglass has escaped from slavery in 1838 and became a popular speaker, traveling in the northern United States and to Great Britain.

In the prospectus, Douglass wrote that "the objective of *The North Star* will be to attack slavery in all its forms and aspects; advocate universal emancipation; exact the standard of public

Frederick Douglass

morality; promote the moral and intellectual improvement of the colored people; and to hasten the day of freedom to our three million enslaved fellow-countrymen."[37]

After four years, *The North Star* was merged with the *Liberty Party Paper* in Syracuse, New York, and renamed the *Frederick Douglass' Paper.* It continued publishing until 1860.

David Sloan, *The Media in America: A History,* 6th ed. (Northport, AL: Vision Press, 2005), p. 150.

[37]Carter R. Bryan, "Negro Journalism Before Emancipation," *Journalism Monographs,* 25 (1969), p. 19.

Chapter 4

MEDIA BARONS AND THE CORPORATE NEWSPAPER

Henry Raymond and George Jones had a dream.

Someday they would publish a great newspaper. But during the early 1840s, neither of them had any money. Raymond was chief assistant to Horace Greeley, the famous publisher of the *New York Tribune* and *The New Yorker*, and Jones worked in the Tribune's business office.[1]

But Raymond would not be under Greeley's thumb for long. Greeley was mentally erratic, and Raymond left the *Tribune* in 1843, working as a correspondent for several other newspapers and building a reputation as an orator and savvy politician. In 1851, Raymond and Jones got enough capital together to launch the *New York Daily Times*. Raymond managed the newsroom and Jones the business office.

The *Daily Times* sold for one cent, but it did not stoop to the sensationalistic practices of most of its competitors, including the *Tribune*. The *Daily Times* quickly developed a reputation for accuracy, truthfulness, fairness and objectivity — despite Raymond's passion for and involvement in politics (he eventually became a state legislator and U.S. Congressman) — and for insightful analyses of foreign news events. A year later the newspaper had a

---

[1] Sources for this institutional biography include Michael Emery, Edwin Emery and Nancy L. Roberts, *The Press and America: An Interpretive History of the Mass Media* (Boston: Allyn and Bacon, 2000), pp. 107-108, 147-149, 234-240; 457-460; Jean Folkerts and Dwight L. Teeter, Jr., *Voices of a Nation: A History of Media in the United States* (New York: Macmillan Publishing Co., 1989), p. 493; Thomas A. Schwartz, "Raymond, Henry Jarvis," pp. 572-575 in Joseph P. McKerns (ed.), *Biographical Dictionary of American Journalism* (New York: Greenwood Press, 1989); Janet E. Steele, "Jones, George," pp. 370-372 in McKerns (ed.), *Biographical Dictionary of American Journalism*; Kristen Dollase, "Ochs, Adolph S.," pp. 521-523 in McKerns (ed.), *Biographical Dictionary of American Journalism*; James Aronson, *The Press and the Cold War* (New York: Bobss-Merrill, 1970), p. 146; *Hoover's Guide to Media Companies* (Austin, TX: Hoover's Business Press, 1996), p. 128-129; and *The New York Times* Web site: <www.nytimes.com/adinfo>.

circulation of 25,000. In 1857, Raymond and Jones changed the name to *The New York Times*.

Today the *Times* consistently ranks in polls of journalists as the best newspaper in the United States — and many would say "the world." The newspaper and its staff have earned 79 Pulitzer Prizes, 36 more than any other news organization. The newspaper has more than 1,000 reporters and editors, nine bureaus and 29 international bureaus. *Times'* circulation also has been growing in recent years. The newspaper has the third highest daily circulation in the United States (about 1,095,000) and the highest Sunday circulation (1,650,000).

The Times Building in New York in 1908.

But the *Times* didn't acquire its top "guard dog" ranking overnight.

In 1867, Raymond retired from politics to devote his attention to turning the *Times* into a national newspaper. The newspaper began exposing corruption in government and crusaded for tariff reduction and monetary and civil service reforms. But Raymond became despondent when several friends and two of his children died. He died in 1869 from a stroke.

Jones was not a journalist, but he had been in the news business for more than a quarter century and he assumed control of the newsroom. In 1870, he launched an attack on the infamous Tweed Ring, a corrupt network of Democratic politicians and bureaucrats that bilked the New York City government of $200 million. The newspaper and *Harper's Weekly* succeeded in driving the Tweed Ring from power. Jones died in 1891.

The *Times* foundered after Jones' death and was on the brink of bankruptcy until Adolph S. Ochs, the son of Bavarian immigrants, purchased the newspaper in 1896. Ochs was not a very good writer, but he was outstanding as a leader and organizer. After several months of negotiations, he managed to persuade a number of investors, including tycoon J. P. Morgan, to invest in the deal. Ochs put up $75,000 of his own money. On October 25, 1896, the *Times* published its now-famous motto in the masthead: "All The News That's Fit To Print."

To raise circulation and decrease debt, Ochs published a pictorial Sunday magazine and created the "Review of Books," which continues to be a regular feature of the Sunday edition of the *Times*. In 1898, he reduced the price of the paper to one cent, and circulation tripled. But the real strength of the paper lay in the staff and the editorial philosophy. Ochs went to great lengths to hire the best reporters and editors in the field. In 1904, he hired Carr Vattel Van Anda (see biography later), who implemented Ochs' philosophy of publishing a newspaper with solid news coverage and editorial opinion.

But during the latter part of the 19th century, not all newspapers showed this commitment to quality. In large cities, many faced stiff competition and, to attract readers, exaggerated or distorted facts to attract attention. Joseph Pulitzer and William Randolph Hearst both became known as media barons, a derogatory name for publishers who place more emphasis on sensationalism than on facts and news.

CHAPTER OVERVIEW

This chapter examines the development of the press in the latter half of the 19th century. Newspapers were growing and becoming more structurally complex, offering more specialized content to an increasingly diversified public. Weeklies became dailies, and dailies began publishing on Sundays. The division of labor and role specialization expanded concomitantly.

According to Emery and Emery, regularly employed reporters were rare even after the penny press had become well established in the 1840s. However, by the 1850s, chief reporters — forerunners of city editors — had emerged at larger newspapers. In 1854, for example, the *New York Tribune* had 14 reporters and 10 editors.[2]

At the large dailies, the publisher or owner played a lesser role in day-to-day operations. Editors were increasingly drawn from the ranks of the formally educated and, in many cases, knew little about printing, advertising or circulation. Their role was to fill the newspaper with news and commentary in the most efficient manner possible. The advertising and circulation tasks, in turn, were handled by other individuals who had specialized knowledge in those areas.

On the eve of the Civil War, the *New York Herald* was the world's largest daily at 77,000 circulation. Emery and Emery point out that the paper had developed the best financial section of any paper in the country,[3] which supports the notion that the penny press, as an institution, was serving the interests of the growing capitalist class.

---

[2]Michael Emery and Edwin Emery, *The Press in America: An Interpretive History of the Mass Media*, 6th ed. (Englewood Cliffs, NJ: Prentice Hall, 1988), p. 212.

[3]Emery and Emery, *The Press in America*, pp. 120-123.

Bennett, himself once an economics teacher, wrote the "money page." The paper had a letters-to-the-editor column, a critical review column and a society news section. The paper also covered sports and church groups. It was, in other words, emerging as a highly diversified product that catered to the interests of an increasingly diverse audience.

In short, newspapers were beginning to exhibit the characteristics of the corporate form of organization. Understanding the historical development of the corporate form of organization is crucial for understanding the role and function of corporate and global media today. The central theme of this chapter is that the transition is part of an ongoing process of social differentiation, fueled by increasing urbanization and industrialization.

EFFECT OF CIVIL WAR

The American Civil War brought major changes in news writing styles, including the development of more fact-oriented stories, the summary lead and the inverted pyramid style of writing (putting the most important facts first).

To save telegraph toll costs, correspondents strived to be more concise. One way to accomplish this was to eliminate opinion and

Newspapers in camp during the Civil War, depicted in 1884.

coloration from stories. Reporters from the battlefield also relayed the most important information first for fear that complete dispatches might not make it through the telegraph lines.[4] Some scholars document how "objectivity" in news reports increased during the war.[5]

However, as noted earlier, it is important to point out that this "objectivity" is relative, not absolute. Newspapers on both sides of the conflict frequently distorted the truth. For example, newspapers almost always underestimated casualties on their own side and overestimated casualties on the enemy's side. Although military elites were often the source of these lies, during wartime

[4]See Emery and Emery, *The Press in America*, p. 170-171.
[5]Donald L. Shaw, "News Bias and the Telegraph: A Study of Historical Change," *Journalism Quarterly*, 44:3-12, 31 (1967).

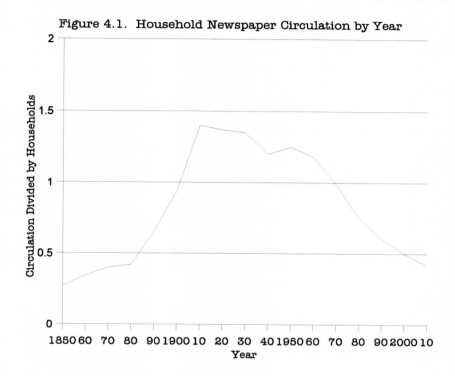

Figure 4.1. Household Newspaper Circulation by Year

mass media often censor themselves or publish half-truths in the interest of national security or to keep up morale at home.

GROWTH AFTER THE CIVIL WAR

The most explosive growth in the newspaper industry came after the Civil War.

Between 1870 and 1900, the number of general-circulation daily newspapers quadrupled, going from 574 to 2,226, and the number of weekly newspapers tripled, going from 4,000 to more than 12,000.[6] Daily circulation increased five-fold, from 2.6 million copies to 15 million, and household penetration (the number of newspapers sold divided by the number of total households) nearly tripled, from .34 to .94 copies per household (see Figure 4.1).

---

[6]U.S. Department of Commerce, *Historical Statistics of the United States, 1789-1945* (Washington, DC: U.S. Government Printing Office, 1949).

One of the major consequences of this massive growth in the newspaper industry in the late 1800s was increased competition. In 1880, about 239 of the 850 cities with an English-language daily newspaper had two or more dailies. The number nearly tripled by 1910, when 689 of the 2,202 cities had competitors.[7] Competition was greater in the larger cities, especially New York City, which had 15 general circulation dailies in 1890.

Newspapers also faced competition from magazines, which were taking in 60 percent or more of the national advertising revenue in 1900.[8] To survive and grow, newspapers needed to increase circulation, and one way to attract more readers was through sensationalistic coverage.

The dramatic growth in the newspaper industry in the closing decades of the 19th century can be attributed largely to industrialization and urbanization.[9] Total manufacturing production increased seven-fold from 1865 to 1900, and the total number of industries tripled, going from about 140,000 to 500,000. Population also increased from 31 million to 76 million.

The growth of industry and urban populations contributed directly to the growth of newspapers. Manufacturers needed efficient ways to reach buyers. Urban residents, especially the emerging middle and upper middle classes, needed access to information that could help them through everyday life in an increasingly interdependent, complex society. Newspapers were one mechanism for meeting both of these needs.[10]

---

[7]Raymond B. Nixon, "Trends in Daily Newspaper Ownership Since 1945," *Journalism Quarterly*, 31:3-14 (1954). See Table 4.1. Data are for English language dailies.

[8]Emery and Emery, *The Press in America*, p. 222.

[9]Education and declining illiteracy also were contributing factors. Between 1870 and 1900, the percentage of children attending public school increased from 57 to 72 percent, and illiteracy declined from 20 to 11 percent. For a sociological perspective on industrialization and urbanization, see Marvin E. Olsen, *The Process of Social Organization* (New York: Holt, Rinehart and Winston, 1968), especially Chapter 17.

[10]Newspapers are not the only way of integrating people into a community (e.g., occupation, church membership). In fact, research suggests that they may not be very important for newcomers (see Keith R. Stamm and Avery M. Guest, "Communication and Community Integration: An Analysis of the Communication Behavior of Newcomers," *Journalism Quarterly*, 68:644-56 [1991]). However, a large body of research evidence suggests that among established residents newspaper use is strongly correlated with community ties. See, e.g., Morris Janowitz, *Community Press in an Urban Setting*, 2nd ed. (Chicago: University of Chicago Press, 1967 [1952]).

Ownership Structure

Although the typical newspaper was still owned and managed by individuals (sole proprietors) or families and friends (partnerships) after the Civil War, more and more were becoming legally incorporated.

In legal terms, a corporation is an entity that has powers similar to an individual — it can borrow money, enter into contracts, and file lawsuits. From an investor's standpoint, the main advantage of a corporation is limited liability. If the corporation goes bankrupt, the investor loses only his or her investment. She or he does not have to pay off other debts. Another advantage of the corporation is that, when its owners die, the corporation does not have to liquidate its assets and typically continues to do business as usual.

Entrepreneurs still owned and managed most newspapers in the late 1800s, but chain or group newspaper organizations were gaining a foothold. A chain newspaper organization is usually defined as two or more newspapers in separate cities owned by the same individual or company. A newspaper not owned by a chain is called an independent newspaper organization.

Concentration of Ownership

In a study of Wisconsin newspapers, media historian Carolyn Dyer found that about one-fourth of the newspapers published between 1833 and 1860 were operated as parts of chains or other forms of groups.[11]

She divides the group-owned newspapers into five types of ownership structures: joint-operating agreements; chains; one community, two newspaper groups; family groups; and complex family groups. About a dozen of the groups resembled modern chains in that they involved the simultaneous publication of two or more general-circulation newspapers in different communities. She notes that the distance between the two communities in "many instances" would have permitted the sharing of presses and type.[12]

Dyer argues that the depiction of "frontier journalism as the solitary pursuit of heroic individuals" is basically a myth. Very few of the newspapers she studied were capitalized solely by their operators[13] or through pre-publication subscription contributions.[14] Most depended on at least one or two other

[11]Carolyn Stewart Dyer, "Economic Dependence and Concentration of Ownership Among Antebellum Wisconsin Newspapers," *Journalism History*, 7(2):42-46 (1980), p. 43.
    [12]Ibid, p. 45.
    [13]Dyer uses this term to refer to the person in charge, who had various titles, including publisher, printer and editor.
    [14]Dyer, "Economic Dependence and Concentration of Ownership," p. 43.

sources: chattel mortgages, in which the investment was secured by the equipment purchased, and joint-stock companies, in which ownership was sold as stock to investors. The mortgages were available from banks and printing equipment manufacturers, and the stock was usually sold to political parties and other special interest groups.

Dyer argues that the price paid for capitalization through these organizations was loss of editorial control, particularly in the case of joint-stock companies. Dyer also contends that the joint-stock company, the precursor to today's modern corporation, was "not generally a satisfactory way to run a paper."[15] Although more likely than other types of newspapers to hire technically competent printers, the joint-stock newspaper was less able to keep them. Operator turnover was quite high because, according to Dyer, the shareholders often gave little editorial autonomy to the operator. Shareholders, she argues, usually saw the newspaper as a vehicle for promoting their political views and were often involved in day-to-day operations.

This control very well may have existed. But it is important to point out that this does not necessarily mean a loss of diversity of opinion. The present-day criticism of corporate newspapers revolves around the question of whether those newspapers place greater emphasis on profits at the expense of a robust debate of public issues. The description that Dyer gives of joint-stock newspapers suggests that, to the contrary, many were pursuing political, not just economic, goals because they were capitalized by political parties. If this is the case, one might expect that such joint-stock ownership could contribute to increased diversity.

Although chains existed before the Civil War, what distinguished the groups after the war is that they survived long beyond the death of the original owners. The Scripps family is often credited with creating the first major newspaper chain.[16] In 1880, for example, the Scripps family owned newspapers in Cleveland, Cincinnati, St. Louis, and Buffalo. Today the Scripps chain still continues to be one of the largest in the country. It owns newspapers in 18 markets.

MEDIA BARONS AND YELLOW JOURNALISM

The upshot of all these changes is that the newspaper industry was becoming a field where fortunes could be made. In the 1890s, for example, the

---

[15]Ibid, p. 44.

[16]Alfred McClung Lee, *The Daily Newspaper in America: The Evolution of a Social Instrument* (New York: Macmillan, 1937), p. 211.

New York World was valued at $10 million and was pulling in an annual profit of $1 million a year.[17] Joseph Pulitzer and William Randolph Hearst became the media barons of their day.

Joseph Pulitzer

Pulitzer was born in 1847 and reared in Budapest. He emigrated to the United States in 1864 as a recruit for the Union Army during the Civil War.[18] After the war he became a reporter on a German-language newspaper in St. Louis. He bought a share of the newspaper and resold it at a profit.

He was elected to the Missouri state legislature in 1869 and helped to organize the Liberal Republican Party, which in 1872 nominated Horace Greeley for president. After the party's demise, Pulitzer became a Democrat.

In 1878 Pulitzer gained control of the *St. Louis Dispatch* and the *Post* and merged them. The *Post-Dispatch* became the city's dominant evening newspaper.

On May 10, 1883, he purchased the *New York World*, a morning paper, and soon turned it into the leading journalistic voice of the Democratic Party in the United States. Pulitzer also founded the *World*'s evening counterpart, the *Evening World*, in 1887.

His newspapers contained a unusual mix of high-quality investigative journalism and sensationalism. He was known as the "people's champion," but he often engaged in publicity stunts and blatant self-promotion to attract readership. His newspapers contained a lot of entertainment content, including comics, sports news, women's fashion coverage, and illustrations.

The *World* eventually went head-to-head with Hearst's *New York Morning Journal*, and the grandstanding and sensationalistic coverage, especially surrounding the Spanish-American War of 1898, led the coining of the term *yellow journalism*. Poor health forced Pulitzer to abandon the management of his newspapers in the late 1880s, but he continued to exercise a close watch over their editorial policies.

Pulitzer died in 1911. His will endowed the Columbia University School of Journalism in 1912 and established the Pulitzer Prizes, which have been awarded annually since 1917. They are the most prestigious awards in journalism.

---

[17] Emery and Emery, *The Press in America*, p. 218.

[18]Sources for this summary of Pulitzer include W. A. Swanberg, *Pulitzer* (New York: Scribner, 1967) and Julian S. Rammelkamp, *Pulitzer's Post-Dispatch, 1878-1883* (Princeton, NJ: Princeton University Press, 1967).

William Randolph Hearst

Hearst was born in 1863 and was the only child of George Hearst, a multimillionaire miner and rancher, and Phoebe Apperson Hearst, a school teacher. Hearst attended but dropped out of Harvard University. In 1887, at age 23, Hearst became "proprietor" of the *San Francisco Examiner*, which his father accepted as payment for a gambling debt.

In 1895, Hearst purchased the *New York Morning Journal* and entered into a circulation war with Pulitzer, his former mentor and owner of the *New York World*. Both newspapers wrote stories that exaggerated facts to stimulate newspaper

William Randolph Hearst

sales. This was particularly the case before the Spanish-American War in 1898. The newspapers implied that the Spanish had blown up the battleship Maine in Cuba, but there was no evidence to support such claims. The competition between the newspapers was so intense that Hearst hired away many of Pulitzer's top journalists.

Hearst was elected to the U.S. House of Representatives in 1903, but failed in his attempts to win the mayorship of New York City and the governorship of New York. He built a national chain of 28 newspapers and 18 magazines, some of which are still part of the Hearst Corporation (including *Cosmopolitan* magazine). The Great Depression weakened his empire and by 1940 he had lost control of his company.

Hearst was widely criticized for using his media empire to advance his own personal interests. This abuse of power was illustrated in Orson Welles' film "Citizen Kane," which was loosely based on Hearst's life (see Chapter 9). Hearst tried to discredit Welles and stop production and distribution of the film. These efforts were not successful, but the film on its initial release lost money and was shelved by RKO Pictures. Hearst died in 1951.

INVESTIGATIVE REPORTING AND CRITICAL NEWS

Pulitzer and Hearst are often criticized for sensationalizing and distorting the news. But their newspapers also published investigative stories that exposed injustice and corruption in government and business. In other words, their newspapers were guarding the system against abuse of power.

This is not the first time newspapers played the role of guardian for the community. However, Pulitzer and Hearst helped institutionalize investigative reporting as a reportorial tool of daily journalism. Its social control function was to expose people and organizations that violated community or national values, laws or norms.

The emergence of investigative reporting as a mainstay in American journalism at that time in history was no accident. It was a sign that newspapers were beginning to exhibit the characteristics of the corporate form of organization. They were growing and becoming more structurally complex. They were becoming "big business."

By the turn of the century, a typical metropolitan newspaper, for example, was staffed with a chief editor, a managing editor or night editor, a city editor, two dozen reporters, a telegraph editor, a financial editor, a drama critic, a literary editor and editorial writers.[19] The production side of the business included printers, pressmen, typographers, and photoengravers, each of whom was represented by different unions.[20]

Specialized roles had developed more fully, and at large newspapers functional areas such as advertising, circulation and news were increasingly being managed by individuals who had developed specialized skills and knowledge in those areas. At the large dailies, role specialization meant that the publisher or owner played a lesser role in day-to-day operations. Editors were increasingly drawn from the ranks of the formally educated and, in many cases, knew little about printing, advertising or circulation. Their role was to fill the newspaper with news and commentary in the most efficient manner possible.

As control of news production shifted from owners to professional managers, so did coverage of news and the content of the editorial pages. Because professional journalists tended to have fewer ties to the community, they were freer to criticize local community leaders. The journalists and their organizations also developed professional norms and eventually formal codes of ethics, which helped insulate the newspaper from local, state or national parochial political pressures.

In short, as the organizations became more complex, the more critical the news became of mainstream groups and values. Contemporary research shows, in fact, that corporate newspapers produce editorial content that is much more critical of mainstream institutions, elites and values than their entrepreneurial counterparts. And local community leaders also see corporate newspapers as

---

[19]Emery and Emery, *The Press in America*, p. 214.
[20]Emery and Emery, *The Press in America*, p. 223.

being more critical of them and their policies.[21] These studies are discussed in more depth later in this book.

A Brief History of the Corporate Newspaper

As noted above, the birth of the corporate news organization in the United States is often traced to the late 1800s. This was a time, many mass communication scholars point out, that the press as well as other capitalist enterprises began to exhibit the characteristics of "big business."

Mass communications historian Hazel Dicken-Garcia writes that the "emphasis shifted from news *persons* to news *selling,* and an editor-centered, personal structure gave way to corporatism, focused on advances in technology, increased competition, large circulations, diversification, and advertising as a means to profit" (emphasis in original).[22]

Media historians Michael Emery and Edwin Emery argue that the transition from the entrepreneurial to the corporate form of organization began at the close of the Civil War and was reflected in the writings of Henry Watterson of the *Louisville Courier-Journal* and Harvey W. Scott of the *Portland Oregonian.*[23]

> Both enjoyed long careers that began at the close of the Civil War and continued until World War I, but both belong primarily in this transitional period of journalism history. Arthur Krock, an associate of Watterson on the *Courier-Journal* staff before becoming a *New York Times* fixture, offers one reason for setting Watterson apart from later editors: "... he was the last of those editors who wrote with the power of ownership." The same was true of Scott. Other editors, like [Edwin Lawrence] Godkin, exercised free rein because of their relationship to the owners of their papers, and

---

[21]David Demers, "Who Controls the Editorial Content at Corporate News Organizations? An Empirical Test of the Managerial Revolution Hypothesis," *World Futures: The Journal of General Evolution, 57*:103-123 (2001); David Demers and Debra Merskin, "Corporate News Structure and the Managerial Revolution," *Journal of Media Economics,* 13(2):103-121 (2000); David Demers, "Structural Pluralism, Corporate Newspaper Structure and News Source Perceptions: Another Test of the Editorial Vigor Hypothesis," *Journalism & Mass Communication Quarterly, 75*:572-592 (1998); and David Pearce Demers, "Corporate Newspaper Structure, Editorial Page Vigor and Social Change," *Journalism & Mass Communication Quarterly,* 73:857-877 (1996).

[22]Hazel Dicken-Garcia, *Journalistic Standards in Nineteenth-Century America* (Madison, WI: University of Wisconsin Press, 1989), p. 20. Also see pp. 56-62.

[23]Emery and Emery, *The Press in America,* p. 182.

they have continued to do so since, but admittedly with increasing difficulty as the newspaper became a corporate institution.[24]

The notion that the transition to corporate ownership occurred on such precise terms could be contested.[25] The transition was gradual and was associated with the growth of cities, industries and, more specifically, retail advertising. The penny papers, in particular, might be called the first corporate newspapers because they were the first media to attract mass audiences. Yet the history of the corporate form of organization is actually much older than that.

Early History of Corporate Groups

Although corporate groups existed during the Roman empire, social theorists usually trace the origins of the modern corporation to the late Middle Ages and the rise of major trading centers.[26]

Before then, work and other social activities revolved almost exclusively around the family and the local community. The economic and social division of labor was very limited. The vast majority of people worked the land or tended herds, and the availability of work outside of agriculture was limited in part because there was little surplus in food production. People shared a common value system and work environment.

But with advances and improvements in agriculture, which increased food production, more and more people were freed from the land. Artisan guilds, local boroughs and ecclesiastical bodies were some of the earliest corporate

---

[24]Emery and Emery, *The Press in America*, p. 182.

[25]The argument that corporate newspapers give editors less autonomy than other forms of organization also is empirically questionable. See David Pearce Demers, "Effect of Corporate Structure on Autonomy of Top Editors at U.S. Dailies," *Journalism Quarterly*, 70:499-508 (1993).

[26]This early history of corporate organizations is drawn from a number of sources, including Adolf A. Berle, Jr. and Gardiner C. Means, *The Modern Corporation and Private Property* (New York: Macmillan, 1932), pp. 127-52; Emile Durkheim, *The Division of Labor in Society*, trans. W. D. Halls (New York: Free Press, 1984 [1933]), see preface to the second edition; Daniel Bell, *The End of Ideology* (Cambridge, MA: Harvard University Press, 1988 [1960]), pp. 39-45; Daniel Bell, *The Coming of the Post-Industrial Society* (New York: Basic Books, 1973), pp. 269-98; S. Prakash Sethi, "Corporation," in *Academic American Encyclopedia*, electronic version (Danbury, CT: Grolier, 1992); and William H. McNeill, *History of Western Civilization*, 6th ed. (Chicago: The University of Chicago Press, 1986). There is no historical record of whether ancient Greece had corporate groups.

groups. Two key factors distinguished corporate groups from other social formations.

The first was that they were consciously created instruments of self-governance designed to promote the interests of their members. Many justified their existence in part through claims that they served in the public interest and would protect the public from charlatans and quacks. They often monopolized markets, controlled prices, decided who could join their groups, and reproved members who violated organizational norms and goals. Sociologist Emile Durkheim also argued that the primary functions of these groups were to curb individual egoism, foster solidarity among workers, and act as a check on the abuses of employers, industrial organizations and the state.[27]

The second factor distinguishing the corporate groups from other groups was that they survived beyond the lifetime of any single member. This permanency enhanced the power of corporate groups relative to individuals and other, more transitory social formations (i.e., kinship, friendship systems).

Contemporary professional groups, such as doctors and lawyers, and modern business corporations can trace their roots to these early corporate groups. One of the earliest forms of the business corporation was the joint-stock company, which was created in the 16th and 17th centuries to fund large public works projects, such as canal or sewer construction, or overseas trading expeditions.

Through the sale of stock, such organizations could accumulate large sums of capital in a short period of time. Shares of these companies could be easily transferred from one person to another. However, unlike the modern legal corporation, the owners of joint-stock companies were personally liable for the company's debts, and many lost money because of unscrupulous promoters and risky ventures.[28]

In response to these events, England, the United States and other Western nations passed laws during the late 1700s and early 1800s limiting the liability of a stockholder to the actual amount of money invested. If the corporation went bankrupt, the personal assets of the investor were protected. The laws also were changed to give the corporation a legal personality so that it could enter into contracts, sue or be sued, and enjoy other privileges of legal citizenship.

In 1837, Connecticut became the first state in the United States to pass a statute which allowed incorporation "for any lawful business."[29] These changes promoted capital investment, which, in turn, had a profound effect on the development of the business organization.

---

[27]Durkheim, *The Division of Labor in Society,* see preface to the second edition.
[28]McNeill, *History of Western Civilization,* p. 507.
[29]Berle and Means, *The Modern Corporate and Private Property,* p. 136.

In the early 1800s, most businesses were very small relative to other competitors in the market, but by the late 1800s, many had grown to powerful proportions, wielding substantial market power. At the turn of the century, for example, Standard Oil Company controlled 90 percent of the refined petroleum sold in the United States.[30]

In terms of controlling a market, newspaper chains were never that powerful, nor are they today. But in the late 1800s, they were becoming big businesses, or what German sociologist Max Weber called "corporations" or "bureaucracies." They employed hundreds of people and some were owned by absentee stockholders. Professional managers ran the companies. The division of labor was often extensive, with many workers doing very highly specialized work.

What Is a Corporate News Organization?

More specifically, Weber defined a corporate organization as a group controlled by an administrative staff engaged in a continuous purposive activity.[31] Corporate organizations may or may not pursue economic profits, but they all establish and maintain boundaries for admission and continued membership. In other words, one must be hired or be allowed to join the group to become a member, and one is expected to abide by its rules. The rules are enforced either by a head or by an administrative staff.

Weber defined a bureaucracy as a corporate organization in which behavior is goal-directed and decision making is rational. By rational decision making, he means that bureaucratic

Max Weber

---

[30]C. Joseph Pusateri, *Big Business in America: Attack and Defense* (Itasca, IL: F. E. Peacock Publishers, 1975), p. 12.

[31]Sources for this discussion include Peter M. Blau and Marshall W. Meyer, *Bureaucracy in Modern Society*, 3rd ed. (New York: Random House, 1987); David Pearce Demers, *The Menace of the Corporate Newspaper: Fact or Fiction?* (Ames: Iowa State University Press, 1996); David Demers, *Global Media: Menace or Messiah?* (Cresskill, NJ: Hampton Press, 1999); H. H. Gerth and C. Wright Mills (eds.), *From Max Weber: Essays in Sociology* (New York: Oxford University Press, 1946); and Max Weber, *The Theory of Social and Economic Organization*, trans. A. M. Henderson and Talcott Parsons (New York: The Free Press, 1964 [1947]).

organizations try to reduce the production and distribution of goods or services into routines so as to find the most efficient and effective way to reach a goal. The reader can see that this use of the term rational is clearly different from the common sense meaning of "reasoning" or "reasonableness." The focus is on how to find the most efficient way to produce a product or service.

In addition to (1) rationality, Weber argues that bureaucracies are characterized by a (2) hierarchy of authority, (3) employment and promotion based on technical qualifications, (4) a set of rules and procedures that define job responsibilities and show how tasks are accomplished, (5) formalistic impersonality and (6) a highly developed division of labor and role specialization.

Weber pointed out that authority in a bureaucracy is vested in the position rather than in the individual. This minimizes the disruption that occurs when an individual leaves the organization. Selection for employment or promotion is based on technical competence or expertise rather than patronage or social position, and loyalties are given to the organization and its set of rules and procedures, not to individuals. In exchange, employees are given monetary compensation, promotions or other rewards.

Interpersonal relations in bureaucracies are more impersonal than those in nonbureaucratic organizations, but Weber argued that such impersonality was necessary to efficiently accomplish the goals of the organization. In other words, when people are too close to or friendly with each other, this can interfere with job performance (e.g., too much socializing). Tasks in a bureaucracy are highly specialized and delegated to individuals who ultimately are accountable for their performance. Rules and regulations control and standardize behavior, enabling managers to control the actions of a large number of workers. And the division of labor and role specialization generate economies of scale and increase the productive capacity of the organization.

Although Weber believed bureaucratic organizations are very efficient, he did not see them as a panacea. He believed they tend to monopolize information, resist change and threaten individual freedom and democratic principles. Many critics of media corporations, especially global media, strongly agree. A number of empirical studies also have questioned the extent to which bureaucracies are rational or efficient. Others even argue that bureaucracies are self-destructive.

All these criticisms have some merit. Who among us hasn't experienced the coldness of bureaucratic red tape? Time, however, has demonstrated that despite these problems corporate organizations often are capable of adapting to changes in the environment, and they still remain the most effective and efficient way to coordinate the work of large numbers of people. In fact, no other organizational form has displaced the corporate form, and nearly all aspects of modern life are interpenetrated by it.

Global media organizations are the most extreme form or example of a corporate media organization. For comparison purposes, the opposite of the corporate form of media organization is the entrepreneurial media organization, which scores low on the six characteristics listed above and has operations in only one country.

Although professionals and scholars often talk in terms of these dichotomies (corporate vs. entrepreneurial, global vs. nonglobal), in the real world these ideal types are better conceptualized on a continuum, in which all media organizations may be ranked as higher or lower than each other. Thus, global media represent one extreme end of the continuum — they are the largest, most complex corporations in the mass communication industry — and a media organization owned and managed by just one person would anchor the other end of the continuum.

Today's Modern Business Corporation

Today, of course, the modern business corporation is the dominant form of organization. In 1980, the 100 largest corporations in the United States held nearly 50 percent of the manufacturing assets.[32]

Although the corporate organization is often praised for its efficiency and increased productive capacity, it is also strongly criticized for having too much power.[33] The major fear is that the corporate organizations will act only in their own self-interest, not in the interest of the community or their customers.

Despite many complaints about corporations, and global mass media corporations in particular, the evidence thus far does not strongly support the critics' perspective. Indeed, large-scale media appear to enhance rather than detract from diversity in the marketplace of ideas, as is shown in subsequent chapters.[34]

---

[32]Campbell R. McConnell, *Economics* (New York: McGraw-Hill, 1987), p. 118.

[33]See, e.g., Pusateri, *Big Business in America.*

[34]David Demers, *Global Media: Menace or Messiah?* (Cresskill, NJ: Hampton Press, 2002, revised edition).

Chapter 5

STRUCTURE OF
MODERN NEWSPAPERS

Carr Vattel Van Anda loved journalism.[1]

At age 6, he produced a mock newspaper that indulgent relatives bought for 10 cents a copy. At age 10, he built a makeshift printing press out of wood, using a broom handle for the roller, and type salvaged from the local newspaper. During his teens, he published his own newspaper. At age 19, he began working as a typesetter for a Cleveland newspaper. In his twenties and thirties, he worked as a printer, reporter and editor for several newspapers before joining *The New York Times* in 1904 as managing editor. In fact, Van Anda loved the newspaper business so much he continued working as night editor at the *Times*.

So it's not too surprising that Van Anda also became one of the world's most respected journalists during the early 20th century. Under his tutelage, the *Times* was transformed into one of the world's most respected news organizations — and many would say "the most respected." In the bigger scheme of things, it's no exaggeration to say that Van Anda helped legitimize journalism as a profession, because he encouraged reporters to employ research and scientific-like precision to the news-gathering process.

Van Anda was born December 2, 1864, in Georgetown, Ohio, to Frederick C. and Mariah E. Davis Van Anda. His mother died when he was an infant. His father, a lawyer, remarried. The family moved to Wapakoneta, Ohio, when Van Anda was in his early teens. While there, he purchased a printing press for $5. In addition to doing some job printing, he wrote and published the *Boy's*

---

[1]Sources for this brief biography of Van Anda include Michael Emery, Edwin Emery and Nancy L. Roberts, *The Press and America: An Interpretive History of the Mass Media* (Boston: Allyn and Bacon, 2000), pp. 237-240, 282; Kristen Dollase, "Van Anda, Carr Vattel," pp. 711-712 in Joseph P. McKerns (ed.), *Biographical Dictionary of American Journalism* (New York: Greenwood Press, 1989); and E. W. Scripps School of Journalism Web site <www.scripps.ohiou.edu>.

Gazette. He used his profits to buy materials for chemistry and physics experiments, one of his other interests.

At age 16, Van Anda enrolled in Ohio University, where he studied chemistry and physics. In his spare time, he worked as a correspondent for newspapers in Cleveland and Cincinnati. Van Anda was a brilliant man. Later in his career, he discovered an error in one of Albert Einstein's equations. He might have become a famous scientist. But his love for journalism overpowered his love for science, and after two years of college he dropped out to take a job as foreman for a weekly newspaper.

In 1883, Van Anda became a typesetter for the now defunct

The Titanic story on the Front page of *The New York Times,* May 12, 1912.

Cleveland Herald and also wrote stories for the paper in his spare time. He was promoted to telegraph editor but eventually left that position and worked as a reporter and copy editor for several newspapers, including the *New York Sun,* the first successful penny paper. In 1885, Van Anda married, but his wife died two years later while giving birth to their daughter. In 1893, he was named night editor for the *Sun.* He made his final career move in 1904, when he accepted the managing editor position at *The New York Times.*

The *Titanic* disaster of 1912 was a turning point for his career. Van Anda managed the news staff that produced two full pages of copy for the morning edition in just two hours. The *Times* became the first newspaper to report the tragedy and scooped competitors on several other stories as well. Six years later, with Van Anda still at the helm, the *Times* won its first Pulitzer Prize for coverage of World War I.

Co-workers said Van Anda had a cold, steel gaze that they jokingly called the "Van Anda death ray." But he was widely admired and respected. He was known as "the chief architect of the superior news department." While other newspaper editors were encouraging their staffs to write sensational stories, Van Anda was directing his staff to cover science, exploration, aviation and archaeology. This included substantial coverage of Einstein and the opening of King Tutankhamen's (popularly known as King Tut's) tomb in Luxor, Egypt, in 1922. Van Anda also encouraged reporters to do their research in advance.

By 1920, circulation of the *Times* had grown to more than 300,000 daily and 500,000 Sunday. In 1925, ill health forced Van Anda into semi-retirement. He formally retired in

A sidewalk newsstand in New York City, 1901.

1932. His second wife died in 1942, and his daughter died in 1945. Upon hearing the news of his daughter's death, Van Anda suffered a heart attack and died two hours later.[2]

CHAPTER OVERVIEW

The era during which Van Anda lived and worked marked some major changes for newspapers and journalism in general.

The first was that journalism became increasingly "professionalized." One sign of this was the development of formal codes of ethics. In 1922, the American Society of Newspaper Editors approved its first code, which stated that (1) journalists who use their power for selfish reasons violate a public trust; (2) freedom of the press is a vital right of "mankind"; (3) journalists should not accept bribes or money from news sources; and (4) journalists should be sincere, truthful, accurate, impartial and fair. Another sign of increasing professionalism was the institutionalization of the *ethic of objectivity*,[3] which admonished reporters to (1) keep their personal opinions and their newspaper's opinions out of their news stories (the editorial pages were the appropriate place for that); (2) cover all sides to a story; and (3) give all sides to a story an equal amount of

---

[2]Ohio University's E. W. Scripps School of Journalism issues The Carr Van Anda award annually for "enduring contributions to journalism." Past recipients include Walter Cronkite, Helen Thomas, William Raspberry, Harry Reasoner, Pierre Salinger, and Ted Turner.

[3]See Michael Schudson, *Discovering the News* (New York: Basic Books, 1978) and Barbara M. Kelly, "Objectivity and the Trappings of Professionalism, 1900-1950," pp. 149-166 in Steven R. Knowlton and Karen L. Freeman (eds.), *Fair & Balanced: A History of Journalistic Objectivity* (Northport, AL: Vision Press, 2005).

coverage.[4] Van Anda, more than anyone, embodied these principles, and he also encouraged his reporters to collect the news like a scientist would.

But at the same time the industry was becoming more professionalized, it was also becoming more concentrated in terms of ownership. After 1910, some daily newspapers across the country began going out of business, and more and more newspapers were being purchased by chains or large corporations. The number of owners — or those entities (e.g., individuals or organizations) that own newspapers — declined despite substantial growth in the population, the number of urban places, daily circulation and advertising revenue. Between 1910 and 1930, the population increased from 92 to 122 million. The number of cities with 8,000 or more population rose from 768 to 1,208. Circulation went from 22.5 million to 40 million. And newspaper advertising tripled between 1915 and 1929, going from $275 million to $800 million.[5] But the newspaper industry still lost newspapers.[6]

The daily newspaper industry reached maximum diversity in about 1910, when there were 2,202 English-language daily newspapers operated by 2,153 owners (see Table 5.1). But by 1940 the number of owners had declined to 1,619, and by 2000 the number of owners stood at 436, an 80 percent decline since 1910. Over the 90-year period, the number of dailies dropped 33 percent, going from 2,202 to 1,480. Needless to say, many journalists and social observers were concerned. During the mid-1800s, the famous radical Karl Marx had predicted that ownership of industry under capitalism would become more centralized. As this happened, he argued, workers would be able to see how they were being exploited by the capitalists. This awareness, in turn, set the stage for revolutions against capitalist governments. Were his predictions coming true?

The purpose of this chapter is to examine the loss of dailies and the growth of chains and corporate news organizations during the 20th century. This will include an analysis of the impact of radio and television competition on newspapers. This chapter also examines the social control and social change functions of mass media in the 20th century. A "guard dog" metaphor is used to explain the role and function of the press.

---

[4]See Chapter 16 for an in-depth analysis of the concept of objectivity.

[5]Lee, *The Daily Newspaper in America*, see appendices. Advertising revenue figures are taken from the ANPA Bureau of Advertising.

[6]That is, the number of individual proprietorships, partnerships and legal corporations that own newspapers declined. However, it is important to point out that the number of people who own stock or other equities in newspapers has increased with the rise of the legal corporation, mutual funds and pension funds.

TABLE 5.1
GROWTH OF CHAIN OWNERSHIP IN THE UNITED STATES

Year	No. of Dailies	No. of Groups	No. of Dailies in Groups	Percent Group Owned	Avg. No. per Group	No. of Inde- pendent Dailies	No. of Owners
1900*	1,967	8	27	1.4	3.4	1,940	1,948
1910	2,202	13	62	2.8	4.8	2,140	2,153
1920	2,042	31	153	7.5	4.9	1,889	1,920
1930	1,942	55	311	16.0	5.7	1,631	1,686
1940	1,878	60	319	17.0	5.3	1,559	1,619
1950*	1,772	86	427	24.1	5.0	1,345	1,431
1960	1,763	109	552	31.3	5.1	1,211	1,320
1970	1,748	157	879	50.3	5.6	869	1,026
1980	1,745	154	1,139	65.3	7.4	606	760
1990	1,611	129	1,217	74.8	9.4	409	538
2000	1,480	124	1,184	80.0	9.5	312	436

Sources: For 1900 data, Michael Emery and Edwin Emery, *The Press in America* (Englewood Cliffs, NJ: Prentice-Hall, 1988), p. 335 and Frank Luther Mott, *American Journalism* (New York: Macmillan, 1962), p. 648; for 1910 and 1920 data, Raymond B. Nixon and Jean Ward, "Trends in Newspaper Ownership and Inter-Media Competition," *Journalism Quarterly*, 38:3-24 (1961); 1930 to 1960 data, Benjamin M. Compaine, "Newspapers," pp. 27-93 in Benjamin M. Compaine, Christopher H. Sterling, Thomas Guback and J. Kendrick Noble, Jr., *Who Owns the Media: Concentration of Ownership in the Mass Communications Industry* (White Plains, NY: Knowledge Industry, 1982), p. 30, 39; for 1990 data, *Editor and Publisher International Yearbook*; and for 2000 data, David Demers, *Media Concentration in the United States*, proprietary paper prepared for Centre D'Études sur les Médias, University of Laval, Quebec, Canada (February 2001) available online at <www.cem.ulaval.ca/CONCetatsUnis.pdf>.

*Number of chains and newspapers in chains estimated for these years.

EXPLAINING THE DECLINE IN NEWSPAPER OWNERS

The decline in the number of owners can be broken down into two separate trends. The first is the loss of competing newspapers through mergers or suspensions. The second is the growth of the chain newspaper.

Mergers and Chains

In 1900, 559 cities with a daily, or 61 percent of the total, had two or more competing newspapers. But by 1930 the number of cities with competing dailies fell to 288, or 29 percent.[7] New York City lost nearly half of its dailies during this time period. And by 1986 only 28 cities, or 2 percent, had competing papers.[8]

A study by Royal Ray in the early 1950s found that between 1910 and 1930 1,495 dailies were founded, 1,391 newspapers suspended publication or shifted to weekly status, and 362 merged with rival papers.[9] The net result was a loss of more than 250 dailies. From 1909 to 1950, 559 dailies disappeared through consolidation or merger. According to Ray, the period 1937 to 1943 accounted for more than half of the decline.

Girls selling newspapers in 1910.

The second trend contributing to concentration of ownership — and a more important one than the first — is the growth of the chain newspaper. Table 5.1 shows that the number of newspapers under chain or group ownership increased substantially from 1900 to 1930, going from 1.4 percent to 16 percent of the total number of dailies. The Great Depression brought the growth of chain ownership to a virtual standstill; some large national chains, including Hearst and Scripps-Howard, lost some papers.[10] But, overall, the newspaper industry held up quite well.

Table 5.1 shows that between 1930 and 1940 the industry lost a net total of only 64 newspapers — fewer than it did during the previous or succeeding decade. Chains were even losing papers.[11]

---

[7]Emery and Emery, *The Press in America*, p. 334.

[8]John C. Busterna, "Trends in Daily Newspaper Ownership," *Journalism Quarterly,* 65:831-8 (1988).

[9]Royal H. Ray, "Economic Forces as Factors in Daily Newspaper Concentration," *Journalism Quarterly*, 29:31-42 (1952).

[10]Commission on Freedom of the Press, *A Free and Responsible Press* (Chicago: University of Chicago Press, 1947), p. 42.

[11]Ibid.

Yet, despite this stagnation, the number of specialists working in the newspaper organization continued to grow. In the newsroom, reporters were assigned to cover a variety of beats, including labor, science, agriculture, social work, foreign affairs and the usual political and economic beats. The political column began in the early 1920s with the writings of David Lawrence, Mark Sullivan and Frank R. Kent. The political cartoon also became institutionalized.[12]

The Impact of Radio

Ray attributes the decline in the number of owners in the late 1930s to the loss of advertising revenue as a result of the "recession," competition from radio, and increasing wages and newsprint prices. The loss during World War II he attributes to increased operating costs, caused by price rises, shortages and rationing of newsprint and other materials, and higher wages because of shortages of labor.[13]

> The dramatic rise of radio as an advertising medium during the 1930s and the consequent loss of advertising to radio by newspapers understandably causes publishers to seek shelter through integration. Post-war expansion of radio and television only serves to intensify the competition for advertising appropriations.[14]

But is radio responsible for concentration of ownership in the newspaper industry? Other historical data are not clear on this point.

Radio made its commercial debut in the 1920s but did not become a major medium until the depression years. As might be expected, some newspaper owners perceived the new medium as a competitive threat. Others, however, saw it as a marketing tool. The American Newspaper Publishers Association's radio committee issued a report in 1927 which showed that 48 newspapers owned radio stations, 69 sponsored programs on unowned stations, and 97 gave news programs over the air. Many newspapers were using radio to sell themselves, and the committee concluded that it worked.[15]

Nevertheless, by the late 1920s many newspaper publishers perceived radio as a competitive threat. Chester argues that there are three major reasons for

[12]Emery and Emery, *The Press in America*, p. 336.

[13]Ray, "Economic Forces as Factors in Daily Newspaper Concentration," pp. 33-4.

[14]Ray, "Economic Forces," p. 41.

[15]Edwin Emery, *History of the American Newspaper Publishers Association* (Minneapolis: University of Minnesota Press, 1950), Chapter 13.

this.[16] One was the expansion of chain broadcasting by the National Broadcasting Company and the Columbia Broadcasting System. The second was the growth of radio advertising. And the third was the drop in newspaper lineage and circulation in the early years of the depression. In 1932 the American Newspaper Publishers Association formed the Publishers' National Radio Committee to develop ways to limit competition from radio.

The committee drafted a "10-point agreement" in 1934 that, among other things, required CBS to withdraw from the news collection field, prohibited NBC from entering the field, and set up a Press-Radio Bureau that would control the collection and dissemination of news to radio stations.[17] The plan was implemented, but it failed to gain the support of many independent stations, especially outside of New York City, and the effort was abandoned in 1938, when the major networks withdrew their financial support and set up their own news gathering services to supplement the wire services.[18]

But was the competitive threat from radio real or imagined? A recent study by Lacy found that change in the absolute and per capita number of radio stations in 72 cities between 1929 and 1948 had no effect on whether competition between daily newspapers declined in those cities.[19] Furthermore, despite the growth of radio during the 1920s, newspaper penetration grew.

Figure 4.1 (see Chapter 4) shows that the number of newspapers per household peaked at 1.32 copies in 1930. Household circulation declined somewhat during the depression and began rising again in the 1940s, reaching another high point in the mid-to-late 1940s. And this growth occurred despite opinion polls by Lazarsfeld and Kendall, which showed that during World War II 61 percent of citizens got most of their news by radio, and that during the late 1940s 44 percent obtained most of their news by radio.[20]

Whatever anxieties publishers had about radio in the early 1930s appeared to have subsided during the 1940s, as most dailies were publishing radio program listings without charge.[21]

---

[16]Giraud Chester, "The Press-Radio War: 1933-1935," *Public Opinion Quarterly*, 13:252-264 (1949), pp. 252-253.

[17]Ibid, pp. 256-7.

[18]Ibid, p. 263.

[19]Stephen Lacy, "The Effect of Growth of Radio on Newspaper Competition, 1929-1948," *Journalism Quarterly*, 64:775-81 (1987).

[20]Paul F. Lazarsfeld and Patricia Kendall, *Radio Listening in America* (New York: Prentice-Hall, 1948), p. 34.

[21]Chester, "The Press-Radio War," p. 264.

POST WORLD WAR II

The trend toward chain ownership picked up after World War II. By 1950, one-fourth of all dailies were owned by chains or groups. But newspaper penetration began to decline in the late 1940s and has continued to decline ever since (see Figure 4.1). The newspaper industry's share of total advertising dollars also has declined since the 1940s.[22]

The Impact of Television

The declines coincided with the emergence of television as a mass medium, and, needless to say, many scholars and journalists believe the trends are no coincidence — that television adversely impacted newspaper circulation. However, strong empirical evidence is still lacking, and some scholars argue that the two media are more complementary than competitive.[23]

The trend toward group ownership continued in the 1950s and 1960s. Former newspaper editor-turned-scholar Ben H. Bagdikian argues that this growth was fueled by high taxes and tax laws that favor investing the profits elsewhere. Newspapers, he adds, made about 12 to 15 percent profit on assets after taxes. "Tax regulations permit accumulation of undistributed earnings free of the usual tax on undistributed earnings of 38½ percent for amounts over $100,000 — if the accumulation is for buying another property of the same type," he writes. "Thus, accumulated newspaper profits tend to be used to buy other papers in other places."[24]

Chain Ownership and Profits

Bagdikian argues that one of the most harmful effects of chain ownership may be that profits are not reinvested in the paper. He also contends that even though families still own a large share of the stock in many chain organizations, the idea of "a crusading proprietor" whose main interest is civic betterment, not profits, is basically a myth.

Profits in the 1960s averaged 20 percent of gross before taxes. Most families had little role in the day-to-day operations. The transition from local to absentee ownership, he argues, has two major consequences for the industry.

---

[22]Robert J. Coen, "Estimated Annual U.S. Advertising Expenditures 1935-1985," unpublished report (New York: McCann-Erickson Advertising, Inc., 1986).

[23]The literature on this topic is discussed in more depth later.

[24]Ben H. Bagdikian, *The Information Machines* (New York: Harper & Row, 1971), p. 131.

First, it means that a conventional corporate newspaper will be less concerned about local issues. "There are many cases of negligent local owners and conscientious absentee ones, but on the whole absentee owners are less sensitive to local nuances," he writes. "A locally rooted family or a personal operator whose family is part of the community is more susceptible to the social and informational needs of the paper's surroundings."[25] Second, the transition produces a lower quality product.

> The tradition of the personally involved owner is strong and, while it produces numerous cases of entrenched morbidity, it also is the most important single factor in papers of excellence. ... Modern corporate pressures are beginning to erode the tradition of personal direction and family control of newspapers.[26]

These charges are examined in more depth in Part III of this book. What's important here is that Bagdikian became, and remains, the best known critic of corporate media and concentration of ownership.

During the 1960s, 1970s and 1980s, dailies under direct competition continued to die here and there, but, overall, the newspaper industry was relatively stable. Established papers in most communities — especially those in communities without competition from another daily — were on solid ground. And, unlike the earlier part of the century, there were few attempts to start newspapers, especially dailies.

Barriers to Entry

A major part of the problem was cost. Bennett founded the *New York Herald* in 1835 for $500. The capitalization of a major city daily in 1960 was about $6 million.[27] But even a small weekly would easily have run into the hundreds of thousands of dollars in start-up costs.

The diffusion of offset printing and computerized composition equipment during the 1960s and 1970s had a profound impact on staffing and role specialization at most dailies. One study of newspapers found that from 1959 to 1980 a typical 20,000-circulation daily reduced staffing in the mechanical

---

[25]Bagdikian, *The Information Machines*, p. 117.

[26]Bagdikian, *The Information Machines*, pp. 117-8.

[27]Ray Eldon Hiebert, Donald F. Ungurait and Thomas W. Bohn, *Mass Media II: An Introduction to Modern Communication* (New York: Longman, 1979), p. 224.

department (e.g., printing, typesetting) by 50 percent, but it increased the number of reporters and editors by 40 percent.[28]

Role Specialization

Not unexpectedly, this increase has been accompanied by increased role specialization. Most large newspapers now have environmental, science and technology reporters, and almost every reporter has some specialty. Some even have an information technology beat, covering such topics as the Internet and e-mail.[29]

For example, at the *Star Tribune* in Minneapolis during the early 2000s, the business news section — just one of several functional areas in the news department — had 18 specialized roles, including a business editor, two general assignment reporters, Monday business editor, business forum editor, workplace reporter, retail and commercial development reporter, news assistant, technology reporter, research assistant, small business reporter, food reporter, business-calendar correspondent, national economics correspondent, manufacturing reporter, management reporter, travel and hospitality reporter, housing reporter, consumer affairs reporter, and two columnists. Such specialization appears to correspond to increasing differentiation in business and industry in the Twin Cities metropolitan area.

Concentration and centralization of ownership also has continued. In 1900, the typical daily had a circulation of 7,500; only 27 of the 1,967 dailies, or 1.4 percent, were owned by a chain or group. But by 1990, the typical daily had a circulation of 38,000 and was owned by a chain or group headquartered in another city or state. About 80 percent of the 1,611 dailies, or 1,217, were part of a chain or group.[30]

Although newspapers have become more differentiated in content since World War II, they have not been able to eliminate the decline in penetration per household, which is at its lowest point since 1890 (see Figure 4.1).

---

[28]B. E. Wright and John M. Lavine, *The Constant Dollar Newspaper: An Economic Analysis Covering the Last Two Decades* (Chicago: Inland Daily Press Association, 1982). Offset printing and computerized composition saved the 20,000-circulation daily about $200,000 a year. Profits did not increase substantially during the early 1980s, however, because of increased costs of newsprint.

[29]The Minneapolis *Star Tribune* created the beat in February 1994. Joel Kramer, "Beats Open a Window Onto How a Paper Sees the News," *Star Tribune* (February 28, 1994), p. A29.

[30]Data from Emery and Emery, *The Press in America*, p. 335, and *Editor & Publisher International Yearbook* (New York: Editor & Publisher, 1991).

HOUSEHOLD PENETRATION CONTINUES TO DECLINE

Aside from chain ownership and increasing specialization, one of the most notable trends in the newspaper industry in the 20th century has been a decline in daily newspaper penetration. Penetration increased throughout the 19th century and peaked in the 1920s, when there were about 1.3 newspapers for every household in the United States (see Figure 4.1).

Since then, however, penetration has declined. Only about 4 of 10 households today subscribe to a daily newspaper. Research also shows that only about 5 of 10 of adults read a daily newspaper during the week, compared with about 8 of 10 in the 1970s.[31] And total daily circulation has dropped since 1987, when it peaked at about 63 million. Total U.S. daily newspaper circulation stands at about 50 million.

The precipitous decline in household penetration in the 1950s suggests that television played a key role. Indeed, most people now get their news from television. It takes much less effort to watch television than to read a newspaper. However, both mediums have survived because they do not perform identical functions. The newspaper contains a lot more information and news than television, which is primarily a source of entertainment programming.

Another significant trend in recent decades has been the switch from an evening to a morning publication schedule. In 1950, only about one of five newspapers published in the morning. Today about half of all dailies publish in the morning. The most dramatic change came from 1980 to 1990, when nearly 200 dailies made the switch. Many dailies switched to lessen competition from early evening television news, which had the advantage of providing more up-to-the-minute news reports.

JOINT-OPERATING AGREEMENTS

In an attempt to stem the decline of competing dailies in large cities, Congress passed the Newspaper Preservation Act of 1970. The Act enables two different newspapers in a city to enter into a joint-operating agreement, which allows them to share staff in terms of production, circulation and advertising but to keep editorial operations separate.

---

[31]W. R. Simmons & Associates Research Inc., 1970-1977, and Scarborough Research, *Top 50 DMA Market Report*, 1995-1998.

The program has been only a partial success. About a dozen joint-operating agreements still exist, but those numbers are expected to decline because it is still much more efficient economically to publish one newspaper than two.

Only very large cities, like New York City and Chicago, can financially support more than one daily, and the newspapers that have survived in those cities reach different markets. (*The New York Times* and *Chicago Tribune* are preferred by a more white-collar reader and the New York *Daily News* and the *Chicago Sun-Times* are preferred by a more blue-collar reader).

Newspaper Technology Improves

In terms of technology, the most dramatic change in the 20th century was the diffusion of offset printing and computerized composition equipment during the 1960s and 1970s. Prior to such technologies, newspapers used Linotype machines and hot metal type to set copy, processes that were very labor intensive.

But offset printing and computerized composition reduced costs substantially and enabled newspapers to hire more reporters. One study found that from 1959 to 1980 a typical 20,000-circulation daily reduced staffing in the mechanical department (e.g., printing, typesetting) by 50 percent, but it increased the number of reporters and editors by 40 percent.[32]

Not unexpectedly, this increase has been accompanied by increased role specialization in the newsroom. Most large newspapers now have environmental, science, health, and information technology beats, the latter covering such topics as the Internet and e-mail.[33]

Are Newspapers in Crisis?

DeFleur and Ball-Rokeach argue that the rise and fall of the press, as measured by penetration, follows the familiar S-shaped "curve of adoption" that is typical of growth patterns for a variety of cultural innovations.[34] They

---

[32]B. E. Wright and John M. Lavine, *The Constant Dollar Newspaper: An Economic Analysis Covering the Last Two Decades* (Chicago: Inland Daily Press Association, 1982). Offset printing and computerized composition saved the 20,000-circulation daily about $200,000 a year. Profits did not increase substantially during the early 1980s, however, because of increased costs of newsprint.

[33]The Minneapolis *Star Tribune* created the beat in February 1994. Joel Kramer, "Beats Open a Window Onto How a Paper Sees the News," *Star Tribune* (February 28, 1994), p. A29.

[34]For additional literature on the diffusion of innovations, see Everette M. Rogers,

contend that limited education, transportation and printing facilities played a part in keeping the number of "early adopters" small.

By 1910, many of these constraints had been overcome. During the next three decades new innovations in media — including film, radio, news magazines, and television — began to appear, competing with newspapers for audience attention. According to media historians Arthur J. Kaul and Joseph P. McKerns,

> To a greater or less extent, each of these functional alternatives to the newspaper has eaten into the circulation of the daily press. Each, in some sense, provides news, information, or entertainment in a way that once was the exclusive province of the newspaper.[35]

Kaul and McKerns argue that the evolution of the newspaper industry can be divided into four major historical periods: a prevariation stage (before 1825), in which newspapers existed as "small, formally unorganized enterprises"; a variation stage (1825-1845), when major technological and cultural changes affected the development of newspapers; a selection stage (1845-1900), in which the number of newspaper competitors grew dramatically and became crowded; and a retention stage (post 1900), in which ownership became increasingly concentrated.

In 1985, they argued that newspapers are "dying in a crisis generated by the disjunction of material and knowledge technologies. In a very real sense, today's newspapers are trapped in the contradictions of their evolution."[36] They also argue that contemporary mass communication history and theory cannot explain "the decline of the newspaper and its displacement by newly evolving communication media."[37] They propose a "dialectic ecology" model, which synthesizes the ideas of Charles Darwin and Karl Marx. Basically, the model focuses attention on contradictions and crises generated with the life history of organizations.

The historical stages articulated by Kaul and McKerns appear to provide a reasonably accurate description of the changes that the newspaper industry has undergone. The newspaper as it is currently packaged and delivered to

---

Diffusion of Innovations, 3rd ed. (New York: The Free Press, 1983).

[35]Melvin L. DeFleur and Sandra Ball-Rokeach, *Theories of Mass Communication*, 5th ed. (New York: Longman, 1989), p. 60.

[36]Arthur J. Kaul and Joseph P. McKerns, "The Dialectic Ecology of the Newspaper," *Critical Studies in Mass Communication*, 2:217-233 (1985), p. 217.

[37]Kaul and McKerns, "The Dialectic Ecology of the Newspaper," p. 217.

consumers may also disappear with the advent of electronic technologies such as interactive video on the Internet.

But this does not necessarily mean that the organizations that publish the papers are doomed as well, because organizational forms are not simply reducible to technology. Indeed, the history of the newspaper organization has shown that it can adapt to a variety of social, economic and cultural changes, including competition from broadcast media. An alternative scenario for the future is that, although the current physical form of the newspaper may perish, newspaper organizations will use the Internet to deliver the product electronically to the consumer.[38] To date that hasn't worked well because advertisers and consumers have not yet fully adapted to the "new" medium (see Chapter 12 for more details on the impact of the Internet).

---

[38]John Rodden, "Ma Bell, Big Brother and the Information Services Family Feud," *Media Studies Journal*, 6(2):1-16 (1992), p. 8.

Chapter 6

ROLE AND FUNCTION OF MODERN NEWSPAPERS

Security guard Frank Wills never thought of himself as a hero. But don't try telling that to the Democrats.

On June 17, 1972, Wills was making his nightly rounds when he discovered a piece of masking tape over the lock of a door on the first floor of the building he was patrolling. He removed the tape and discovered several other doors that were taped to stay open. When he returned to the first door, he found the tape he removed had been replaced. Wills called police at 1:47 a.m.

When police arrived, they followed the trail of tape to the Democratic National Committee headquarters, whose offices were located in Wills' building, the Watergate office-apartment-hotel complex in Washington, DC Police arrested five men who had broken into the offices. Later it turned out four of the burglars were Cuban exiles and one was a former CIA surveillance expert. They were carrying cameras, pens filled with tear gas, eavesdropping equipment and $6,500 in crisp $100 bills.

For two years newspaper reporters followed the story, which eventually tied the burglary to President Richard Nixon. The burglars, acting under orders of Nixon's re-election campaign, had been searching for information to embarrass Democratic presidential candidate George McGovern. They also intended to bug the phones and offices. But the dirty tricks didn't end there. The reporters also discovered that Nixon's administration had been spying illegally on U.S. citizens, harassing political opponents, forging campaign literature, and attempting to obstruct justice through a cover-up.

Nixon won the 1972 election, but he resigned two years later, on August 8,

Nixon just after his resignation.

1974, under pressure of impeachment and conviction. A number of his assistants were convicted and spent time in prison. Nixon, however, never went to prison because he was pardoned by Vice President Gerald Ford, who became president after Nixon resigned. The pardon angered many Americans, and Ford lost the 1976 presidential election to Democrat Jimmy Carter. For a brief time, security guard Frank Wills, who earned $80 a week, was a hero. But today his whereabouts are unknown.

No story in the history of journalism has generated more praise for U.S. mass media. Bob Woodward and Carl Bernstein of *The Washington Post* took the lion's share of credit, helping their newspaper win a Pulitzer Prize. They also wrote a best-selling book, called *All the President's Men,* which was made into a successful movie starring Robert Redford and Dustin Hoffman.[1]

The Watergate story seemed to confirm watchdog theory. This is the notion that the news media are supposed to be watchdogs for the people, especially the powerless and those who have no organized voice in the system. News media are adversaries, not advocates, of the government and the powerful. They are supposed to challenge authority and promote democratic ideals.

But how accurate is this ideal? Do newspapers really challenge the dominant power groups, as suggested by the watchdog notion? Moreover, what is the primary function of newspapers and other mass media in a community or society?

CHAPTER OVERVIEW

Most professional journalists do not see themselves as advocates of government or big business, or as agents of social control. They see themselves as defenders of truth and justice. They believe they represent the interests of ordinary citizens, not government bureaucrats or corporate elites.

But, interestingly, many historians and scholars who study newspapers and news media reach just the opposite conclusion. Some even believe journalists act more like lap dogs for the rich and powerful than watchdogs for the poor and weak. The lap dog theory, which draws from Marxist theory, sees newspapers and other media as powerful agents of social control.

The truth, I shall argue in this chapter, lies in-between the watchdog and lap dog models — in what three mass communication researchers at the University of Minnesota have called the guard dog model of the press. In a nutshell, this theory contends that newspapers clearly generate content that

---

[1]Carl Bernstein and Bob Woodward, *All the President's Men* (New York: Simon and Schuster, 1974).

supports dominant values and institutions. The 20th century is filled with examples of the newspaper performing the social control function (i.e., supporting the status quo and the powerful institutions and groups in a community). But they also publish content that, at times, criticizes or challenges those in positions of power and occasionally benefits the less powerful, the less privileged. Watergate is a good example.

Watergate and Social Control

On the surface, it may seem strange to argue that Watergate is a good example of how newspapers reinforce the status quo. After all, didn't the news media bring down the most powerful individual in the world?

Yes, but Nixon's resignation did not lead to radical change in the structure of the American political system. In fact, Watergate is a prime example of how media helped maintain that system. And to understand why this is the case, one first needs to make a distinction between individual problems and social structural problems.

Almost from the beginning, the problem of Watergate was defined primarily as an individual problem, not as a problem of the social structure. In other words, the media spotlight was focused on the illegal actions of various individuals connected with the Nixon administration, who were defined as "bad actors." The media did not focus on the social structure as the source of problem, or the idea that something was wrong with the laws or structure of the American system of democracy.

This distinction is important. When problems are defined in individual terms, problems are resolved by punishing or controlling the individuals. This generally does not lead to much social change. But when the problem is defined as systemic, or part of the social structure, then the social system must be changed to correct the problem, and this can have a much greater impact on people's lives now and in the future.

Most societies, including the United States, have rules and laws to punish people who burglarize offices, tap telephones, engage in political espionage or lie. The system also is composed of institutions, organizations and special interest groups — such as Congress, the FBI and the Supreme Court — that have the power to create and enforce those values and laws. By drawing attention to the "abuses of power" that occurred during Watergate, the media played an important role in reminding others about the rules and reinforcing the power of these institutions to control people. Media coverage, in other words, reinforced the status quo.

Guard Dog Theory

More formally, University of Minnesota mass communication researchers Phillip J. Tichenor, George A. Donohue and Clarice N. Olien liken the media to a guard dog. The basic idea is that media serve as a guard dog not for the entire community per se, but for the political and special interest elite groups that hold power.

The "Minnesota Team" argued that the watchdog theory — which sees media as representing the average citizen — is fundamentally a myth, "in the sense of a sentinel of the general community keeping watch over central powers of government." The Minnesota Team also rejected the neo-Marxist or critical theory perspective, which tended to see media as lap dogs of political or economic elites. This couldn't be the case because, the Team pointed out, the media often attack or criticize powerful elites (Watergate is a good example), and elites in turn often are critical of the mass media.

Instead, the researchers argue that mainstream media are "a sentry not for the community as a whole, but for those particular groups who have the power and influence to create and command their own security systems."[2] Guard dog media "are conditioned to be suspicious of all potential intruders, and they occasionally sound the alarm for reasons that individuals in the master households, that is, the authority structure, can neither understand nor prevent. These occasions occur primarily when authority within the structure is divided."

The press is most likely to "bark" at elites when they are attacked by another powerful elite group (such as when Democrats criticize Republicans), or when elites in power violate the laws and norms (as in Watergate). The media's role is not to protect individual elites or organizations per se, but, rather, to protect "the system." Any individual actor is expendable, but attacking or challenging the system itself (e.g., values, norms) is much more problematic. Mainstream media provide broad-based support for dominant institutions and values, such as responsible capitalism, representative democracy and family values.

From a broader perspective, the Minnesota Team sees the mass media as one institution among many (police, courts, schools, churches, businesses) that plays an important role in helping maintain society and the status quo. Media provide information that social actors use to achieve their personal and

---

[2]George A. Donohue, Clarice N. Olien and Phillip J. Tichenor, "A Guard Dog Conception of the Mass Media," paper presented to the Association for Education in Journalism and Mass Communication (San Antonio, Texas, August 1987), p. 10.

professional goals. Thus, the guard dog model is fundamentally a social control model.[3]

One implication of the guard dog model is that social change comes slowly, because elites usually resist changes that might affect their power and wealth. Also, change usually comes only when elites have an interest in changing the system. If elites have no interest in change, then there often is little media coverage.

Watergate and Guard Dog Theory

Watergate is a good example of how guard dog theory works. If the media were like a watchdog, they would have directed a lot of criticism at the system (its structure) that gives power to some groups and individuals and not to others. But that was not their main focus. They were focused on individuals. Conversely, to be a lapdog, the media coverage would have supported Nixon and his administration. But this clearly was not the case.

The claim that media coverage of the Watergate scandal is an example of social control ironically was confirmed by Vice President Gerald Ford the day after Nixon resigned and Ford became president. "Our long national nightmare is over," Ford said, adding that Watergate demonstrates "our system (of governance) works." He praised the press, and then urged the country to turn to other issues.

In short, the problem of Watergate did not stem from the system itself — it stemmed from a handful of individuals who violated the rules. The media played a crucial role in defining which rules were broken, and to that extent reinforced the status quo.

From a broad perspective, all investigative reporting can be seen as helping to support the social system. That's because all investigative stories have a moral lesson embedded within them. They either draw attention to the violation of some law or norm or they suggest that the system needs a law or norm to correct a wrong. In Watergate, the moral lesson was that politicians should not engage in dirty tricks, or violate the trust of the people, or cheat, lie or steal.[4]

---

[3]George A. Donohue, Phillip J. Tichenor and Clarice N. Olien, "Mass Media Functions, Knowledge and Social Control," *Journalism Quarterly*, 50:652-9 (1973).

[4]Ironically, though, investigative journalists appear to be unaware of the morality tales in their stories, according to mass communication researchers James S. Ettema and Theodore L. Glasser. "These reporters do acknowledge that their stories do not 'speak themselves,' but they maintain that their narrative skills are employed strictly in the service of cognition. ... the selection and sequence of facts is determined by a 'logical

But social systems are not static. They change, and investigative reporting can help promote change that contributes to social order.

Watergate and Social Change

Admittedly, the Watergate scandal did not change the social system a whole lot. The institution of the Presidency continues to be very powerful — in fact, probably more powerful today than at any time in history. And many politicians still engage in dirty tricks (e.g., negative political advertising).

But it would be unfair to say the Watergate story had no effect on the system. In the months and years after Watergate, Congress (and many states) passed a series of "good government" bills or rules designed to restore faith in the political process. Among other things, these actions

- limited individual contributions to candidates for federal office to $1,000 for each primary, election and runoff, and to $5,000 for political action committees;

- required candidates running for federal office to identify people and organizations that contribute $100 or more to a campaign;

- eliminated office "slush" funds, limited spending on direct mail to constituents, and eventually banned honoraria;

- required elected officials to file annual reports detailing some aspects of their income and investments; and

- resulted in the enactment of an independent prosecutor law.

To be sure, none of these changes has radically altered the distribution of power in American society. As a consequence, some scholars even argue that investigative journalism is politically conservative. They point out that stories rarely address questions of what has gone wrong in the system, who should be accountable, and how things should be changed. In many cases, journalists consider such matters as going beyond the bounds of "objectivity" in reporting.

---

progression,' not, of course, by any moral order." In other words, reporters see themselves as fact gatherers, not as preachers of right and wrong. James S. Ettema and Theodore L. Glasser, "Narrative Form and Moral Force: The Realization of Innocence and Guilt Through Investigative Journalism," *Journal of Communication*, 38(3):8-26 (Summer 1988), p. 23.

Many other examples in which investigative reporting has had little or no impact on the system could be cited. However, there also are many examples that have contributed to significant social change — change that has benefited disadvantaged and disenfranchised groups and, paradoxically, contributes to social order.

NEWSPAPERS, SOCIAL CONTROL AND SOCIAL CHANGE

The muckraking era in the early 1900s provides one the best examples of the press as an institution of control and change.[5] Many magazines and newspapers published stories about corruption in government, poor working conditions, unfair business practices, and unhealthy conditions in meat-processing plants. The stories prompted authorities to prosecute law-breakers, and, more importantly, they stimulated a public debate that indirectly led to a number of reforms, including the breaking up of monopolies, more sanitary regulations on the meat-packing industry, improved working conditions for factory workers, allowing laborers the right to unionize, more limitations on working hours for children, improved housing conditions, and increased penalties for government abuse of power. From a systemwide perspective, these reforms no doubt helped to "cool down" radical groups and reduced the potential for violent or revolutionary change.

Another good example of the role of newspapers as an agent of control and change is the coverage of the sinking of the Titanic in 1912. Stories in *The New York Times* and other newspapers reinforced values about the sanctity and dignity of human life. For instance, the Boston *Daily Globe* reported that the wealthy and poor "were in deep grief" and "the disaster stunned" theater-goers.

The newspapers also published stories of heroism, which included the "brave" wireless man who continued sending wireless radio messages even as water filled the cabin; the orchestra playing music to calm the passengers right up to the end; the "dedicated" members of the electrical engineering crew, who stayed at their posts knowing they would die; the captain of the *Carpathia*, who "raced" his ship to the scene to pick up survivors; and the "unsinkable" Molly Brown. At the same time, the stories also created villains, such as the *Titanic* captain who used "poor judgment"; another ship captain who failed to respond to distress calls; and a ship company administrator who saved himself before saving women and children.[6]

---

[5]More details about the muckraking era are contained in Chapter 8.
[6]In times of disaster or the threat of it, people often turn to the mass media to get a

The stories mobilized political and maritime elites to enact a number of reforms to maritime law, including requirements that all ships carrying enough life jackets and life boats for everyone on board and all ships must monitor their wireless telegraph machines 24 hours a day.

During World War I, the press published numerous stories that helped President Woodrow Wilson and other government officials raise bonds and recruit volunteers to fight the war. After the war, America became increasingly concerned about communism as a political force in the world. Newspapers, taking their cues from U.S. leaders, published many stories critical of Russia and the Bolsheviks, essentially creating America's first "red scare." The concern was so great that Italy's fascist leader Benito Mussolini, who was combating communism in his own country, received more favorable media coverage than any other world leader, even though Mussolini often censored the press. The coverage did not become critical until Mussolini linked arms with German's Adolf Hitler in 1936.[7]

In the 1920s, the press also played a major role in publicizing the "Teapot Dome" scandal, in which U.S. Secretary of the Interior Albert Fall secretly leased oil reserves on public land to the Sinclair Consolidated Oil Company and obtained kickbacks in return. When news of the scandal broke, top administration officials resigned and Fall was convicted of bribery. Like Watergate, the press served the function of identify "bad actors" who eventually were punished. Mass media historian Dolores Flamiano also found that during the early part of the 20th century mainstream newspapers and magazines "helped to bring the concerns of the birth control movement to a larger, more heterogeneous audience."[8]

The 1930s provides one of the most compelling cases of the press' role as a supporter of the status quo. One might have expected that, during the Great Depression, newspapers would have raised major concerns about the viability

---

better sense of what is happening and, in some cases, to take precautionary measures. More specifically, mass communication researchers Douglas Blanks Hindman and Kathy Coyle studied the role of local radio news during the April 1997 Red River Valley floods in North Dakota and concluded that media coverage helped mobilize volunteers, helped citizens monitor the threat to their own property and helped enhance the sense of primary group solidarity that is often observed during natural disasters. See Douglas Blanks Hindman and Kathy Coyle, "Audience Orientations to Local Radio Coverage of a Natural Disaster," *Journal of Radio Studies*, 6(1):8-26 (1999), p. 22.

[7]James D. Startt and Debra Reddin van Tuyll, "The Media and National Crises, 1917-1945," pp. 319-342 in Wm. David Sloan (ed.), *The Media in America: A History*, 5th ed. (Northport, AL: Vision Press, 2002), p. 328.

[8]Dolores Flamiano, "The Birth of a Notion: Media Coverage of Contraception, 1915-1917," *Journalism and Mass Communication Quarterly*, 75(3):560-571 (1998), p. 567.

and future of capitalism as an economic institution. After all, nearly one-third of adults were unemployed, and efforts to revive the economy proved relatively fruitless until World War II, when deficit spending stimulated the economy. But concerns about the viability of capitalism were never seriously raised during the depression. In fact, historian Richard Rubin argues that the press was reluctant "to politicize economic issues and bring new, unorthodox solutions into the political area."[9] Instead, media historians James D. Startt and Debra Reddin van Tuyll point out that some evidence even suggests the press contained "strong anti-labor prejudices ... and was more interested in saving the nation's business than in reporting what had happened."[10]

During World War II, the press also helped the government achieve its goals of maintaining morale at home and raising funds and an army to fight the war effort. Although censorship existed at a formal level and some newspaper journalists violated the rules, there was little need to formally censor journalists. Journalists policed themselves. They knew where the boundaries were. And they were patriotic.

During the 1950s, the civil rights movement also got more attention from the news media. The Nashville *Tennessean*, *The New York Times*, *The Atlanta Constitution* and a handful of other newspapers were regularly publishing news reports about acts of discrimination against African Americans.[11] Some reporters went undercover, exposing the role of the Ku Klux Klan. The coverage increased in part because the U.S. Supreme Court helped legitimate the civil rights movement through a series of court rulings, particularly the Rosa Parks back-of-the-bus case and the *Brown v. Board of Education* school desegregation case. By the early 1960s, *The News York Times* was giving prominent coverage to the civil rights movement, which included Martin Luther King's famous "I Have a Dream" speech.

During the 1960s and 1970s, mainstream media coverage of the status quo became somewhat more critical. In addition to the civil rights movement, newspapers and other media began giving more coverage to the anti-Vietnam War movement, the women's movement and the environmental movement. In 1968, journalists in Vietnam rebuffed U.S. military propaganda about the Tet Offensive, and their reports helped turn public opinion against the war — so much so that after those reports a majority of citizens opposed the war.[12] "The

---

[9]Richard I. Rubin, *Press, Party, and Presidency* (New York, 1981), p. 124.

[10]Startt and van Tuyll, "The Media and National Crises, 1917-1945," p. 330.

[11]The role of the press in promoting civil rights is documented in David Halberstam, "The Education of a Journalist," *Columbia Journalism Review* (November/December 1994).

[12]After 1968, a majority of Americans said the war was "a mistake." Harold W.

media's negative assessment proved more convincing than Washington's statements of victory because it confirmed the sense of frustration that most Americans shared over the conflict," according to Vietnam historian Sandra C. Taylor.[13] Although journalists such as David Halberstam played a key role in drawing attention to problems in Vietnam, the real story of change was occurring in Washington, DC, where moderate members of Congress and the Senate were increasingly becoming more critical of America's involvement in Vietnam. In other words, the journalists were simply passing on the concerns of elites in their news stories. Once the war ended, so did most of the protests; in fact, the women's and civil rights movements lost some of their "steam" after the end of the war.

In the 1970s, journalists at many large, corporate newspapers across the United States began investigating reports of police brutality, and their stories helped contribute to the formation of many civilian review boards. *Philadelphia Inquirer* reporters Donald L. Barlett and James B. Steele also made a name for themselves with a number of investigative reports on the criminal justice system and Washington's relationship with special interest groups. Today, the interests of investigative reporters are championed by an organization called Investigative Reporters and Editors (IRE), which is based at the University of Missouri.

In the 1980s, the press focused a great deal on the Iran-Contra scandal, in which the administration of President Ronald Reagan secretly funded U.S. backed Contras in Nicaragua, who were fighting the Marxist-backed government, through the illegal sale of arms to Iran. The Iran-Contra scandal, which led to some convictions, and the investigation of President Bill Clinton's involvement in "Whitewater," a real estate deal in Arkansas, and his sexual affair with Monica Lewinsky show how the press helps define the boundaries of illegal and immoral behavior. The role of the press as an "agent" of control also is evident in the coverage of the 1991 Iraq War, which was very favorable toward the U.S. military and government even though the press was granted only limited access to the battlefields.

Virtually all news and entertainment content has implications for social control. But this is particularly the case when a social system is threatened by war or terrorist acts. In fact, *the greater the perceived threat, the greater the potential for social control.* The attacks of September 11, 2001, provide strong support for this proposition. That was the day 19 so-called "suicide terrorists"

Stanley and Richard G. Niemi, *Vital Statistics on American Politics*, 4th ed. (Washington, DC: Congressional Quarterly Press, 1994), p. 356.

[13]Sandra C. Taylor, "Vietnam," *New Grolier Multimedia Encyclopedia* (1993).

commandeered four U.S. commercial airliners and about 9 a.m. flew two of them into the 110-story twin towers of the World Trade Center in New York City, killing nearly 3,000 people. A third plane was flown into the Pentagon, killing 200 more people. The fourth plane crashed in a Pennsylvania field, killing all 45 on board.

The next day, newspaper headlines reflected outrage and anger:[14]

"Acts of Mass Murder" –*Newsday*
"It's War" –*New York Daily News*
"Acts of War" –*San Jose Mercury News*
"A Day of Infamy" –*Tulsa World*
"Terror Beyond Belief" –*Newark Star Ledger*
"Who Would Do This?" –*Oakland Press*
"Day of Evil" –*Orange County Register*
"A Day of Horror" –*Reno Gazette-Journal*
"Evil Acts" –*Southeast Missourian*
"Bring Them to Justice" –*South Bend Tribune*
"Bush Vows Revenge" –*Ventura County Star*

The authorities eventually placed responsibility for the attacks on Afghanistan-based Osama bin Laden and his al Qaeda terrorist network. For weeks and months afterward, news stories, editorials, commentaries and letters to the editor condemned the attacks and the "terrorists," and praised the actions of the firefighters, police and passengers on the hijacked plane. New York Mayor Rudolph Giuliani also was elevated to the status of hero for his leadership during the crisis.

In short, news media coverage of 9/11 was not "objective" in any absolute sense of the word. It defined who was "good" and who was "evil." The content helped mobilize public opinion against terrorism and the eventual military offensive in Afghanistan that led to the ousting of the Taliban, which had supported bin Laden, from power. Public opinion polls showed Americans strongly supported the U.S. military intervention in Afghanistan.

After that war, the Bush administration also placed part of the blame for the attacks on Iraqi President Saddam Hussein, even though it was later revealed there were no significant connections between the terrorists and Hussein. In fact, none of the terrorists was from Iraq, even though public opinion polls showed nearly half of all Americans thought there was a connection. In early 2003, the Bush administration launched a public relations

---

[14]The front pages of hundreds of newspapers published at the time of the September 11 attacks are available at <www.September11news.com>.

campaign to drum up support for ousting Hussein from power. The news media played a key part in mobilizing public opinion to support the attack on Iraq, according to researchers and analysts.[15]

When the United States launched a military strike in Iraq in March 2003, the U.S. public was solidly behind the effort. That support began to fade in early 2004, when it became evident that Hussein did not have weapons of mass destruction or direct links to al Qaeda. By the Spring of 2006, public opinion had turned against the war effort, as more evidence emerged that the Bush administration had misled the American public about the reasons for invading Iraq.

In short, newspaper and other news media coverage of key events during the 20th century demonstrates that the media can have a significant impact on reinforcing and changing the social structure, value systems and public policy. The ebb and flow of control and change helps explain the persistence and stability of modern capitalism. Without such stories and investigative reports, the United States undoubtedly would have experienced even greater levels of social unrest throughout the century.[16]

SUMMARY OF ROLE OF NEWSPAPERS

From a historical perspective, it is fair to say that newspapers — more than any other medium — have broadened the role that ordinary citizens can play in political affairs. Three hundred years ago people around the world had very little say in their own governance. Power was extremely centralized. Kings, emperors, nobles, despots, military leaders and tribal chiefs ruled. But, as noted in Chapter 1, the printing press helped decentralize control over knowledge and

---

[15]Ralph D. Berenger (ed.), *Global Media Go to War: Role of News and Entertainment Media During the 2003 Iraq War* (Spokane, WA: Marquette Books, 2004).

[16]The discussion thus far appears to assume that newspapers and other media are incapable of producing adverse effects for people or society. That isn't true. Newspapers and other media are capable of producing stories that can help destroy social or political institutions (e.g., British control of the colonies until the Revolutionary War) or have other "dysfunctional" effects, such as manipulating public opinion or a debasing of culture. Violent content, for example, has been shown to produce aggressive behavior in children (e.g., Albert Bandura, *Social Learning Theory* [Englewood Cliffs, NJ: Prentice-Hall, 1977]) as well as perceptions of the world as a mean and scary place (George Gerbner, Larry Gross, Marilyn Jackson-Beeck, S. Jeffries-Fox, and Nancy Signorielli, "Cultural Indicators: Violence Profile No. 9," *Journal of Communication*, 28:176-207 [Summer 1978]). But when taken as a whole, media content clearly supports powerful groups and their interests, even while criticizing them.

information, and newspapers in many countries played a key role in giving ordinary citizens a greater role in everyday political affairs.

Metaphorically, the newspapers helped create a "public sphere," one in which political ideas and social problems could be discussed and debated. Newspapers helped create a world of "politics for everyone," although it is important to point out that the political role of ordinary citizens still continues to be limited — elites continue to hold a disproportionate amount of power. Thus, in absolute terms, political and economic power remains highly centralized in the United States, but in relative terms newspapers and other media contributed to a slow decentralization of power — an issue that will be explored in more depth in the latter part of this book. First we'll finish out the history of print media by examining the role and function of books and magazines.

Chapter 7

BOOKS, IDEAS AND
SOCIAL CHANGE

Mathew Carey had a choice. Stay in Ireland and probably go to jail. Or flee to America and start a new life. Guess which one he chose?

Carey fled Ireland because he had been arrested and imprisoned for publishing a newspaper whose purpose, in his own words, "was to defend the commerce, the manufacturers and the political rights of Ireland against the oppression and encroachment of Great Britain."[1] He was released after a change in political leadership, but new charges were expected to be filed against him. So, in 1784 he dressed like a woman to avoid capture and boarded a ship for the new land.

Mathew Carey

When Carey stepped foot on Pennsylvania soil several months later, he found a new country with only a handful of printers and newspapers. But lots of opportunities. With a $400 loan from the famous Frenchman Lafayette, who helped the colonists win the Revolutionary War, he established the *Pennsylvania Herald*. The paper aligned itself with colonists who supported a strong central or federal government (Constitutionalists). The paper was very successful because Carey reported on the Pennsylvania Assembly. But he sold it in 1788.

A year later he published his first book — the Douay (Catholic) Bible. It was a hit. He found his niche. And he got rich doing it.

Carey founded the first general publishing house in the United States. He also was a book seller. His achievements were so numerous that one historian had difficulty choosing which to mention.[2] He published Protestant bibles,

---

[1]J. E. Hagerty, "Mathew Carey," in *The Catholic Encyclopedia, Vol. III* (New York: Robert Appleton Co., 1908; Online Edition, 1999, Kevin Knight).

[2]John Tebbel, *A History of Book Publishing in the United States: Volume I, The Creation*

nature books, science books, literature, fiction, autobiographies, and children's books. He earned $300,000 in nine years, an amount that in today's dollars would be worth tens of millions.

Carey established a statewide network of booksellers. He also wrote several books himself, including *The Olive Branch*. He helped establish the Hibernian Society, which aided destitute Irish people. And he drew up a constitution for the American Company of Booksellers, the first professional book association.

But one of Carey's most important contributions was that he was one of the first publishers to create within his organization a division of labor − that is, specialized roles for employees. He had so much business that some employees just set type, others set up and ran the printing presses, and then others spent most of their time proofreading. The proofreader role, in fact, became a recognized trade after the turn of the century.

CHAPTER OVERVIEW

As noted above, the book publishing industry was the first mass medium to show how the division of labor could reduce costs and increase the productive capacity of an organization. The economies of scale derived from the division of labor are largely responsible for the growth of large-scale corporate mass media.

Like newspapers, books can produce content that focuses on politics, science, human interest, entertainment and a host of other topics. However, the most distinctive feature of books is that they can offer much more in-depth analysis of ideas than newspapers and other mass media. This makes books the ideal format for scientists, scholars, biographers and novelists.

The capacity to analyze ideas in depth also means that books often have a greater capacity than most other forms of mass media to facilitate social change. The history of book publishing is filled with numerous examples of books having a significant impact on public policy and public opinion.

THE DIVISION OF LABOR

The division of labor was not a new idea. Adam Smith wrote about it in 1776 in his famous book, *An Inquiry Into the Causes of the Wealth of Nations*. He argued that a nation's wealth was not to be found in gold or agriculture, but

---

of an Industry 1630-1865 (New York: R.R. Bowker, 1972), p. 109.

rather in the productive capacity of labor. Create a division of labor and production will increase. This, in turn, produces wealth.[3]

To illustrate this argument, Smith begins the first page of his book with an example of a pin factory. He points out that 10 laborers working independently of each other can scarcely produce 10 stick pins in a day. But when the tasks are broken down into a number of distinct operations and the work is coordinated, 10 men can produce as many as 48,000 pins a day.

> One man draws out the wire, another straights it, a third cuts it, a fourth points it, a fifth grinds it at the top for receiving the head; to make the head requires two or three distinct operations ... and the important business of making a pin is, in this manner, divided into about eighteen distinct operations, which, in some manufactories, are all performed by distinct hands ... .[4]

According to Smith, three factors explain why the division of labor increases human production. First, specialization increases dexterity. When production is separated into simple tasks, a laborer becomes more proficient in performing that task. Second, the division of labor saves time that would normally be lost in passing from one job to another. "It is impossible to pass very quickly from one kind of work to another that is carried on in a different place and with quite different tools."[5] And third, when production is separated into simpler tasks, machines can be constructed that enable one person to do the work of many. "Men are much more likely to discover easier and readier methods of attaining any object when the whole attention of their minds is directed towards that single object than when it is dissipated among a great variety of things."[6]

Adam Smith

Increased production was the major consequence of the division of labor, but it did not cause the division of labor, according to Smith. Nor was the division of labor the product of a conscious process, at least in the beginning.

---

[3]Adam Smith, *An Inquiry Into the Nature and Causes of the Wealth of Nations* (Buffalo, NY: Prometheus Books, 1991 [1776]).

[4]Ibid, p. 3.

[5]Ibid, p. 5.

[6]Ibid, p. 5.

Smith argued that "the power of exchange" created the division of labor.[7] Humans have "a propensity" to barter and exchange one thing for another. And the motivation to make contracts for exchange, he added, comes not from benevolence but from self-interest, or the desire to increase one's own happiness. Thus, at the primitive level of production, a division of labor ensues when one individual, pursuing his or her own self-interest, finds that he or she can produce a product that can be exchanged for other desired products. Under capitalism, this productive process is moved to a higher level — it is institutionalized. Capitalists consciously seek to increase efficiency by creating a division of labor.[8]

Although Smith was not specifically concerned with developing a theory of the organization, his theory incorporates the notion that organizations grow as the division of labor increases.[9] In order to increase output, capitalists must invest more and more money to pay for the machinery and other equipment. This resulted in what Smith called accumulation, or capital investment. Although demand for labor and, concomitantly, the cost of wages would increase as businesses grow, accumulation would not fizzle out because Smith believed increasing wages also would produce an increase in the number of laborers. Increasing wages would improve living conditions. This would reduce infant mortality, which was quite high in Smith's day, and, thus, increase the supply of workmen, which in turn would push down the costs of labor. The accumulation process could proceed in cycles of greater and lesser production, but the process would continue basically until all of the earth's resources were consumed.

Ironically, Carey was not a big fan of Smith's theory, but it didn't really matter. The specialized roles that Carey created in his organization lowered costs and generated economies of scale, which in turn helped him become a success.

---

[7]Ibid, pp. 6-8.

[8]Ibid, p. 37. Smith also argued that increased demand for products and services and foreign trade promote a division of labor (see, p. 327 and pp. 190-1, respectively).

[9]For a more complete exposition of this model, see A. Lowe, "Adam Smith's System of Equilibrium Growth," and W. A. Eltis, "Adam Smith's Theory of Economic Growth," in Andrew S. Skinner and Thomas Wilson (eds.), *Essays on Adam Smith* (Oxford: Clarendon Press, 1975).

BOOK PUBLISHING IN THE COLONIES

In 1755, only about 50 printing offices were operating in the colonies. A hundred years later, there were 385. They were producing about 1,000 books a year, valued at about $13 million.[10]

In the early 1800s, most of the books published — 70 percent or more — were written by British authors. But by 1850, most — 80 percent — were written by Americans. Many of these authors became famous. They included James Fenimore Cooper, Ralph Waldo Emerson, Nathaniel Hawthorne, Henry Wadsworth Longfellow, Walt Whitman, and Edgar Allen Poe.

The first half of the 19th century produced a number of companies that are still around today. They include John Wiley & Sons (1828), Little, Brown & Company (1837), and Houghton Mifflin Company (1849). By the end of the 19th century, the book publishing industry had more than 25,000 printing houses, which generated nearly $170 million in sales.[11] The growth in book publishing in large part stemmed from a series of technical developments that lowered costs. Steam power and cylinder drums (as opposed to the flatbed press) made presses faster. Machines called "Linotype" were developed to set type.

New methods of reproducing illustrations were introduced. And paper, which had been made by hand until the 1800s, was now produced mainly with machinery. Paper made up 20 percent of the costs of producing a book in 1740 but only 7 percent in 1910. Cloth also replaced leather for the book covers after 1820, which reduced costs considerably.

Other nonprinting technological and social changes were also helping to grow the book publishing industry. Rapid growth in the number of railroad lines during the mid-1800s, for example, made travel much easier and cheaper, and this in turn increased demand for books because people needed something to do while they traveled. Perhaps more importantly, mandatory education raised literacy levels and increased demand for textbooks as well as fiction and nonfiction works.

BOOK PUBLISHING AND SPECIALIZATION

The book industry in the 19th century also was becoming more specialized in two ways. The first involved a separation of publishing from bookselling. The second major trend was specialization in content.

---

[10]Tebbel, *A History of Book Publishing in the United States, Vol. 1*, p. 221.

[11]John Tebbel, *A History of Book Publishing in the United States: Volume II, The Expansion of an Industry, 1865-1919* (New York: R.R. Bowker, 1972-1981), pp. 63, 67.

Bookselling

In the 18th century, a book publisher generally marketed and sold his or her own books. Many owned bookshops or hired salespeople, who traveled around the countryside. They also would take out ads in newspapers.

In the 19th century, book publishers increasingly began to specialize in publishing, leaving the marketing and selling to independent booksellers. The publisher would sell the books to the book store owner at a discount, who would then mark up the books to make a profit.

Specialization in Content

Some publishers focused on the paperback fiction trade market. Others specialized in religious books or school textbooks. Specialization enabled publishers to reduce marketing and distribution costs. A publisher that focused on educational textbooks could send one salesperson to a school or university and sell a variety of textbooks to teachers in different departments.

Paperbacks became very popular after the 1840s. During the Civil War they were shipped to soldiers' camps. Their popularity waned a bit in the late 1800s because of excessive competition and passage of the Copyright Act of 1891, which punished publishers for pirating English titles. Prior to passage of the law, publishers on different sides of the Atlantic Ocean would often pirate each others best sellers and not pay the author or original publisher.

Literary Agents

The literary agent also added more complexity to the book publishing industry. The first literary agent set up shop in 1875.

Literary agents represented writers and would attempt to secure publishing contracts with publishers. This freed up writers to concentrate on their craft. Publishers sometimes resented the agents because they would negotiate for higher royalties as well as their own cut of the profits However, respectable agents also saved publishers time.

Many agents, then as today, signed contracts only with writers who showed promise or were competent at their craft. Today, some publishers will not deal directly with writers. They only deal with agents.

The Social Impact of Books

Throughout history, it is fair to say that the content of most books generally has reinforced dominant values and institutions in a society. But many books also contained themes that challenged the status quo and conventional ways of thinking.

Challenging the Status Quo

For example, the main characters of Cooper's *The Last of the Mohicans* (1826) include noble Indians, not just villainous ones. At the end, the "evil" Mangua pays for his crimes when he is shot and killed by one of the heros. One of the main theme's of Emerson's *Self-Reliance* (1841) is that humans should trust their own intuitions and resist the limitations of mainstream institutions and conventional ideas.

In *The Scarlet Letter* (1850), Hawthorne condemns the Puritan ethic because it cannot forgive missteps from the path of virtue. Forgiveness, in other words, is a virtue. And in *Walden* (1854), Thoreau, a student of Emerson, attacks America for its emphasis on materialism and a restrictive work ethic. The emphasis on materialism turns men into "machines" who "lead lives of quiet desperation." Structural theorists, by the way, sometimes use this analogy to explain the limited role of free will in explaining human action.

Outside the United States, the most powerful nonfiction book of the 19th century was Karl Marx's *Das Kapital* (1867), which was a stinging indictment of capitalism as an economic system. Marx basically argued that capitalism involves a process in which a small number of capitalists (bourgeoisie) exploit the labor of millions of workers (the proletariat) for their own benefit. He argued that revolution was inevitable and that the new economic order (communism) would signal an era of freedom for ordinary people. The revolutions never took place in capitalist economies, but the book did inspire many revolutions in noncapitalist systems (Russia and China being the most important), and the writings of Marx continue to inspire many scholars and people who see faults in modern capitalism.

After 1850, American women began making a mark as novelists. Louisa May Alcott wrote *Little Women* (1868), one of the first books to suggest that women can earn their own living and have an identity separate from their husbands, fathers or brothers. And Harriet Beecher Stowe is often given credit for inadvertently starting the American Civil War.

Harriet Beecher Stowe as a Social Change Agent

"So you're the little woman who started this great war!"[12]

That's what Abraham Lincoln reportedly told Harriet Beecher Stowe when he met her during the U.S. Civil War in the 1860s.

Ironically, Stowe didn't look like a rabble rouser. She was less than five feet tall and the mother of seven children. But her book, *Uncle Tom's Cabin* (or *Life Among the Lowly*), helped mobilize public opinion against the injustice of slavery. The book sold more than a half million copies in the United States within five years and was translated into more than 20 foreign languages. Historians and scholars widely agree it is one of the most influential books in American history.

Harriet Beecher Stowe

Stowe was born in 1811 in Litchfield, Connecticut. She was the daughter of a liberal clergyman. Stowe was very bright. She learned Latin before age 10 and was teaching it at age 12. She helped her sister open a school and wrote a geography textbook before moving to Ohio at age 25. Stowe was very religious and promoted feminist causes as well. Many of the female characters in her writings are presented as equals to men.

Her husband, a teacher, was also an ardent opponent of slavery. To supplement his income, Stowe began writing short stories dealing with domestic life. The royalties enabled her to hire household help to assist with raising their seven children.

In Cincinnati, which was separated only by the Ohio River from a slave-holding community, Stowe met many fugitive slaves and listened to their stories. She also visited Southern states.

Uncle Tom's Cabin was published in episodes in the *National Era* in 1851. The book was published the following year.

Religion plays a prominent role in the book. Stowe urges people to maintain a personal relationship with God and to love and care for others even

---

[12]Sources for this section: John R. Adams, *Harriet Beecher Stowe* (New York: Twayne Publishers, 1963); Harriet Beecher Stowe, *Uncle Tom's Cabin* (New York: Macmillan Publishing Company, 1994 [1852]); and Noel Bertram Gerson, *Harriet Beecher Stowe: A Biography* (New York: Praeger Publishers, 1976).

if they are cruel and mean. *Uncle Tom's Cabin* is the first book to feature a black person as the hero. But Tom did not fight for his freedom; rather, he sought freedom to serve God, an even more noble cause. Although religion plays a prominent role in the book, Stowe builds a strong case for the emancipation of slaves.

Stowe also wrote *The Key to Uncle Tom's Cabin* (1853), which reinforced her arguments with a large number of documents and testimonies against slavery. Stowe also wrote many other articles, books and poems.

She died in 1896 at the age of 85.

Influence of Mark Twain

By the end of the 19th century, the most influential novelist in America was Samuel Clemens, better known by his pen name Mark Twain. In fact, Ernest Hemingway and many other writers argued that *The Adventures of Huckleberry Finn* (1885) was the most influential book of the 20th century.

Several common themes run through this book and Twain's other masterpieces, which include *The Adventures of Tom Sawyer* (1876), *The Prince and the Pauper* (1882), and *A Connecticut Yankee in King Arthur's Court* (1889). Some of those themes — which include the importance of friendship, freedom and independence, justice and compassion — reinforce society's dominant values and norms. In *The Prince and the Pauper,* Twain also criticizes people who judge others by the clothes they wear, rather than by what's in their hearts and minds.

Mark Twain

But Twain also attacked some powerful traditional institutions and values. In *The Adventures of Tom Sawyer,* he takes aim at organized religion, which he believes is based on control and power and does little to stimulate true spirituality. In *The Adventures of Huckleberry Finn,* Twain attacks traditional values about chivalry, arguing that the American Civil War itself was partly caused by romantic notions of honor and a false sense of glory.

BOOKS ARE BIG BUSINESS

By the end of the 19th century, the book publishing industry was beginning to take on the characteristics of the modern corporate form of organization, or the bureaucratic organization (see Chapter 4). In other words, publishing companies had a highly developed division of labor, a hierarchy of authority, and lots of rules and procedures.

At the beginning of the 20th century, the U.S. population stood at about 92 million. About 40 percent of those people lived in cities, and about 10 percent of the population over age 10 was illiterate. By 1940, the population had increased by more than 50 percent, to 151 million. About 60 percent of them lived in cities. And illiteracy dropped to about 3 percent, primarily because of mandatory state education.

Incomes were also rising because of increasing industrialization. People had more disposable income to buy books. And new labor laws also reduced the number of hours people had to work, giving them more leisure time to read books.

These five factors — growth in the population, increasing urbanization, increasing literacy, increasing income, and more leisure time — all contributed to increased demand for books, despite the Great Depression of the 1930s. The total number of books sold went from 201 million in 1925 to 551 million in 1943.

Book Industry Prospers

The book publishing industry generally prospered during this period. The number of publishers issuing new books doubled, going from 431 in 1924 to 955 in 1941. Total value of products sold went from about $44 million in 1914 to $110 million in 1939. The number of new titles published per year increased from about 8,000 in 1925 to about 10,000 in 1939.

The pre-World War II period was generally a good time for publishers. Many new companies were being started and many established ones got bigger and bigger. This was an age that produced many household names in the book publishing business: Alfred A. Knopf, Alfred Harcourt, Donald Brace, Richard Simon, Max Schuster, William Morrow, and W. W. Norton. Their companies still survive today.

The first book clubs — Book-of-the-Month Club and Literary Guild — were founded in the 1920s. They sold books by subscription on a national scale. The first comic books appeared just before World War I. One of the most popular was "Mutt and Jeff." Paperback books made a revival after World War II. Advances in printing techniques and mass promotion reduced costs considerably. By the 1980s, nearly three-fourths of all books sold were paperbacks.

"The Great Change"

After World War II, things changed dramatically. In fact, mass communication historian John Tebbel calls this time period "The Great Change."[13] Some of the changes included:

- *Bigger Fees for Film Rights.* Hollywood began paying increased prices for the film rights to books and Broadway plays, especially mystery novels. Before the war, the rights were usually sold for $2,500 to $5,000. Afterward, filmmakers were paying $25,000. Today they often pay in the millions.

- *Rising Book Prices.* The cost of books began increasing and has continued to increase ever since. Today, some college textbooks and monographs (academic books not necessarily intended for classroom use) sell for $100 and more.

- *Perfect Binding.* To bind books, publishers increasingly were using a relatively new production technique called perfect binding. This process uses glue rather than sewing and reduces costs substantially. Most books today are perfect bound.

- *Mass Market Publishing.* This took off after World War II and established itself as the dominant force in the trade market by the 1970s. The goal was to sell as many books as possible to general audiences. Volume was the key. Mass paperbacks — the kind of books sold at supermarkets and drug stores — were the most popular. They included primarily fiction works, especially romance novels and mysteries. Next most popular were the trade paperbacks, which included nonfiction works for general audiences. For every book published in 1927, ten were available in 1947.

- *Increasing Specialization.* Publishers increasingly became specialized in the types of books they published. Avon Books, for example, specialized in romantic novels for women, many of them set in the 18th and 19th centuries. The novels of Kathleen Woodiwiss, Rosemary Rogers and Patricia Gallagher sold millions. The Harlequin Romance, a romantic suspense novel in which the lovers didn't reach kissing stage until the last page, was introduced during this period.

[13]John Tebbel, *A History of Book Publishing in the United States: Volume IV, The Great Change, 1940-1980* (New York: R.R. Bowker, 1972-1981).

Other categories of specialization included children's books; educational, business, scientific, technical and reference books; and religious books.

- *Growth of Book Clubs.* Book clubs grew dramatically after World War II, and by the 1970s they accounted for nearly 1 of every 10 books sold in the United States. The most popular were Book-of-the-Month Club, Literary Guild and Reader's Digest Book Club.

- *Concentration of Ownership.* More than 300 mergers took place between 1958 and 1970, many of which involved companies outside of book publishing.[14] Today many of the mergers are taking place on a global level. The biggest publishing house in the world is Bertelsmann, a German company that ranks among the top five global media corporations.

Concentration of Ownership

The last change — concentration of ownership — has perhaps raised the most concern about the future of book publishing. Like other industries in modern capitalism, increasing competition in the field of publishing drove some book publishers out of business and forced others to sell out. Avon, for example, was eventually purchased by the Hearst Corporation; Random House and Doubleday Direct by Bertelsmann; Bantam by IFI International; and so on.

"The immediate effect of these ownerships," writes Tebbel, "was to provide paperback publishers with enough capital to give them a marked competitive edge over the hardcover people in the drive for profits in a market that was narrowing down to competition for 'better' if not 'best' sellers."[15] The competition was so intense, in fact, that Avon paid $1.9 million for the rights to Colleen McCullough's *The Thorn Birds*, which was made into a very popular television mini-series.

Today mergers and acquisitions are taking place on a global scale. This scares many people, because they believe "corporate owners might dictate the content of lists, preventing some books they might not like from being published, or might insist that only books in more profitable categories be published."[16] Yet, to date, critics have offered little hard evidence to support such charges. In fact, a growing body of research shows that large-scale media

---

[14]Ibid, p. 723.
[15]Ibid, p. 352.
[16]Ibid, p. 723.

organizations produce content that is more diverse and critical of established groups (a theme we'll explore in more depth in the second part of this book).

Book Publishing in the 1990s

The book publishing industry got a big boost in the late 1990s with the publication of *Harry Potter and the Sorcerer's Stone*. The book, written by J. K. Rowling, was a phenomenal success and has been credited with getting millions of children interested in reading again. The social control messages in this and other books in the Harry Potter series are very heavy — Harry and his friends battle evil wizards and witches.

J. K. ROWLING: MAGIC AS SOCIAL CONTROL

In the mid-1990s, Joanne Rowling was so poor that she had to skip meals to provide enough food for her daughter.[17] Five years later she was one of the richest women in the world, earning hundreds of millions of dollars a year.

Better known as J. K. Rowling, Joanne is the author of the Harry Potter book series, whose hero is a boy with the powers of a wizard. The books draw upon social control themes as old as the lessons in Homer's *Iliad*. Potter continually confronts evil and defeats it.

Religious groups have criticized the books for promoting witchcraft. But the public has generally ignored such criticism, and the books have been credited with stimulating reading among young people.

The books have been translated into more than 60 languages and combined have sold more than 250 million copies in 200 countries. Rowling's fifth installment, *Harry Potter and the Order of the Phoenix*, broke all records with a first print run of 6.8 million copies and a second print run of 1.7 million copies.

Rowling has won many honors and has been featured on many national television programs. But a decade ago she was single mom caught in a classic Catch-22. She couldn't work because she couldn't afford daycare, and she couldn't afford daycare because she wasn't working. So she and her daughter survived on $105 a week in public assistance.

---

[17]Sources for this brief biography include Scholastic Books, "Meet J. K. Rowling," <www.scholastic.com>; and J. K. Rowling, "The Not Especially Fascinating Life So Far of J. K. Rowling," <www.cliphoto.com/potter/rolwing.htm>.

She was born in England in 1965. From an early age, she enjoyed telling stories to her sisters. She wrote her first story, about a rabbit, when she was 5 or 6 years old.

In school, she was terrible at sports but loved English and foreign languages. She wrote a lot in her teen years but never showed much of it to her friends. She attended Exeter University, where she studied French, presumably to enter a career as an administrative assistant. But that was a disaster, she said, because she was a very disorganized person. "The worst secretary ever."

When she was 26, she went abroad to teach English. She married and had a daughter, but the marriage ended and she found herself having difficulty making ends meet.

The idea for the Harry Potter books came to her in 1990, while she was riding a train. "Harry just strolled into my head fully formed," she said. She worked on the book for several years, often while her daughter napped. Several publishers rejected the manuscript.

But in 1998, Bloomsbury (UK) and Scholastic Books published *Harry Potter and the Sorcerer's Stone*. The book was a huge success and has been credited with getting kids back into reading.

Harry Potter and the Goblet of Fire was released in 2000 and sold 3 million copies in its first 48 hours of release, making it the fastest-selling book in history. In 2005, *Harry Potter and the Half-Blood Prince* sold 9 million copies in the United States and Great Britain in 24 hours — once again breaking records. In 2007, *Harry Potter and the Deathly Hallows*, the last book in the Potter series, sold 8.3 million copies in 24 hours. Warner Brothers has produced four Harry Potter films, all of which were box-office hits. Rowlings currently lives in Scotland with her husband and two children.

Despite the success of the Potter books, books sales as a whole grew slowly during the 1990s and even declined slightly from 2002 to 2003. Part of the problem was increased competition from other forms of mass media, particularly the Internet.

IMPACT OF BOOKS DURING THE 20TH CENTURY

Assessing or measuring the impact of books on public policy or society is never an easy task. This is especially true of fiction works, which are sometimes dismissed simply because they are fiction. But during the early 1900s, several nonfiction books provided more direct evidence of the power of books to influence social policy (i.e., produce social change).

Perhaps the best example was Upton Sinclair's *The Jungle,* which chronicled unhealthy conditions in meat-packing plants in the United States. A socialist, Sinclair hoped his book would persuade people that such abuses would not occur under socialism.[18] But instead of affecting them in the heart (i.e., turning them into socialists), his book hit them in the stomach. Congress and state legislatures responded by passing laws that improved methods of meat-packing and inspection. Thus, one might argue Sinclair's book indirectly helped to shut down the socialist movement, which sought more radical changes. Sinclair wrote many other books and eventually won a Pulitzer Prize in 1942 for *Dragon's Teeth*, a book about the rise of Hitler.

W. E. B. Du Bois, a Ph.D.-educated sociologist, became the best-known champion of civil rights before World War II. He edited a magazine and wrote numerous papers and books, including *The Souls of Black Folks* (1903), which criticized Booker T. Washington's more conservative, or accommodating, approach to securing equal rights. Later, he was able to influence the U.S. Congress to pass laws that established legal action against lynchers, among other things.

W. E. B. Du Bois as a Champion of Civil Rights

In May 1919, William Edward Burghardt Du Bois was angry.[19]

Although many African Americans had served in the U.S. Armed Forces during World War I and some had lost their lives, those returning were treated like second-class citizens at home. They were denied jobs because they were black. Some were lynched by white mobs for taking jobs in the north. And those that remained in the military were denied promotions.

"By the God of Heaven, we are cowards and jackasses if now that the war is over we do not marshal every ounce of our brain and brawn to

Du Bois in 1907

fight the forces of hell in our own land," Du Bois wrote in a famous editorial titled, "Returning Soldier," and published in the magazine *Crisis*, which he edited. "We return. We return from fighting. We return fighting! Make way for Democracy! We saved it in France, and by the great Jehovah, we will save it in the United States of America, or know the reason why."

---

[18]Upton Sinclair, *The Jungle* (New York: The New American Library, 1960 [1905]).

[19]Sources for this biography on Du Bois include Gerald C. Hynes, "A Biographical Sketch of W. E. B. Du Bois," available at <www. Duboislc.org>; Manning Marable, *W. E. B. Du Bois, Black Radical Democrat* (Boston: Twayne, 1986); David L. Lewis, *W. E. B. Du Bois: Biography of a Race, 1868-1919* (New York: H. Holt, 1993).

Congress listened. It passed legislation to inaugurate black officer training schools, establish legal action against lynchers and set up a federal work program for returning veterans.

Du Bois was a famous sociologist and black protest leader. But it was his journalism and books that moved people to action.

Du Bois was born in 1868 in Massachusetts. He endured many racial insults as a child. At age 15, he became the local correspondent for the *New York Globe,* a position he used to urge Blacks to politicize themselves.

Two years later he attended college in Nashville, and it was there that he witnessed discrimination and racism in its most extreme forms. After graduation, he entered Harvard graduate school, attended school in Germany and became the first black man to earn a Ph.D. at Harvard. His dissertation, *The Suppression of the African Slave Trade in America,* remains the authoritative work on that subject.

He took a teaching job and conducted empirical research on African American life in America, writing numerous papers and books, including *The Souls of Black Folks,* which criticized Booker T. Washington's conservative approach to securing equal rights. Du Bois became more radical as time passed, but he never joined the communist party.

He founded and edited for 25 years *Crisis* magazine, which was published by the National Association for the Advancement of Colored People (NAACP), a group he helped create in 1909. Du Bois was a superb writer. His mission was to make people aware of the problems that faced African Americans. He wanted racial equality and he fought tirelessly all his life to achieve that goal. But he became disillusioned at the end of his life, and he renounced his U.S. citizenship and moved to Ghana, where he died in 1963.

Historians today widely agree that Du Bois is the most important black protest leader in the first half of the 20th century, and he continued to influence many contemporary civil rights leaders and writers, including Alex Haley, who wrote *Autobiography of Malcolm X* (1965), which chronicles the life of an African American who draws upon Islamic religion to solve problems facing Black Americans, and *Roots* (1976), which chronicles a slave family before and after emancipation. Both of these books helped mobilize the civil rights movement during the 1960s and 1970s.[20]

---

[20]*Roots* was turned into a popular and award-winning television mini-series. Polls at the time showed that the series also had a tremendous affect on sensitizing White Americans to the historical struggles of African Americans.

Rachel Carson and Silent Spring

Another example of a book having a dramatic and measurable effect on public policy is Rachel Louise Carson's *Silent Spring*.[21]

In 1957, a friend of Carson's wrote to her telling how the chemical insecticide DDT was killing song-birds in her backyard. She asked Carson, who was a biologist, to find someone in Washington, DC who could help.

At the time, the public knew little about the dangers of DDT and other pesticides. Although many biologists and environmental scientists were aware of the dangers, the mainstream mass media had ignored many pleas to look into the problem.

Rachel Carson

In 1945, for example, Carson herself proposed writing an article on the dangers of DDT for *Reader's Digest*. The magazine turned her down.

But Carson, who had worked for the U.S. Fish and Wildlife Service, could not ignore her friend's plea. She contacted *The New Yorker* magazine, which suggested that she write the article herself. Carson ended up writing a book.[22]

Carson's basic theme was that indiscriminate use of pesticides and other chemicals could destroy life on earth. Chemicals were getting into the food chain and threatening all forms of biological life. She criticized the government for spraying without first informing citizens so they could take precautions. She also criticized the government for not conducting more research into the impact of chemicals on wildlife and ecosystems. And she criticized the practice of applying more chemicals when insects develop resistance to chemicals.[23]

When word got out that Carson was writing *Silent Spring*, the U.S. chemical industry launched an aggressive public relations campaign, criticizing Carson and the book. The chemical companies also threatened to withdraw advertising from media that favorably reviewed the book. A government official also criticized Carson, calling her a "spinster."

But the negative publicity backfired. It created even more interest in her book, which generated a whopping 40,000 in advance sales. President John F.

---

[21]The full name is dichlorodiphenyltrichloroethane.

[22]Rachel Carson, *Silent Spring* (Greenwich, CT: Fawcett Publications, 1962).

[23]Carson was not opposed to the use of chemicals to control pests. Indeed, DDT was credited for saving millions of lives around the world, because it killed malaria-carrying mosquitoes. However, she believed that too little concern had been given to the adverse environmental effects of the chemicals.

Kennedy asked the Science Advisory Committee to examine the effects of pesticides, and the Committee issued a formal report that backed up most of Carson's claims. By the end of 1962, more than 40 bills had been introduced in various states to regulate the use of pesticides. In 1970, the U.S. government created the Environmental Protection Agency. In 1973, DDT was banned in the United States. And perhaps most importantly, *Silent Spring* helped mobilize environmental groups and movements around the world.

Unfortunately, Carson did not live long enough to see most of these social changes. She died of cancer in 1964.[24]

Impact of Fiction During the 20th Century

Fiction books also made their mark on changing the world. Most notably, John Steinbeck's *Grapes of Wrath* (1939) took aim at the California agricultural industry and stimulated a number of reforms that helped protect migrant workers in California.

Ernest Hemingway also became one of the best known and loved writers of the century. His *Farewell to Arms* (1929) is a powerful anti-war story, and it argues that there is no glory in modern warfare, where men are reduced to helpless targets. This argument has angered military institutions, which depend heavily on duty and glory to recruit new soldiers and maintain morale. His *For Whom the Bell Tolls* (1940) was more mainstream, criticizing fascism and brutality and extolling the virtues of commitment and camaraderie. Similarly, *The Old Man and the Sea* promotes more traditional values of courage, manhood, and respect for nature.

In 1988, Toni Morrison's book *Beloved*, which chronicled the story of an escaped slave woman who killed her baby to save it from slavery, won the Pulitzer Prize for fiction. In 1993, Morrison became the first African American woman to win the Novel Prize in Literature. Oprah Winfrey was so moved by the book that she bought the movie rights, adapted it for television, and starred in the lead role.

---

[24]In 1963, Betty Friedan's *Feminine Mystique* also stimulated a national debate about the role and treatment of women in society and helped mobilize the women's movement.

Chapter 8

MAGAZINES AND COMMUNITIES
OF SPECIAL INTEREST

Success never came easy in the magazine business. By the late 1700s, more than 100 magazines had been started, but none had succeeded.[1]

Charles Brockden Brown was well aware of this situation when, in 1803, he founded *Literary Magazine and American Register*. One might call him the "Stephen King of the late 18th and early 19th centuries." His first novel, *Wieland* (1798), is the story of Theodore Wieland, a religious enthusiast seeking direct communication with divinity. Wieland's father violates a vow to God and dies by spontaneous combustion. Wieland mistakenly assumes a ventriloquist's utterances are supernatural. Wieland goes insane and, acting upon the prompting of an "inner voice," murders his wife and children. When he learns about his deeds, he kills himself.

Charles Brown

Brown called himself a "story-telling moralist." This shows that he recognized his role as a agent of social control. Many literary scholars today also call him the founder of the American novel. And in the magazine field, he is known as the first publisher to clearly articulate a philosophy for the field.

The purpose of a magazine, he said, was to enlighten and amuse. In fact, in the first issue of *Literary Magazine and American Register*, he said he had called upon his literary friends to contribute articles that "warm and enlighten." He

---

[1]This historical review is mainly drawn from John Tebbel and Mary Ellen Zuckerman, *The Magazine in America: 1741-1990* (New York: Oxford University Press, 1991); Frank Luther Mott, *A History of American Magazines, 1741-1885,* 3 Vols. (New York: D. Appleton and Co., 1930); Emery, Emery and Roberts, *The Press in America*; Matthew Schneirov, *The Dream of a New Social Order: Popular Magazines in America: 1893-1914* (New York: Columbia University Press, 1994); and James Playsted Wood, *Magazines in the United States: Their Social and Economic Influence* (New York: The Ronald Press Company, 1949).

added that many magazines had failed financially because of lack of commitment to a set of principles, but that the "public is always eager to encourage one who devotes himself to their rational amusement."[2] He also noted that magazines, because they publish less frequently than daily newspapers, had more time to reflect and comment on the news.

Unfortunately, his own magazine only lasted four years. But his philosophy helped justify the role and function of magazines in society — a perspective that lives on today.

CHAPTER OVERVIEW

From a structural perspective, the most notable characteristic of magazines is specialization. The history of magazines, in fact, is one of specialization. Magazines create and maintain communities of interest, and that's why they've been able to survive.

Like other forms of media, magazines provide content that helps social actors achieve their goals. In other words, they play an important social control, or system maintenance, function.

However, magazines also can challenge the status quo and facilitate social change. The most notable example of this occurred in the muckraking era of the early 1900s, which exposed corruption and incompetence in American business and government. One might even go so far as to argue that the muckrackers helped prevent a revolution in America.

MAGAZINES IN THE EARLY 19TH CENTURY

Magazines acquired longer lives after the 1820s. Several factors contributed. One was technology. Breakthroughs in printing technology — especially the cylinder press — reduced the costs of publishing. Another factor was literacy, which was increasing dramatically as more and more people attended formal schooling. A third factor was the railroads, which encouraged transportation and gave people free time to read. Magazines were ideal reading on the train.

The number of magazines in the United States grew dramatically between 1825 to 1850. One historian estimates that up to 5,000 magazines were started. Of course, most failed. But the total number of magazines in existence did increase six-fold, going from about 100 to 600.[3]

---

[2]Cited in Wood, *Magazines in the United States*, p. 37.
[3]Tebbel and Zuckerman, *The Magazine in America*, p. 11.

Three of the longest-lived and most popular magazines of the 19th century were *North American Review*, *Saturday Evening Post*, and *Youth's Companion*. The *Review*, which published the works of intellectuals and scholars on a variety of subjects, was founded in 1815 and survived until the late 1930s.

The *Post* was founded in 1821 and published family-oriented content. It became even more famous in the 20th century for its Norman Rockwell covers. The magazine went out of business in 1969, but it was revived by a nonprofit corporation in 1971 and is currently published quarterly.

Youth's Companion was founded in 1827 and was, as the title suggests, targeted to boys and girls. Parting ways with previous publications, the magazine placed less emphasis on moral and religious instruction and gave more attention to entertainment.

MAGAZINES AND MASS CIRCULATION

Following the lead of the penny press (see Chapter 3), many magazines dropped their prices in the 1830s, which bolstered their circulations. This, in turn, increased the amount of advertising, which became a much more important source of revenue than subscriptions. In fact, advertising revenues made it possible to sell a magazine for less than its cost of production.

Increasing Specialization

Prior to the 1820s, magazines tended to be weeklies. Most were intended for general audiences and contained a variety of essays on the arts, politics and history. But after 1850 most magazines were monthly, and their content became increasingly specialized.

The Dial (1840-1844), for example, was the journal of the New England Transcendentalists. It was edited by author Margaret Fuller and later by Ralph Waldo Emerson. *Harper's* and *Scribner's* also were geared to intellectuals and contained high-brow literary content and political essays.

In contrast, *Munsey's* and *Cosmopolitan* focused more on the needs of working- and middle-class families. To attract such readers, the magazines cut their cover prices by as much as 20 cents. Many sold for 10 or 15 cents. This strategy worked. By the end of the century, a number of magazines had circulations that exceeded 250,000.

Illustrations and Photographs

Lower postage rates and the increasing use of illustrations and pictures also contributed to higher circulations. The Postal Act of 1879 gave second-class mailing privileges to magazines, which enabled magazines to charge less for subscriptions.[4]

Illustrations and photographs also were extremely popular. Before the Civil War, woodcuts were used to illustrate landscapes and people. This required hiring highly skilled artisans. *Harper's Weekly*, which was founded in 1857, made extensive use of woodcuts, especially during the Civil War, when its artists would recreate war scenes.

However, the photograph gradually replaced woodcuts as the century came to a close. This transition was made possible by the halftone, which was a continuous tone picture converted into small black and white dots. The dots were large enough to be inked on printing presses but small enough to appear invisible to the naked eye.

Magazines for Women

Magazines targeted to the needs of women had been around since the 18th century. By 1830, nearly 50 women's magazines had appeared and disappeared.

Among them was Mary Chase Barney's *Ladies Magazine*, which was intended to provide political information to women and give them a place to express their views. She refused to publish romantic fiction, telling them they must "make love for themselves."[5] But her magazine didn't last long. During the 19th century, women preferred literary contributions, along with fashion, travel, biography and etiquette. Focusing on these topics eventually paid off.

Among the successes were *Harper's Bazar* (1867; *Bazaar* after 1929, with two "aa's"), *McCall's Magazine* (1876), and *Ladies Home Journal* (1883), all of which have survived to the present. *Good Housekeeping*, founded in 1885, initiated a testing station for consumer goods. Obtaining the "Good Housekeeping Seal of Approval" became and still is an important objective of companies that produce consumer goods.

But not all magazines were oriented to the domestic side of women's lives. Feminist Amelia Bloomer's *Lily, A Ladies Journal Devoted to Temperance and Literature* (1849-1856) advocated female voting rights and dress reform. Other women's rights magazines in the Antebellum period included *Genius of Liberty, Una,* and *Women's Advocate,* with the latter "designed to present the wrongs of women and to plead for their redress."[6]

---

[4]Wood, *Magazines in the United States*, p. 100.
[5]Quoted in Tebbel and Zuckerman, *The Magazine in America*, pp. 36-37
[6]Quoted in Tebbel and Zuckerman, *The Magazine in America*, p. 38.

Magazines, Civil Rights and Politics

Before the Civil War, a number of magazines also promoted the abolition of slavery and the rights of African Americans. They included *National Era*, *National Anti-Slavery Standard*, *Saturday Visiter* (sic), and *Anglo-African Magazine*. Harriet Beecher Stowe's *Uncle Tom's Cabin* first appeared in serial form in the *National Era*. The book is credited with helping to generate strong public opinion against slavery (see Chapter 7 for more details).

Another good example of an abolitionist publication was the *National Reformer*, which was the organ of the American Moral Reform Society, an interracial organization. It was edited by William Whipper, the son of a black servant and her white employer. The Reformer advocated a number of reforms, including abolition, equal rights for blacks and women, temperance and nonviolence. Arguing the cause of slavery for the South was *DeBow's Magazine*.[7]

Although the magazine industry continued to become more specialized as the 19th century came to a close, political and social commentary, which had always been a staple of magazines, remained popular, too. In fact, a number of magazines devoted to critical review prospered during this time and are in existence. They include *Atlantic Monthly* (1857), *Harper's New Monthly Magazine* (1850, now called *Harper's Magazine*), and the *Nation* (1865).

There was, indeed, no shortage of political and social issues to write about. In fact, many people felt capitalism was out of control, and industrialization and urbanization were creating more problems than they were solving. The analysis of political issues reached an apex in the early 1900s, with the so-called muckraking magazines.

CAPITALISM OUT OF CONTROL

At the turn of the century, capitalism was on a roll.[8] Business was booming. Railroads were expanding. Industrial output was growing rapidly. Factories were turning out all kinds of new products and time-saving devices.

Many people dreamed of leading the life of a Horatio Alger book character — a person who would become fabulously rich through hard work. Of course, some did. John D. Rockefeller, Andrew Carnegie, Jay Gould, J. P. Morgan,

---

[7]Tebbel and Zuckerman, *The Magazine in America*, pp. 15-17.

[8]For a general historical review of the turn of the century, see Harry J. Carman, Harold C. Syrett, and Bernard W. Wishy, *A History of the American People: Volume II – Since 1865* (New York: Alfred A. Knopf, 1967).

Cornelius Vanderbilt and Daniel Drew built financial empires in the oil, railroad, steel, shipping and banking industries.[9]

But appearances can be deceiving. In fact, life for many urban residents was less than ideal. Poverty was widespread, even among employed workers. Many factories and businesses paid low wages and required their workers to work 14 or more hours a day, six to seven days a week. The wages were so low in some cases that everyone in a family, including children, had to work in order to survive.

Housing conditions were awful. Access to health care was often nonexistent. New immigrants especially suffered. They were forced to accept the worst and lowest paying jobs. Labor unions were despised, and most newspapers seldom sympathized with striking workers, who they usually described as anarchists or dangerous radicals.[10]

The burgeoning factory system was producing wealth, as Adam Smith had predicted in his 1776 classic book, *The Wealth of Nations*.[11] But, as Karl Marx correctly pointed out in the mid-1800s,[12] the wealth went not to the workers or ordinary people — it went to the capitalists, or what he called the "owners of the means of production." The "robber barons" got richer and richer while many workers, or proletariat, lived in poverty.

All was not well in America. In fact, at the turn of the century, millions of Americans — perhaps as many as 30 million — called themselves "socialist" or "communist" or identified with left-wing political parties. To them, capitalism was out of control. It could not solve many economic, political and social problems, despite what the free-market economists said. And it could not be trusted to police itself.

One consequence of this discontent was the progressive social movement, which lasted from about 1890 to 1915.[13] Although the term has its roots in religious ideas, the progressive movement wanted greater democratic participation for individuals. It also believed in science. And it wanted to check

---

[9]Matthew Josephson, *The Robber Barons: The Great American Capitalists, 1861-1901* (New York: Harcourt, Brace and Company, 1934).

[10]The negative coverage of labor unions reflects the dependence that newspapers had on powerful political and economic elites of the time. Politicians and police were solidly behind the capitalists who ran the factories. The muckraking magazines offered one of the few sympathetic voices for the workers.

[11]Adam Smith, *An Inquiry Into the Nature and Causes of the Wealth of Nations* (Buffalo, NY: Prometheus Books, 1991[1776]).

[12]Karl Marx, *Capital: A Critique of Political Economy*, Vols. 1-3, trans. by Samuel Moore and Edward Aveling (New York: International Publishers, 1987).

[13]Richard Hofstadter, *The Progressive Movement, 1900-1915* (Englewood Cliffs, NJ: Prentice-Hall, 1963).

the power of large corporations and restore the power of the individual entrepreneur or craftsman.

This, then, was the state of affairs when an unassuming magazine reporter named Ida Tarbell began investigating one of the most powerful men and corporations in America.

IDA TARBELL AND STANDARD OIL

When Tarbell's father heard she was going to write a series of articles about The Standard Oil Company for *McClure's* magazine, he pleaded with her not to do it.[14]

In 1897, Standard Oil controlled 90 percent of the oil production in the United States. The company, headed by John D. Rockefeller, had run many competitors out of business, including her father's business partner, who had shot himself to death. Now Frank Tarbell was struggling to pay off his partner's debts.

"Don't do it, Ida," he pleaded. "They will ruin the magazine." Other friends and associates gave similar warnings.

Ida Tarbell

But Ida was not easily frightened. She was independent, college-educated, and talented. She believed injustice should be confronted and defeated.

So, with the support of S. S. McClure, her magazine publisher-boss, Tarbell began investigating Standard Oil. For five years she dug into files of previous lawsuits and obtained a copy of a congressional investigation that had been suppressed. She interviewed scores of current and former business partners and clients.[15]

---

[14]The following sources were used for this introduction: Fred J. Cook, *The Muckrakers: Crusading Journalists Who Changed America* (Garden City, NY: Doubleday & Company, 1972), see Chapter V; Michael Emery, Edwin Emery and Nancy L. Roberts, *The Press and America: An Interpretive History of the Mass Media,* 9th ed. (Boston: Allyn and Bacon, 2000), pp. 223-226; and Ida M. Tarbell, *The History of the Standard Oil Company* (New York: McClure, Phillips & Co. 1904). Also see Ida M. Tarbell, *All in the Day's Work: An Autobiography* (New York: Macmillan, 1939) and Kathleen Brady, *Ida Tarbell: Portrait of a Muckraker* (New York: Seaview/Putnam, 1984).

[15]When Standard Oil heard it was being investigated, the company hired Mark Twain to be its public relations front-man. Twain contacted McClure and asked whether *McClure's* magazine intended to run a story. "You will have to ask Miss Tarbell," he said.

The end result was one of the greatest and most powerful investigative stories of all time — a 19-part series that set into motion a series of events that led to the break-up of the world's greatest oil trust. Tarbell's first story appeared in *McClure's* magazine in November 1902. She profiled Rockefeller, who was conniving, deceitful, greedy and dishonest.[16]

Tarbell's articles revealed that Rockefeller had made secret deals with the railroad companies to have his company's oil shipped at discount. This was illegal, because the railroads were monopolies and were required by law to charge the same rates to everyone. But Rockefeller's underhanded scheme enabled him to bankrupt or buyout scores of smaller refineries. Rockefeller even had deals with newspapers. More than 100 newspapers in Ohio, for instance, had signed contracts with Standard Oil, guaranteeing that they would print editorials and news in favor of the company in exchange for advertising.

Standard Oil tried to discredit Tarbell after the stories began appearing. Rockefeller and company spokesmen called her "Miss Tarbarrel." They fed stories to newspapers that belittled and criticized her. When her articles were published in a book two years later, an oil industry publication subsidized by Standard Oil headlined its review: "Hysterical Woman Versus Historical Facts." A Harvard University economist criticized Tarbell's book and called her "a mere gatherer of folklore." Standard Oil distributed 5,000 copies of his attack.

But all of these attempts to destroy Tarbell failed. She had truth on her side, and the public could sense that. They loved her and for a time she was one of the most famous women in America.

Nearly two dozen anti-trust lawsuits were filed against Standard Oil from 1904 to 1906. The U.S. Bureau of Corporations launched an investigation and in 1906 handed a report to President Theodore Roosevelt that confirmed Tarbell's findings.

The tide had turned against Rockefeller and Standard Oil, and the bad news kept pouring in. Newspaper publisher William Randolph Hearst came into possession of documents which showed that Standard Oil had been bribing judges, Congressmen and U.S. Senators. Finally, in 1911, the U.S. Supreme Court issued a decree ordering the breakup of Standard Oil, because the court determined that the company's goal had been "to drive others from the field and exclude them from their right to trade."[17]

McClure was a reporter's publisher. He supported numerous investigative projects and earned a reputation as one of the finest publishers in the history of magazine journalism.

[16]This image of Rockefeller contrasted sharply with his role as a father. He is described as extremely devoted and loving with his children.

[17]The irony is that after the break-up of Standard Oil, John D. Rockefeller became even richer. As he predicted, the company was worth a lot more broken up than it was

McClure's magazine prospered during this time. Its circulation eventually exceeded 500,000, making it one of the two biggest magazines in America. Tarbell and other journalists at the magazine had a disagreement with McClure and left in 1906. They purchased and edited *American Magazine*. Tarbell also lectured and wrote several popular biographies, including eight books on Abraham Lincoln. She served on numerous governmental committees throughout her life.

She remained single to preserve her independence and freedom. She died in 1944 at the age of 87. *McClure's* magazine went out of business in the 1930s.

ROLE AND FUNCTION OF MAGAZINES

Few stories in the history of magazine journalism have had as much impact on the political process as Tarbell's "History of the Standard Oil Company." Her stories prompted government authorities to break-up Standard Oil, and they also indirectly prompted changes in anti-trust laws that gave the U.S. government greater authority to regulate monopolistic practices in the private sector.

Like newspaper investigative stories, Tarbell's exposé on Standard Oil may be seen as performing a guard dog function for society (see Chapter 4 for discussion of the guard dog concept). It helped construct (or reconstruct) a social problem (abuse of power by big business) that policy makers were encouraged to solve for "the good of the entire community or society."

Yet magazines have a social control function that is distinct from newspapers and other media. Most notably, magazines typically offer more specialized content and more in-depth coverage.[18]

For example, in terms of political content, magazines clearly offer a wider variety of choices than daily newspapers, radio or television. There are

---

as one single trust. To make matters worse, the new companies also engaged in price-fixing, thwarting some of the anti-trust efforts. However, the investigation took a psychological toll on Rockefeller and his family. Rockefeller experienced such stress that all of the hair on his body fell out. When Tarbell met him, she was shocked at his appearance — he looked liked a very old man. Rockefeller's son, John D. Rockefeller Jr., also had several mental breakdowns.

[18]Unlike newspapers, magazines also have had the ability to reach national audiences. The problem for newspapers was technical: How could a newspaper be published daily and distributed nationally? Until recently, this was not economically feasible (*USA Today* is an exception). But timeliness is less important for magazines, which generally publish weekly or monthly. Many magazines, in fact, depend on national or international distribution to survive.

magazines that cater to political activists or junkies on the extreme left end of the spectrum (communist) as well as on the extreme right (fascist), and the middle, too. Although many people abhor extremist perspectives, civil rights advocates point out that freedom of expression can be likened to a "safety valve" that reduces the potential for violence and revolution.

Of course, books can compete with magazines in terms of specialization and depth. However, magazines publish more regularly and, thus, create "ongoing communities of special interest" — something that is more difficult to do with books. Every week or month those communities are given a fresh supply of information or entertainment content on that topic of interest. And for almost every unique interest, there seems to be a magazine out there to serve it.

For example, magazines like *Time* and *Newsweek* specialize in news and politics, while *Good Housekeeping* and *Redbook* provide a wide range of advice on domestic living and home life. There are serious literary magazines, like *The New Yorker*, and those that spoof culture, such as *Mad* magazine. There are magazines that cater to car lovers, literary afficionados, quilt makers, sailors and body builders. Some magazines also keep people up to date on the latest celebrity gossip and give them advice on parenting and coping with life changes.

Of course, all of these magazines — even the nonpolitical ones — have implications for social control. Entertainment and hobby magazines help people relax and escape from the stresses of life.

But magazines can, from time to time, also shake things up.

Ida Tarbell's story was only part of the picture in the early 1900s. Dozens of other journalists were investigating unfair businesses practices, as well as corruption in city and state government, poor sanitation in meat packing plants, fraud in patent medicines, and poor housing, working and health conditions. They included:

- David Graham Phillips (1867-1911), a former newspaper reporter, book author and freelance writer who exposed graft and corruption in the U.S. Senate in his 10-part series, "The Treason of the Senate," which was published in *Cosmopolitan* magazine. The series documented how rich businessmen bribed senators.

- Jacob Riis (1849-1914), a New York newspaper reporter who exposed child labor abuses, industrial water pollution, and slum housing conditions. Riis mastered photography and his pictures convinced others the problems were real. He wrote and took pictures for several books, including *How the Other Half Lives*, *The Children of the Poor*, and *The Battle with the Slum*.

- Lincoln Steffens (1866-1936), a former newspaper reporter and managing editor of *McClure's* magazine who investigated corruption in government in numerous cities (Chicago, Cincinnati, Cleveland, Minneapolis, New York, and Pittsburgh) and in state government (Illinois, Missouri, New Jersey, Ohio, Rhode Island, and Wisconsin). His 1904 book on corruption in city government, *The Shame of the Cities*, was a best-seller.

These and other exposés encouraged legislation that protected children and the environment, gave women the right to vote, reformed the judicial system, increased anti-trust prosecutions, and improved the safety of food and drugs.

Today few magazines specialize in investigative reporting. One notable exception is *Mother Jones*, which was launched in 1976 by the nonprofit Foundation for National Progress. But, ironically, the decline of muckraking since the turn of the century may stem in part from its own success. The reforms instituted in response to the muckrakers' exposés helped cool down some protest groups and social movements. Since then, other reforms — such as expanding rights for labor unions, women and minorities — also have been interpreted as playing a role in cooling down radical elements of some social movements.[19]

MAGAZINES AFTER WORLD WAR I

The muckrakers' investigations and the progressive era effectively came to a close with the start of World War I. The nation's attention shifted to the war in Europe and to stopping Germany's imperialist policies. During times of war, research has shown that social movements usually are forced to put their goals on hold for the good of the entire country.[20] The number of new magazine start-ups also dropped.

---

[19]See, e.g., Marco Giugni, Doug McAdam and Charles Tilly (eds.), *How Social Movements Matter* (Minneapolis: University of Minnesota Press, 1999).

[20]William Gamson, *The Strategy of Social Protest*, 2nd ed. (Homewood, IL: Dorsey, 1990).

Reader's Digest

But after the war several new magazines offering specialized content or a unique approach emerged on the scene. One of those was *Reader's Digest*, which appeared in 1922 and carved its niche by purchasing the rights to books and articles from other publishers and condensing them for easy reading. The magazine was very conservative, moralistic and anti-communist, but it was extremely successful. At one point, it achieved a circulation of 20 million.

News and Business Magazines

The first modern news magazines were founded in the 1920s. Henry Luce created *Time* in 1923. His successful formula involved summarizing the big news stories of the week and classifying them into more than 20 different departments or sections. *Time* also had conservative leanings.

Newsweek, which had more liberal and Democratic ties, was founded in the early 1930s. In contrast to newspapers, which were closely tied to the ethic of objectivity, news magazines sprinkled opinions, analysis and viewpoints in their stories. In 1929, McGraw-Hill Publishing Company founded *Business Week*, which is the leading business and financial news magazine.

The New Yorker

The New Yorker, which positioned itself as a magazine of humor and literary fare for the sophisticated urbanite, was founded in 1925. Some of the best writers in this country have written articles for it, including James Thurber and E. B. White, who together coauthored in 1933 a tongue-in-cheek piece titled, "Is Sex Necessary?" Today *The New Yorker*, which also publishes nonfiction articles on current affairs, is considered by many critics to be the best literary magazine in the world.

Magazines for African Americans

None of the magazines targeted to African Americans and founded before the Civil War survived it. Several other magazines founded in the early 1900s — *Voice of the Negro* and *Colored American* — had financial difficulty.

But in 1910, W. E. B. Du Bois, an executive for the National Association for the Advancement of Colored People, founded *The Crisis*, which achieved a circulation of more than 100,000 in eight years. Du Bois, who is revered today as one of the greatest civil rights champions in the history of the United States, edited the magazine until 1934 (see Chapter 7 for more details). *The Crisis* challenged the concepts of white supremacy and black inferiority at a time when these ideas were widely accepted. The National Association for the Advancement of Colored People still publishes the magazine.

Picture Magazines

Photojournalism came of age in the 1930s. Although magazines had been publishing woodcuts and pictures since the 19th century, the notion that photos themselves could tell a story really began with several European magazines and Henry Luce's *Life* magazine, which was founded in 1936. *Life*, a weekly magazine, was so successful in the 1950s that it alone generated one-fifth of all U.S. magazine advertising revenues. *Look*, another photo magazine, appeared the following year. *Ebony* magazine copied the formula and applied it to black life in America.

John H. Johnson as a Reformist

When John H. Johnson told civil rights leader Roy Wilkins about his plans to create a magazine for black Americans, Wilkins told him to forget it. It was the early 1940s, and the idea of a black publishing company was widely dismissed because blacks' incomes were far below whites, but Johnson wouldn't listen.[21]

He obtained a $500 loan secured by his mother's furniture and in 1945 published and distributed 25,000 copies of *Ebony*, a monthly magazine created to counter stereotypical portrayals of blacks in white-owned mass media. The magazine focused on the positive in black life.

"We try to seek out good things, even when everything seems bad," Johnson once said. "We look for breakthroughs — we look for people who have made it, who have succeeded against the odds, who have proven somehow that long shots do come in."

Ironically, Johnson could have been talking about himself. He parlayed that $500 into a publishing and cosmetics empire with annual sales of more than $500 million and 2,000 employees. He became the first black American to make Forbes' list of the richest Americans. Johnson Publishing Co., Inc. is the world's largest black-owned and -operated publishing company. The company also publishes *Jet*, a weekly newsmagazine.

---

[21]Sources for this biography of Johnson include Herbert G. McCann, "Pioneering Publisher Johnson Dies," Associated Press (published in the Spokane *Spokesman-Review* August 9, 2005), p. A6, and "John Johnson, Publisher of Ebony and Jet, Dies at 87," *Reuters* (August 8, 2005).

Johnson's magazine philosophy was to reflect the "happier side" of black American life. But *Ebony* and *Jet* didn't shy away from controversy. During the 1950s and 1960s, the magazines gave extensive coverage to the civil rights movement, including vivid pictures of police beating blacks and the assassinations of Martin Luther King and Malcolm X. *Jet's* historic photograph of the teenager Emmett Till, who was brutally murdered in 1955 for whistling at a white woman, helped galvanize the civil rights movement. The photograph also reportedly inspired Rosa Parks, who refused to give up her seat on a bus to a white woman. The U.S. Supreme Court eventually struck down the segregationist transportation law used to punish Parks.

John H. Johnson

Yet, despite this, some critics have charged that Johnson's magazines have focused too much on entertainment and not enough on promoting the civil rights movement. Johnson responded in his 1989 autobiography, *Succeeding Against the Odds:*

"Whenever I got sick, my mother gave me castor oil. And I'd run and hide and squeal and holler. Finally, she got smart. She gave it to me in orange juice. And it was more acceptable then. I tell people all of the time, we run a lot of entertainment, but it's orange juice. If you look inside, there's always castor oil."

In 1996, President Bill Clinton gave Johnson the Medal of Freedom. "He gave African Americans a voice and a face, in his words, 'a new sense of somebody-ness,' of who they were and what they could do, at a time when they were virtually invisible in mainstream American culture," Clinton said. Johnson died in 2005 at the age of 87.

TRUTH IN CIRCULATION

In 1932, the magazine publishing industry faced a major problem. Many publishers were exaggerating the circulations of their magazines in order to secure advertising contracts. An independent "watchdog" was needed to verify the circulation of publications.

So advertisers, advertising agencies and publishers formed the Audit Bureau of Circulation, often referred to as ABC (not to be confused with the television network), which audits and verifies circulation claims. Participation was and still is voluntary, and publishers pay a fee to the nonprofit organization to use its services. Today about 900 of the 22,000 magazines in the United States are ABC participants. Most major magazines participate.[22]

MAGAZINES AND THE IMPACT OF TELEVISION

When television arrived on the scene in the 1950s, the most popular magazines were *Reader's Digest, Life, Look, Collier's,* and *Saturday Evening Post.* Like television, all of them appealed to large, general audiences.

But only one of them — *Reader's Digest* — survived beyond the 1970s. *Collier's* closed in 1956, the *Post* in 1969, *Look* in 1971, and *Life* in 1972.[23] The irony is that all of the magazines had large circulations when they folded.

Saturday Evening Post, for example, had a circulation of about 6 million and a pass-along rate of 14 million readers (meaning each magazine was read by more than two people). The main problem was a loss of advertising. Advertisers dropped general magazines and went to television, partly because it drew extremely large audiences, was more engaging and more cost effective per consumer.

But not every manufacturer wanted to reach large audiences. As people's needs for goods and services became more unique and specialized, manufacturers began producing more specialized products and services to meet those needs. Manufacturers needed cheap and efficient ways of reaching their specialized target markets, and magazines were ideally suited to meet that need. Thus, television had relatively little impact on specialized magazines, because those magazines could deliver specialized audiences to advertisers for a much lower cost.

MAGAZINES AND SPECIALIZATION

One of the best success stories, as mentioned earlier, was *Ebony.* Another successful specialized magazine established after World War II was the *National Review,* launched in 1955 by conservative William F. Buckley, Jr. The *Review* was targeted to conservatives and had a circulation of more than 100,000 by 1977.

---

[22]See the Audit Bureau of Circulation Web site: <www.auditbureau.org.au/abcstory/intro.html>.

[23]*Life* and *Saturday Evening Post* were resurrected as a monthly and quarterly, respectively, in the 1970s, but *Life* was permanently shut down in 2000 and the *Post,* which is being published by a nonprofit organization, has never been able to achieve the glory it once had.

But perhaps the most phenomenal success story of the 1950s was Hugh Hefner's *Playboy*, a magazine launched in 1953 and targeted to men. *Playboy* featured partially nude photos of women and articles written by leading writers. The first issue featured Marilyn Monroe on the cover and sold more than 51,000 copies.

Playboy's circulation reached 7 million in 1972, but afterward began to decline because of competition from *Penthouse* and *Hustler*, which offered more explicit erotic photography. But Hefner, who had built a financial empire that included "Playboy Clubs" around the world, stuck with his soft-core approach. In the 1980s, all of the "Playboy Clubs" were closed and many other operations were curtailed. Ironically, Hefner, who had once been perceived as a liberator of sexual repression, also was now being cast by feminist groups as the repressor.

In 1982, his daughter, Christie, was named president of Playboy Enterprises. A Playboy Channel was launched and closed down. The company now operates a successful pay-per-view cable television venture called *Playboy at Night*. The circulation of *Playboy* has remained steady at about 3 million, which means it continues to be one of the largest magazines targeted to men in the world.

MAGAZINES AND THE "NEW GENERATION"

Magazines on the left wing of the political spectrum struggled during the conservative, anti-communist 1950s. But they made a comeback during the 1960s and 1970s, when sentiment against conservative politics and the Vietnam War grew. *The Nation* (1865) and *The New Republic* (1914), for example, attracted new customers, especially from younger, college-educated people.

Magazines geared to serve the interests of young people also emerged during the 1960s and 1970s. *Rolling Stone*, which focused on music and politics, was founded in 1967. By 1977, the magazine had a circulation of 500,000 and was a $10-million-a-year operation.

In 1965, *Cosmopolitan* magazine, faced with declining circulation, hired Helen Gurley Brown to remake the magazine. Brown, the author of the best-selling book *Sex and the Single Girl*, turned the literary *Cosmopolitan* into a magazine for young, career-minded women. Circulation began climbing and today *Cosmopolitan* has a circulation of about 3 million.

Occasionally, magazines on the left could also shake up the status quo. One of those was *MS* magazine, which was launched in 1971 and promoted the belief that when women are liberated, men will be too. The magazine was edited by Gloria Steinem, who became famous after she went undercover as a "bunny" in a Playboy club and later wrote about her "degrading" experience.

MS magazine reached a circulation of 500,000 by 1983, but eventually went out of business and since has been revived as an adless monthly.

Another magazine that bucked the status quo was *The Progressive*, which became internationally famous when it tried in 1979 to publish an article titled, "The H-bomb Secret: How We Got It — Why We're Telling It." Although the article was based mainly on public sources and experts said no one could build a bomb with just the information in the article, the U.S. government filed a lawsuit to block publication. A U.S. district court sided with the government but the case became moot after another publication published the article and the government dropped its lawsuit.

SPECIALIZATION AND "ZINES"

As the 20th century came to a close, the trend toward specialization in the magazine industry accelerated. From 1990 to 2000 alone, there was a net gain of more than 6,000 new magazines. Nearly all of these magazines were targeted to specialized as opposed to general audiences.

One of those was *Brill's Content*, a magazine launched in Summer 1998 by Steven Brill, creator of Court TV. The purpose of the magazine, he writes, is to serve as a critic of the mass media. "It's time to hold journalists accountable, it's time we embarrass them into doing their jobs the way they're supposed to — with integrity, honesty, fairness and accuracy." But *Brill's* only lasted five years.

The 1990s was also the decade of zines (pronounced "zeens") — low cost magazines that focus on alternative cultures and offbeat subjects. One example was *Kicks*, a magazine about obscure 1960s rock groups and grade-B horror movies. Another is *The Optimistic Pezzimist*, which is for people who collect Pez dispensers. Desktop publishing and copy machines have made small-press runs financially viable.

As the magazine industry entered the 21st century, most major publishers began offering online versions of their hard-copy product. Newsletters and scientific journals also were following suit. And now some newer magazines are publishing exclusively on the Internet, raising questions about the future of the industry.

But one fundamental function hasn't changed: Magazines still play an important role in helping social actors achieve their goals. The attacks of September 11, 2001, provide a good example.

Newsweek Helps Mobilize Opinion

On the morning of September 11, 2001, *Newsweek* editor Mark Whitaker was assembling a team of reporters and assigning stories when Donald Graham, chairman and CEO of the Washington Post Company, which owns *Newsweek*, called.[24]

"Buddy, this is going to be one of the biggest stories you'll ever cover," Graham said. "Do what you have to do."

Whitaker later said the comment giving him carte blanche to cover the terrorist attack "was hugely inspiring." The magazine published a special newsstand issue titled "Attack on America" two days after the attacks. This was followed up with three regular issues: "God Bless America," which examined of the after-effects of the attacks under the photo of firefighters raising the flag at the World Trade Center ruins; "Trail of Terror," which examined Osama bin Laden's organization; and "Why They Hate Us," a look at the Arab perspective on America.

Newsweek's coverage earned it the prestigious National Magazine Award for "General Excellence." The coverage also demonstrated how news magazines helped mobilize public opinion against the so-called terrorists and boosted morale at home.

In the "Attack on America" issue, a *Newsweek* writer wrote that "Tuesday, September 11, 2001, will indeed be a 'date which will live in infamy,' as Franklin Roosevelt said almost 60 years ago, after the bombing of Pearl Harbor. But the analogy ends there. Last Tuesday's events are even more gruesome and tragic than what happened on December 7, 1941."

For the "God Bless America" issue, *Newsweek* editor at large Kenneth Auchincloss wrote a piece ("We Shall Overcome") on patriotism and the nation's renewed sense of unity.

In the "Trail of Terror" issue, *Newsweek* quoted President George W. Bush, who gave nations around the world an ultimatum: "Either you are with us or you are with the terrorists." *Newsweek* also wrote that, "In the coming months, years and perhaps decades, America's global war against terrorism will demand radical thinking on how to fight an enemy whose goal is to instill fear and confusion, whose armies are militia networks strewn across the globe and whose war finances are untraceable bundles of cash. The American people must

---

[24]Sources for this section on *Newsweek* include Lisa Granatstein, "National Magazine Awards," *Mediaweek* (May 6, 2002), and various issues of *Newsweek* between September 13, 2001, and October 15, 2001.

accept at the outset that capturing or killing one individual will not rid them or the world of the scourge."

And this, from a reader in the October 15, 2001, issue: "Thank you for publishing in your last three issues the pictures of the terrorist attacks and their aftermath that kept me from sleeping. I needed to see the reality of the horror. I am moved that you did not decide that your readers could not handle the reality of this unspeakable terror."

SUMMARY OF ROLE OF PRINT MEDIA

Before Gutenberg's printing press, political and religious leaders controlled ordinary people through a variety of mechanisms, including brute force. But another more subtle and perhaps more powerful weapon was knowledge. They controlled access to and production of knowledge — and they used that knowledge to control people. After all, ignorant people are easier to control.

But the mass production of books, newspapers and pamphlets — made possible after the invention of Gutenberg's printing press — began chipping away at elite power structures. The process was slow at first. Political and religious authorities tried to control the distribution of printed material, especially material critical of them. Nevertheless, by the 1700s the sheer amount of material being produced outpaced the ability of censors to control it. Literacy spread. So did ideas about democratic government, which helped ignite revolutionary movements in many European countries and the New World.

The development of the printing press and other forms of mass communication have not eliminated social inequities or injustices, to be sure. Great disparities continue to exist within and between countries. The "information revolution" also has not ushered in direct democracy, a political system in which all citizens have a direct say in the day-to-day happenings in government. In the so-called "democratic" countries around the world, the ordinary citizen's role is still limited to electing a handful of representatives at local and national levels every couple of years. These politicians and the professional government bureaucrats hold most of the power.

The development of print mass media also hasn't led to calls for radical change. Indeed, the content of the press generally provides support for the status quo and helps social actors achieve their goals. But history shows that print media in the United States have often produced content that has facilitated many economic and political reforms — reforms that have improved conditions for many disadvantaged groups and people and have had a modest impact on decentralize economic and political power. These trends also are being reinforced today by the electronic mass media and the Internet, whose histories we will now explore.

Part II

A Brief History of Electronic Mass Media

Chapter 9

MOTION PICTURES AND
MORALITY TALES

George Orson Welles was only 24 when he signed a contract with RKO Radio Pictures in the Summer of 1939 to produce his first movie.

To say he was talented is a gross understatement. He had already become famous in the New York theater community for his creative and offbeat productions of classic plays. He also became nationally known after his October 1938 Mystery Theater radio production of *War of the Worlds*, which was so realistic that nearly a million people across the country panicked, believing the earth was being invaded by Martians.

Orson Welles

Yet Hollywood didn't exactly greet Welles with open arms. Welles was called an "upstart" because he had no film-making experience. But to his credit, he ignored the insults. Instead, he hired respected screenwriter Herman J. Mankiewicz to help him develop the idea for his motion picture. Mankiewicz and Welles went through seven re-writes. But the hard work paid off. *Citizen Kane* is today rated the greatest motion picture of all time, including by the American Film Institute.

The film tells the story of Charles Foster Kane, an aging newspaper tycoon whose arrogance alienates him from everyone who loved him. The movie was loosely based on the life of William Randolph Hearst, who had built a newspaper empire in the late 19th and early 20th centuries (see Chapter 4). On his deathbed in his Gothic mansion in Florida, Kane utters his last word, "Rosebud."

What is "Rosebud?" Through the use of flashbacks, a magazine reporter covering the life of Kane searches doggedly to discover the meaning of the word and the man behind it.

This author won't reveal the movie's ending for the benefit of those who haven't seen it. But "Rosebud" has become the most famous prop in

149

Hollywood. It was sold to producer/director Steven Spielberg in 1977 for $60,500.[1]

For two years Welles hid the fact that the movie was based on the life of Hearst. He was worried in part about what Hearst would do. And this was no exaggerated fear.

When word leaked out just before completion of the film in 1941, Hearst newspapers, wire services and radio stations banned all mention of *Citizen Kane* as well as all other films produced by RKO and refused to accept advertising for the movie. A group of Hollywood executives, fearing the wrath of Hearst on their operations as well, even offered RKO a cash settlement to destroy the film.

But it was too late. Welles had sneak-previewed the film to so many prominent people that it was impossible to expunge it. The film opened in theaters in 1941 and received good reviews and did well in large cities. But the Hearst boycott and Hollywood control of theater bookings hurt the debut. RKO eventually reported a loss of $150,000.

The film was re-released in the mid-1950s, and in the early 1960s an international panel of leading film critics selected *Citizen Kane* as the No. 1 film of all time. The film is acclaimed not only for its script and acting (Welles played Kane), but for its wondrous use of light and photography. The angles, shadows and perspectives in this black-and-white movie are still widely copied by cinematographers today.

Welles had a fabulously successful career as a movie producer, director, actor and writer, although he was never again able to match the acclaim he achieved with *Citizen Kane*. Welles also came to symbolize the successful Hollywood outsider — the man who placed art above profits and commercial success. Welles died in 1985.[2] RKO Radio Pictures struggled financially for most of its 25-year existence. The company ceased production in 1953 and was sold to Desilu Productions in 1957.

---

[1]Interestingly, Mankiewicz appears to have gotten the idea of "Rosebud" from Hearst's real-life mistress, Marion Davies, who told Mankiewicz that "rosebud" was the nickname Hearst had given to an intimate part of her body. For the record, though, the prop in the movie is quite different.

[2]Welles worried that media mogul Ted Turner, who had purchased the rights to *Citizen Kane*, would "colorize" his black-and-white masterpiece — that is, transform the movie into full color. Welles, like many purists, see black and white film as a more abstract art form. The movie has not been colorized as of this writing.

CHAPTER OVERVIEW

No motion picture in the history of film-making has generated more acclaim and attention than *Citizen Kane*. The technical aspects of the film — such as the camera angles, lighting, and set details — are, indeed, masterful.

But the heart of this film is not in the technical details. It's in the story. And this is a story about a man who climbs the ladder of success only to find he is alone at the top. Wealth and power cannot buy happiness. True happiness can be found only in loving others and in enjoying the simple things in life.

If that sounds moralistic, that's because it is. *Citizen Kane* is a great morality play. In other words, it deals with questions of right and wrong. And the moral lesson in this movie is an old one. Greed and arrogance are bad. For thousands of years, artists and playwrights have employed similar themes in their works of literature and art, including popular works such as the sinking of the *Titanic* (see Chapter 6 for more details). *Citizen Kane* is unique only in that it conveys the moral lesson through the life of Charles Foster Kane, a newspaper tycoon.

Almost all motion pictures contain messages about right and wrong, good and bad. This includes serious films like *American Beauty* and popular movies like *The Lord of the Rings*. *American Beauty* is the story of a man going through a mid-life crisis, but in the end he finds redemption. Redemption — or the idea that people who stray from the "path of righteousness" can redeem themselves — is a major and powerful theme in many motion pictures. The *Lord of the Rings* movies pit "evil" forces against the "good" forces, and "good" always wins in the end. It's also a story about friendship.

Thus, motion pictures — like many other forms of mass media, art and literature — are morality plays. They tell stories that deal with issues of right and wrong. In general, these stories promote or reinforce dominant norms and values in a culture, such as love, friendship, trust, and honesty. They define the boundaries of acceptable behavior and they reinforce social order. And, at times, they can challenge the status quo and facilitate social reform.

Of course, motion pictures aren't the only mass medium that tells stories and deals with questions of right and wrong. As pointed out in in earlier chapters, investigative news stories contain moral lessons as well. But in terms of teaching those lessons, no mass medium format is more compelling than motion pictures. This power is so widely recognized that even encyclopedia entries pay homage to it: "Motion pictures are the most important narrative art form of the 20th century, having taken on the functions served earlier by dime novels, serial novels, staged melodramas, wax museum displays, epic paintings, and professional storytelling. These earlier forms ... were supplemented by comic books, radio, and television, but it is the motion picture that came to dominate them all."[3]

Motion pictures have this power partly because they engage not one but two human senses — seeing and hearing. Print media engage only the former and radio only the latter. Television engages both senses and that certainly accounts in part for its power and popularity.

But motion pictures are even more engaging than television because they are shown on a "big screen," which draws the viewer into the experience even more. Movie critic Roger Ebert even argues that *Citizen Kane* can only be fully appreciated on the big screen, because there are many props and items that cannot be easily seen on the small (broadcast television) screen.[4]

EARLY HISTORY OF MOTION PICTURES

Most people think of Thomas Alva Edison as a great inventor. But when it comes to motion picture technology, he played only a supporting role.[5]

The scene begins in 1877, after Edison invented the phonograph. Within a decade, this became the most popular home entertainment device of the 19th century. But Edison wasn't satisfied. He wanted moving pictures to accompany the sound.

So in the 1880s, he commissioned one of his laboratory assistants to build a Kinetograph, a machine that used a clock to ensure intermittent but regular movement of a perforated film strip through the camera. The machine exposed 40 frames per

Thomas Edison

---

[3]"Motion Pictures: The Art of Film: Types of Motion Pictures: Fictional Genres," *Encyclopedia Britannca* (Chicago: CD Rom version, 1999 edition).

[4]Roger Ebert, "Citizen Kane," *Roger Ebert's Video Companion 1998 Edition* (Kansas City, MO: Andrews McMeel Publishing, 1998), p. 147.

[5]For general histories of the motion picture industry, see Jack C. Ellis, *A History of Film* (Englewood Cliffs, NJ: Prentice-Hall, 1979); Arthur Knight, *The Liveliest Art: A Panoramic History of the Movies*, rev. ed. (New York: Macmillan, 1978); Paul Rotha, with Richard Griffith, *The Film Till Now: A Survey of World Cinema* (London: Spring Books, 1967); and Gerald Mast, *A Short History of the Movies*, 4th ed. (1986). For a history of the technology, see Raymond Fielding, *A Technological History of Motion Pictures and Television: An Anthology from the Pages of the Journal of the Society of Motion Picture and Television Engineers* (Berkeley: University of California Press, 1983). Material for this section was also obtained from film studio web sites and from Mr. Showbiz <www.mrshowbiz.com>.

second and used up to 50 feet of film. Edison then had the assistant invent another device, called the Kinetoscope, to show the film. The Kinetoscope was a large box weighing about a thousand pounds that projected the film for individual viewing.

Although the machines worked well, Edison and his assistant were never able to create a practical machine that could synchronize sound with pictures. They gave up on that project. But in 1894, the Kinetoscopes were commercially produced and marketed, and the machines were very popular. Kinetoscope parlors charged 25 cents for admission to about five machines, each of which showed short clips of circus or vaudeville acts.

THE CINÉMATOGRAPHE

Although Kinetoscope parlors were popular, they didn't last long. They only allowed one person to view the image at a time. What really launched the motion picture industry was the film projector — a device that would project the image in a room so that many people could watch at the same time. And credit for that invention goes to French brothers Auguste and Louis Lumiére, who invented the Cinématographe, a device that also functioned as a camera and projector.

The Lumiére brothers

The Cinématographe was much more economical than the Kinetograph, because it ran at a speed of 16 frames per second rather than 40, using much less film. The Cinématographe also was lightweight (less than 20 pounds) and portable, which meant that film making could leave the studio. In fact, most of the early Lumiére films were shot outdoors. They were called documentaries, or "actualities."

Although Edison's motion picture inventions lost favor, his role in the motion picture industry did not end there. In the mid-1890s, he purchased the rights to another state-of-the-art projector, which was called the Vitascope, and began mass producing it. Soon many Vaudeville houses were showing Edison and Lumiére "films," although the modern concept of the motion picture as a story or narrative had not yet taken shape. The public saw them as animated photographs or living pictures.

As the film industry grew, film producers began leasing projectors, operators and film shorts to vaudeville operators and entrepreneurs. This eventually led to the separation of production from exhibition — a division of labor had emerged in the film industry.

Early Filmmaking

Although early filmmakers experimented with a number of techniques, the notion that motion pictures could be used to tell a story didn't emerge until the late 1800s. French magician Georges Méliès pioneered the way. He purchased film making equipment and constructed a glass studio on the grounds of his house at Montreuil.

Between 1896 and 1913, Méliès produced, directed, photographed and acted in more than 500 films. In 1899, he produced *L'Affaire Dreyfus* (*The Dreyfus Affair*), a film that told the story of a French Jewish officer wrongly convicted of treason.[6]

An Industry Grows

The first major box-office success, however, was *The Great Train Robbery* — a 12-minute film that depicted a train robbery, the formation of a posse, and the demise of the gunmen. The film contained the first "close-up" and set the pattern for the "western."

In the same year, a film exchange opened in San Francisco, linking producers and exhibitors. Exhibitors could buy or lease films, and eventually rental fees were calculated based on individual production costs and box-office receipts.

By 1908, about 9,000 small theaters called nickelodeons (often converted store fronts) were operating in the United States. More than 20 million people were going to the movies. They each paid 5 cents to see about an hour's worth of short films.

Motion Picture Associations

About 20 motion-picture production companies were operating in the United States in 1908. The companies were highly competitive and fought over patent rights, but they eventually formed the Motion Picture Patents Company to resolve some of their differences and fend off problems from the growing distribution and exhibition industries.

The MPPC pooled 16 patents on motion-picture technology and gave Eastman Kodak Company an exclusive contract to supply raw film stock. The MPPC effectively operated as a trust, controlling who could purchase film and

---

[6]Dreyfus later was exonerated and the scandal helped propel left-wing politicians into power.

obtain royalties. Two years later the MPPC formed the General Film Company, which combined licensed distributors into a single corporate entity.

These associations increased the efficiency of the industry, but they sparked a counter-reaction from independent filmmakers, who themselves formed the National Independent Moving Picture Alliance (earlier called the Independent Film Protective Association). The NIMPA embraced the idea of longer, multi-reel films — a move MPPC resisted and that eventually contributed to the MPPC's demise.

THE SILENT FILM ERA

Multiple reel films began appearing in 1907 and caught on very quickly. People liked the longer, story-oriented films, and they soon began calling them "feature" films. Exhibitors and producers also liked them, because they could charge more for admission and because it was less costly to advertise one long film rather than a number of short ones.

Movie Palaces

With attendance and revenues increasing, exhibitors began building more elaborate movie palaces — theaters that were larger and more comfortable than the nickelodeons. Some also included live orchestral music to accompany the production. Feature films also drew more attendance from the middle classes, who saw them as "legitimate theater" (or "high culture").

By 1916, more than 21,000 movie palaces were operating in the United States, and the nickelodeon was in decline. About 60 percent of film production was based in Hollywood, and the industry employed more than 15,000 workers and invested more than $500 million annually.

Early Stars and Directors

The star system of marketing also began to take shape during this time period. Borrowing the idea from Broadway and theater, the star system involved using famous actors to stimulate demand for films. Douglas Fairbanks, Sr., Mary Pickford, Buster Keaton and Charlie Chaplin became big box-office draws.

Many directors also became famous. In particular, D. W. Griffith helped establish motion pictures as an art form in the United States with his production of *The Birth of a Nation* (1915). This was the case even though the film was heavily criticized for being racist and was withdrawn from some theaters in urban areas (Griffith, by the way, was the son of a Confederate colonel). Other prominent directors included Cecil B. deMille, who staged a number of big productions like *The Ten Commandments* (1923), and Mack Sennett, who created *Keystone Kops* and is called the father of slapstick comedy.

Early Mergers and Specialization

During the 1920s, a number of mergers and acquisitions took place in the motion picture industry. By the early 1930s, eight major companies controlled 95 percent of the film production market.

The film industry was very vertically integrated, meaning studios controlled not only the production but also the distribution network for films and the theaters which showed them. Interestingly, most investment went not to film production, which only consumed about 5 percent of corporate assets, but to distribution and exhibition. The film companies, in other words, were basically theater chains and produced films to fill those houses.

The film companies also began specializing. Metro-Goldwyn-Mayer was the largest and produced many films that focused on middle-class life in America. Paramount produced sophisticated, more high-brow films. Universal Pictures was known for its horror films. Warner Brothers produced films targeted to working-class audiences. Twentieth Century Fox was known for making films with state-of-the-art special effects. RKO Radio was the smallest and struggled the most, but produced the classics *King Kong* (1933) and *Citizen Kane* (1941). It also distributed Disney's pictures.

Smaller studios produced the so-called B-rated film, a low budget production. But the B films often served as a spring-board for new stars, like John Wayne.

The silent film era reached its peak in the 1920s. About 700 silent films were produced in the United States in 1925. Average weekly movie attendance was about 50 million, and hundreds of millions of people around the world were going to the movies.

CALLS FOR REFORM

Controversy also began to envelop the film industry during the 1920s. Then as today, the movies focused on three major themes: sex, crime and violence. And then, as today, many movie goers were minors. Religious organizations and parents were concerned about the effects these movies were having on young people, and there were threats of boycotts and protests.

To head off the criticism, the studio heads in March 1922 formed a self-regulatory organization called the Motion Picture Association of America (formerly called the Motion Picture Producers and Distributors of America).

Although it didn't have the power to censor, the MPAA promoted a "Production Code" that placated critics for a time.

However, the controversy boiled over again with the release in the early 1930s of the Payne Fund Studies, the first social scientific studies of the effects of movies.[7] These studies showed that movies which contained scenes of horror and violence scared many children, giving them nightmares. The studies also found that movies presented moral standards that were more progressive and more sexually liberating than traditional values. The film industry responded again by strengthening its Production Code, which quieted critics for a time.

But conservatives and religious groups have never stopped complaining completely about the alleged "immoral" content in movies and television programming. Liberals also complain that too much emphasis is placed on materialism and commercialism.

The MPAA continues to function as a "protectorate" and "safety valve" for the U.S. film industry. It represents the seven major producers and distributors: The Walt Disney Company; Sony Pictures Entertainment, Inc.; Metro-Goldwyn-Mayer Inc.; Paramount Pictures Corporation; Twentieth Century Fox Film Corp.; Universal Studios, Inc.; and Warner Brothers.

TALKING PICTURES

Although silent films were popular in the 1920s, they could not survive the technology of sound, which was finally refined in the mid-1920s. At first, the major studios snubbed the technology. But in 1926, Warner Brothers, a minor studio at that time, began synchronizing orchestral music to its silent films. The public loved it and exhibitors loved it even more, because they didn't have to pay for live musicians.

The first movie to include dialogue in addition to a musical score was *The Jazz Singer* (1927). Walt Disney produced the first animated sound cartoon, *Steamboat Willie* (1928), which debuted Mickey Mouse. In less than two years, the entire American film industry converted to talking pictures. By 1930, silent pictures were extinct.

Sound enabled directors to make more realistic dramas. There was no need to switch back and forth from action sequences to frames of text. Orchestral music also was added to the sound track to create moods, which eliminated the need for in-theater musical performers.

---

[7]For a review, see Shearon A. Lowery and Melvin L. DeFleur, *Milestones in Mass Communication Research*, 2nd ed. (New York: Longman, 1988).

Sound launched the age of musicals. Dancers Fred Astaire and Ginger Rogers topped the genre (*Flying Down to Rio*, 1933; *The Gay Divorcee*, 1934). Sound also launched the gangster movie, with Edward G. Robinson (*Little Caesar*, 1930) and James Cagney *(The Public Enemy*, 1931) taking top billing. Sound changed the comedy. Humor now depended as much on a good script as on physical (visual) action. The Marx Brothers (*A Night at the Opera*, 1935), Laurel and Hardy (*The Music Box*, 1932), and W. C. Fields (*The Man on the Flying Trapeze*, 1935) were good at both.

Change always brings uncertainty, and some of the silent film directors didn't adapt well to the new sound technology. But in their place emerged a new generation of directors, who exploited sound and increasingly sophisticated visual techniques to produce highly acclaimed movies.

They included: Frank Capra, who directed *It Happened One Night* (1934), *Mr. Smith Goes to Washington* (1939) and *It's a Wonderful Life* (1946); David O. Selznick and Victor Fleming, whose *Gone with the Wind* (1939) was a huge box office success and won 10 Academy Awards; John Ford, who won Best Director Oscars for *The Informer* (1935), *The Grapes of Wrath* (1940), *How Green Was My Valley* (1941), and *The Quiet Man* (1952); and Alfred Hitchcock, who directed *Blackmail* (1929), the first successful British talking picture, and many other thrillers, including *The Man Who Knew Too Much* (1934), *The Thirty-Nine Steps* (1935), and *Rebecca* (1940), which won an Oscar for Best Picture.

COLOR MOVIES

Techniques for coloring photographs had been around since the 19th century. The first color films were hand-colored frame by frame, but this was not very cost effective for longer films. Other techniques produced only partial color.

But in the early 1930s, the Technicolor Corporation introduced a three-color system that produced full-color film photography. The system was introduced in the 1933 Disney cartoon, *The Three Little Pigs*. Toward the end of the 1930s, the three-color system was being used on full-length feature films, including *Gone With the Wind* (1939) and the *Wizard of Oz* (1939).

Although the public loved full-color movies, by the end of the 1940s fewer than one in eight were filmed in Technicolor because it was expensive. However, in 1950 a federal court broke up Technicolor's monopoly and Eastman Kodak introduced a much less expensive color film process. Within five years, half of all movies were being made in color, and by 1970 all but about 5 percent were color.

THE (TEMPORARY) DECLINE OF HOLLYWOOD

Many motion picture historians argue that Hollywood studios reached their zenith during the late 1930s and the 1940s. The studios were producing nearly 500 movies a year.

Although World War II curtailed film production in Europe, it was a lucrative time for film studios in the United States. Studios cooperated with the U.S. government and churned out pro-American and anti-Nazi and anti-Japanese films. They included *Casablanca* (1942), which starred Humphrey Bogart and Ingrid Bergman and has been called the second best movie ever made, *The Devil With Hitler* (1942), *Blondie for Victory* (1942), *This Land Is Mine* (1943), *Destination Tokyo* (1944), and *The Purple Heart* (1944).

In 1946, the year after the war had ended, more than two-thirds of the population went to the movies at least once a week. The studios were making lots of money. But this didn't last long. Four factors intervened.

End of Monopolies

The first came in the late 1940s, when the U.S. government forced the studios to sell their theater chains and monopolistic controls over film distribution. The government also ended the practice of block booking, which had forced independent theaters to exhibit lower quality films, or B-rated films, to get A-rated films (expensive productions with top stars). These changes gave independent and foreign filmmakers greater access to movie theaters.

Inflation

The second factor leading to the decline of the film industry was inflation, a post-war economic condition that ate into profits. Many studios responded with smaller scale productions. This didn't always mean lower quality. Post-war films focused more on real-life social problems and addressed such issues as racism (*Gentleman's Agreement*, 1947; *Lost Boundaries*, 1949), mental illness (*The Snake Pit*, 1948) and alcoholism (*Smash-Up*, 1947).

Right-Wing Extremism

The third factor affecting the film industry were attacks from right-wing politicians, especially Sen. Joseph McCarthy of Wisconsin, who accused the film industry of being sympathetic to communists. The House Un-American Activities Committee called more than 100 Hollywood witnesses, some of whom testified against their colleagues. However, eight screen writers and two directors, later known as the Hollywood Ten, refused to testify and were sentenced to serve up to a year in prison.

Fearing repercussions, the Association of Motion Picture Producers fired the Hollywood Ten and expressed their support for the HUAC. The studios then blacklisted many producers, writers, directors and stars who were suspected of communist associations. This destroyed the careers of many innocent people. During this time, the studios began producing motion pictures with conservative, anti-communist overtones, or they avoided politics altogether. The "red scare" didn't subside until 1954, when broadcaster Edward R. Murrow challenged McCarthy and showed that many of his accusations were false.

Despite the red scare, the studios produced some notable movies in the 1950s. They included *The Robe* (1953), *Around the World in Eighty Days* (1956) and *The Ten Commandments* (1956). These films were longer than traditional films (three to four hours) and were produced on cameras with a wider aspect ratio, meaning the width of the screen was proportionately much wider than the height. CinemaScope, SuperScope, WarnerScope and Panavision were some of the names the studios gave to the process. Although the wider screens injected more realism into the image, they could not combat the competitive effects of television.

The actor James Dean also became a legend in the 1950s, even though he only had three major movie roles (*East of Eden*, 1955; *Rebel Without a Cause*, 1955; *Giant*, 1956) before dying in automobile accident in 1955. Dean came to symbolize a restlessness that eventually took hold in the 1960s social movements that opposed the Vietnam War and favored equal rights for women and minorities. Films such as *Dr. Strangelove* (1963), which condemned nuclear weapons, reinforced the goals of these movements.

Television

But the studio system continued to go into decline during the 1950s because of a fourth factor: television. In 12 years, the small screen went from being a novelty to being a necessity in the American home. By 1960, nearly 90 percent of homes had a television.

Television was not a perfect substitute for films. For one, it was initially only available in black and white. The screen also was much smaller. But the programming was free and more diverse. Television offered daily news programming, half-hour comedies, hour-long dramas (police dramas, westerns), and variety shows. Perhaps even more important, television was convenient. People could watch it from the comfort of their home.

As a consequence, movie attendance dropped dramatically. In fact, attendance dropped 64 percent from 1950 to 1960. In 1950, a typical citizen went to the movies 30 times a year. In 1960, the typical person went only about 7 times a year. Attendance declined again from 1960 to 1970, but leveled off and has increased slightly in the past two decades.

One consequence of declining movie attendance was that the film studios became takeover targets. In fact, nearly all of the major studios were acquired by other, larger nonmedia corporations. Paramount was purchased by Gulf and Western Industries, United Artists by Transamerica Corporation, Warner Bros. by Kinney National Services, and MGM by Las Vegas financier Kirk Kerkorian. Walt Disney was the only "survivor."

The uncertainty also led the studios to cut film production by nearly 50 percent. In 1950 the industry made 483 films, compared to 248 in 1960. Production remained relatively low until 1990.

THE REBIRTH OF HOLLYWOOD

During the early 1960s, the prevailing wisdom in Hollywood to maximize profits was to produce movies that appealed to the entire family. However, this approach was not working well, because parents and older people were going to the movies a lot less often. The typical movie-goer was becoming younger and had different tastes than older people.

So, by the late 1960s, the studios violated the traditional formula and began producing movies geared to the interests of younger people. This approach worked. *Bonnie and Clyde* (1967), *2001: A Space Odyssey* (1968), and *The Wild Bunch* (1969) were big box office successes. Some were spectacular successes. Dennis Hopper's *Easy Rider* (1969) cost $375,000 to make and returned $50 million at the box office.

To counter the effects of television, filmmakers included more scenes of nudity (e.g., *Midnight Cowboy*, 1969; *Carnal Knowledge*, 1971), which was made possible after the MPAA discarded the Production Code in 1968 and created the voluntary movie rating system. Needless to say, this worked for a time.

During the 1970s, a younger generation of directors dubbed the "movie brats" emerged on the scene. Most had learned film making at film school or in college. But the studios weren't complaining. Francis Ford Coppola's *The Godfather* (1972), Martin Scorsese's *Mean Streets* (1973), Steven Spielberg's *Jaws* (1975) and *Close Encounters of the Third Kind* (1977), and George Lucas' *Star Wars* (1977) generated tens of millions of dollars in profits. John Carpenter's *Halloween* (1978) also encouraged some studios to produce low budget slasher and horror films. In fact, by 1981 horror films made up half of the 50 top-grossing movies.

During the 1980s, the Reagan administration deregulated the film making industry, allowing the major studios to own theaters.

Because of these changes, the film industry held its own during the 1970s and 1980s. Although attendance rates remained relatively flat, revenues rose partly because of higher admission costs and population growth. In 1950, one could still attend a movie for less than a buck. By 1980, the ticket price had risen to about $3. From 1960 to 1980, the population increased by nearly 50 million. The industry was making money again. The seven MPAA studios grossed $1.4 billion in 1970 and $2.7 billion in 1980.

VIDEO AND CABLE HELP MOVIES

During the 1980s, video cassette recorders (VCRs) and cable television began generating new sources of revenues for filmmakers. At first the studios were worried that movies on video cassette tapes would cut into movie attendance. However, videos expanded the film industry's market, in some cases generating more revenues than the first-run showing. Many people, in fact, preferred to watch videos in the comfort of their homes.

The growth of cable television also was a bonus to some of the film studios. Before cable, the studios depended on one of the three major television networks for re-broadcasting a movie after its first-run showing. After cable, studios had many more outlets, and some — like Disney and Fox — even set up their own networks.

These new sources for marketing films also helped the independent film industry. In 1985, the independents for the first time released more motion pictures than the major studios.

FILMS SINCE THE 1980s

At the same time, film making became even more sophisticated and eclectic. Musicals made a comeback (*Flashdance*, 1983; *Footloose*, 1984; *Dirty Dancing*, 1987); science fiction used more advanced special effects (*Blade Runner*, 1982; *Aliens*, 1984); and war movies were much more realistic (*Platoon*, 1986; *Gardens of Stone*, 1987; *Full Metal Jacket*, 1987). This decade also produced some of the most creative and thought-provoking films, such as Joel and Ethan Coen's *Blood Simple* (1984) and David Lynch's *Blue Velvet* (1986).

The 1990s started big with Kevin Costner's *Dances With Wolves* (1990), which earned a Best Picture Oscar and a Best Director Oscar for Costner. But there were some flops. Costner's *Waterworld* (1995), for example, reportedly cost more than $150 million to make and only earned $88 million at the box office.

Cutthroat Island (1995), which starred Geena Davis, cost more than $110 million and took in only $10 million at the box office, earning it the distinction of the first movie to lose more than $100 million.

But these losses were more than offset by revenues from the movies of Steven Spielberg, Spike Lee, and Jodie Foster, who emerged as the top producers/directors in Hollywood. And the decade ended with an astonishing success story: James Cameron's *Titanic* (1997), which was the most expensive film ever made (more than $200 million) but returned nearly $2 billion in worldwide ticket sales, making it the highest grossing movie of all time.

At the start of the 21st century, the film industry was relatively healthy. Film production has increased to 1950s levels (see Table 6.3). Movie attendance also has increased slightly during the last decade (going from 4.5 to 5.1 movies per year per person; see Table 6.2), even though ticket prices climbed to an average of about $5 in 2000 ($7 for first-run movies).

In 2000, revenues reached $7.7 billion. Officials attribute the increased attendance to higher quality movies, better marketing and more comfortable theaters. In May 2005, George Lucas' *Star Wars: Episode III — The Revenge of Sith* broke two-day, three-day and four-day box office records, raking in $158 million in the first four days. The movie was the last in Lucas' six-movie Star Wars epic. In 2006 and 2007, the second and third installments in the *Pirates of the Carribean* series were released. Both earned more than $1 billion worldwide, as well as third and fifth place rankings in terms of total revenues.[8]

Concentration of Ownership

In terms of revenues, the movie-making industry has always been highly concentrated in terms of ownership. Although it is estimated that there are 10,000 to 20,000 independent filmmakers in the United States, about seven Hollywood studios rake in about 80 percent of all film revenues.

The film industry is the most highly concentrated media industry in the United States because it has the highest barriers to entry. It costs tens of millions of dollars to start a studio. The average cost of producing and marketing a Hollywood film is $75 million.

However, concern about concentration of ownership in this industry is still rather low because some independent films are able to obtain national distribution, which was not the case in the 1930s and 1940s. The Internet also is reducing concern because it is being viewed as a potential new source for

[8]The rankings are available at the Internet Movie Database, <www.imdb.com/boxoffice/alltimegross?region=world-wide>.

distribution and exhibition. Still, critics point out that independent filmmakers have limited access to the market, because the major studios have an 80 percent market share.[9] Distribution is still a problem for independent filmmakers, who are often at the mercy of theater chains.

THE ROLE AND FUNCTION OF MOTION PICTURES

People often complain about the motion picture industry. Many argue that movies make children aggressive, stereotype certain groups, and promote commercialism and materialism.

It would be difficult to argue that movies do not have these dysfunctional effects on some people on some occasions. However, it would be difficult to argue that all of the effects of movies are dysfunctional for society. If that were so, then one might expect complete social decay and disorder in a short period of time.

Instead, when viewed from a distance, it is clear that the greatest effect of movies is reinforcement of dominant norms and values in a society. Like other forms of art and literature, movies usually tell a story that contains a moral lesson.

Movies that Reinforce Social Values

For example, in the Christmas classic *It's a Wonderful Life*, George (played by Jimmy Stewart) faces a financial crisis and wishes he had never been born. An angel grants his wish and then shows George what the world would have been like without him. The experience transforms George and he appreciates his life. As the angel puts it: "See George, you've really had a wonderful life. See what a mistake it would be to throw it away?"

This film is just one example of the power that motion pictures play in reinforcing dominant values in society. During World War II, Hollywood made movies to help the war effort and maintain morale "back home." During the Vietnam War, Hollywood produced *The Green Beret*, which starred John Wayne and idealized the U.S. military. In recent years, the new enemy in movies are "the terrorists."

---

[9]Although some independent films have national distribution, the vast majority do not. The big studios still dominate and engage in anticompetitive activities. See John W. Cones, *Hollywood Wars: How Insiders Gained and Maintain Control over the Film Industry* (Spokane, WA: Marquette Books LLC, 2007).

Movies, like other forms of mass media, reinforce values about the importance of family and friends, obeying the law, and being honest and grateful. In fact, it is very difficult to find a movie that does not support these values.

Movies also can have other prosocial effects. The Paine Fund Studies showed that movies, like television, have taught many children how to groom and dress, play sports, and interact with others. Although not all of the content of motion pictures results in prosocial effects, movies in general reinforce dominant values of a society and, as such, their biggest impact is maintenance of society.

Of course, most people do not think about social control when they go to the movies. To them, the movies are simply entertaining — a form of relaxation. But it is important to point out that "being entertained" is itself an effect. To the extent that movies help people relax, then they are contributing, however subtly, to social order. Steven Spielberg's films are good examples of the social control function of movies.

Steven Spielberg and Family Values

Even before turning 18, Steven Spielberg was a success. At age 12 he had completed his first scripted amateur film. At age 13 he won a prize for a 40-minute war movie called *Escape to Nowhere*. And at age 16 his 140-minute science-fiction production, *Firelight*, generated a $100 profit in a local theater.[10]

Yet Spielberg's application to film school in the 1960s was rejected because his grades weren't good enough. As a youth, Spielberg was more interested in watching television and producing amateur films than in studying. But failure to gain entry to film school didn't deter Spielberg.

He enrolled as an English major at California State University in Long Beach, and after scrounging up $15,000 from friends, Spielberg produced *Amblin'*, a 24-minute film about a pair of hitchhikers. *Amblin'* won several film awards and was shown at the Atlanta Film Festival in 1969. Executives at Universal-MCA were so impressed that they gave him a seven-year contract in the television division. Spielberg, only 20 years of age, made history as the youngest person to obtain a long-term contract from a major production studio.

---

[10]Sources for this biography of Spielberg include Joseph McBride, *Steven Spielberg: A Biography* (New York: Simon & Schuster, 1997); Philip M. Taylor, *Steven Spielberg: The Man, His Movies and Their Meaning* (London: Batsford, 1999); and Anthony Breznican, "Spielberg's Family Values," *USA Today* (June 23, 2005), p. A1.

Today Spielberg is consistently rated one of the top producers/directors in the world. He earned Best Director and Best Picture Oscars for *Schindler's List*, which details the true-life story of a German factory owner who saved thousands of Jewish citizens during World War II, and a Best Director Oscar for *Saving Private Ryan*, which chronicles the efforts of a group of World War II soldiers whose mission is to find and bring home the only surviving son of a family whose three other sons were killed in action. *The Color Purple*, which told the story about two African sisters separated at an early age, earned 11 Oscar nominations.

Steven Spielberg

Many Spielberg movies contain a lot of action and adventure. But the key value promoted in these movies, as well as many of his other movies, is family values. This is very transparent in *E.T.: The Extra-Terrestrial* (1982), as well as *War of the Worlds* (2005), which was an adaption of H. G. Wells' classic book that focuses on a divorced father who regains the love and respect of his children after fighting to keep them safe from cannibalistic aliens. His movies also have promoted civil rights. This includes not only *Schindler's List* but also *Amistad*, a movie about an 1839 shipboard revolt by African slaves, and *Minority Report* (2002).

Movies and Social Change

Although all mass media produce content that generally supports the dominant values and norms in a society, in relative terms motion pictures often "push the envelope" even more. Part of this tendency stems from the fact that filmmakers and script writers on the whole tend to be more liberal than the population at large. Art and literature have always attracted people who are critical of the status quo. Film offers a way to air alternative ideas.

During the 1920s and 1930s, for example, the movies helped acclimate people to an increasingly urban and industrialized society. Although half of the population of the United States lived in rural areas, the settings for most movies took place in big cities and usually portrayed cosmopolitan life in a glamorous way. Needless to say, this encouraged many people to move to urban areas in search of a better life. By the 1960s, only five percent of the population earned a living through farming and the nation was overwhelmingly urbanized.

Another good example of the social change function took place during the 1960s and 1970s, when many independent filmmakers (not associated with one of the seven big film studios) produced movies that were critical of U.S.

involvement in the Vietnam War and supported the women's and civil right's movements. More recent movies like Sherman Alexie's *Smoke Signals* (1998) also help to dispel myths about Native Americans. Al Gore's *An Inconvenient Truth* (2006) is being given credit for mobilizing public opinion against the administration of President George Bush, which has refused to recognize global warming as a major problem facing the world.

But perhaps no contemporary filmmaker has done more to shake up the status quo than former print journalist Michael Moore, whose documentaries on General Motors, the gun industry, and the Bush Administration and 9/11 have raised people's consciousness about abuse of power in the system.

Michael Moore and Social Change

Michael Moore is a journalist who likes to do things his way.[11]

When the chairman of General Motors refused to respond to his requests for an interview, he took his camera crew to GM headquarters and tried to ride the elevator to the chairman's office. He was turned away.

When Moore, as editor of *Mother Jones* magazine, refused to publish an article critical of the Sandanista rebels in Nicaragua because he thought the article was inaccurate, the magazine fired him.

When Random House considered scrapping publication of Moore's book *Stupid White Men* because it was too critical of President George W. Bush, Moore revealed the plan to a convention of librarians, who initiated an e-mail campaign that forced the publisher to release the book. The book became a No. 1 best-seller.

When Moore won an Academy Award in 2003 for his documentary, *Bowling for Columbine,* he used his acceptance speech to criticize President Bush. This angered many people on both the left and right, who believe recipients of Oscars should not mix politics with acceptance speeches.

But Moore didn't care. "I don't compromise my values and I don't compromise my work," he says. "That's why I've been kicked from one network to the next. I won't give in."

Moore's brand of journalism also violates the ethic of objectivity, which requires journalists to remain on the sidelines when they cover stories. Some critics argue that Moore is too ideological, too liberal, and that he sometimes ignores the facts.

---

[11]Sources for this biography of Moore include "Biography of Michael Moore," Yahoo.com and "Biography of Michael Moore," The Biography Channel, <www.thebiographychannel.com>.

But Moore's approach also has produced many admirers around the world. What they like most is that his journalism supports the working class and the poor over corporations and powerful political elites. Not since the Vietnam War have people seen this kind of populist journalism. Mass communication scholars also point out that the ethic of objectivity isn't really neutral at all — it actually produces a mainstream bias, one that tends to support the status quo (see Chapter 5 for more details).

But whether one likes or dislikes Moore's brand of journalism, there is no denying that he is having a tremendous impact on journalism and documentary filmmaking around the world. He is especially liked overseas, where foreigners often see the United States government as arrogant and elitist.

Moore was born in 1954 in Davison, Michigan. His father and grandfather both worked for General Motors. As a Boy Scout, he won a merit badge for creating a slide show that exposed environmentally unfriendly businesses in Flint. At age 18, he became one of the youngest people in the United States to be elected to political office (school board).

He dropped out of college and began writing for an alternative weekly newspaper, eventually becoming its editor. He worked briefly for *Mother Jones* and the Ralph Nader organization. He used his settlement money from the magazine to produce *Roger and Me* (1989), a humor-laced documentary that skewered General Motors and its chairman, Roger Smith, for laying off 30,000 auto workers in Flint, Michigan. Moore nearly went bankrupt producing the film, which took three years. The film won a number of honors and went on to become one of the most financially successful documentaries ever made.

In the 1990s, Moore produced several television shows, but none lasted long. He wrote another book in 1996, titled *Downsize This!*, before writing *Stupid White Men*.

In 2002, he won the Oscar for *Bowling for Columbine,* a film that criticized the gun industry and right-wing groups. In 2004, he released *Fahrenheit 9/11,* a film that indicted the Bush administration for its close financial ties to Saudi Arabia and relatives of terrorist Osama bin Laden. The film was the first documentary to win the Cannes Film Festival's Palm D'or, the festival's top prize.

When Disney refused to distribute the film, apparently because of concerns over the political fallout, the rights were sold to Miramax heads Bob and Harvey Weinstein, who then were able to secure theatrical release in the United States. In three days, *Fahrenheit 9/11* grossed more money than *Bowling for Columbine* and also became the first documentary in history to be crowned the top money-maker of the weekend.

In 2007, Moore released *Sicko,* a documentary that compares the highly profitable privatized American health care industry to other nations' public health care systems and contains Health Maintenance Organization horror stories. The film stimulated a national debate over the question of how the world's most prosperous nation can also be the only industrialized country in the world without universal health care. Nearly 50 million Americans have no health insurance.

Moore has made millions of dollars from his movies, but he also has given millions to charitable causes, including unemployed workers in Flint.

Chapter 10

RADIO, RECORDINGS, LOVE AND POLITICS

Edward R. Murrow stood on the roof of a building near the British Broadcasting Corporation in London as the German bomber passed overhead. The year was 1940, and Adolf Hitler's air force was bombing the city night after night in what came to be known as the "Battle for Britain."

"Off on my left, I can see the faint-red angry snap of anti-aircraft bursts," Murrow said, speaking into a microphone that transmitted his live radio report to millions of people back in the United States, which was not yet involved in World War II. "Four searchlights are swinging over in this general direction. The plane's still very high. ... Just overhead now the burst of the antiaircraft fire. Still the nearby guns are not working. The searchlights now are feeling almost directly overhead. Now you'll hear two bursts a little nearer in a moment. ... There they are. That hard, stony sound."[1]

For five years Murrow reported the war. He began his broadcasts with the simple declaration: "This is London." He spent several more evenings reporting from rooftops as the bombs burst around him and ignited numerous fires that did massive damage to London and other English cities from June 1940 to April 1941. Thousands of civilians and several hundred British fighter pilots were killed. On December 25, 1940, he reported, "This is

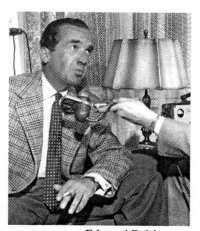

Edward R. Murrow

---

[1]A book of Murrow's broadcasts from London was published in 1941. Edward R. Murrow, *This is London* (New York: Simon and Schuster, 1941). Also see Joseph E. Persico, *Edward R. Murrow: An American Original* (New York: Dell, 1988), p. 173.

not a merry Christmas in London. I heard that phrase only twice in the last three days."

On one occasion, the BBC Broadcasting House suffered a direct hit. The bomb smashed through an upper story window and came to rest on the floor. The bomb squad attempted to defuse the bomb, but it went off, killing seven people and injuring several others. Murrow knew most of them. He was on the radio as the wounded and killed were taken out of the studio. He described the scene and the smell of iodine that permeated the studio.

Murrow also flew more than 40 combat missions aboard Allied bombers and paratrooper planes. After the war, he visited a recently liberated concentration camp and reported: "I pray you believe what I have said about Buchenwald (concentration camp). I reported what I saw and heard, but only part of it. For most of it, I have no words."

Murrow went on to become the most famous and trusted U.S. journalist of the war. His quiet, monotone voice enhanced his credibility. The poet Archibald MacLeish would later tell Murrow, "You burned the city of London in our houses and we felt the flames that burned it."[2]

After the war, Murrow was promoted to vice president and director of public affairs of CBS. In 1951, he took his radio program "Hear It Now" to television and called it "See It Now." His television show made history in 1954 when it condemned Sen. Joseph R. McCarthy for falsely accusing people of being communists (see next chapter for details).

Murrow, who smoked three packs of cigarettes a day, died of lung cancer in 1965 at the age of 57.[3]

Many historians argue that Murrow's live radio reports from London played the crucial role in swaying American public opinion against Nazi Germany. But Murrow's broadcasts almost didn't happen. When Murrow first proposed the idea, the British Air Ministry turned him down, because it was worried Murrow might say something to compromise British national security. Control of information is a primary concern during times of war.

But Murrow wouldn't take "no" for an answer. He went to the top of the political power structure — to Winston Churchill, the British Prime Minister. Churchill also recognized the value of controlling information. But, instead, he saw Murrow's reports as an opportunity to generate sympathy in America for the British.

---

[2]Erik Barnouw, *The Gold Web* (New York: Oxford University Press, 1968), p. 151.

[3]Janet Murrow kept a diary that has been an invaluable source of information to historians about Ed. She died in 1999. Ed attended Washington State College, which is now Washington State University and houses the Edward R. Murrow School of Communication.

Of course, this was not the first time mass media was used to influence public opinion during a war. In the late 1890s, New York newspapers played a major role in drumming up support for U.S. involvement in the Spanish American War.[4]

But never before had a major war been reported "live," as it happened. Leaders around the world quickly seized upon this new-found power. Radio was used to drum up sympathy for the home country and hate for the enemy. In other words, radio became a tool of propaganda for both sides. It was a mechanism of social control.[5] And it still is, even during peacetime.

CHAPTER OVERVIEW

Radio continues to be an important medium of politics and social control. This doesn't mean the content of news programs and talk shows always supports the interests of elites. A lot of news and talk radio is critical of powerful people, partly because even elites don't always agree with each other.

But the content of these programs rarely supports extremist positions like fascism or communism. Like other forms of media content, radio content leans more toward the center of the political spectrum, or perhaps a bit to the right (especially talk radio).

But politics isn't the only content on radio. In fact, radio's most unique niche today is music. Needless to say, most people enjoy listening to music because it entertains and relaxes them. And music is no less important as a means of control than news programs or talk shows. Entertainment is, indeed, a form of control. People who are entertained and relaxed have fewer reasons to stir up trouble (e.g., join anti-establishment or revolutionary movements). Moreover, the lyrical content of music generally reflects and reinforces the values and beliefs of a society.

---

[4]During times of war especially, mass media almost always rally behind the national interest (see, e.g., discussion in Chapter 9 about filmmakers supporting the U.S. government during World War II). This is the case even in countries whose journalists adhere to the so-called "ethic of objectivity" (see Chapters 5 and 16 for more discussion of this topic). Media help build and maintain morale and, thus, play a social control function.

[5]A more formal definition of "propaganda" is the dissemination or promotion of ideas or doctrines, often deceptive or distorted, to further a cause.

Early History of Recording

"Mary had a little lamb."

With those five words, Thomas Alva Edison launched a recording industry in 1877.[6] He had just invented a tinfoil phonograph, which consisted of a cylinder, a hort and a hand crank.

A decade later it was one of the most popular devices of the 19th century. In 1888, he made the first "celebrity" recording of a 12-year-old pianist virtuoso.

In 1894, Charles and Émile Pathé built a small phonograph factory near Paris and began recording singers. They had 12,000 recordings within a decade.

Also in 1894, in the United States Emile Berliner filed a patent on a Gramaphone, which used a disc rather than a cylinder. Discs were much easier and less expensive to produce. He expanded operations in Europe and his company eventually became Victor.

Early Recordings

In the early days, the recordings were made acoustically as opposed to electronically. A singer would project her or his voice into a horn, which was then transformed into grooves on a cylinder or disc. This and other early recording technologies could not reproduce all sounds faithfully, but this didn't lessen public enthusiasm about the product.

During the 1890s, people could put a coin in a slot to hear a short song or skit come out of a Gramaphone, which used discs 10 or 12 inches in diameter and contained several minutes of recorded music. During the early 1900s, the recording industry began mass producing records, mostly classical recordings.

Recording Becomes a Mass Medium

The recording industry, which was dominated by Victor and Columbia, became a mass medium for popular music after 1910. Ragtime music gets some of the credit. It launched a dance craze. Jazz and blues music closely followed. Symphonies were being recorded in Europe. Beethoven's *Fifth* symphony was immensely popular. In the United States, Leopold Stokowski and the Philadelphia Orchestra became famous.

---

[6]General histories of the recording industry can be found in Michael Chanan, *Repeated Takes: A Short History of Recording and Its Effects on Music* (New York: Verso, 1995) and Michael Campbell, *And the Beat Goes On: An Introduction to Popular Music in America, 1840 to Today* (New York: Schirmer Books, 1996).

By the 1920s, the music companies were producing tens of millions of recordings a year in the United States. The quality improved dramatically after the introduction of the microphone and electrical recording process about 1925. The music industry was selling more than 100 million records a year.

In the mid-1920s, radio offered free, live music. When the country entered the Great Depression in 1929, this cut into sales of records. Most people couldn't afford to own a phonograph and purchase records as well. So many just bought the radio. In fact, to keep up with demand for radios, RCA converted most of its phonograph factories into radio production facilities.

Total revenues in the recording industry dropped from $46 million in 1930 to $6 million in 1933. Despite tough times, the recording industry survived, in part because of the popularity of the jukebox, or coin-operated phonograph. For a nickel, patrons could hear and dance to their favorite tunes. Thousands of eating and drinking establishments installed a jukebox, and dance crazes like the jitterbug kept the public coming back

The recording industry was hit hard again during World War II, when the U.S. government declared shellac, the main ingredient in records, a substance vital to the war effort. The industry was also set back by a musicians' strike. Sales of records increased only slowly during the war.

Improving Technology

But the recording industry rebounded after World War II because of three factors: better marketing, better technology and an improved economy.

The marketing idea — to mail free records to radio stations in hopes of getting free air play — was first used by Capital Records during the war. The idea was simple but it worked.

Radio stations did not have to spend money on records. But more important, they did have to hire live bands, which was expensive. Soon all of the major labels were supplying radio stations with free records.

Later, during the 1950s, the industry would come under attack for a practice known as payola, in which record companies paid disc jockeys to play their records.

The Communications Act of 1934 was eventually amended to eliminate this practice. However, today record companies can still get their records played if the radio station announces who paid for the air time (pay-for-play) or if companies pays for 10-second commercials that run with their songs (pay-for-say).

Recording technology also improved during the 1940s. Companies began manufacturing records from vinyl, a plastic resin made from petroleum. This was more durable and produced a better sound than shellac. Vinyl also enabled production of larger, long-playing (LP) records that could record the contents of an entire symphony on one side (up to 30 minutes).

LPs ran at a speed of 33 revolutions per minute, which was much slower than 45s and 78s. In the late 1940s, the 45 rpm became the standard for singles and the 33 rpm for albums. The 78 eventually became extinct.

The quality of the sound also was improved with multiple track recording and stereo. Multiple track recording involved recording instruments and voices through separate microphones and tracks. The tracks were then mixed to produced the final song.

Stereophonic sound was produced by sending the sounds of some instruments or vocals to one channel, or speaker, and the sounds of the others to the other channel or speaker. Taken together, the industry called these technical improvements high-fidelity (hi-fi) sound, which meant the recorded sound approached the original.

Finally, the recording industry got a boost from the economy, which rebounded after the war. People had more money to buy records.

Radio stations began playing more records because it was cheaper than hiring live performers. Record companies also began courting radio stations, often bribing station managers and disc jockeys to play their records. During the 1940s, radio stations played records of six major recording companies: Capital, Columbia, Decca, Mercury, MGM and Victor.

EARLY HISTORY OF RADIO

Radio traces its roots to the electric telegraph.

In 1837, Samuel Morse developed a device that could transmit electric impulses into a series of dots and dashes on paper. The dots and dashes represented letters and numbers in Morse Code. By the 1890s, telegraph lines were transmitting messages to thousands of places around the world. But the telegraph, which relied on wires and lines, was expensive to install and maintain. Also, the telegraph never became a mass medium, because it was impractical for people to learn Morse Code.[7]

---

[7] A telegraph can be more broadly defined as a system that allows the transmission of information across a distance. The French, for example, developed a semaphore system in the late 18th century, which enabled messages to be transmitted from hilltop to hilltop using flags or a fox with panels and telescopes. For general histories of radio, see Gleason L. Archer, *History of Radio to 1926* (New York: The American Historical Society, 1938); Alden R. Carter, *Radio: From Marconi to the Space Age* (New York: F. Watts, 1987); Paul F. Lazarsfeld, *Radio and Printed Page* (New York: Arno Press, 1971); Stanley Leinwoll, *From Spark to Satellite: A History of Radio Communication* (New York: Scribner,

The idea of transmitting signals without wires took shape in 1873 with the publication of James Clerk Maxwell's theory of electromagnetic waves. About 15 years later Heinrich Hertz, a German physicist, electronically generated such waves. However, not until 1895 was the first practical wireless telegraph developed. Guglielmo Marconi, an Italian, couldn't interest the Italian government in his wireless device. But the British gave him a patent. Marconi eventually won the Nobel Peace Prize and became rich from his invention.

Marconi

In 1899, the first wireless message was sent across the English Channel. The first transatlantic wireless telegraph message was sent in 1901 from England to Newfoundland. One of the first popular applications for the telegraph radio was shipping. Boats, including the *Titanic*, were equipped with them for safety and navigational reasons. Additional advancements in technology during the early 1900s, such as the vacuum tube and the electronic-tube oscillator, helped boost signal strength.

On Christmas Eve 1906, Reginald Aubrey Fessenden broadcast the first known radio program in the United States from his experimental station at Brant Rock, Massachusetts. This consisted of two musical selections, the reading of a poem and a short talk. Wireless operators on ships within a radius of several hundred miles heard the program.

From then until World War I, the airwaves were populated mostly with amateur operators. Most broadcasters and listeners tuned in with homemade radio sets. A radio could be easily and inexpensively built with an empty Quaker Oats carton, cotton-covered wire, tinfoil, galena, a thin piece of wire called a cat's whisker and a pair of headphones.

But the growing interest in radio created a major problem: There were more people who wanted to broadcast than there were frequencies to carry them. The airwaves were so congested in some areas that radios could only pick up static.

Airwave Regulation

The government responded with legislation, but it would take 15 years to clear the air.

The first law was the Radio Act of 1912, which was passed in the aftermath of the *Titanic* disaster. The law required ships to leave their radios on 24 hours

1979); and Christopher Sterling, *History of Broadcasting: Radio to Television* (New York: Arno Press, 1996).

a day and required federal licensing of all transmitters. All broadcasters were required to identify themselves with call letters (which begin with "W" for stations east of the Mississippi River and "K" for stations west of the river) when they went on the air,[8] but no specific frequencies were assigned and everyone who applied was given a license. The airwave congestion got so bad in large cities that sales of radios began to decline in 1927.

Congress responded with the Radio Act of 1927, which gave the Federal Radio Commission the power to grant and revoke licenses on specific frequencies to those who broadcast in "the public interest, convenience or necessity." The FCC gave licenses to about 600 broadcasters and denied licenses to 150 others. But this resolved the congestion problem.

Seven years later, Congress passed the Communications Act of 1934, which converted the FRC into the Federal Communications Commission, an agency that survives to this day. The new law gave the FCC control over wireless as well as wired communications, such as the telephone. The law also gave the FCC power to place limits on how many radio (and eventually television) stations one individual or company could own. One individual or company was not allowed to own more than seven AM radio stations and seven FM stations, and no more than one AM and one FM in the same market. The seven-station limit also was placed on the television industry in the 1950s.

Commercial Radio

The commercial potential of radio was recognized long before its reality. In 1916, David Sarnoff, a former wireless telegraph operator who routed messages to families during the sinking of the *Titanic*, believed radio could become a "household utility" for pumping music into American households. After World War I, Sarnoff emerged as a major executive in the radio and later television industries.

But credit for the first commercial venture is given to Frank Conrad, an engineer at Westinghouse in Pittsburgh. Conrad had constructed a small transmitting station in his garage and was broadcasting phonograph records. Soon thereafter, people began asking him to play specific songs. He began broadcasting twice a week for two hours in the evening. A local department store then took out advertisements in local newspapers, telling readers they could buy a receiver to listen to Conrad's programs.

---

[8]The rule applied to new stations. Stations that had already been established, such as KDKA in Pittsburgh, were allowed to keep their call letters.

Recognizing the market potential of broadcasting, Westinghouse, which was already manufacturing radio equipment, asked Conrad to build a 100-watt broadcast station on top of the company's factory. The first commercial radio station, KDKA, went on the air in Pittsburgh on November 2, 1920. The station broadcast the news that Warren Harding had defeated James Cox for president of the United States. By the end of 1921, eight radio stations were operating in the United States.

AT&T Corporation launched its first radio station, WEAF, in New York City in 1922. The station broadcast the first paid commercial, which cost $50 and promoted a real estate company. By the end of 1922, the government had granted licenses to more than 550 radio stations. By 1925, more than two million radio sets were being sold a year, and the nationwide radio audience numbered 30 million.

By 1930, more than 600 radio stations were on the air in the United States, and radio was the most popular leisure-time activity. The technology was also improving. Edwin Howard Armstrong invented FM radio in the early 1930s, which offered much clearer reception. But FM would not emerge as an important medium until the late 1950s.

Broadcast Networks

A broadcast network is a group of stations that share programming. The stations may be owned by the network or they may be independent.

The first network, National Broadcasting Company, was established by Radio Corporation of America (RCA) in 1926. NBC supplied programming to 16 stations. Two years later the network had 56 stations. The major advantage of networks was that it provided less expensive programming.

The Columbia Broadcasting System (CBS) was founded in 1927. CBS grew quickly because, instead of charging affiliates for programming as NBC did, it supplied the programming free in return for five hours of affiliates' time. This approach was so effective that NBC adopted the same policy during the 1930s.

The Mutual Broadcasting System, which served a coalition of independent radio stations, was founded in 1934. Within six years it had 160 members. The American Broadcasting Corporation was created in the mid-1940s, after the U.S. government forced RCA to sell one of its two networks (NBC Blue) because of concerns about too much control over the public airwaves.

Entertainment Programming

Live music was the most popular form of programming in the 1920s. RCA hired the Philadelphia Orchestra under Eugene Ormandy, and NBC created its own orchestra under the leadership of Arturo Toscanini. Jazz, big bands, and country music also became very popular. Dance crazes, such as the Charleston, stimulated demand for records. Then, as today, the lyrical and thematic content of music focused heavily on love, relationships, having a good time and how to get over bad times.

However, in the late 1920s, the networks began producing more dramas, comedies, soap operas, game shows, talk shows, and news programming. Many of these programs attracted larger audiences, which in turn generated higher advertising revenues. One of the most popular programs was "Amos 'n' Andy," which was based on the life of two black men (although the real-life actor-comedians were white). The comedy more recently has been severely criticized for portraying racial stereotypes. But during the Great Depression the problems of the black man were generalized to other citizens as well.

Other comedic programming quickly followed. Former vaudeville comedians Fred Allen ("Town Hall Tonight" and "The Fred Allen Show"), Jack Benny ("The Jack Benny Program"), and George Burns and Gracie Allen ("The George Burns and Gracie Allen Show") became national stars, and later transferred their radio programs to television. The light-hearted nature of their programs offered many people respite from the tough economic times — a decade in which up to a third of the population was unemployed.

Dramatic and mystery programming, such as "Charlie Chan," "Sherlock Holmes" and "The Shadow" were also very popular. "The CBS Mystery Radio Hour" made history in 1938 with its dramatic adaptation of H. G. Wells' science-fiction story, *The War of the Worlds*. The program was so realistic that, despite disclaimers, one million people in the United States panicked, believing the Martians were invading earth. This incident reinforced the idea that radio had powerful effects and stimulated research into the effects of mass media.

Radio News

Radio news also became more sophisticated throughout the 1930s, but it was an uphill battle.

Many newspapers felt threatened by radio, which could broadcast free up-to-the minute news reports. Some newspapers felt so threatened they stopped publishing radio programming schedules. In 1933, under pressure from newspapers, the wire services stopped selling news to radio stations. The dispute was eventually resolved when radio owners agreed to broadcast only brief news reports. Newspapers would then provide in-depth coverage.

But newspapers couldn't compete with radio in terms of breaking news, or news reported as it happens. One of the most memorable radio broadcasts occurred in 1937, when the German dirigible Hindenburg burst into flames as it was landing in New Jersey, killing 36 people. Announcer Herb Morrison was recording the event for his radio station and began crying as the dirigible crashed, but he regained his composure and provided an incomparable news account of the tragedy.

The threat of World War II stimulated the development of network news departments. Edward R. Murrow was a pioneer, covering Hitler's march into Vienna in 1938 for CBS.

During the war, radio provided news and entertainment programming that helped maintain morale at home and in the battlefield. President Franklin D. Roosevelt's famous "fireside chats" helped mobilize support for his policies and maintain public morale before and during World War II. The U.S. government also created The Voice of America in 1942 to broadcast news and information to Europe that supported U.S. policies. Today VOA broadcasts reach 86 million people around the world.[9]

Voice of America: News or Propaganda?

During times of crisis, such as a war, one of the first things governments do is make plans to control the press and the dissemination of information and ideas.[10] But in the late 1930s, the United States wasn't at war. So New York Congressman Emmanuel Celler had difficulty mustering enough support for legislation that would have created a government-funded international radio service to combat Adolph Hitler's propaganda radio service.

All that changed after the bombing of Pearl Harbor on December 7, 1941. On February 24, just 79 days after the attack, the U.S. Foreign Information Service began transmitting radio news in German to Germany and other European countries. Announcer William Harlan Hale opened with these words: "Here speaks a voice from America." The name stuck and Voice of America was born.

From the outset, the VOA promised to tell listeners the truth, regardless of whether the news was good or bad. But there was no doubt that the United States, following in the footsteps of other major world powers, created the radio

---

[9]For more information, see the International Broadcasting Bureau's Web site at <www.ibb.gov>.

[10]Sources for this report on VOA include Robert S. Fortner, *International Communication: History, Conflict, and the Control of the Global Metropolis* (Belmont, CA: Wadsworth, 1993), pp. 8-9; the Voice of America Web site <www.voanews.com>; and Jerry White, "Bush Administration Moves to Silence Dissent," World Socialist Web site <www.wsws.org/articles/2001/sep2001/cens-s29.shtml> (originally published September 21, 2001).

service with the primary purpose of controlling information about it and its allies. For example, during the war, the VOA didn't report news that officials thought could jeopardize the security of U.S. troops or the U.S. government.

Today the VOA broadcasts more than 1,000 hours of news, informational, educational, and cultural programs every week to an audience of more than 100 million people worldwide. VOA programs are produced and broadcast in 44 languages through radio, satellite television, and the Internet.

The content of VOA reads and sounds much like that in any other Western news agency (see the VOA Web site, www.voanews.com, for samples). On the surface, there doesn't appear to be any blatant attempt to fabricate information or ideas. Yet the organization receives it share of criticism that its content is loaded with propaganda.

"The programs on VOA or Radio Moscow, designed to present official points of view or to analyze world events from a U.S. or Soviet viewpoint, are obviously politically motivated," writes Robert S. Fortner, a professor and expert on the history of international communications. "The United States often complained about alleged Soviet disinformation campaigns, but it used disinformation itself to mislead Iraq prior to beginning the February 1991 ground offensive in Kuwait."

Officials in less developed countries also often criticize the VOA for broadcasting reports that promote the interests of the United States. But the complaints aren't always from the political left. In September 2001, soon after the attacks on the Pentagon and the World Trade Center, the VOA was criticized by the Bush administration and other conservatives for broadcasting an interview with an alleged terrorist leader. Ironically, some observers note, the Bush administration was in essence encouraging the VOA to be less objective when covering the news and to produce only content that serves the interests of the United States.

The "Golden Age of Radio"?

The 1930s and 1940s are said to be the "golden age of radio."

Indeed, by 1940, the industry was selling more than 50 million radios a year. More than 80 percent of the 35 million U.S. homes had a radio, and nearly 40 million people were listening each week.

Radio was, indeed, the country's favorite pastime. Families spent their evenings huddled together around the radio listening to their favorite programs. Radio made stars of singers Perry Como, Bing Crosby, Doris Day and Frank Sinatra, most of whom also built even bigger careers on television or in the movies.

But not every social group had an equal footing on radio. Advertisers would not sponsor programs directed at African American audiences. Despite this, some black singers and musicians had attained a level of success. Critics raved over stage and screen actor Ethel Waters, and musicians Duke Ellington and the Mills Brothers made appearances on many programs.

The first radio stations geared toward the interests of African American audiences emerged in the late 1940s in large cities like New York. WWRL of New York and other black-oriented stations played rhythm 'n' blues and gospel music and broadcast news and features for the black community.

But, overall, there were few opportunities for African American actors. The most successful black actor on radio was Eddie Anderson, who played Rochester, a supporting actor on the Jack Benny Program from 1937 to 1950. Anderson also played the same role when the show was turned into a TV series in 1950, but he and the show were criticized because the character often engaged in stereotypical behaviors.

Women's roles in radio weren't much better. Most of the programs were oriented around the lives of men. Women often were cast in the traditional roles of wife and mother. And when they weren't, they usually were portrayed as being dependent upon or serving men.

IMPACT OF RADIO AFTER WORLD WAR II

The 1950s cemented the relationship between the radio and recording industries. A key factor pushing them closer together was television.

Television, which emerged as a commercial entity in the early 1950s, was more engaging than radio as a medium for dramatic and comedic programming. It could do everything radio could do (produce sound) and more (produce visuals to accompany the sound). Television became what sociologists call a *functional substitute* for radio. Within several years, almost every major radio drama and comedy program had been converted into a TV program.

The impact of television on radio was so great that many people predicted the end of radio as a medium. But that never happened. Radio found its niche by specializing even more in music, news and talk show formats, and also by becoming more localized. Nearly half of the radio stations dropped their affiliations with the national radio broadcast networks. They no longer needed dramatic and comedic programming.

To fill air time, most radio stations turned to music and many began offering more specialized music formats. For example, some played primarily country music, while others focused on jazz, big band or classical. Specialization is a trend that has continued to the present. In large cities today, one can find a format for almost every major genre of music. Because FM radio offered better sound reproduction and less static than AM radio, during the 1950s radio stations that offered a music format increasingly turned to FM, while those with news and talk increasingly dominated AM radio. This distinction continues today. About one-fourth of the AM stations focus on news and talk, versus only about 7 percent of FM stations.

In terms of news, radio's big advantage over television and newspapers was immediacy — it provided the fastest up-to-the-minute newscasts, sometimes reporting live. In recent decades, television has erased some of this advantage because of 24-hour news programs like CNN. But radio continues to have an edge because it is more widely available and allows a listener to engage in other activities, such as driving a car, at the same time. Television demands more attention from a viewer.

The transistor radio, which was invented in 1948, also helped radio broadcasting survive the impact of television. The transistor radio was much smaller and lighter than the vacuum tube radio and could be carried anywhere, such as the beach or park. The transistor radio, which was being sold in stores and installed in automobiles in 1954, also was much less expensive. Finally, the recording and radio industries were given another boost in the 1953. A new musical sound was about to shake up America.

The Rock 'n' Roll Era

In 1953, Bill Haley and his band, "The Comets," were struggling musicians. They had one moderate hit, "Rock the Joint," which sold 75,000 records. But their next release, "Crazy, Man, Crazy," shot into the U.S. Top 20 and gave the group national recognition. More importantly, it launched a new music genre, rock 'n' roll.

Rock 'n' roll was a term allegedly used to describe the movements of sexual intercourse. But today it is associated with the most commercially successful trend in modern music.

The roots of rock 'n' roll go back to classical blues, gospel and country western music. But most people didn't care about that. They liked "rock" because it was fun to dance to. Within a year or two, teenagers abandoned the more traditional music of Patti Page ("Tennessee Waltz"), Doris Day and Bing Crosby, and began listening to a new band of musicians.

Early Rock Stars

In 1954, Bill Haley and the Comets released "Shake, Rattle and Roll" and "Rock Around the Clock." The latter sold more than 25 million copies, a phenomenal number, and ensured that "rock 'n' roll was here to stay."

Other performers quickly followed and had even more success. Two were African Americans. Chuck Berry wrote the hits "Maybellene," "Sweet Little Sixteen," "Rock and Roll Music," "Roll Over, Beethoven," and "Johnny B. Goode." Little Richard wrote the hits "Good Golly Miss Molly," "Long Tall Sally," "Tutti-Frutti," and "Lucille."

But Elvis Presley became the king of rock 'n' roll. Before he became famous, Presley used to listen to the "Grand Ole Opry" and watch black musicians perform the blues live. In 1954 Presley recorded the first of 15 songs, five of which had considerable local success. In 1956, Elvis recorded "Heartbreak Hotel," the first of 45 rpm records that sold more than a million copies.

Elvis Presley in the 1957 movie Jailhouse Rock

He appeared on television but the networks would show him only from the waist up because gyrating hip action on stage was considered too controversial. "Elvis the Pelvis" drove audiences wild when he performed live. During his life, Elvis sold more than 500 million records. He died of an accidental drug overdose in 1977.

Rock and Social Protest

Rock 'n' roll became a dominant music genre on radio during the 1960s, a time of increasing social unrest. Social movements that promoted civil rights, women's rights, and environmental protection and criticized U.S. involvement in the Vietnam War became increasingly vocal. These and other liberal groups demanded more justice and equality. Young people also were experimenting with marijuana, LSD and other drugs. They rejected traditional values that frowned on sex before marriage. Needless to say, music reflected and reinforced these changing values and trends.

The Beatles — John Lennon, Paul McCartney, George Harrison and Ringo Starr — led the way with songs about justice, equality, love, peace, sex and drugs. In the early 1960s, the group wrote love song songs, such as "Love Me Do," "Please Please Me," "She Loves You," and "I Want To Hold Your Hand."

Later, the Beatles turned to writing more serious and controversial works. In 1967, the group released the album, "Sgt. Pepper's Lonely Hearts Club

Band," which became the definitive psychedelic soundtrack. Today many critics consider "Sgt. Pepper" to be the best rock album of all time. Beatlemania lasted until 1970, when the band broke up after McCartney left to pursue a solo career.

Specialization

The 1960s and 1970s saw the emergence of new, more specialized forms of music, including the hard-driving dancing beat of disco (The Bee Gees), the soulful sounds of Motown (Diana Ross and The Supremes), the aggressive urban dance beat of funk (Sly and the Family Stone), the iconoclastic sounds of punk (Sex Pistols), the social conscious lyrics of folk-rock (Bob Dylan), and the Afro-Jamaican sounds of reggae (Bob Marley).

In the 1980s, rap/hip-hop (LL Cool J) became popular and has remained one of the dominant music genres throughout the 1990s and early 2000s (Puff Daddy and DMX). The term hip-hop, by the way, refers to a cultural movement that contains four major elements: deejaying, rapping, graffiti painting, and b-boying (a dance style).

RADIO AND RECORDING SINCE THE 1970S

One consequence of this specialization in music has been a decline in rock 'n' roll's share of the recording industry's revenues. At its heyday, rock music generated 60 percent of recording industry revenues. By 1990, its share of the pie had dropped to 42 percent, and by 2000 rock's share had slipped to 25 percent.

Yet, despite the decline, rock 'n' roll continues to be the most popular music genre in terms of total sales. Country music, which was the second most popular genre in 1995 (17%), slipped to third place in 2000 (11%). Rap/hip hop took over the second spot, capturing 13 percent of all sales. Rhythm and blues was fourth with 10 percent. Sales of pop and jazz music have declined slightly since 1990, whereas sales of gospel/religious (including Christian rock) have increased slightly.

As the number and variety of different music genres has expanded, so have the number of commercial radio stations, especially FM stations. In 1930 there were 612 AM radio stations. That number increased to more than 2,000 in 1950 and more than 4,000 in 1970. The total number of commercial AM stations has remained about the same since 1980, at about 4,500.

In contrast, the total number of commercial FM stations continues to grow. Since 1960, the total number has grown by about 1,000 every 10 years. In 2000, the number of commercial FM stations overtook the number of AM stations for the first time (5,892 FM compared with 4,685 AM). The total number of educational FM stations also has increased substantially over the past two decades. There were 2,140 in year 2000.

Opportunities for minorities and women on radio improved during the 1960s and afterward, partly because of judicial and legislative actions that lessened discriminatory practices. FCC rules reinforced these decisions. Terry Gross, a highly respected radio talk show host on National Public Radio, got her start in 1973.

Terry Gross: Interviewing Society's Elites

Terry Gross is 5-feet-tall.[11] But on the air she has a towering presence. In fact, Gross, the host of National Public Radio's hour-long "Fresh Air" talk-interview program, is a giant in the radio talk show industry. She garners respect from just about everyone, including her guests.

"When I'm with Terry, I know I'm in good hands," science writer Timothy Ferris, who has been on her show three times, tells a *Los Angeles Times* reporter. "It's like sparring with Muhammad Ali. It's not so much that I've never seen anybody throw a jab over the top before. It's the way that it's thrown that makes it different."

"What makes her such an exceptional interviewer is her intelligence coupled with her sense of curiosity," says Jennifer Roth, a radio station general manager who has worked with Gross. "She can be tough but she also has empathy with other people and the ability to see things through their eyes."

Like other talk show hosts, most of the guests that Gross has on her show are society's elites (e.g., politicians, musicians, poets, artists, celebrities, filmmakers and authors). Ordinary people rarely get interviewed on her program. In this respect, her program is no different from the way other news media cover the news — elites always have more access to the press.

But Gross says she tries to give her 3 million listeners something they haven't already heard about her guests. "Anyone who agrees to be interviewed must decide where to draw the line between what is public and what is private," she says. "But the line can shift, depending on who is asking the questions. What puts someone on guard isn't necessarily the fear of being 'found out.' It sometimes is just the fear of being misunderstood."

Gross began her radio career in 1973 hosting and producing arts, women's and public affairs programs for a public radio station in Buffalo, New York.

---

[11]Sources for the Terry Gross biography include National Public Radio's Web site <www.npr.org>; Eleanor Yang, "NPR's Terry Grosss: Asking the Smart Questions," *Los Angeles Times* (April 15, 2000), p. F20; and Anthony Violanti, "A Breath of Fresh Air," *The Buffalo News* (December 17, 2000), p. 4F.

Two years later she joined the staff of "Fresh Air," which was then a local interview and music program at WHYY-FM in Philadelphia. In 1985, the program was distributed nationally, and it now airs on more than 160 public radio stations. Her 5,000 guests have included Nancy Reagan, Ice-T, Tom Hanks, Monica Lewinsky, Jerry Seinfeld, Toni Morrison, and Studs Terkel.

Recording Formats

Audio recording formats have changed dramatically over the years. In the 1890s, shellac replaced wax as the material preferred for producing records. In the 1940s, vinyl replaced shellac. In the 1960s, eight-track tape players were introduced and were popular because they could be used in cars. But they were quickly overtaken by the smaller, more reliable audiocassette tape player.

Each of these changes improved audio technology. But the single most important change in the last 50 years has been digital audio recording. Digitization involves breaking down sounds and notes into a binary system of 0s and 1s (offs and ons) for processing by a computer. The key advantage of digital recording is that the quality of sound does not deteriorate with each reproduction — it remains as good as the original. In contrast, the quality of analog recordings, such as that found on vinyl records and metal tapes, breaks down the more they are played and when they are recorded from one medium to another.

In the early 1980s, the recording industry began producing music on plastic compact discs (or CDs), which contained digitally encoded music read by lasers. The discs can be played over and over again without any loss in quality or sound. CDs quickly replaced vinyl records as the dominant format. By 1990, CDs were generating more revenue than vinyl records and cassette recordings combined. During 2000, 93 percent of all sales in the recording industry came from CDs. Other formats, such as the digital audio tape (DAT), have appeared on the market but have not been as popular.

Digitization also has filtered into the music video market as well as radio broadcasting. Digital video discs (DVDs) were introduced in 1997 and sales increased seven-fold from 1998 to 2000, to $80 million. DVDs are more reliable and durable than VHS tapes, and can hold a lot more data and have much better quality. In addition, DVDs can be programmed in multiple languages. Users simply select the language they want.

The digitization movement also is spreading to radio. Digital radio has higher quality sound than analog broadcasts. Digital signals can be transmitted via the Internet or satellite. About 4 million people subscribe to XM or Sirius radio, the two satellite providers. In 2007, the two companies announced they were interested in merging, partly because neither company has been earning a profit. The FCC is expected to support the merger.

OWNERSHIP RULES

During the 1980s and 1990s, the FCC began relaxing ownership rules. These changes stimulated mergers and acquisitions and greater concentration of ownership in the industry.

More specifically, in 1983 the 7-7-7 rule (one company could own a maximum of seven AM, seven FM and seven TV stations in different markets) was upped to 12-12-12. Then, in 1992, the limits for radio stations were upped to 18 AM and 18 FM. The FCC also allowed ownership of two AM and two FM stations in the same market as long as that market had at least 15 competing stations and the new local operation did not account for more than one-fourth of the total listening audience. In 1994, the radio ownership limits were increased to 20 and 20 (television remained at 12).

Ownership limits were again eased in 1996 with the passage of the Telecommunications Act of 1996. In large markets with 45 or more stations, one company could now own up to eight stations but no more than five AM or five FM stations in one market. In markets with 30-44 stations, the limits were set at seven stations (up to four AM or FM); in markets with 15-29 stations, six stations (up to four AM or FM); and with fewer than 15 stations, five stations (up to three AM or FM).[12]

In 1999, the FCC once again relaxed ownership rules, allowing a company to own up to eight broadcast stations (two of which may be television) in larger markets. The FCC reasoned that duopolies (two TV stations in one town) and multiple-station ownership decrease production costs and, therefore, enable the stations to provide more resources to improve news and public affairs programming.

The upshot of all these changes has been a tremendous increase in the number of stations owned by chains or groups. Before passage of the Telecom Act, about 1,000 stations a year changed hands and the total value of the transactions ranged from $1 billion to $5 billion. After passage, about 2,000 stations were sold a year and the value of the transactions ranged from $9 billion to $25 billion.[13] Large companies are buying up more radio stations because it is more efficient to operate multiple radio stations in one market or

---

[12]Mark Fratrik, *State of the Radio Industry: Radio Transactions 2000* (Chantilly, VA: BIA Financial Network, 2001), pp. 6-7.

[13]Ibid, p. 8.

in multiple markets. The stations can share advertising and administrative staffs.

CONCENTRATION OF OWNERSHIP

The number of radio stations increased by 18 percent from 1990 to 2000, going from 10,819 to 12,717. However, between 1996 and 2000, more than 2,000 radio stations were purchased by chains, which reduced the number of owners from about 5,200 to 4,000. About 500 of the 4,000 owners are chain organizations, meaning they own more than one radio station. On January 1, 2007, there were a total of 13,836 stations.[14]

As noted earlier, the mergers and acquisitions were sparked by the Telecommunications Act of 1996, which removed most restrictions on ownership. The most dramatic merger took place in 2000. Clear Channel Communications purchased AMFM, Inc., for $24 billion. Clear Channel and four other companies earn about three-fourths of all money spent on radio advertising in the United States.

Scholars and media critics are also concerned about an FCC decision in 2003 that allows companies to own more radio and television stations in local markets. However, concerns about concentration of ownership in the radio industry are less acute than they are for the newspaper industry. There are three reasons for this.

The first is the tremendous growth in the number of Internet digital radio stations. More than 9,000 radio stations around the world are currently broadcasting on the Internet, many of which have no over-the-air operations and, thus, are not subject to FCC regulations. Analysts believe that digital Internet radio represents a major threat to over-the-air broadcast radio.

The second reason for less concern about concentration of ownership in the radio industry is the FCC's decision to approve more low-power FM radio station licenses. The FCC announced in December 2000 that it would approve about 250 additional noncommercial educational low-power (2-3 miles) radio station licenses.

Finally, there also is less concern about concentration of ownership in the radio industry because newspapers have historically played a more important role as a disseminator of public affairs information. The content of a half-hour news program on radio does not even fill the front page of a newspaper. Also,

---

[14]These data come from the Federal Communications Commission.

there are fewer daily newspapers owners (less than 450) than radio station owners (about 4,000).[15]

Historically, concern about concentration of ownership also has been lower when a Republican occupies the White House. That's because Republicans tend to prefer less government control of business and the market.

ROLE AND FUNCTION OF RADIO AND RECORDINGS

When scholars talk about the social control aspects of radio, the first thing that usually comes to mind is talk radio, which usually involves a host who interviews guests and takes listeners' calls.

Talk radio hosts always have a point of view, sometimes controversial. Rush Limbaugh and Dr. Laura Schlessinger, for example, promote conservative values. They differ only in that Limbaugh deals primarily with political issues, whereas Dr. Laura's program dispenses conservative personal advice on love, marriage, family and relationships.

Of course, not all of the political content on radio is controversial. Radio is often the first place people turn to in times of crisis, such as threatening weather conditions. Radio news, like newspaper and television news, often is viewed as "objective" and informative.[16] Indeed, National Public Radio, which provides programming to the nation's noncommercial and educational radio stations, and commercial radio networks like ABC and CBS, are highly respected for their news coverage (see discussion below).

But, as will be discussed in depth later (see Chapter 16), even so-called "objective" news is not really objective in any absolute sense. News reports tend to frame the world from the perspective of those who are in power, because journalists rely heavily on them for the news. Murrow's reports are a good example. He depended upon British authorities for information, and this explains in part why his reports reflected a pro-British point of view.

Music, Social Control and Social Change

But politics and news aren't the only content on radio. In fact, radio's most unique niche today is music. More than 80 percent of on-air radio content is

---

[15]David Demers, *Media Concentration in the United States:* Proprietary report prepared for the Centre D'Études sur les Médias (Quebec, Canada: University of Laval, 2001).

[16]See Chapter 16 for an in-depth discussion of the ethic of objectivity.

music.[17] Listening to music is the No. 1 pastime activity while driving or riding in a car. Millions of people wake up to radio music and news. And millions more listen to it throughout the day as they work.

Needless to say, most people enjoy listening to music because it entertains and relaxes them. But this does not mean music has no implications for social control, or that it is less important in this regard than news programs or talk shows. As noted earlier, entertainment is also a form of control. People who are entertained and relaxed have fewer reasons to stir up trouble (e.g., join anti-establishment or revolutionary movements). Moreover, the lyrical content of music generally reflects and reinforces the values and beliefs of a society.

Musicians write about the beauty of love, friendship, honor, respect, peace and duty, and the ugliness of war, discrimination, hate, and dishonor. Of these, the most prominent value in music is romantic love. Love sells. That's because a sizable portion of tape and compact disc buyers are young people, who often are searching for love or for a marriage partner. At any one point in time, about three-fourths of the songs on the best selling lists are about love and relationships. Every genre of music — jazz, blues, rock-n-roll, bluegrass, rap, hip-hop, classical, pop, punk, country, folk, swing — sings about the beauty as well as the trials and tribulations of love.

To be sure, not all music supports dominant values and institutions. Punk and rap musicians, for example, are criticized occasionally for producing lyrics that challenge or attack traditional values or institutions, such as the police. One example is the rapster Eminem, whose songs have denigrated women and homosexuals. Many musicians also compose lyrics that glorify or encourage sex out of wedlock, which angers some people who hold traditional religious values.

However, it is important to point out that these same songs almost always support a more fundamental value: love. And this is a value upon which almost everyone can agree.

Music genres reflect the integrating power of music. Many working-class people like country music; highly educated and upper class people often like classical music; young people are drawn to rock, punk, hip-hop, alternative, rap and grunge; and minorities are disproportionately drawn to blues, jazz, rap and hip-hop. These genres create a community and often help make people feel more connected to society. In fact, music plays such an important role in most people's lives, that it is difficult to conceive of a life without it.

---

[17]I generated this estimate from statistics on radio station formats. About 23 percent of AM radio stations and 7 percent of FM stations focus primarily on news and talk, whereas the others focus on music.

Music also can serve as an agent of change. One of the best examples of this occurred during the 1960s, when folk and rock musicians wrote songs criticizing U.S. involvement in the Vietnam War. Their songs reinforced the goals of the anti-war movement and protest groups. Although it would be inaccurate to say that protest music alone helped bring an end to the Vietnam War, it clearly helped bond people together in a common cause and, thus, indirectly facilitated social change (e.g., an end to the war). Today, some forms of folk, rock, and rap/hip hop continue to challenge traditional values or dominant institutions.

National Public Radio

During the 1950s and 1960s, many educators and citizens were extremely displeased with the content on commercial radio and television. They even called television the "boob tube," meaning it was stupid and foolish. Then as today, commercial broadcasting places a high priority on entertainment programming and a low priority on educational programming. That's the best way to attract audiences and earn advertising revenues.[18]

But critics believed that broadcasting should provide more than "low-brow" entertainment programming. A vital, healthy "public" also needs access to high culture, such as in-depth news and information, serious documentaries, classical music, opera and literature.

So Congress passed the 1967 Public Broadcasting Act, which created the Corporation for Public Broadcasting. Its mission was to provide citizens with access to high-quality news and cultural programming. CPB founded National Public Radio in 1970 to provide programming to the nation's fledgling noncommercial radio stations, many of which were located on college campuses.

NPR's first program — live coverage of the U.S. Senate deliberations on the Vietnam War — aired on April 19, 1971. Two weeks later NPR broadcast the first edition of "All Things Considered," an afternoon news and talk program. Its morning counterpart, "Morning Edition," was launched in 1979. These two programs provide some of the most listened to programming on public radio.

In the 1980s, NPR also provided educational programming, including original plays, adaptations from novels, and jazz, folk and classical concerts. However, funding has always been a problem. In the 1980s, the U.S. government drastically reduced its support, and under the weight of a $7

---

[18]Ralph Engelman, *Public Radio and Television in America: A Political History* (Thousand Oaks, CA: Sage, 1996).

million debt, the network abandoned almost all of its non-news programming. The network was financially restructured and today receives most of its funding from member stations, individuals, foundations and corporations. Only 4 percent comes from government sources.

The NPR network includes more than 500 noncommercial stations in the United States and Europe, which receive the programming via satellite. Some of the other popular programming on NPR includes Fresh Air, Car Talk and Talk of the Nation, which are interview programs; and Marian McPartland's Piano Jazz and The Thistle and Shamrock, which are music programs. The news staff of NPR is highly respected in the field of journalism. Some of the more prominent members include Noah Adams, Bob Edwards, Daniel Schorr, and Cokie Roberts.

One of the most popular public radio programs is *A Prairie Home Companion*, which is produced by Minnesota Public Radio and distributed by Public Radio International to more than 460 radio stations worldwide. Says program creator and host Garrison Keillor, "When the show started, it was something funny to do with my friends, and then it became an achievement that I hoped would be successful, and now it's a good way of life." The show revolves around the fictional town of Lake Wobegon, Minnesota, where the people are full of insecurities about life.

Despite the emphasis on educational programming and news, public radio (as well as public television) has come under attack in recent years for pandering too much to corporate sponsors. The networks, in an effort to lure corporate sponsors, now offer sponsors longer "spots" to promote their products and services. Some critics see this as advertising, and it's hard to disagree.

Although critics have not been able to produce direct evidence that corporate sponsorship has adversely influenced programming, public radio, like all mass media, provides content that generally supports mainstream values and institutions. Overall, though, the news and documentary content tends to be more sensitive to the concerns of minorities, disadvantaged groups and environmentalists than other mainstream media. On the political spectrum, NPR tends to be slightly more liberal than commercial networks, offering some balance to the conservative commercial talk shows.

Chapter 11

TELEVISION AS THE
GREAT ENTERTAINER

At age 13, Oprah Winfrey got into trouble and was sent to a juvenile detention center. Some people say it was the best thing that ever happened to her.[1]

The center was too crowded to accept her, so she was sent to live with her father, a strict disciplinarian. He forced Oprah to learn five new words before dinner each day and to read a book and write a report on it once a week.

Three years later Oprah won an oratorical contest that gave her a scholarship. Fifteen years later she received Golden Globe and Oscar supporting actress nominations for her performance as Sofia in Steven Spielberg's adaptation of Alice Walker's masterpiece, *The*

A Polish made television from the '50s.

Color Purple. Twenty years later she would host the most popular syndicated television show in the world — one that is focused mainly on entertaining women and helping them solve their problems. Thirty years later her media empire would be valued at more than $1 billion, making her the most successful female entertainer in U.S. history and the most influential.

Oprah credits her father with turning her life around. "My father, Vernon Winfrey, is one of the most honorable men I know," she said before he died in 2005. She was born in 1954, the daughter of Vernita Lee and Vernon, who were not married. At age 4, she began her public speaking career. She toured

---

[1]Sources for this biography of Oprah include Deborah Tannen, "The TV Host Oprah Winfrey," *Time* (January 19, 2000), available at <www.time.com/time/time100/artists>; "The Cult of Oprah," *The Irish Times* (August 5, 2000), p. 61; Richard Huff, "The Power of Oprah: From Beef to Books, Americans Experience a Formidable Force," (New York) *Daily News* (January 28, 1998).

churches in Nashville, reciting sermons of James Weodon Johnson while other children sang. Vernita and Vernon separated and Oprah lived on a pig farm in Mississippi with her maternal grandmother until age 6, when she went to Milwaukee to live with her mother. Oprah had little supervision and got into trouble. A cousin also sexually molested her. When she went to live with her father in Nashville, she was pregnant. The child died shortly after birth.

But her father, who was a barber and city council member, laid down some rules. Oprah responded. She became a good student. At age 17, she was crowned "Miss Fire Prevention" in Nashville. While visiting a radio station one day, she was invited to read copy. The station hired her to read news on the air. At 19, Oprah, who was now a sophomore at Tennessee State University, was crowned Miss Black Tennessee. In the same year she was hired as Nashville's first female and first black TV-news anchor. After graduation she took an anchor position in Baltimore, but she wasn't well suited for the job. Sometimes she would cry when reading sad news. The station moved her into their morning talk show program. She found her niche. In 1984 she became host of A.M. Chicago, a morning talk show. The name eventually was changed to *The Oprah Winfrey Show*, and in 1986 the program was syndicated. Soon thereafter her program surpassed Phil Donahue as the nation's top rated talk show.

Oprah, who was 32, went on to star in many prime-time TV specials, home videos and movies. She also set up her own television, film, video and print production companies (all of which have "Harpo" — Oprah spelled backwards — in the name). In 1996, Oprah set up a book club that catapulted virtually every selection to the top of the best-selling list. She has won scores of awards and contributes 10 percent of her fortune to charitable causes.

In 2000, Oprah launched a magazine, titled *O: The Oprah Magazine*. In the same year, she co-founded Oxygen, a U.S. cable television network targeted to women. In September 2002, she debuted in *Oprah After The Show* on Oxygen. But the foundation of her empire has been the *The Oprah Winfrey Show*, which is seen by more than 30 million viewers in 160 countries. More than 1 million people also visit her Web site, Oprah.com, every day. "She's certainly the most influential person on television," said Dick Kurlander, vice president of Petry Television, a company that consults to TV stations. "She's extremely credible."

Many people have analyzed Oprah's success. *Time* magazine, which selected her as one of the 100 most influential people of the 20th century, perhaps put it best: "Women, especially, listen to Winfrey because they feel as if she's a friend. Although Phil Donahue pioneered the format she uses (mike-holding host moves among an audience whose members question guests), his show was mostly ... 'report-talk' .... The overt focus is on information. Winfrey transformed the format into ... 'rapport-talk,' the back-and-forth conversation that is the basis of female friendship, with its emphasis on self-revealing intimacies. She turned the focus from experts to ordinary people talking about personal issues."

CHAPTER OVERVIEW

No program on television better illustrates the social control function of that medium than "Oprah." The show promotes a number of dominant values in American society, such as the importance of living responsibly, being kind and giving to others, education and multiculturalism as a means to solve social problems, and protecting and nurturing children. The show combines entertainment with information and, thus, captures the major and minor functions of television as a mass medium: to entertain and inform, respectively.

Broadcast television may also facilitate social change, but its role here is generally more circumscribed than it is for books, newspapers, and magazines. The history of broadcast television shows that it rarely criticizes powerful elites and dominant institutions and values, and when it has (such as the Smothers Brothers Comedy hour in the 1960s) television is often criticized for being too liberal. In defense of their practices, broadcast TV and network executives point out that their programming is subject to regulation from the Federal Communications Commission. As such, many sociologists believe television is the most powerful medium of social control, especially because people spend more time with television than with any other medium.[2]

However, the potential of television as an agent of social change is increasing as more and more television channels become available through cable, satellite and eventually the Internet. The FCC does not have the power to regulate the content of this programming.

THE ORIGINS OF TELEVISION

David Sarnoff got his start in radio (see previous chapter).[3] But it was television that took him to the top of the broadcasting profession.

---

[2]The typical child and adult in the United States spends about 25-30 hours a week watching television.

[3]This historical review draws from a number of sources, including Giraud Chester, Garnet R. Garrison, and Edgar E. Willis, *Television and Radio*, 3rd ed. (New York: Appleton-Century-Crofts, 1963); Michael Emery and Edwin Emery, *The Press and America: An Interpretive History of the Mass Media*, 6th ed. (Englewood Cliffs, NJ: Prentice Hall, 1988); Sydney W. Head, Thomas Spann and Michael A. McGregor, *Broadcasting in America: A Survey of Electronic Media* (Boston: Houghton Mifflin Company, 2001).

During the 1930s, Sarnoff was president of RCA, which was racing to develop the first viable commercial television system in the United States. One of the best decisions he made was hiring Vladimir K. Zworykin, a Russian immigrant who had invented the iconoscope, the first electronic camera suitable for a television studio. Zworykin and his team were entrusted with developing a system acceptable for public viewing.

In 1939, they publicly unveiled the system. Sarnoff wanted a lot of publicity, so he selected the New York World's Fair for the debut. The demonstration was a big success. Two years later the Federal Communications Commission adopted what basically amounted to RCA's standard for black-and-white television. Sarnoff also played a key role in the development of color television. He rose to the position of chairman of the board of directors of RCA. He retired in 1969 and died in 1971.

William Paley

But it was William S. Paley, owner and chairman of CBS radio and television, who became known as the "godfather of American broadcasting."

Paley purchased CBS radio in 1929 and built the failing company into a profitable nationwide network of hundreds of radio and television station affiliates. He helped launch the careers of many Hollywood stars, including Frank Sinatra, Bing Crosby, and Kate Smith.

In the 1940s, he expanded into television, and by 1950 CBS emerged as the leader in ratings and programming — a position it held for 25 years. CBS television introduced such stars as Lucille Ball and Ed Sullivan and recruited Jack Benny and Jackie Gleason from other networks.

Paley also supported some controversial programs, such as "All in the Family" and "M*A*S*H," and news programming, including Edward R. Murrow's "See It Now" and "60 Minutes." But he was criticized severely for pulling Edward R. Murrow's "See It Now" program off the air in 1958 because of concerns of alienating advertisers (see discussion later in this chapter). Paley died in 1990.

Experimental Television

The Columbia Broadcasting System (CBS) began broadcasting in 1939 and the DuMont network went on the air in 1940. However, World War II halted production of consumer electronics and slowed the diffusion of television. During the war, six experimental stations were on the air — one each in Chicago, Philadelphia, Los Angeles, and Schenectady (New York) and two in New York City. The stations only broadcast a couple of hours a week and the content consisted mainly of civil defense programs. Only about 10,000 television receivers were in use at the time.

Post-War TV

Although 158 station applications had been filed with the FCC at the end of the war, television did not expand quickly. There were three major concerns: (1) Would consumers purchase the expensive television receivers (more than $1,200 in today's currency)? (2) Would advertisers pay for air time, which was expensive? (3) Should the television industry wait until color television was perfected?

However, within three years it became clear that consumers would buy and watch black-and-white television sets and that advertisers would pay for air time. At the beginning of 1948, 16 stations were on the air. Nine months later more than 400,000 television sets were in use, and the FCC approved 108 more station applications. In fact, the demand for station licenses was so great that the FCC placed a freeze on new applications because it was running out of channels. This freeze was lifted four years, in 1952, after the FCC added 70 channels to the 12 it had approved in the early 1940s.

At the beginning of 1950, 96 stations were on the air and two million television sets were in use. By the end of the year, nearly four millions sets would be in use, in about 9 percent of all U.S. households. Network services also were created for some stations on the East coast. Originally there were four networks, ABC, CBS, NBC and DuMont. DuMont failed in 1956. By 1951, coast-to-coast broadcasting had been made possible with the development of coaxial cables and microwave relay systems. In the same year, 94 stations carried a speech by President Harry Truman to the San Francisco peace conference.

TV Expands

By 1952, more than 100 television stations were on the air. About a third of the 45 million homes in America had a television set. By 1960 — about a dozen years after commercial television became viable — more than 500 stations were on the air and nearly 9 of 10 homes (87.1%) had a television set. No mass medium before or after television has been diffused and adopted more quickly.

In 1953, the Federal Communications Commission approved a color television system advanced by RCA that also worked on black-and-white sets. In 1958, NBC became the first network to offer programs in color. But full network color television would not be adopted until 1966, and by 1972 only half of U.S. households had a color television set. They were more expensive than black-and-white sets and color television was not a priority for many consumers.

EARLY PROGRAMMING

The technology of black-and-white television was refined in the 1940s. But it would take more than technology to get people to watch it. The networks were searching for programming that would attract viewers. They found it in a cross-dresser.

Milton Berle

His name was Milton Berle. They called him "Mr. Television" and "Uncle Miltie."[4] He was the first TV superstar. On June 8, 1948, he first appeared as host of "The Texaco Star Theater," a comedy-variety program that aired on NBC on Tuesday nights at 8 p.m.

Berle was already a star of stage, film and radio. But radio was not his best medium. His comedy was partly physical. He had a toothy grin and wore wacky costumes. He was the first man to dress as a woman on television. People loved it.

The ratings for his television program were as high as 80 percent, which meant that four out of five households watching television were watching his show. Needless to say, NBC loved him, too. They gave him a contract in 1951 that paid him $200,000 a year for life (later reduced to $120,000 in exchange for allowing him to appear on other television networks).

Ironically, though, Berle's success on television didn't last long. "The Texaco Star Theater" was dropped in 1953. Berle hosted several other television programs; his last was in the 1960s. After that he appeared as a guest performer in films and on many television programs, and also appeared in night clubs. He died in 2002 at the age of 93.

Other Entertainment Programs

In the early years, television was broadcast live. This included entertainment programming as well as news programs. Of course, things didn't always go by the script. But the guffaws were often more funny than the

---

[4]J. Y. Smith, "Milton Berle, 'Mr. Television,' Dies at 93," *The Washington Post* (March 28, 2002), p. A1.

original script, and viewers loved it. *The Red Skelton Show* became famous for this.

As mentioned briefly in the Chapter 10, much of the early TV entertainment content was transplanted from radio. This included the talent shows of Arthur Godfrey and Ted Mack; the comedy of Bob Hope, Jack Benny, George Burns and Gracie Allen, and Edgar Bergen; and light-hearted dramatic/comedic shows such as *The Adventures of Ozzie and Harriet, Amos 'n' Andy* and *The Life of Riley*. Children's programming included *Howdy Doody* and *Kukla, Fran and Ollie*.

But the most spectacular success of the early 1950s was the *I Love Lucy* show, which attracted about 7 of 10 viewers when Lucille Ball, the show's star and pregnant in real life, gave birth to a son. *I Love Lucy* contained many stereotypes and portrayed Lucille as a well-intentioned but bumbling housewife. However, the show, which ran from 1951 to 1956, also portrayed her as a strong-willed woman who could not be easily manipulated by her husband.

In 1955, the most highly rated program on television was a quiz show (*The $64,000 Question*). But this and 20 other programs were canceled in the late 1950s when it was revealed that many of them were rigged. In 1994, Robert Redford produced and directed *Quiz Show*, a hit movie that dramatized the scandal on the quiz show *Twenty-One*.

Westerns (*Gunsmoke, Bonanza* and *Death Valley Days*) and crime dramas (*Perry Mason* and *Dragnet*) became extremely popular in the mid- to late 1950s, when the production facilities were moved from New York and other cities to Hollywood. More than 30 Westerns were being aired in 1959. *Gunsmoke* was the most popular, lasting an amazing 20 years.

News Programs

In 1952, NBC launched from New York the *Today* show, which began at 7 a.m. Eastern time and was first hosted by Dave Garroway. Two years later the network debuted the *Tonight* show, whose first host was comedian Steve Allen. Jack Parr replaced Allen and Johnny Carson eventually replaced Parr.

Edward R. Murrow first appeared on television in 1951, hosting *See It Now*, a news-oriented program based on his popular radio show *Hear It Now*. The TV program was one of the first regular network shows to be broadcast nationally. In 1953, Murrow also hosted a popular interview show called *Person to Person*, in which he interviewed movie stars and famous people. That program lasted until 1959. But it was the *See It Now* program that contributed to his reputation as the most trusted journalist in America.

Murrow Marginalizes a Radical

In February 1950, a quiet and undistinguished senator from Wisconsin charged that 205 Communists had infiltrated the U.S. State Department.[5]

Although Joseph R. McCarthy could not identify a single "card-carrying Communist" in the U.S. government, he was able to generate a great deal of publicity and public support for his anti-Communist campaign. Many innocent people were forced to resign from their jobs, including Hollywood screen writers and directors.

Sen. Joseph P. McCarthy

At the time, many political elites knew McCarthy was a liar and self-appointed witch-hunter. However, few, including President Dwight D. Eisenhower, were willing to criticize him. They feared reprisals and a public backlash.

But broadcaster Edward R. Murrow wasn't one them.

On March 9, 1954, he publicly criticized McCarthy on his television news program *See It Now*. That show was based on four months of research. Fred Friendly, Murrow's colleague and co-producer of *See It Now*, put together a mountain of evidence against the Republican senator.

"We will not walk in fear, one of another," Murrow told his 12 million viewers. "We will not be driven by fear into an age of unreason if we dig deep in our history and doctrine and remember that we are not descended from fearful men, not from men who feared to write, to speak, to associate and to defend causes which were for the moment unpopular."

Murrow concluded: "The actions of the junior Senator from Wisconsin have caused alarm and dismay amongst our allies abroad and given considerable comfort to our enemies, and whose fault is that? Not really his. He didn't create this situation of fear; he merely exploited it, and rather successfully. Cassius was right: 'The fault, dear Brutus, is not in our stars but in ourselves. ... Good night, and good luck."

---

[5]Sources for this story about Murrow include Joseph Wershba, "Edward R. Murrow and the Time of His Time," *Eve's Magazine* (www.evesmag.com/murrow.htm; ©2000); and "Senator Joseph R. McCarthy," *See It Now*, CBS News (March 9, 1954). Crosby's quote taken from Erik Barnouw, *The Image Empire* (New York: Oxford University Press, 1970), p. 116.

McCarthy's influence diminished substantially after that program and after a nationally televised, 36-day hearing on McCarthy's charges of subversion. In late 1954, the Senate finally condemned him by a vote of 67 to 22 for conduct "contrary to Senate traditions." McCarthy died in 1957, a discredited man.

The *See It Now* program, which first aired in 1951, was popular with everyone except CBS executives, who were concerned about alienating corporate sponsors. CBS Board Chairman William S. Paley pulled the plug on the program in 1958. Many supporters of the program were outraged.

New York Herald Tribune television critic John Crosby wrote that "See It Now ... is by every criterion television's most brilliant, most decorated, most imaginative, most courageous and most important program. The fact that CBS cannot afford it but can afford *Beat the Clock* is shocking."

Murrow continued broadcasting his nightly radio news show and appeared on television regularly on *Person to Person* and on CBS Reports. In 1960, he left CBS to take charge of the U.S. Information Agency. But illness forced him to retire in 1963. Murrow, who was a heavy smoker, died of cancer in 1965 two days before his 57th birthday.

TV News and Presidential Election Coverage

In 1956, NBC assigned two broadcast journalists to cover the Democratic and Republican presidential political conventions. Chet Huntley and David Brinkley would go on to become two of the most respected journalists in the country, co-anchoring the NBC evening news for 14 years. NBC became the first network to offer a 30-minute evening news broadcast. Huntley retired in 1970. He was replaced with John Chancellor. Brinkley left to do a commentary program and appeared on many television news programs until 2003, when he died.

In 1960, television for the first time broadcast the presidential debates. Media and political experts then as today widely agree that John F. Kennedy outshone Richard Nixon during the debates, largely because of his cool demeanor and good looks. Since then, political campaign managers have made "television image" a major part of their marketing campaigns.

Although Huntley and Brinkley were popular newscasters in the 1960s, the biggest star was Walter Cronkite, who was promoted from reporter to the evening anchor position at CBS in 1962. Cronkite eventually would become the "most trusted journalist" in America, according to polls. He resigned from the anchor position in 1981 but continued to give commentaries and host documentary specials. Dan Rather, who earned distinction for his coverage of the Vietnam War, replaced Cronkite, and served as anchor until 2005, when he resigned after he and CBS were criticized for airing a series of stories allegedly based upon fabricated documents that raised questions about President George Bush's performance in the National Guard during the Vietnam War.

During the 1950s and 1960s, ABC's evening news program struggled to compete with CBS and NBC. The network went through a number of anchors, including Peter Jennings (1965 to 1968), who would in the 1970s co-anchor the program from London and become sole anchor from New York in 1983. In recent years, Jennings has been rated in polls the most popular evening news anchor.

The most popular woman newscaster of the 1970s was Barbara Walters. She co-starred on NBC's *Today* show and later co-anchored the evening news with Harry Reasoner. Reasoner became upset when he learned that Walters was being paid $5 million to co-anchor the show for five years, more than he was being paid. Walters went on to host many other television programs, interviewing hundreds of famous personalities and world leaders.

TELEVISION GROWS UP

In the late 1950s and early 1960s, one of the most popular television entertainment programs was *Leave It Beaver*, a family situation comedy seen through the eyes of a small boy named "Beaver Cleaver." Beaver lived in an idyllic household, where his mother wore dresses when she cleaned, his father never raised his voice in anger, and his older brother almost always treated him with respect. When the show ended in 1963, it seemed that America itself had also lost much of its innocence.

President John F. Kennedy was assassinated in 1963, and for the next 15 years Americans would be divided by a number of controversies, including the Vietnam War, racial and gender discrimination, and environmental degradation.

Television was not untouched by these events. For the first time, Americans were first-row spectators to riots in major U.S. cities and to a war in a foreign land. The images of injured and dead U.S. servicemen were particularly disturbing to the American public. Many historians and scholars believe such images helped sway public opinion against the war.

But it would be incorrect to say that television deliberately set out to challenge U.S. government policy or to sway public opinion against the war. Television then, as now, was a business, run by executives who sought to make a profit. TV executives were not eager to broadcast news or entertainment programming that criticized powerful people or alienated lots of viewers or advertisers. In fact, the networks were quick to censor programs that criticized the so-called "establishment," which included president, the government, and the military and industrial complexes.

Smothers Brothers

Perhaps the best example was the *Smothers Brothers Comedy Hour*, which starred Dick and Tom Smothers and aired on CBS from 1967 to 1969. In folks songs and comedy sketches, the brothers and their guests poked fun at the military, the police, middle-class America, President Lyndon Baines Johnson and the government. Almost everyone thought it was funny except CBS censors. For example, they cut

Smothers Brothers in 1969

- one scene from a Mother's Day special which ended with the words, "Please talk peace" (reference to Vietnam War);

- an interview with Dr. Benjamin Spock, who was an advocate for draft evaders;

- images from the 1968 police-instigated riot outside the Democratic Party convention in Chicago;

- a folk song by Pete Seeger that told the story of a World War II soldier killed because of a stupid order from his commanding officer (he was able to perform the song on a later episode);

- many scenes that made mild reference to sex or drugs.

Although the Smothers Brothers show had high ratings, it was canceled in 1969. The network justified its decision by making reference to a network policy that "prohibits appeals for active support of any cause" (even if it was "peace"). But the real reason was that CBS executives were worried about alienating advertisers and losing their broadcast licenses.[6]

---

[6]But the censors at CBS helped canonize the Smothers Brothers as symbols of the struggle for free speech on television. To this day, Dick Smothers lectures on the topic to groups across the country. On December 4, 2002, Bravo aired *Smothered*, a documentary special about the Smothers Brothers' censorship struggles.

Other '60s Shows

The *Smothers Brothers Comedy Hour* was, however, an anomaly. Most entertainment television during the 1960s and 1970s ignored the Vietnam War and civil rights, women's and environmental movements altogether. Those topics were too controversial and could jeopardize a television station's license or alienate advertisers.

Instead, entertainment programming was dominated by comedy and science fiction shows. The latter included *The Andy Griffith Show, The Beverly Hillbillies, The Addams Family, My Favorite Martian, Bewitched* and *I Dream of Jeannie*. The sci-fi list included *Star Trek, Outer Limits,* and *Twilight Zone.*

The first prime time cartoon show, *Rocky and His Friends*, appeared in 1959. The second was the *Flintstones*, which began broadcasting in 1960 and appealed to both children and adults. This spurred a number of other half-hour cartoon programs, including *Alvin and the Chipmunks, The Jetsons* and *Mr. Magoo.*

Westerns, crime dramas and variety shows also were popular on prime-time television. But CBS's *60 Minutes*, which debuted in 1968 and featured investigative news reports, also was one of the most popular. A decade later *60 Minutes* would become the first news program to be No. 1 in the ratings.

In 1969, the landing of Apollo 11 on the moon was watched by 94 percent of households, making it the most viewed event in the history of television.

Public Television

In 1961, FCC chairman Newton Minow called television a "vast wasteland." That criticism was nothing new. Frieda Hennock, a former member of the FCC, had complained about the lack of educational programming in the late 1940s and early 1950s. Although she was able to get the FCC to set aside a number of frequencies for educational use, many of the educational stations lacked the resources to produce high-quality programming.

This problem was partially solved in 1967, when Congress created the Corporation for Public Broadcasting, which in turn created the Public Broadcasting System (PBS) — a noncommercial, public television network serving many of the educational nonprofit stations already in operation in the United States. PBS doesn't produce original programming. Instead, it serves as a distributor of programming that is produced abroad (English programming) or at major public television stations in the United States. WGBH in Boston, for example, produces about a third of the programming on PBS stations.

Educational shows for children and news and documentary programming have been among the most popular. In the children's genre, *Sesame Street*, which first appeared in 1969 and is produced by the Children's Television Workshop at WNET in New York, leads the pack. *The MacNeil/Lehrer NewsHour* (now *The NewsHour with Jim Lehrer*) was first broadcast in 1975 and became immensely popular for its in-depth (one-hour) coverage of national and international affairs. One of the most successful documentary programs was *The Civil War*, a five-part series that appeared in 1990. *Nature*, a documentary program that explores the natural world, also has had an extremely loyal following.

Although public television offered more sophisticated programming to American audiences, it also has faced its share of criticism. Conservatives, in particular, have tried on occasion to cut federal funding to PBS because they believe it has a liberal bias. Those criticisms are not without merit, as education in general and higher education in particular tend to tolerate a greater diversity of ideas and different points of view (conservatives tend to emphasize tradition and often oppose change).

But in recent years, PBS also has been accused of being soft on corporations, which have been contributing an increasingly greater amount of money to public television programming. PBS executives concede they have had to rely more heavily on corporate funding to generate high-quality programming, but deny such dependence biases PBS programming.

Minorities and Women on Television

As was the case with radio, the opportunities for women and minorities on television were limited when television first came on the air. In the 1950s, advertisers would not sponsor programs hosted by minorities.

However, Hugh Hefner's *Playboy's Penthouse*, a syndicated television program that began broadcasting in 1960, often featured black musicians, including Sammy Davis Jr., Nat King Cole and Ray Charles. In 1968, singer Diahann Carroll became the first black female to star in a comedy series. *Julia* was a young, independent, widowed nurse (her "husband" had been killed in Vietnam) who was raising a little boy. The series lasted until 1971.

Opportunities for women were greater than for minorities in the 1950s and 1960s. Lucille Ball served as a model. *The Lucy Show* (without ex-husband Desi Arnez) ran from 1962 to 1968. *The Ann Sothern Show*, a comedy, ran from 1958 to 1961. Carol Burnett also hosted a variety show on CBS from 1967-1978.

Black Entertainment Television (BET), the first cable network targeted to African American audiences, was launched in 1980. The network is now owned by Viacom, which continues to produce television and radio programming targeted to black audiences.

The first Spanish-speaking television station, KMEX (Univision) was founded on September 29, 1962. KMEX won the first Edward R. Murrow Award and is the first TV station to create a Spanish-language morning talk show ("Los Angeles al Dia"). The Radio and TV News Directors Association also nominated the station as "America's Best Newscast."

On June 27, 2006, Broadcasting Media Partners Inc., an investor group, acquired Univision. Today, Univision Communications Inc. of Los Angeles is the No. 1 Spanish-language media company in the United States. It's holdings include: Univision Network, which reaches 97 percent of U.S. Hispanic households, TeleFutura Network, a 24-hour general-interest Spanish-language broadcast television network reaching 72 percent of U.S. Hispanic households; Univision Television Group, which operates 22 television stations; TeleFutura Television Group, which operates 28 television stations; Galavision, the country's leading Spanish-language cable network; and Univision Music Group, which includes the Univision Music and other labels.

TELEVISION GETS MORE CONTROVERSIAL

Entertainment television shows began to deal with more controversial topics during the 1970s.

At the head of the pack was the satirical comedy *All in the Family*, whose lead character (Archie Bunker) was a blue-collar bigot. The show dealt with many sensitive issues, including abortion, racism and homosexuality. Although the program was clearly intended to be a parody, research showed that, ironically, many politically conservative viewers identified with Bunker's archaic value system.

Saturday Night Live also satirized many topics and people, including religious leaders. *Roots*, a miniseries based on Alex Haley's popular book about several generations of black Americans, fostered greater appreciation for the plight of blacks. So did *Good Times*, a gritty comedy about a black family living in a ghetto. Also popular but much less political were the comedies *Happy Days*, which followed the lives of a group of fifties-era teenagers, and *The Brady Bunch*, a sappy comedy about a family with six children.

Rise of Cable Television

In 1970, 677 commercial television stations were on the air. Most of them were affiliated with one of the three major television networks (ABC, CBS and NBC), which dominated television. On average, 90 percent of the people viewing prime-time television were watching one of the three big networks. But the networks' share of the viewing audience began to decline with the ascent of cable television.

Cable television had been around since 1950. Originally, Community Antenna Television (CATV) was designed for remote areas in Arkansas, Oregon and Pennsylvania that had difficulty receiving over-the-air television signals. But cable companies were now aggressively marketing in metropolitan areas, where cable was less costly to install per household and, thus, much more profitable. By 1970, about 4 million homes nationwide had cable, which would soon offer more channels than broadcast television.

Home Box Office, the premium cable movie channel, began broadcasting in 1972. Turner Broadcasting System (TBS) was launched in 1976. In 1979, C-Span (Cable-Satellite Public Affairs Network), which included live broadcasts of the House of Representatives, the sports channel ESPN, and the children's network Nickelodeon began broadcasting. USA Network debuted in 1980 and MTV in 1981. A&E Television, Lifetime Television, TNN, and The Discovery Channel were added between 1983 and 1985. In 1987, Rupert Murdoch's News Corporation launched Fox Broadcasting Company, the fourth major television network.

Cable television subscriptions grew rapidly during the 1970s and 1980s. From 1970 to 1980, the percentage of homes connected to cable nearly tripled, going from about 7 percent to 20 percent. The percentage doubled from 1980 to 1985, with 43 percent having access. By 1990, more than half of all television households were wired for cable.

Many people and companies profited from cable television. But the most spectacular success story of the time was Ted Turner, who founded Turner Broadcasting System and the Cable News Network. Turner is today one of the richest men in America and one of its greatest philanthropists, having donated billions to charitable causes.

The proliferation of cable television stations meant that people had more choices, and with that audiences for the three major networks began to decline. Where they once commanded 90 percent of the audience, the three major networks now capture about 40 percent, and their share continues to decline.

Situation Comedies Rule

Historically, situation comedies have been the most popular fare on television. This was also the case during the 1980s. The (Bill) *Cosby Show* led the pack. It was a wholesome comedy that featured an upscale African American family. But television as a whole would never return to the "innocent" 1950s. *Cheers*, for example, featured the escapades of an unmarried, sexist, womanizing bar owner called "Sam Malone" and his voyeuristic patrons. *Roseanne* portrayed a working-class family in which the mother and father often argued and shouted at the kids and dealt with real-world problems like drugs and sex.

But the most outrageous comedy of the time was *Married...with Children*, which featured a father who was a professional failure, a vain mother, the lustful son, and a promiscuous daughter. Although critics attacked *Married...with Children* as being anti-family, closer inspection shows that virtually every episode contained a moral lesson that reinforced traditional family values or other system values.

Medical and crime dramas also were popular in the 1980s. *St. Elsewhere* was a critically acclaimed "realistic" medical series that won eight Emmy awards. *Miami Vice* fused rock music into its sound track and started a pastel-color fashion trend in clothes for men.

NIMH Study

Through the years, critics always complained that television shows had too much violence. In defense, TV executives would often respond that the violence was make-believe and that there was no evidence to show that violent programming had adverse effects on children or adults.

For all practical purposes, this debate came to an end in 1982, when the National Institute of Mental Health published *Television and Behavior: Ten Years of Scientific Progress and Implications for the Eighties.*[7] This report reviewed more than 3,000 scientific studies of television violence and concluded that the evidence overwhelmingly supported the conclusion that televised violence increases aggressive behaviors in many children.

Ironically, though, the report has had relatively little impact on programming. In fact, mass communication researchers report that there is more violence on television today than 25 years ago.

However, the report did help the position of educators and parents who wanted television manufacturers to install the V-chip, a device that allows parents to block offensive programming on television sets. All televisions 13 inches and larger are now equipped with the technology, which blocks undesired programs using a rating system developed in 1996 by The National Association of Broadcasters, the National Cable Television Association and the Motion Picture Association of America. "The TV Parental Guidelines" system is as follow:

---

[7]D. Pearl, L. Bouthilet, and J. Lazar (eds.) *Television and Behavior: Ten Years of Scientific Progress and Implications for the Eighties*, Vols. I & II (Washington, DC: U.S. Government Printing Office, 1982).

- TV-Y. Appropriate for all children.
- TV-Y7. Appropriate for children age 7 and above.
- TV-G. Suitable for all ages, not specifically children.
- TV-PG. Unsuitable for younger children; parental guidance suggested.
- TV-14. Unsuitable for children under 14 years of age.
- TV-MA. Unsuitable for children under 17. This program contains one or more of the following: graphic violence (V), explicit sexual activity (S), or crude indecent language (L).

Although most television are now equipped with the V-chip, studies show that most parents do not use it. But the V-chip has blunted criticism of the networks.

Talk Shows

Talk shows have been around since the origins of television. For example, Steve Allen and Ernie Kovaks hosted "Tonight," which aired on NBC from 1954 to 1957. Phil Donahue launched the first audience-participation show in 1967, and his show is still being broadcast on MSNBC. But talk shows didn't draw a lot of attention until the 1980s, when Oprah Winfrey took her Chicago show national in 1984. Oprah's show quickly overtook Donahue's show in the ratings, and she has gone on to become the most successful woman in television history.

Other talk shows appeared on the scene, but most (*Geraldo, Sally Jesse Raphael, Maury Povich*) had to employ gimmicks or sensational tactics to attract audiences. These, in turn, have been upstaged by Jerry Springer, whose show, which was launched in 1991 and is still in syndication, became infamous for featuring guests who assault each other with fists and chairs.[8]

Springer's show and others frequently are criticized for promoting anti-social values. But a close viewing shows they almost always reinforce traditional norms and values.

---

[8]*The Jerry Springer Show* was seen in more than 190 U.S. markets and was a hit in 40-plus foreign countries. It was the first talk show to beat Oprah Winfrey in more than a decade.

ARE TV TALK SHOWS DESTROYING MORALITY?

The episode on the *Jerry Springer Show* was called "Secret Mistresses Confronted."[9]

The syndicated television show, which was tape recorded in May 2000, featured Ralf Panitz, his ex-wife Nancy Campbell-Panitz and his current wife Eleanor. All three had been living together since Ralf and Nancy divorced. But Nancy didn't know that Ralf secretly had married Eleanor. To get Nancy on the show, Ralf told her that he was going to publicly renounce Eleanor on air.

But that never happened. Instead, Ralf and Eleanor announced they had been married two months earlier. Eleanor then hurled insults at Nancy. "Are you going to leave us alone? I want you to leave us alone ... You're old. You're fat." Nancy left the stage and the audience booed her.

Three months later, Ralf went home after watching the program on television in a local bar. He and Nancy had an argument. He beat her to death, according to police. Ralf was convicted of second-degree murder and sentenced to life in prison. In July 2002, Nancy's family filed a lawsuit against Springer and his company, claiming they contributed to Nancy's death.

The incident brought back memories of a 1995 Jenny Jones Show program, in which a man murdered another man after learning on the show that he was the subject of his victim's homosexual fantasies. A jury ordered *The Jenny Jones Show* to pay $25 million in damages to the family of the murdered man.

Critics call Springer's show "trailer trash television" because, according to the *Los Angeles Times*, it "deifies dysfunction, exploits unsophisticated guests and gives a promotional forum to the sexually confused and promiscuous, porn stars, adulterers, criminals, Ku Klux Klan member and various other ne'er-do-wells."

The show titles seem to support these criticisms: "I Am Pregnant by a Transsexual," "I Want Your Man," "Paternity Test: I Slept With Two Brothers," and "Prostitutes vs. Pimps!" And producers don't mind when fights break out on the show, because they know that increases the show's ratings.

But it would be inaccurate to argue that Springer's show or other talk show programs like it are destroying morality. In fact, they actually reinforce dominant values. Even Springer recognizes this.

---

[9]Sources for this discussion of talk shows includes Greg Braxton, "Them's Fightin' Words," *Los Angeles Times* (April 5, 1998), p. 4 (Calendar); Jeff Daniel, "Springer Fights His Way to the Top of the Trash Heap," *Everyday Magazine* (February 1, 1998), p. D3; Michael Cameron, "Springer TV Show Murder Charge," *The Sunday Telegraph* (July 30, 2002), p. 3; Paul Gallagher, "Springer Sued Over 'Murderous' Show," *The Scotsman* (July 12, 2002), p. 5.

"Our audience always boos the bad guy and cheers the good guy," he told the *Los Angeles Times*. "Our show becomes a little morality play. ... if you are concerned about what lessons come out of our show, we make it clear that violence is no good. We make it clear that infidelity, promiscuity, drugs and prostitution are bad."

Of course, this doesn't appease critics. They prefer more talk shows like Oprah, which consciously avoid lurid topics. But all talk shows and "real-life" courtroom dramas such as *People's Court* and *Judge Judy* perform the function of reinforcing dominant values about right and wrong. If they didn't, nobody would advertise on them.

TELEVISION TECHNOLOGY ADVANCES

In 1969, Sony Corporation introduced the first low-cost videocassette recorder, a device for recording, storing and playing back television programs on a magnetic cassette tape. But Betamax was never very successful in the United States. Instead, consumers in the 1980s turned to VHS, a format developed by Matsushita Corporation.

Videocassette Recorders

In 1980, only about 1 percent of households in the United States had a videocassette recorder. But five years later a fifth of all homes had a VCR, and by 1990 two-thirds (69 percent) had one. The growth of VCRs spurred a new industry in the 1980s: home movie rentals.

Hollywood Video, which has 1,800 stores, was founded in 1984. Blockbuster Video, which is the largest video rental chain with more than 8,000 stores, was founded in 1985.

During the 1990s, some industry analysts predicted that video rental stores would go out of business when cable and satellite television systems began offering movie rentals on demand. However, this has not happened, partly because the "on demand" services offer a limited number of movies for viewing. Consumers also need to subscribe to premium services to get the movies on demand, and many are not interested in paying the extra costs.

During the late 1990s, VHS technology was replaced by DVD (Direct Video Disc) technology, which offers a much higher quality picture. DVD rentals overtook VCR rentals in 2003.

Satellite Television

The first commercial satellite was launched in 1965. It relayed TV, radio, telephone and data communication signals. But it wasn't until the 1980s that consumers began to receive the signals directly from the satellite companies.

The first satellite home systems required a very large "dish" to capture the signal. They were also very expensive, costing up to $15,000. The satellite industry almost collapsed, because consumers began pirating signals and cable television companies launched a major anti-satellite campaign. Half of the satellite companies went out of business.

But four factors helped save the industry in the 1990s. The first was new encryption technology, which eliminated most of the pirates. The second was a higher quality signal, which offered clearer reception than conventional cable wire systems. The third was reduced costs — homeowners could now get a system installed for less than $100. And the fourth was the introduction of the small-dish Direct Broadcast Satellite (DBS) system in 1994, which was much more convenient and could be installed almost anywhere.

Today more than 20 million homes, or about one in six homes in America, are hooked up to satellite television. The two biggest companies are DirecTV, which has 12 million subscribers, and the DISH Network, which has 7 million. The latter, which was controlled by Rupert Murdoch's News Corporation, tried to purchase the former in 2002, but the FCC blocked the deal, calling it monopolistic.[10]

LIVE WAR COVERAGE

In 1991, Iraqi dictator Saddam Hussein ordered a military invasion of Kuwait. Several weeks later, a U.S.-led coalition launched a counterattack. President George Bush's administration asked American television networks to leave Iraq. All complied except Ted Turner's Cable News Network.

While the other major networks presented a lot of "talking heads," CNN was broadcasting live reports 24-hours a day from Bagdad, where coalition planes were dropping bombs and Iraqi anti-aircraft guns were firing back. It was high drama, and CNN's ratings soared. Almost overnight, CNN had established itself as the television news leader, eclipsing the three big networks (ABC, CBS and NBC), which had big-name stars like Dan Rather, Peter Jennings, and Tom Brokaw.

---

[10]Stephen Labaton, "FCC Blocks EchoStar Deal with DirecTV," *The New York Times* (October 11, 2002), obtained from *NYT* Web site.

The Gulf War guaranteed a place for 24-hour-news programs in American culture. But this was just the tip of the specialization iceberg.

INCREASING SPECIALIZATION

During the 1990s, dozens of other specialized television networks emerged as subscriptions to cable and satellite television soared. This included in 1994-95 two new networks geared toward younger audiences — Warner Brothers Network (WB) and United Paramount Network (UPN). In 1998, Lewell "Bud" Paxson, a TV station group owner, started PAX TV, the seventh major commercial network. It focused on family programming.

Cable television was now offering channels devoted exclusively to a wide variety of specialized topics, including business news, sports (including golf and outdoor channels), nature, cooking, women's interest, home improvement, travel, romance, history, entertainment, science fiction, cartoons, shopping, religion, arts, re-runs of old TV programs, old movies, pay movie channels, and pay-per-view movies.

This specialized programming was made possible in large part because of the growth of satellite and cable television subscriptions. In 1990, more than half of all households in the United States subscribed to cable or satellite television. Ten years later, at the beginning of the 21st century, three-fourths would be subscribers.

As in previous decades, the most popular shows in the 1990s continued to be comedies. This included *Seinfeld, Cheers, Home Improvement, Friends, Veronica's Closet* and *Frasier.* Other popular shows included *60 Minutes, E.R., Touched by an Angel,* and *NFL Monday Night Football.*

On May 31, 2000, CBS aired a television program in which 16 people were sequestered on an isolated island for 39 days and had to work together to survive. One by one they voted each other off the island. The last person standing would win $1 million. *Survivor* was an instant hit and ushered in a new program genre — reality TV. The list included *Who Wants to Marry a Millionaire, The Mole, The Osbournes, The Anna Nicole Show,* and *Big Brother 3.*

There was no shortage of critics for these shows. However, the TV networks and the viewing public didn't care much what they thought. Reality shows were profitable. They cost an average of $400,000 per episode compared with $2 million for a dramatic series. Audiences liked them partly because the outcomes were not predictable.

In late 2002, CBS was planning to launch *The Beverly Hillbillies,* a reality-based show in which a real Appalachian family was moved to Beverly Hills, where the network would film their experiences. The show, which didn't expect to begin filming until 2003, was already generating criticism for perpetuating stereotypes and was canceled.[11] This incident illustrates how general values may play a role in regulating television content.

In the early 2000s, other popular shows included *CSI: Crime Scene Investigation*, *Everybody Loves Raymond*, *Sopranos* and *Law & Order*. But none of these shows, even the most-watched, could command as many viewers as shows did in the 1960s. There were just too many alternative choices on cable and satellite television.

The trend toward specialized programming is expected to continue in the 21st century. New channels geared to the interests of women, minorities, sports enthusiasts, and people interested in politics, crafts and business are expected.

TELEVISION ANGERS CONSERVATIVES

Entertainment television programming during the 1990s couldn't be called radical by any measure. It rarely challenged powerful corporate and political groups. In fact, it usually glorified corporate life and high-powered politicians. However, television did produce some programming that angered conservatives and religious leaders.

This included *Ellen* and *Will and Grace*, which featured homosexuals in lead roles. *NYPD Blue* contained nudity and foul language. *Friends* revolved around sexual themes and innuendoes. *Men Behaving Badly* and *South Park* contained a lot of crude behavior. *Politically Incorrect with Bill Maher* was, indeed, often politically incorrect. *Seinfeld* even had one show devoted to the topic of masturbation (i.e., who could hold off the longest before doing it). Public television also has angered some conservatives, because it draws much of its content from intellectuals and universities, which generally are more liberal than mainstream America.

However, none of the criticized programs provided any kind of sustained critique of the status quo. In fact, the shows generally supported dominant values, such as the importance of love and friendship.

ROLE AND FUNCTION OF TELEVISION

In the 1950s, sociologists Paul F. Lazarsfeld and Robert K. Merton argued that radio and newspapers could have an adverse impact on citizen involvement in public life. They argued that people who spent too much time with news media could actually become less politically active, substituting

---

[11]"CBS Hunts 'Hillbillies' for Reality-TV Transplant," *The* (Spokane) *Spokesman-Review* (November 3, 2002), p. A12.

consumption of media and knowledge of public affairs for actual political involvement. They called it the narcotizing dysfunction of the mass media.[12] "It is termed *dys*functional rather than functional on the assumption that it is not in the interest of modern complex society to have large masses of the population politically apathetic and inert," the sociologists wrote[13] (italics in original). Mass media make people apathetic and inert because, according to Lazarsfeld and Merton, it decreases the amount of time "available for organized action." They wrote:

> The individual reads accounts of issues and problems and may even discuss alternative lines of action. But this rather intellectualized, rather remote connection with organized social action is not activated. ... Mass communications may be included among the most respectable and efficient of social narcotics. They may be so fully effective as to keep the addict from recognizing his own malady.[14]

Television and Social Control

Although Lazarsfeld and Merton were writing before television became a powerful force in society, the narcotizing dysfunction has been associated with television more than any other medium. That's partly because people spend more time with television than with any other mass medium and because many scholars say it is the most powerful medium. The entertainment programming on television is often viewed as "low culture." In fact, during the 1950s and 1960s, many people referred to television as the "boob (slang for 'stupid') tube."

During prime-time evening hours, more than 75 million Americans are "glued to the tube." The typical child over age 4 watches more than 20 hours a week, or about four hours a day. The typical adult watches more than 30

---

[12]Lazarsfeld and Merton did not specifically discuss the narcotizing effects of mass media on children. However, I argue that the concept is no less applicable to children, who may whittle away their time in front of the television instead of being involved in other activities that contribute more effectively to their social and intellectual development.

[13]Paul F. Lazarsfeld and Robert K. Merton, "Mass Communication, Popular Taste, and Organized Social Action," pp. 554-578 in Wilbur Schramm and Donald F. Roberts (eds.), *The Process and Effects of Mass Communication*, rev. ed. (Urbana: University of Illinois Press, 1971, originally published in 1954), p. 565.

[14]Lazarsfeld and Merton, "Mass Communication, Popular Taste, and Organized Social Action," pp. 565-566.

hours a week, or about 4½ hours a day.[15] Television is the No. 1 leisure time activity among both children and adults. In fact, many children spend more time watching television than they do in the classroom.

Why do people watch so much television?

The No. 1 reason is to relax or be entertained. Research shows that television viewing can reduce stress and help some people escape loneliness and boredom. Thus, it would be grossly unfair to argue that watching television has only adverse effects. Watching television is not necessarily a bad thing. People need to relax to be healthy, physically and mentally. Commercial television and public television also provide public affairs and educational programming that many critics find appealing.

But "being entertained" also is a way of controlling people. If people are content watching television, then they are less likely to be socially and politically active, as Merton and Lazarsfeld point out. This becomes more problematic as viewing time increases. People who watch a lot of television are often called "couch potatoes," meaning they are lazy and passive. They are less likely to question injustice and wrongdoing, and, thus, they are easier to control.

Perhaps more important, entertainment television often avoids controversial issues, such as poverty, lack of universal health care, racial discrimination and corporate abuse of power. Television also rarely criticizes powerful institutions and value systems. Instead, shows like *West Wing*, which revolves around life in the White House, help legitimize powerful institutions, even through in reality they do not always act in the interests of ordinary people.

Television and Social Change

Although television programming generally reinforces the status quo, some of it provides images and ideas that are contrary to traditional — especially conservative — values and beliefs.

For example, the 1970s television miniseries, *Roots*, examined the problems that African Americans faced in white America. Research showed that white people who saw the program were more sympathetic to the plight of black Americans. TV families also do not fit the archetypical ideal of a wife, husband and children. The families on many TV programs have one parent or have more than one unmarried adult living in a household. In recent years, even

---

[15]Statistics on viewing are from Nielsen Media Research-NTI (2001), Veronis, Suhler and Television Bureau of Advertising, Inc.

homosexuality has gained greater acceptance in prime-time entertainment programming.

The psychological and social effects of programs that present alternative, nontraditional lifestyles are not clear. But at least one study suggests they contribute to the decline of traditional family values[16] and that, in turn, may lead to increasing tolerance for alternative lifestyles. In a changing world, many people see this as a good thing.

Much of the content on cable television also challenges traditional norms and values. This includes shows like "Sex in the City" and "Queer Eye for the Straight Guy." They contain frank discussions about sex and sexuality. This is possible partly because the Federal Communications Commission does not regulate cable TV. It only regulates broadcast television because only a limited number of stations can broadcast over the air. There is, theoretically, no limit to the number of cable, satellite or Internet stations.

The potential of television as a agent of social change should increase as more and more television channels become available through cable and the Internet (see next chapter). The FCC does not regulate these channels, so they have greater freedom to produce programming that challenges dominant values and institutions. And public television also provides a source of inspiration for some social change agents.

Frieda Hennock and Public Television

Big Bird owes a debt of gratitude to Frieda Hennock. So does Kermit the Frog and Mr. Rogers.[17]

That's because Hennock, the first woman appointed to the Federal Communications Commission in 1948, was a tireless advocate of educational television. In fact, many people today believe educational television might not even exist had it not been for Hennock.

Hennock was born in Kovel, Poland, in 1904. She was the youngest of eight children. In 1910, she immigrated with her family to New York City. Her father was a real estate broker and banker.

---

[16]Michael Morgan, Susan Leggett and James Shanahan, "Television and Family Values: Was Dan Quayle Right?" *Mass Communication & Society*, 2(1/2):47-63 (1999), p. 47.

[17]Sources: Maryann Yodelis Smith, "Frieda Barkin Hennock" in Barbara Sicherman and Carol Hurd Green (eds.), *Notable American Women: The Modern Period — A Biographical Dictionary* (Cambridge, MA: Belknap Press of Harvard University Press, 1980).

Hennock entered Brooklyn Law School after high school. She graduated in 1924 but had to wait a year before being admitted to the bar because she was only 21.

Hennock became one of New York's most successful female lawyers. She began her practice in 1926 with $56. A year later she formed a partnership with a man partly because of discrimination against women lawyers. The two dissolved the firm about seven years later because of disagreements.

Hennock then took a job as assistant counsel to the New York Mortgage Commission from 1935-1939. She also lectured on law and economics at the Brooklyn Law School. In 1941, Hennock became the first woman and the first Democrat to associate with Choate, Mitchell and Ely, one of New York City's most prestigious law firms.

Hennock was appointed to the FCC in 1948, partly because of her support for the Democratic Party. Hennock relinquished a substantial income from her law practice to take the FCC position. "It seems fundamental that in this field [communications] — so peculiarly affecting women — the viewpoint of this sex should be represented," she said, in accepting the position.

She also told a *Milwaukee Journal* reporter: "Women haven't had nearly the recognition they deserve. If they have brains and ability they should not be penalized merely because they wear a skirt."

Hennock worked long hours and devoted much of her effort to reserving channels for educational use. She wanted 500 channels reserved for noncommercial purposes. The commission eventually settled on 242 channels.

Hennock also encouraged educators to apply for the channels even if they didn't have the funds to operate them. She spent many weekends traveling to cities and promoting educational television in speeches and in magazine articles. Hennock also sought stricter controls on children's programming, because she was concerned about the effects of violence, crime and horror.

In 1951, Hennock was nominated for a federal judgship, but the American and New York City bar associations refused to endorse her because she was a woman. She also came under intense scrutiny for a friendship she had with a married federal judge. Although no evidence of an affair was ever presented, she withdrew her name.

Hennock left the FCC in 1955 and married a real estate broker. She went back into corporate law and then started her own firm. She died in 1960 of a brain tumor.

Chapter 12

THE INTERNET AND MASS COMMUNICATION FOR EVERYONE

O n April 2, 2003 — the same day U.S. soldiers rescued Private First Class Jessica Lynch and three days before U.S. tanks rolled into Baghdad — Salam Pax, a resident of Baghdad, entered the following comments in his Web site:

> Two hours ago we could hear the rumbling of the planes over us and it took them ages to pass. Afraid is not the right word. Nervous, edgy, sometimes you just want to shout out at someone, angry. I wish the Iraqi and the American governments would stop saying they are doing this for the people. I also want to hold a "not in my name" sign. ...
>
> Nonstop bombing. At the moment the US/UK are not winning any battle to "win the heart and mind" of this individual. No matter which way this will go, my life will end up more difficult. You see the news anchors on BBC, Jazeera and Arabiya so often you start dreaming of them, noticing when they get a hair cut and, in one case on Jazeera, a bad dye job.

Pax, a 29-year-old Iraqi architect who kept an online journal of the events happening during the 2003 Iraqi War, has been called the most celebrated reporter of the war, even though he didn't work for a news organization. His Weblog, which he called *Where is Raed?*,[1] offered first-hand, clandestine observations of the bombing of Baghdad. It attracted more than 100,000 visitors a day. His site was so popular that his Internet provider upgraded his account without charge so he could continue posting messages and photographs.

Supporters of Weblogs (or Warblogs, which are Weblogs that chronicle war-related events) argue that they provided some of the most thoughtful and insightful analyses of the war. Indeed, many mainstream journalists visited the Warblogs to get additional information. Critics, however, argue that bloggers

---

[1]The Web site is still operating at <http://dear_raed.blogspot.com>.

(the person who write a Weblog) are often politically biased and that the quality of their writing is often poor because it usually is not formally edited. *American Journalism Review* writer Catherine Seipp summed up the debate well when she wrote: "Just as many bloggers view the mainstream media as elitists, mainstreamers generally look upon bloggers as a bunch of mutts crashing the dog show."[2]

More specifically, bloggers can point out that mainstream journalism also has a bias — one that promotes mainstream values and powerful elite groups. A good example of this, as Pax pointed out, was the message repeated over and over in Western media that ordinary Iraqis would be much better off after being liberated from Saddam Hussein. Of course, that has not been the case for the vast majority of Iraqis.

CHAPTER OVERVIEW

Irrespective of whether one likes or dislikes Weblogs, it is clear that they are having a major impact on the dissemination of news and information. Several surveys show that some people rely on Weblogs more than traditional media and find them to be more credible.

From a broader perspective, Weblogs can be interpreted as having two major effects: They can lessen dependence on traditional media for news and information, and They can produce content that challenges traditional, mainstream journalism and views of the world. Thus, Weblogs, like the Internet in general, represent a threat to the power that traditional mainstream media.

This chapter examines the history of the Internet, which is the newest technology capable of accommodating mass communication messages. Although the Internet and World Wide Web have grown quickly, they are not likely to replace traditional media very quickly. The Internet is best viewed not as a replacement for traditional media but rather as a supplement. It adds another layer of complexity in the social world — one that, from a broad perspective, helps many people and organizations achieve their goals more easily and efficiently. And this, in turn, contributes to social order.

However, the long-term effects of the Internet and World Wide Web on mass communication may be even greater than the invention of the printing press. That is a bold statement to make, but the Internet has one big advantage

---

[2]See Barbara K. Kaye and Thomas J. Johnson, "Weblogs as a Source of Information about the 2003 Iraq War," pp. 291-301 in Ralph D. Berenger (ed.), *Global Media Go to War: Role of News and Entertainment Media During the 2003 Iraq War* (Spokane: Marquette Books, 2004).

over the printing press: It gives individuals the ability to mass communicate for the first time in history. It also gives them the power to circumvent traditional mass media, both in terms of obtaining information and disseminating it.

At the end of the this chapter, I argue that the Internet is slowly whittling away at the mediating power of mass media — a process that parallels the effects that the printing press had on traditional political and religious elites in the 16th-19th centuries.

A Brief History of the Internet

Cuban Dictator Fidel Castro doesn't like the Internet very much. In fact, until recently, his country wouldn't allow its citizens access to the Internet. Ironically, though, he played a key role in creating cyberspace.

This story begins in 1962, when Castro invited the Soviet Union to set up military bases in Cuba, which is only 90 miles from Florida.[3] The Soviet Union brought in nuclear missiles and pointed them at the United States. That angered President John F. Kennedy, who gave the Soviet Union an ultimatum: remove the missiles or prepare for war.

The Soviets backed down and removed the missiles. But the action exposed a serious weakness in the U.S. military: One nuclear missile could have wiped out the entire American military communications system. The military needed a communications network that would survive a partial nuclear attack.

At the time, the idea of networking computers wasn't new. Airlines had begun using dedicated computer-terminal systems and the military was using a limited defense command-and-control system. But these special-purpose systems were used primarily for calculating mathematical equations or storing data. They were not used for communication. But that would soon change.

ARPA and the Information Superhighway

After the Cuban missile crisis, a U.S. scientific government agency called Advanced Research Projects Agency (ARPA) commissioned Paul Baron of the Rand Corporation to produce a system that would allow the U.S. military to

---

[3]For a thorough but technical history of the Internet, see Barry M. Leiner, Vinton G. Cerf, David D. Clark, Robert E. Kahn, Leonard Kleinrock, Daniel C. Lynch, Jon Postel, Larry G. Roberts, and Stephen Wolff, "A Brief History of the Internet," Internet Society (August 2000), available at <www.isoc.org/internet/ history/brief.shtml>. A readable and moderately in-depth history of the Internet is available from Richard T. Griffiths, *History of the Internet*, Leiden University (October 2002), <www.let.leidenuniv.nl/ history/ivh/chap1.htm>.

maintain control over its nuclear arsenal and planes if a nuclear attack wiped out conventional communication systems.

ARPA set out to create what would later be called the information superhighway. The metaphor was derived partly from the interstate highway system, which President Dwight D. Eisenhower initiated in the 1950s in part to quickly transport military troops and equipment around the country. In the case of computers, however, the goods to be transported was information, and the idea was to transport information from one point to another even if part of the highway system were disabled.

Protocols and Packets

To create the information superhighway, two major things were needed. The first was Protocols, or codes, that allowed one computer to communicate with another. Basically this involved creating a software that allowed computers to talk to each other.

The second thing needed was a way to transmit the information efficiently. Large files could tie up a computer for a long period of time, which in turn could tie up the entire network.

To solve this problem, Baron proposed a "packet switched network."[4] This involved breaking down data into small "packets" and transmitting them from computer to computer until they reach their final destination.

ARPANET Goes Online

In 1969, ARPANET (Advance Research Project Agency Network) went online. It connected computers at government-supported research sites, mainly at universities. Shortly thereafter, simple mail transfer protocols (SMTP or commonly referred to as e-mail) and file transfer protocols (FTP) for longer transmissions were developed.

Within a few years, ARPANET joined with networks developed by U.S. allies overseas and with networks at the Department of Energy, the National Aeronautical and Space Agency, and the National Science Foundation. In 1974, Vinton Cerf of Stanford University and Robert Kahn of the Defense Advanced Research Projects Agency (formerly ARPA) coined the term "Internet," short for "between networks."

---

[4]D. Kristula, "The History of the Internet," (March 1997), available at <www.davesite.com/webstation/net-history.shtml>.

The Civilian Internets

In 1979, Steve Ballovin, a graduate student at the University of North Carolina, created a civilian Internet called USENET. It could do everything ARPANET could do, but it also supported discussion groups, which could communicate in real time, and bulletin boards, which are now called newsgroups. About the same time, the IBM corporation created BITNET, another software system that allowed computer networking, especially for commercial applications.

Within a few years USENET and BITNET joined ARPANET and other university, governmental and commercial networks to form what is now essentially the Internet. However, at that time the users still were mainly scientists, computer experts and others. One needed a knowledge of computers and programming and access to expensive computer equipment.

This began to change in the 1980s, when Apple Computer and IBM (International Business Machine) Corporation introduced easy-to-use personal computers. Some businesses and consumers began logging on.

Hosts and ISPs

In 1984, the number of hosts, or computers linked to the "net," topped 1,000 for the first time. The volume of traffic was growing rapidly, mainly because of the popularity of e-mail and discussion groups. Accessing data and information on the Internet was still a difficult task, often requiring advanced knowledge of archival systems and programming.

To respond to the increasing demand, more domain names were introduced, which gave each Internet address (or URL) in the United States a unique name associated with a numeric address. Government users were given the suffix .gov, businesses .com, educational institutions .edu, nonprofit organizations .org and Internet companies .net. Country suffixes (e.g., .ca for Canada) were also introduced.

Internet Service Providers (ISP) also emerged at this time to meet the increasing consumer demand. They gave users access to the Internet, usually through a telephone line and modem, for a small monthly fee. CompuServe was the first successful ISP. America Online was founded in 1989 as a dial-up information service. It didn't offer Internet access until 1994.

But the so-called "Internet Revolution" really didn't take off until the invention of the World Wide Web and Web browsers. In 1992, there still were only 50 Web sites around the world. Most people used the Internet for e-mail and discussion groups. That was about to change.

Tim Berners-Lee and the WWW

Tim Berners-Lee wasn't thinking about mass media when he invented the World Wide Web in 1990. He was just trying to help scientists exchange data over the Internet. But Berners-Lee's invention did more than solve the problem of transferring documents and data between computers. He turned the Internet into a mass medium.

"It's hard to overstate the impact of the global system he created," declared *Time* magazine, which selected Berners-Lee as one of the 100 greatest minds of the 20th century. "He took a powerful communications system (Internet) that only the elite could use and turned it into a mass medium."[5]

Before the Web, about 600,000 people, mostly scientists and government officials, used the Internet, which was not very user-friendly. But Berners-Lee's software was relatively easy to use and gave Internet users the power to create their own Internet sites and link to other sites.[6] In fact, anyone with a computer and modem (a device for connecting a computer to a phone line) could easily enter cyberspace.[7]

And they did.

Within five years there were 40 million users. Mass media organizations were some of the first. The bigger newspapers and television news organizations set up Web sites and marketed their news directly to online consumers. Journalists also used the Internet for e-mail and to research stories.

Today, about 1.2 billion people around the world — or about 17% of the world's population — are connected to the Internet,[8] primarily through the Web. Most daily newspapers, magazines, book publishers, recording

---

[5]*Time* magazine online, <www.timemagazine.com>.

[6]Berners-Lee made his Web software available to the public in the Summer of 1991. The software had three elements: HTTP, HTML and URL. The software for transferring documents, pages and data was called HTTP, or HyperText Transfer Protocol. HTTP standardized communication between computer servers and clients. In other words, computers with different types of files and operating systems could now communicate with each other. The software for creating Web sites was called HTML, or HyperText Markup Language. The software for identifying and accessing Web sites was called URL, or Uniform Resource Locator. That's the "http://www ... " address that one types in on a browser to access a Web site.

[7]The origins of the term "cyberspace" are usually traced to William Gibson's science fiction novel, *Neuromancer* (New York: Ace Books, 1984), who used the term to refer to the imagined world created by people who communicated with each other via computers.

[8]This estimate comes from Internet World Stats, which is available at <www.internetworldstats.com/stats.htm>.

companies, and radio and television stations and networks have their own Web sites, which combine pictures, graphics, text and sometimes audio-visual content. It's getting harder to tell the difference between media formats.

Berners-Lee could have gotten rich off his invention. In fact, several major computer companies offered him millions of dollars for exclusive rights to develop and sell the software. But he turned them down. He didn't want any company controlling the software that could link the world into one global system. He wanted it to be free. So in 1994 he founded the nonprofit World Wide Web Consortium (W3C) at the Massachusetts Institute of Technology in Cambridge, Massachusetts. The Consortium governs and improves Web technology. Berners-Lee is the director.

"I have profited so much from seeing the system take off and become so remarkable because I chose not to commercialize it," he told *The San Francisco Chronicle*. "If I had tried to commercialize it, it would have prompted people to make separate and incompatible versions of it and it wouldn't have become this marvelous global system."[9]

In July 2004, Queen Elizabeth II knighted Berners-Lee. He also has won numerous awards and been bestowed with several honorary doctorate degrees from institutions around the world. This includes the Finnish Millenium Technology Prize, which included a $1.2 million award. This pleased many people, who believe Berners-Lee deserves some financial compensation for his work.

Web Browsers

Berners-Lee software made it much easier for people to create Web sites and connect to each other. But connecting to Web sites became even easier in September 1993.

That's when Marc Andreessen and others at the National Center for Supercomputing Applications at the University of Illinois introduced Mosaic. This was a browser that used a "point-and-click" mouse interface. It was very user-friendly. In fact, a year later tens of thousands of copies of Mosaic had been installed on computers around the world.

In 1994, Andreessen and others founded Netscape Communications Corporation, which then developed Netscape Navigator, the most popular browser in the 1990s. In 1996, Microsoft Corporation followed with its own version, called Internet Explorer. Explorer eventually eclipsed Navigator as the

---

[9]Laura Evenson, "From the Creator of a Universe; Web Inventor's Book Shares His Goal," *The San Francisco Chronicle* (October 21, 1999), p. B1.

most popular browser, mainly because it was part of the Windows operating systems that were being installed on 90 percent of the world's personal computers.

In 1994, AOL also revised its browser so users could access the Internet. Prior to that users were limited to browsing information the company provided to them. Today there are hundreds of different browsers, but Explorer, Navigator and AOL dominate the market.

In 1994, there were 3,000 Web sites. A year later there were 25,000. In 1996, there were 250,000. In November 2006, there were 110 million Web sites.[10]

Portals and Search Engines

Growth in the number of Web sites created a new problem — how to find information and entertainment content easily and quickly. The answer was Web portals and search engines.

A portal is a Web site that helps users find their way around the Internet. It usually contains advertising banners and links for shopping, news and information, and entertainment. Some portals are also ISPs. AOL is an example. But others, such as Yahoo.com, are not. Anyone can use their Web sites, which also often provide free e-mail accounts and service.

Most portals also include a search engine — an electronic tool that locates information on the Internet. The first engine was Archie, developed in 1990 at McGill University in Montreal. A year later, the University of Minnesota introduced Gopher. These early search engines have been eclipsed by commercial (for-profit) engines, which include Alta Vista, Infoseek, Yahoo!, Northern Light, Excite, MSN Search and Google. Today there are hundreds of search engines.

Growth of the Internet

The Internet grew at an exponential rate during the 1990s, doubling the number of hosts, ISPs and users almost every year. The number of Web sites quadrupled. In 1990, there were 100,000 hosts, several hundred ISPs, 600,000 users and a handful of Web sites. In 2000, there were 55 million hosts, 15,000 ISPs, 300 million users and 15 million Web sites.

---

[10]"World's Web Sites pass 100 Million Mark," *Deutsche Presse-Agentur* (November 1, 2006) retrieved from <http://tech.monstersandcritics.com/news/article_1217195.php> on December 15, 2006.

Most of the ISPs provided local service, but some, like America Online, had built a national audience (25 million subscribers in 2000). Half of the world's ISPs (7,000) were located in the United States.

One factor contributing to growth of the Internet in the late 1990s was the digital subscriber line and broadband technologies. Both terms refer to high-speed transmission of digital (voice, video and text) data on the Internet. In fact, these technologies can be 50 times faster than conventional modem dial-up services.

More specifically, DSL allows high-speed transmission of data over conventional copper telephone lines. Broadband refers to telecommunication technologies that allow multiple channels of data over a single communications medium. The term broadband usually refers to high-speed service provided via a coaxial television cable. Wireless broadband technologies are now becoming available, and may eventually surpass cable because there are no cables to string and maintain.

Commercialization of the Internet

Technology spurred growth of the Internet during the 1990s. However, commercialization of the Internet also played a key role. During the late 1990s, many businesses set up Web sites. They did so primarily for two reasons.

The first reason was public relations. The Web was a place where businesses could inexpensively communicate with and get feedback from customers, clients, investors, media organizations and other businesses. The sites included information about their products and services, market data, corporate reports and investor information.

The second major reason for creating a Web site was to make money. Some businesses sold products and services directly to consumers, who could now go online and purchase everything from cars and clothes to books and compact discs.

One of the most spectacular success stories was Amazon.com, which offered books online and became one of the largest Internet-only-sales companies in the United States. In 1999, the value of the company was $22 billion, even though it had never turned a profit. Other Web portal companies, such as Yahoo.com, offered free services to consumers (e-mail addresses, chat rooms) and then sold links and advertising banners to businesses seeking those consumers.

Although many consumers liked the convenience of shopping online or getting free services, many scholars and consumer groups began complaining about commercialization of the Internet. Would the dot-coms push nonprofit and educational Web sites out of cyberspace? Would the Internet become just another place where people could make a buck?

The Dot-com Boom and Bust

There is no question that the Internet was being "colonized" by business in the late 1990s.

Many companies entered cyberspace hoping to make money either through direct sales to consumers or through the sale of Web advertising. Many of the startups grew quickly, "went public" (sold stock and became a publicly owned corporation), and watched their stock prices soar on speculation of future profits. Their top executives often made millions of dollars. Some of the companies even made money. But many did not.

The Crash

By Spring 2000, investors began pulling their money out of many of the dot-coms, which in turn triggered a major sell-off. Within weeks, the Nasdaq stock market, which hosted many of the Internet technology stocks, lost one-third of its value. In fact, half of all dot-com stocks lost more than 75 percent of their value. Amazon.com, one of the better-faring companies, lost half of its value.

The bubble had burst, sending many of the Internet ventures into bankruptcy. When the dust settled, more than $7 trillion in investor wealth had been lost.

Amazon.com and some other companies survived. Amazon.com actually turned its first profit in Spring 2001. However, as late as 2003, Amazon.com and many other Internet ventures were still having difficulty making money.

Why the Crash?

Many factors have been cited to account for the dot-com crash. A key one was that the advertising and online consumer dollars just weren't there. Although Internet ad revenues and sales had continued to increase in the 1990s, the problem was that the revenues didn't increase fast enough. The same was true for high-speed Internet service.

Advertisers then, as now, were skeptical of the Internet, because there was a lack of research demonstrating its effectiveness, and because Web sites still could not generate the kinds of audiences that one could find for traditional media. Many consumers also were afraid to buy products over the Internet, fearing that someone would steal their credit card information. Some of those fears were founded.[11]

CONVERGENCE OF TECHNOLOGY

In 1997, a broadcasting scholar attending a national conference in Las Vegas boldly declared that newspapers were dead.[12] He probably wishes today that he could retract those statements. But at the time, no one in the audience even thought to question his judgment. They were convinced that new technologies, especially the Internet, would kill off conventional print media.

They were wrong. Print media survived into the 21st century. In fact, daily newspapers (the print versions) continue to be very profitable — much more profitable in relative terms than major U.S. corporations (about 20 percent profit on sales compared with 5 percent for the average major public corporation). The Internet or some other technology some day may eliminate the print newspaper, but there's still no concrete evidence that will happen any time soon.

Much of the euphoria about the Internet has died down. Scholars and professionals still talk about convergence, but they now realize it could be many years and perhaps decades before that happens.

Why Convergence Failed

Many reasons can be cited to explain why convergence didn't occur as quickly as the pundits had predicted. But three stand out: low demand relative to other media; technological problems; and lack of profits.

Low Demand

In 2002, fewer than half of the 105 million U.S. households, or 40 million, were online.[13] Four years later that figure had increased to 70 percent, or

---

[11]I had such an experience in the mid-1990s. My credit card number was apparently stolen by employees of a national ISP provider and was used to charge $15,000 in mail-order computer equipment in Great Britain. Scotland Yard investigated the incident but I never heard whether the culprits were apprehended. The company who sold the computers to the culprits lost out, because mail orders are only covered if the products are shipped to the consumer's home. I didn't have to pay for the bogus charges.

[12]David Demers, "Surviving the Electronic Information Age: Newspapers and Reader-Driven Marketing," *American Editor*, 785 (July/August, 1997), pp. 17-18.

[13]Data are from Decision Analyst, Inc., see <www.decisionanalyst.com>.

80 million households, but only a third of those households had broadband or high-speed access. In contrast, 99 percent of all households have at least one television and one radio, and the vast majority have two or more.

Three major reasons explain why demand for the Internet is low relative to other mass media.

The first is cost. Many low-income families cannot afford them. Although the price of computers has dropped dramatically through the years, even the least expensive desktop computer is still more than $500. But the costs don't stop there. Most consumers must also pay another $10 to $50 a month for Internet access, with broadband access usually above $40 a month.

The second major reason many households are not online is that some people are uncomfortable using computer technology, or they simply have no interest. This is particularly true among the elderly, who are less likely to go online.

The third reason is that the Internet, although offering many conveniences and services, still can't satisfy consumers' needs better than some traditional media. For example, many people still prefer a hard copy newspaper or magazine, because they can find and read what they want very quickly and they can easily transport the printed version from place to place. In contrast, to read a story online, most consumers must sit down in front of their computer and then spend several minutes logging on and waiting for the Web site to load. The seemingly small inconveniences of online media become a major problem for people who are racing to get their families and themselves ready for school or work.

Technological Problems

The fastest way to replace an existing technology or mass medium is to provide a new technology or medium that does everything the old one does, plus more. In other words, a new technology generally will eliminate an old one only when it becomes a functional substitute. The telegraph is the best example. Telephone technology killed it off, because the phone could do everything the telegraph could do and could do it better.

Online technology certainly has come a long way in a short time. However, in 2007 most consumers still could not get high-quality video from cyberspace. High-speed Internet access is a great improvement over modem technology, to be sure. But it typically cannot produce streaming or real-time audiovisual images that could match broadcast television images. Moving images continue to be crude and jerky, primarily because Internet technology needs to be improved (see discussion below).

In addition, accessing audio-visual content on the Internet also can be a very frustrating activity, even with high-speed access service. Users must spend a lot of time clicking and waiting before they can view the audio-visual content.

Lack of Profits

Online mass media have yet to generate substantial revenue and profits for their organizations. This is perhaps the most important factor inhibiting convergence. Only about 7% of all advertising revenue generated in the United States comes from the Internet. Many advertisers are more comfortable with traditional media. They know that anyone can turn on a television and get their messages. The medium is easy to use.

Although online advertising has increased over the years, many advertisers also remain skeptical because the effects of online advertising are not yet well understood. Many consumers dislike online advertising, especially pop-ups, or special boxes that automatically pop up when a Web site or hyperlink is clicked.

The State of Convergence

The fact that convergence has failed to date doesn't mean that it won't happen sometime in the future. Many of the technological problems associated with online media will be solved in the years ahead. Voice-activation technology also may eliminate the need for a keyboard, so typing skills will not be necessary. As more people use the Internet, the advertisers no doubt will follow.

In the meantime, the Internet is best viewed not as a replacement for traditional media but rather as a supplement. Online media offer advantages not available from traditional media. Many online newspapers, for example, offer subscribers a service that will automatically notify them via e-mail of stories of interest. Consumers also can easily search for information and stories at online media sites that archive their issues. And e-mail is an inexpensive way to communicate with people.

In short, the Internet has added another layer of complexity in the social world — one that, from a broad perspective, helps many people and organizations achieve their goals more easily and efficiently. This, in turn, can be seen as generally contributing to social order.

ROLE AND FUNCTION OF THE INTERNET

The Internet may never live up to claims that it will be the "final medium of mass communication." Nevertheless, it will continue to have a profound impact on society and media organizations, serving as both a medium of control and change.

The Internet and Social Control

Millions of people and organizations use the Internet for e-mail, shopping and research. They use the Internet partly because it fulfills needs that traditional media cannot. For example, a long-distance telephone call costs money. E-mail is free. Going the bookstore can take up a whole afternoon. Ordering a book online takes minutes. Researching a specific concept or term can take hours in the library. Doing an online search takes minutes. And e-mail helps people stay in contact with others and even generate new relationships.

The Pew American and Internet Life Project found that 84 percent of U.S. Internet users have contacted an online group.[14] Half say the Internet helped them get to know people they would not otherwise have met. Another third said groups have helped them meet people of different ages. And a fourth said they have met people from different ethnic or economic backgrounds than their own.

The study also found that a fourth go online to connect with their local community, by arranging church meetings, neighborhood gatherings, local sports events, or charity activities. Men were more likely to take part in online groups about professional activities, politics and sports. In contrast, women were drawn to medical support groups, entertainment groups, and local community associations. Six of 10 who visit online groups e-mail the group regularly. A separate Pew study also found that nearly 9 of 10 online users have used the Internet as a research tool.[15]

The content on mass media Web sites, like the content in traditional media, also generally supports and maintains dominant values and social institutions. The sources for online news stories tend to be powerful political and economic elites. The lyrics for songs at a online music site tend to reinforce dominant

---

[14]A summary of the Pew study can be found at <www.nua.ie/surveys/index.cgi?f=VS&art_id=905357358&rel=true>.

[15]John B. Horrigan, "The Internet as a Resource of Information about News and Science," Pew Internet and American Life Project (November 20, 2006), available at <www.pewinternet.org/pdfs/PIP_Exploratorium_Science.pdf>.

values about love and relationships. Advertising encourages people to purchase goods and services that, in turn, help support a free-market system.

In short, the Internet, like traditional mass media, helps people achieve their personal and professional goals more efficiently and effectively. It reduces social distance and helps integrate people and organizations into the dominant culture as well as subcultures.

The Internet and Social Change

In the mid-1990s, the government of South Korea enacted in secret new laws that allowed South Korean companies to lay off union workers, change working hours and hire replacements for union workers who go on strike.

The labor unions, which had been excluded from the meetings, were furious. They staged a strike. But they had a problem. Mainstream media, which were taking their cues from the powerful elites and business leaders, would not help them get their message out to the world. So they did the only thing they could: They created a Web page and sent thousands of e-mails to groups around the world. It worked. Thousands of people and groups around the world condemned the South Korean government.

"E-mail was the only way KCTU could send more than 1,000 copies of letters and petitions overseas every day," one leader of the movement told mass communication researcher Tae-hyun Kim. "Without the Web site," another leader remarked, "the whole strike could have remained as a domestic issue, and might not have been able to attract international attention."[16]

Mass media, particularly news media organizations, are often portrayed in traditional history textbooks as defenders of democracy, life, liberty and happiness. There certainly are some good examples of that (e.g., the muckrakers). But, as this book has shown in previous chapters, mass media do not always identify with the underdog. In fact, more often than not they produce content that supports powerful institutions and elites and dominant value systems. They play a guard dog function (see Chapter 4).

Thus, 20 years ago, when a group without much power wanted to inform others of its plight, there wasn't much that group could do without help from the mainstream media. In fact, historical research shows that mainstream news media marginalized the civil rights, women's and labor movements for many decades.

---

[16]Tae-hyun Kim, "Internet Empowers Korean Social Movement," pp. 231-244 in David Demers (ed.), *Global Media News Reader* (Spokane, WA: Marquette Books, 2002), p. 241.

But the Internet has leveled the playing field a little. Through e-mail and Web sites, groups and individuals can communicate directly with large numbers of people. They can bypass traditional mass media. They can mass communicate. And many are doing that.

For example, during the 1990s many consumers who were victims of consumer fraud or corporate abuse set up Web sites criticizing the offending companies. Some of the businesses capitulated and righted the wrongs. Some did not. But in either case, ordinary people and less powerful groups had a chance to communicate without having to rely on the mass media as the medium.

In recent years, Weblogs, which are essentially online diaries, have become very popular. Weblogs have basically enabled anyone to become a journalist for very little cost. Some people use them to monitor the performance of the mainstream mass media. In 2005, *CBS Evening News* and former anchor Dan Rather were strongly criticized after bloggers raised questions about the veracity of a National Guard document stating that President George W. Bush had failed to perform his duties when he was a pilot during the Vietnam War.[17] In fact, the role of the blogs as a "fifth estate" is now becoming the main topic of some new books.[18]

Of course, the Internet can be used for good or bad purposes. During the 1990s and early 2000s, many terrorist groups around the world used the Internet to communicate and advance their goals. This upset many Western political leaders.

But whether used for good or bad purposes, the Internet has, for the first time in history, given ordinary people the potential to communicate on a mass level. This doesn't level the playing field completely. There is still the problem of getting people to visit Web sites. Political and economic power structures do not change easily, and the mainstream media remain powerful, credible institutions in society.

But from a broad perspective, the Internet may be viewed as another step in the chain of events that has led to decentralization of information and power in the Western world. The printing press helped break the monopoly that political and religious elites had over information and knowledge. And the

---

[17]Howard Kurtz, "After Blogs Got Hits, CBS Got a Black Eye," *Washington Post* (September 209, 2004), p. C01. What is ironic is that the content of the allegedly faked memos was apparently true, according to administrative people who worked with Bush. However, the substantive issue about Bush's performance could not survive the outrage associated with the faked memos.

[18]Stephen D. Cooper, *Watching the Watchdog: Bloggers as the Fifth Estate* (Spokane, WA: Marquette Books, 2006).

Internet now has the potential to take this a step farther — to break the monopoly power of traditional mass media systems.

MASS MEDIA AND THE LOSS OF MEDIATING POWER

Mass media are losing their mediating power.[19]

Many media scholars will find it strange to make this argument at a time when the number and variety of mass media are growing and when criticism of mass media seems to be at an all-time high. But the loss-of-power argument is based on relative, not absolute, change. In other words, although mass media clearly produce more content today than in the past, they are less likely now to be the exclusive or primary source of information and knowledge about the world. The Internet is "stealing" some of their power.

During the 19th and 20th centuries, people and organizations relied heavily, sometimes exclusively, on traditional mass media — newspapers, books, magazines, radio, and television — for information about politics, business, and social affairs. Social movements and organizations also relied upon the mass media to get their messages to the public and to policy makers. If a group was unable to get media coverage, it often had difficulty achieving their goals. This was especially true for groups whose goals fell outside mainstream politics and values.

But the growth of the Internet in the 1980s and the World Wide Web in 1990s has created conditions that lessens dependence on traditional mass media. People and organizations can circumvent mainstream mass media when searching for information or when they need to send a message to the

---

[19]The idea that media are losing their mediating power first came to me in 1997, when I began using the Internet to gather information for my research and writing projects. Typically, I would begin my search with online mass media Web sites, particularly newspaper or magazine archives. Then I would go directly to the Web sites of the sources cited in those newspaper and magazine stories. Before the Internet and the World Wide Web, my search typically would end after examining the mass media sources, which usually involved an in-person visit to a library. Of course, it was too costly or inefficient to directly contact sources that were cited in the mass media stories. Today I still rely heavily on traditional mass media when I research topics. But it is clear that my dependence on them is much less than it was prior to the development of the Internet. The Internet and World Wide Web has given me and other people the ability to go directly to the "horse's mouth," as the cliche goes, and to even circumvent them in some instances. In addition, the Internet gives people and organizations the ability to search out sources excluded from traditional mass media content — an option that also was not very feasible or efficient prior to the Internet.

community or world. Another advantage of the Internet is that it gives social actors the ability to send original, unfiltered, unedited messages directly to target groups and policy makers. Before, they had to rely on journalists to correctly interpret and send the message.

In addition to giving social actors the power to circumvent mainstream media, the Internet has even created new opportunities for social actors to criticize traditional mainstream media. In fact, some blogs focus exclusively on monitoring or criticizing mainstream media. In his book, *Watching the Watchdog: Bloggers as the Fifth Estate*, Stephen D. Cooper provides scores of examples of how blogs have criticized mainstream media news coverage. He argues that the "blogosphere" is emerging as a Fifth Estate — one that is serving as a watchdog of the watchdog. Drawing on systems theory for an analytical framework, Stephen D. Cooper argues that

> The introduction of a new component into the media system — in this case, the blogosphere — would clearly have the potential to reduce the rigidity of all those existing interdependencies. This is not to say that the blogosphere in itself would necessarily remain a permanent outsider to the web of interdependencies ... . But what the blogosphere may indeed do, long term, is to mitigate the severity of those dependencies throughout the entire social system, simply by offering alternative means of gratifying the various information needs of the various social actors.
>
> In short, we might expect the increase in the complexity of the media system brought about by the introduction of the blogosphere to precipitate a corresponding reduction in the strength of media dependencies across the entire social system — at both the individual and institutional levels. And in turn, we might expect the degree of bias in media content attributable to the dependency of any social actors on any other actors to be attenuated, over time.[20]

Mainstream journalists often counter that bloggers are often amateurs who publish unsubstantiated charges and often get the facts wrong. To date, blogs also have had limited impact on public policy making. None has emerged as a major mass media. However, many mainstream media are now monitoring and writing stories about the blog sites, which suggests that they are having an impact, despite the criticisms from some journalists.

Blogs are a visible sign that mainstream mass media are losing some of their power to control news and information. But they are not the only venue challenging mainstream media. Internet sites that allow illegal downloading of

---

[20]Cooper, *Watching the Watchdog*, p. 301.

music have had a major impact on sales of compact disks and other music products. The industry estimates that, in 2006, 1.2 billion illegal downloads were made, which in turn accounts for hundreds of millions in lost revenues. In response, the Recording Industry Association of America has filed thousands of lawsuits against college students and others who are operating sites that allow illegal downloads.

The film industry also is being affected by the Internet. Sites like YouTube are providing content that once was completely controlled by film studios and mainstream television broadcasting and cable companies. Independent filmmakers and others now have a means of distributing their films to audiences without approval or assistance from the traditional film distribution system, which historically has discriminated against the independents and favored the big studios. Similarly, the Internet gives entrepreneurs with a small amount of capital the ability to create their own radio station — an undertaking once reserved only for companies that had a million dollars or more to pay for studio equipment and transmitting towers.

The impact of the Internet on book publishing may be less than on other industries. Part of the reason is that consumers have been slow to adopt e-book technology. Consumers clearly prefer a hard copy book to a electronic one, and they especially do not like reading books on a computer. But the technology for e-books is improving, and more books are being produced electronically and transmitted through the Internet. More importantly, the Internet gives small independent publishers the ability to sell directly to consumers, either through their own Web sites or through online booksellers like Amazon.com. All of this is helping to level the playing field for independent book publishers, who traditionally have had a much more difficult time getting their books in retail outlets.

These changes do not mean that traditional mass media will lose their power quickly or completely. They, too, are harnessing the power of the Internet to achieve their goals, and they will continue to exert a disproportionate influence on the market and on public policy. In absolute terms, political and economic power will remain highly centralized in all Western countries.

However, in relative terms, traditional mainstream media are losing some of their power to mediate information, news and entertainment. Media in the 21st century will no longer be able monopolize information and knowledge to the degree that they did in the 20th century. The printing press stole some power away from political and religious authorities. Now, the mass media are victims of a structural trend that will forever will change the way in which people gain knowledge about the world.

Part III

FUTURE OF MASS MEDIA

Chapter 13

HOW CRITICS ENVISION THE FUTURE OF MASS MEDIA

During the mid-1800s, Karl Marx predicted that growing alienation among factory laborers in capitalist countries would lead to revolution, the overthrow of capitalism and the emergence of the communist state, where everyone would have economic and political equality.[1] This revolution was inevitable, Marx argued, because concentration of ownership would produce great disparities in wealth between rich and poor.

Karl Marx

But by the 1920s, many of Marx's followers conceded that something had gone wrong. There had been no revolutions in capitalist countries. In fact, the only communist-inspired revolution in the world had taken place in a quasi-feudalist state, Russia, where the Bolsheviks overthrew the Czar.

Was Marx wrong?

Many scholars and free-market economists at the time certainly felt so. But Marx's followers disagreed. Drawing on earlier writings of Marx and the Italian anti-Fascist Antonio Gramsci, they argued that the working classes failed to revolt because mass media and other cultural institutions fed them with false ideas, or what Marx called "ideology," about capitalism.[2] More specifically,

---

[1] Karl Marx, *Capital: A Critique of Political Economy*, Vols. 1-3, trans. by Samuel Moore and Edward Aveling (New York: International Publishers, 1987).

[2] The most important critics were associated with the Frankfurt School, a small groups of scholars, loosely organized, who fled Germany before World War II and whose theoretical works draw heavily on Marx's theory of "ideology" and Antonio Gramsci's concept of "hegemony."

some of these ideas were used to explain and justify the economic inequalities.[3] Without class consciousness, workers could not see how the system was exploiting them and why they should revolt.

Today, the descendants of the Frankfurt School are the most powerful and vocal critics of corporate or global mass media,[4] which they see as an unwitting tool of political and economic institutions to keep ordinary citizens from recognizing the evils of capitalism.[5] Moreover, according to the critics, if things continue on their present course, the 21st century will read like the plot line in a George Orwell or Aldous Huxley novel:

> The entire world will be converted into one big capitalist economic system dominated by a handful of global corporations. Only one or two media corporations will be left, and all decisions will be driven by profits and the bottom-line. Media will be filled with entertainment programming but there will be very little serious public affairs content. The emphasis will be on materialism, consumerism and commodification (i.e., turning all aspects of culture into items for sale). Ideas or beliefs critical of capitalism and global corporations will never appear in the media because they will be considered subversive. Groups that oppose the powerful corporations will have no medium through which to express their views. Diversity in the marketplace of ideas will not exist. But most people will be oblivious to these changes. They will be no longer interested in politics. They will spend most of their time watching virtual reality programming and living

---

[3]Economic laws of supply and demand and the functional importance of different occupations are often used to justify economic inequalities. The social value placed on individual mobility, technical competence and achievement — i.e., meritocratic beliefs — makes inequality and income differentials appear to be fair, just and the result of natural law. See David Demers, "Media Use and Beliefs About Economic Equality: An Empirical Test of the Dominant Ideology Thesis," paper presented at the annual meeting of the Midwest Association for Public Opinion Research, Chicago (November 1993).

[4]Global media are simply the most "extreme" case of corporate media; i.e., they are the largest and most structurally complex form of corporate media. See Chapter 4 for a more formal definition of corporate and global media.

[5]Among them are J. Herbert Altschull, *Agents of Power* (New York: Longman, 1984); W. Lance Bennett, *News: The Politics of Illusion,* 2nd ed. (New York: Longman, 1988); Stuart Ewin, *Captains of Consciousness: Advertising and the Social Roots of the Consumer Culture* (New York: McGraw Hill, 1976); Edward S. Herman and Noam Chomsky, *Manufacturing Consent: The Political Economy of the Mass Media* (New York: Pantheon, 1988); Todd Gitlin, *The Whole World Is Watching* (Berkeley: University of California Press, 1980); Fred Powledge, *The Engineering of Restraint* (Washington, DC: Public Affairs Press, 1971); Leon Sigal, *Reporters and Officials* (Lexington, MA: Heath, 1973); and Jeremy Tunstall, *Journalists at Work* (London: The Anchor Press, 1971).

in a fantasy land. And political and economic elites will not mind. It's easier for them to control the populace.

Chapter Overview

Although the scenario above is overly simplistic, it nonetheless captures the essence of what tens of thousands of scholars in the social sciences and humanities around the world believe will happen if globalization in the communications industry continues unchecked.[6] They have developed relatively sophisticated theories and arguments about the future of mass media, which are examined in this chapter.[7] Although the theories and ideas vary, they all share one thing in common: a belief that corporate mass media in general and global media in particular maximize profits and that this has an adverse impact on democratic processes and good journalism.

Inside the Critical Mind

For example, University of Illinois political economist Robert W. McChesney, who also runs Free Press, a nonpartisan organization that has been trying to prevent the Federal Communications Commission from deregulating the broadcasting industry, argues that

> The corporate media are carpet-bombing people with advertising and commercialism, whether they like it or not. Moreover, this is a market-driven system, one based upon one-dollar, one-vote rather than one-person, one-vote. In nations like Brazil or India, this means that a majority of the population will barely be franchised "citizens" in the new global media system. ...
>
> In short, the present course is one where much of the world's entertainment and journalism will be provided by a handful of enormous firms, each with distinct, but invariably pro-profit and pro-global market,

---

[6]Globalization is often associated with economic growth and the exchange of goods and services between countries around the world. But the concept also entails social and political interdependence, meaning that social actors increasingly rely on people around the world to achieve economic, social and political goals. Globalization is defined here as increasing social, economic and political interdependence around the world.

[7]Some of the content in this chapter and the ones that follow was previously published in David Demers, *Global Media: Menace or Messiah?* (Cresskill, NJ: Hampton Press, 1999). However, the chapters in this book include new information and update the literature explored in the earlier book.

political positions on the central social issues of our times. Even allowing for the presence of the occasional dissenting voice, the implications for political democracy, by any rudimentary standard, are troubling.[8]
U.S. media critic Norman Solomon adds that:

In the future, will media coverage be diverse? Prospects are bleak. Consolidation of media ownership has been so rapid in recent years that now just 10 corporations control most of this country's news and information flow. ... Those conglomerates are in business to maximize profits. They're hardly inclined to provide much media space for advocates of curtailing their power.[9]

Ben H. Bagdikian, a former newspaper editor and university professor, writes that

The lords of the global village have their own political agenda. Together they exert a homogenizing power over ideas, culture and commerce that affects populations larger than any in history. Neither Caesar, nor Hitler, Franklin Roosevelt, nor any Pope, has commanded as much power to shape the information on which so many people depend on which to make decisions about everything from whom to vote for to what to eat.[10]

In their edited book on global media, British media studies scholar Annabelle Sreberny-Mohammadi and her co-editors argue that:

Simply put, in the drive for ratings and commercial success, public and private broadcasters have reduced their commitments — financially and ideologically — to news, public affairs and educational programming in favour of entertainment-based programming. In terms of internal diversity, then, commercialization and competition may have narrowed the range of what is on offer.[11]

---

[8]Robert W. McChesney, "The Political Economy of Global Communication," pp. 1-26 in Robert W. McChesney, Ellen Meiksins Wood and John Bellamy Foster (eds.), *Capitalism and the Information Age: The Political Economy of the Global Communication Revolution* (New York: Monthly Review Press, 1998), pp. 15-16.

[9]Norman Solomon, "Corporations Growing Threat to Media Diversity," *The* (Eugene, OR) *Register-Guard* (October 19, 1997), p. 4F.

[10]Ben Bagdikian, "Lords of the Global Village," *The Nation* (June 12, 1989), p. 807.

[11]Annabelle Sreberny-Mohammadi, Dwayne Winseck, Jim McKenna and Oliver Boyd-Barrett, *Media in Global Context: A Reader* (London: Hodder Arnold Publication, 1998), pp. xx.

For decades Noam Chomsky, a world-famous linguist and America's leading leftist dissident, has been criticizing the U.S. news media, which he and his colleague, Edward S. Herman, contend

are effective and powerful ideological institutions that carry out a system-supportive propaganda function by reliance on market forces, internalized assumptions, and self-censorship, and without significant overt coercion. This propaganda system has become even more efficient in recent decades with the rise of national television networks, greater mass-media concentration, right-wing pressure on public radio and television, and the growth in scope and sophistication of public relations and news management."[12]

Noam Chomsky

British media theorist Nicholas Garnham adds that:

In assessing the likely impact of the new information technologies on broadcasting ... we need to remember that the actual history of the press is not one of developing freedoms, but on the contrary that the growth of an advertising-financed, commercial mass circulation press destroyed the independent working-class and radical press (as was the intention), steadily reduced the range of available views and information, incorporated nascent oppositional movements, helped to depoliticize our society and placed control of the channels of information in fewer and fewer hands.[13]

The late political economist Herbert I. Schiller, a vocal critic not only of global media but transnational corporations in general, wrote:

What is happening in Europe and elsewhere represents far more than a continuation of heavy importation of Anglo-American media materials and the exposure of local audiences to this inflow. ... What is now happening is the creation of and global extension of a near-total corporate informational-cultural environment.[14]

---

[12]Edward S. Herman and Noam Chomsky, *Manufacturing Consent: The Political Economy of the Mass Media* (New York: Pantheon Books, 1988), p. 306.

[13]Nicholas Garnham, *Capitalism and Communication: Global Culture and the Economics of Information* (London: Sage, 1990), p. 121.

[14]Herbert I. Schiller, *Culture, Inc.* (New York: Oxford University Press, 1989), p. 128.

And sociologists David Croteau and William Hoynes contend that

> The media's growing hypercommercialism, the concentration of media
> ownership, and the increasing pressure to merge information with
> entertainment, are all examples of how a consumer-friendly media
> industry is indifferent to the needs of citizens. The result is a diminished
> public sphere — the discursive space that is a central component of a
> democratic society — and a weakened democracy.[15] ... In this book, we
> have argued that the corporate commercialism so rampant in today's
> media has dramatically undermined the potential contribution of the
> media to our public life. ... Corporate media has sapped life from civil
> society.[16]

Scores of other critics could be cited. But I think you get the point.

These "critical" scholars come from a broad range of backgrounds and disciplines, but the bulk are in the social sciences, especially communication studies, journalism, sociology and political science. Many are sympathetic to neo-Marxist ideas. They go by a variety of names, including political economists, critical theorists, postmodernists, cultural theorists, media studies theorists and popular culture theorists. The list of critics also includes a substantial number of nonleftist social scientists and professional journalists, who tend to agree with Bagdikian's more moderate perspective — that "bigness" is the problem, not capitalism per se.

The critics' goal is to convince students and the public that mass media, in their present and expected future form, are incapable of serving the needs and interests of the ordinary citizen, or the poor and disenfranchised. Although critics have many different perspectives, they all share the belief that corporate or global media are concerned more about profits than in helping people, especially the disadvantaged, and that a profit-oriented, market-driven medium is a threat to the public interest.

A Brief History of Criticism

Although scholarly criticism of global media corporations is a relatively recent phenomenon, criticism of large-scale corporate media is not. In the early 1900s, Frank A. Munsey, a magazine and newspaper publisher, was widely despised for buying, merging and selling newspapers to make a profit and for

---

[15]David Croteau and William Hoynes, *The Business of Media: Corporate Media and the Public Interest* (Thousand Oaks, CA: Pine Forge Press, 2001), p.208.
[16]Ibid, p. 243.

proposing a national chain of newspapers. He believed there were too many newspapers in the United States and that this was inefficient. When Munsey died in 1925, newspaper publisher William Allen White wrote:

> Frank A. Munsey, the great publisher, is dead. Munsey contributed to the journalism of his day the great talent of a meat packer, the morals of a money changer and the manners of an undertaker. He and his kind have about succeeded in transforming a once noble profession into an eight percent security. May he rest in trust.[17]

During the 1930s, magazine editor Oswald Garrison Villard and radical journalist George Seldes also wrote about the dangers of chain ownership. According to Villard, "Any tendency which makes toward restriction, standardization, or concentration of editorial power in one hand is to be watched with concern."[18] Seldes was much more critical. He called the 21 members of the American Newspaper Publishers Association "the house of lords."[19] He accused them of using their papers mainly to advance the commercial and political interests of themselves and big business.

During the 1940s, the Commission on Freedom of the Press continued this line of criticism, questioning whether freedom and democracy could survive in a system where the communication channels are concentrated in the hands of a few. "Have the units of the press, by becoming big business, lost their representative character and developed a common bias — the bias of the large investor and employer?" Later, the commission added:

> Our society needs an accurate, truthful account of the day's events. ... These needs are not being met. The news is twisted by the emphasis on firstness, on the novel and sensational; by the personal interests of the owners; and by pressure groups. Too much of the regular output of the press consists of a miscellaneous succession of stories and images which have no relation to the typical lives of real people anywhere. Too often the result is meaninglessness, flatness, distortion, and the perpetuation of misunderstanding among widely scattered groups whose only contact is through these media.[20]

---

[17]William Allen White, Editorial, *Emporia* (Kansas) *Gazette* (December 23, 1925).

[18]Oswald Garrison Villard, "The Press Today: The Chain Daily," *The Nation* (May 21, 1930), pp. 597-598.

[19]George Seldes, *Lords of the Press* (New York: J. Messner, 1938).

[20]Commission on Freedom of the Press, *A Free and Responsible Press* (Chicago: University of Chicago Press, 1947), pp. 67-68.

The phenomenal growth of chain ownership in the U.S. newspaper industry during the 1950s, 1960s and 1970s ensured that "the problem" of large-scale media organization would remain on the front burner. Bagdikian emerged as the best-known critic. In the late 1980s, he even predicted that "if mergers and acquisitions continue at the present rate, one massive firm will be in virtual control of all major media by the 1990s." Although this has not occurred, the pace has quickened in the last two decades or so. The top 10 global media organizations account for more than half of all communication industry revenues worldwide. And some analysts now predict that during the next decade only five companies will account for half of all revenues.

CONTEMPORARY CRITICISMS

Contemporary critics have many complaints about corporate mass media. For example, mass communication scholar Robert McChesney argues that corporate media impair the democratic process. According to McChesney, democracy functions best when (1) there are no significant disparities in economic wealth; (2) people have a sense of community well-being; and (3) there is an effective system of political communication. However, he adds,

> The preponderance of U.S. mass communication is controlled by less than two dozen enormous profit-maximizing corporations, which receive much of their income from advertising placed largely by other huge corporations. ... In my view, private control over media and communication is not a neutral or necessarily a benevolent proposition. The commercial basis of U.S. media has negative implications for the exercise of political democracy: it encourages a weak political culture that make depoliticization, apathy and selfishness rational choices for the citizenry, and it permits the business and commercial interests that actually rule U.S. society to have inordinate influence over media content. In short, the nature of the U.S. media system undermines all three of the meaningful criteria necessary for self-government.[21]

From a public policy perspective, the most significant complaint is the allegation that global media are reducing diversity in the "marketplace of ideas." This criticism and other major criticisms — including the charge that corporate and global media are hindering social change, imposing Western

---

[21]Robert W. McChesney, *Corporate Media and the Threat to Democracy* (New York: Seven Stories Press, 1997), pp. 6-7.

ideas on other cultures (media imperialism), and alienating media workers —
are examined below.

Reducing Diversity

During the last 20 years or so, the term "diversity" has entered the
language of everyday life in most Western societies. In most cases, its usage
refers to the extent to which companies, the government, or industry segments
have employees representative of the racial diversity in their communities or
society as a whole.

In the field of communication, the term "diversity" has a much longer
history, and it refers not to racial diversity but to the diversity of ideas,
particularly political ideas. One of the assumptions underlying most Western
notions of political democracy is that voters have access to a broad range of
ideas and opinions. Without such access, they presumably cannot make good
decisions. As former Supreme Court Justice Oliver Wendell Holmes put it, "the
ultimate good desired is better reached by free trade in ideas — that the best
test of truth is the power of the thought to get itself accepted in the competition
of market ... ."[22]

The "marketplace of ideas" metaphor is not an assumption that all critical
scholars find appealing. They point out, quite correctly, that truth does not
always emerge when it competes with falsehood in a private or public forum.
Oftentimes, the group or person that has more money, more resources or more
power wins out. However, critical scholars generally do agree that no political
system would be fair or just if it suppresses ideas that are critical of those in
power or the status quo. As such, the key question becomes: Does the growth
of corporate media organizations lead to suppression of such ideas and hinder
the democratic process? And on this question, there is no doubt about how the
critics answer it.

"The antidemocratic potential of this emerging corporate control is a black
hole in the mainstream media universe," writes Bagdikian. He adds:

> What the public learns is heavily weighted by what serves the economic
> and political interests of the corporations that own the media. Since media
> owners are now so large and deeply involved in the highest levels of the
> economy, the news and other public information become heavily weighted
> in favor of all corporate values.[23]

---

[22]The Holmes quote is from *Abrams v. United States,* 250 U.S. 616 (1919).
[23]Ben H. Bagdikian, *The Media Monopoly,* 2nd ed. (Boston: Beacon Press, 1987), p. x.

More specifically, Bagdikian and other critics cite two major reasons or factors to explain why global and corporate media contribute to the loss of diversity. The first one is concentration of ownership. According to Anthony Smith, a media scholar,

> The public interest, hard always to define, must lie in the provision of a diversity of information from a diversity of sources — and therefore in the limiting of concentration of ownership. Otherwise, the democratic process itself is placed in thrall to a company or individual that may be pursuing, albeit quite legitimately, ends that are at variance with other objectives of a society. Nonetheless, concentration is being driven forward by regulatory and technological forces.[24]

Bagdikian and many other critics argue that the growth of global media and loss of entrepreneurial media are prima facie evidence of a loss of diversity. In some industries, such as the newspaper sector, this charge is true if the criterion for diversity is the actual number of business entities (sole proprietorships, partnerships and corporations) that control the media. However, if actual ownership is the criterion, then media have actually become less concentrated throughout the 20th century. The primary reason is that more and more media organizations are public corporations that sell shares of stock to the public. Although no statistics exist on media corporations per se, about half of all Americans own stock in one or more public corporations, many through pensions or mutual funds. This is the highest level in the world. Stock ownership in Europe is about 25 percent.[25]

Historically, concentration of ownership was greatest during the 19th century, when media (especially print media) were owned by a relatively small number of individuals and families. However, as those organizations grew and their original owners died, they increasingly became the property of a growing number of owners, for two reasons. First, as Karl Marx observed, the original owners would bequeath their property to multiple heirs, who in turn would bequeath their property to multiple heirs. Needless to say, over time ownership usually became dispersed, or less concentrated. Most family-owned media

---

[24]Anthony Smith, *The Age of Behemoths: The Globalization of Mass Media Firms* (New York: Priority Press Publications, 1991), p. 71.

[25]In 1997, 43 percent of all Americans owned stock in U.S. companies either directly or indirectly through mutual funds. The figures are lower in other Western countries: 25 percent in Britain, 16 percent in France, 10 percent in Italy, and six percent in Germany. Source: John Tagliabue, "Selling Europe on the Stock Market," *The New York Times* (March 1, 1998), Section 3, p. 1.

today have dozens of major stockholders, although there are exceptions here and there. Ownership and control of The News Corporation, for example, is highly centralized in Rupert Murdoch and his family. But this is more the exception than the rule, and it becomes increasingly difficult over time for one individual to maintain control of a growing corporation because of the second factor — "going public."

During the 20th century, many media organizations began selling shares of stock to the public in part to generate capital for expansion purposes. Most global media, in fact, are public corporations whose stock is owned by hundreds and, in some cases, thousands of investors. Although top executives at some global media still own or control a very large share of the stock in those companies, over time, as they die, ownership generally will continue to become more diffused or diluted. Also, each time a corporation issues more stock, it tends to have the effect of diluting the power of the outstanding shares.

To get around the problem of ownership diffusion and to support the notion that the mass media industry is becoming more concentrated, critics must assume that control of those media is largely in the hands of a few individuals — such as the board of directors and/or top management. Furthermore, they must assume that these directors or managers are serving their own interests before those of the audience or public.

The first assumption is reasonable — most stockholders have little direct say in the day-to-day operations of media corporations. Only those with substantial holdings have much say. However, the second assumption — that directors and, particularly, professional managers are serving their own interests to the detriment of the public — is more difficult to support. Some research suggests, in fact, that even though publicly owned corporate media organizations are more profitable than owner-managed entrepreneurial media, corporate media actually place less emphasis on profits as an organizational goal and more emphasis on product quality.[26] Why? Because they are more likely to be controlled by editors and professional managers who (1) see their work as an occupation or "calling," not just a job or a source of income, as some owners do; (2) earn most of their compensation through fixed salaries and, thus, do not benefit as directly or as much from profits as the owners (companies are increasingly offering stock options to top managers, but salaries are still the most important source of income for most top-level managers); and (3) place much more emphasis on growing the corporation than on paying profits to the owners, because companies that are too profitable are targets for takeovers and

---

[26]David Demers, "Revisiting Corporate Newspaper Structure and Profit-making," *Journal of Media Economics*, 11(2):19-35 (1998).

growth is one way to expand the power and salaries of professional managers. This debate is taken up in-depth in later chapters.

For now, the important point is that, despite these theoretical problems, critics continue to argue that corporate and global media are greedier and threaten democratic values. To support their argument about the dangers of concentration of ownership, they point to Bertelsmann's purchase of Random House from Advance Publications in Spring 1998 (Bertelsmann at the time was the sixth largest global media company; Advance was 10th). Shortly after the deal was announced, sociologist and media critic Todd Gitlin wrote that

> There's no glossing over that, if this deal is permitted to go forward, authors will have fewer places to sell their books. ... Editors will be dumped — to cut overhead — and more books will be turned over to free-lancers. ... And if consolidation is bad for editors and authors, how can it be good for readers. ... In the longer run, ... when authors can't make a decent living writing necessary books, readers suffer. They may not know they are suffering, but they suffer.[27]

The second factor critics say contributes to the loss of diversity is, crudely put, greed. "The helm is firmly in the grip of commercial and corporate greed," writes British media scholar Peter Golding.[28] More specifically, large, corporate media are believed to place more emphasis on profits than on product quality and information diversity than small, entrepreneurial media. According to Herman,

> The dominant media companies are large profit-seeking corporations, owned and controlled by very wealthy boards and individuals. Many are run completely as money-making concerns, and for the others as well there are powerful pressures from stockholders, directors, and bankers to focus on the bottom line. These pressures intensified over the 1980s as media stocks became stock market favorites and actual or prospective owners of media properties were able to generate great wealth from increased audience size and advertising revenues (e.g., Rupert Murdoch, Time-Warner, and many others). This encouraged the entry of speculators

---

[27]Todd Gitlin, "Eye on the Media: Publishing Deal Can't be Good for Readers," *Newsday* (March 27, 1998), p. A53.

[28]Peter Golding, "Global Village or Cultural Pillage? The Unequal Inheritance of the Communications Revolution," pp. 69-86 in Robert W. McChesney, Ellen Meiksins Wood and John Bellamy Foster (eds.), *Capitalism and the Information Age: The Political Economy of the Global Communication Revolution* (New York: Monthly Review Press, 1998), pp. 84-85.

and takeovers, and increased the pressure and temptation to focus more intensively on profitability.[29]

To support their case, for example, critics can point to an incident that occurred in fall 1998 at ABC News, which is owned by The Walt Disney Company. According to *The Washington Post*, ABC News President David Westin killed a segment produced for the network's *20/20* program because it focused on alleged hiring and safety problems at Disney World in Florida. The segment, which was based on the book *Disney: The Mouse Betrayed*, charged that Disney World fails to perform security checks that would prevent the hiring of sex offenders.[30] ABC denied it killed the story because of the negative publicity for Disney World. Moreover, the company pointed out that its news reports are not soft on Disney. Earlier in the year, for example, another *20/20* segment cited Disney as among a group of American companies that pay very low wages to workers on a Pacific island.

Another example critics can use to support their case that global media are unwilling to report negative news about themselves involved CBS during the 1998 Winter Olympics. A major sponsor of the games was the sports-shoe giant, Nike. CBS reporter Roberta Baskin accused CBS of refusing to rebroadcast her 1997 *48 Hours* report that was critical of Nike's labor practices in Vietnam because, she claimed, CBS did not want to offend Nike. The reporter also said CBS prevented her from doing follow-up stories on Nike and from replying to a *Wall Street Journal* article that criticized her original report. The network denied the charges.

More formally, three major arguments or propositions are used to support the claim that global and corporate media are more profit-oriented than small-scale or entrepreneurial media.

First, global media have more market power, which allegedly enables them to crush the competition and control advertising and subscription rates. The assumption underlying this claim is that those who control the media are profit-maximizers and that competition is necessary to keep them from holding the community hostage. According to the critics, corporate media derive their market power in part from economies of scale, lack of competition at the local level, greater knowledge of the marketplace, tax laws that favor corporate enterprises, and more efficient operations and greater rationality in decision

---

[29]Edward Herman, "Media in the U.S. Political Economy," pp. 75-87 in John Downing, Ali Mohammadi and Annabelle Sreberny-Mohammadi (eds.), *Questioning the Media: A Critical Introduction* (Newbury Park, CA: Sage, 1990), p. 79.

[30]Howard Kurtz, "ABC Kills Story Critical of Owner Disney: Official Denies Corporate Link Influenced Decision," *Washington Post* (October 14, 1998), p. C01.

making. In particular, chains and large-scale media organizations are perceived to be more profit-oriented because they have more market power than independently owned and small media, respectively.

The second argument supporting the notion that the corporate or global media are more profit-oriented revolves around ownership structure. Because corporate media are more likely to be publicly owned than entrepreneurial media, critics believe corporate media must be constantly oriented to the bottom line to keep stockholders happy and investment dollars flowing in. Competition under these conditions is not just a matter of producing a better and less expensive product than a competitor — it also means generating a profit that is higher than at companies in other industries. According to sociologists Paul M. Hirsch and Tracy A. Thompson,

> In this demanding environment, performance is continually assessed by analysts and investors using the quarterly report on earnings. Analysts use information about a firm's operations to generate forecasts about the company's long-term productivity and performance, which are reflected in the stock price. "Working for the numbers" has several important consequences for how newspapers operate. Strategies and activities geared toward creating value in the long run that require heavy investment in the short run become less attractive to executives because they decrease earnings in the current period.[31]

The third argument supporting the idea that corporate or global media are more profit-oriented is based on the belief that they are less responsive to the social and moral concerns of the community.[32] They are believed to be less responsive because their owners and managers are not strongly involved in the local community. Research shows, in fact, that owners of chain newspapers rarely live in the communities their newspapers serve, and managers of chain papers are less involved in local community organizations, are oriented more toward the organization and change jobs more frequently. Without strong ties to the local community, the chain organization is believed to be more interested in pursuing profits than the goals or interests of readers or the community (e.g.,

---

[31]Paul M. Hirsch and Tracy A. Thompson, "The Stock Market as Audience: The Impact of Public Ownership on Newspapers," pp. 142-58 in James S. Ettema and D. Charles Whitney (eds.), *Audiencemaking: How the Media Create the Audience* (Thousand Oaks, CA: Sage, 1994), pp. 145-150.

[32]For a summary of the community involvement debate, see David Pearce Demers, *The Menace of the Corporate Newspaper: Fact or Fiction?* (Ames: Iowa State University Press, 1996), pp. 228-229.

moral development). The notion that corporate media are less oriented to the local community also is expected to diminish community identity and solidarity. One expectation here is that the corporate and global media will publish less local or national news, and more nonlocal or international news.

The critics' charges do not end with profit-making. Because global media are assumed to be profit-maximizers, they also are assumed to place less emphasis on product quality and a diversity of ideas. The logic here is zero-sum: If a media organization maximizes profits, then it has less money to spend on news-gathering, improving the product or serving the public. In particular, critics charge that corporate or global media often sacrifice good journalism for profits. According to Hirsch and Thompson, "the move to public ownership led to the emergence of not only a new set of stakeholders in newspapers but a new logic for managing newspapers. Performance that is measured more in terms of economic than editorial accomplishments undermines newspaper executives' autonomy to pursue nonfinancial goals."

Although the zero-sum argument has a certain amount of intuitive appeal, the paradox is that media which make more money theoretically have more money to spend on improving the operation. Although the evidence is still scanty, research by media economist William Blankenburg suggests that one large (i.e., corporate) newspaper spends more money in absolute and relative terms on the editorial content than two smaller newspapers of equal size.[33] Blankenburg's research does show that publicly owned corporate newspapers are more profitable than privately owned family newspapers — a finding that is consistent with the notion that corporate media, because they are larger and benefit from economies of scale, are structurally organized to maximize profits.[34]

Thus, the question is not just one of maximizing profits but also one of how much and what proportion of profits are spent on improving the media product. Researchers know little about this, however, because information about profits and expenditures is often proprietary.

In addition to more emphasis on profits and less on product quality, critics have argued that corporate or global media rob journalists of their professional autonomy and publish fewer editorials about local issues and fewer editorials that are critical of powerful groups or the status quo. Global media are less vigorous editorially, the critics contend, because they are afraid of offending

---

[33]William B. Blankenburg, "Newspaper Scale and Newspaper Expenditures," *Newspaper Research Journal*, 10(2):97-103 (1989).

[34]William B. Blankenburg and Gary W. Ozanich, "The Effect of Public Ownership on the Financial Performance of Newspaper Corporations," *Journalism Quarterly*, 70:68-75 (1993).

advertisers, readers or sources, who may pull their advertising, buy fewer newspapers or refuse to cooperate with reporters. The effect of this alleged editorial timidity is a loss of diversity in the marketplace of ideas, which in turn is expected to imperil the democratic process.

To back up their claims, critics primarily rely on case studies and personal stories from former journalists and scholars. Typically, these critics recall incidents in which their former media organizations allegedly placed profits above product quality. Some of the titles tell the story: *When MBAs Rule the Newsroom; Read All About It! The Corporate Takeover of America's Newspapers; Networks of Power: Corporate TV's Threat to Democracy; Spiked: How Chain Management Corrupted America's Oldest Newspaper; The Chain Gang: One Newspaper Versus the Gannett Empire,* and *The Business of Media: Corporate Media and the Public Interest.*[35]

Hindering Social Change

Critics say corporate and global media have a conservative bias that impedes social change, which means systematic discrimination against the poor (as well as poor countries), women, minorities, environmentalists, organized labor and people with alternative sexual orientations.[36] For example, British sociologist Peter Golding writes that

---

[35]The full citations for the book titles are as follows: Doug Underwood, *When MBAs Rule the Newsroom: How the Marketers and Managers Are Reshaping Today's Media* (New York: Columbia University Press, 1993); James D. Squires, *Read All About It! The Corporate Takeover of America's Newspapers* (New York: Times Books, 1994); Dennis W. Mazzocco, *Networks of Power: Corporate TV's Threat to Democracy* (Boston: South End Press, 1994); Andrew Kreig, *Spiked: How Chain Management Corrupted America's Oldest Newspaper* (Old Saybrook, CT: Peregrine Press, 1987); Richard McCord, *The Chain Gang: One Newspaper Versus the Gannett Empire* (Columbia: University of Missouri Press, 1996), and David Croteau and William Hoynes, *The Business of Media: Corporate Media and the Public Interest* (Thousand Oaks, CA: Pine Forge Press, 2001).

[36]Some additional examples of case studies or anecdotes that support the critical model can be found in Ben H. Bagdikian, "Conglomeration, Concentration, and the Media," *Journal of Communication,* 30(2):59-64 (1980); Ben H. Bagdikian, *The Media Monopoly,* 2nd ed. (Boston: Beacon Press, 1987); Douglas Kellner, *Television and the Crisis of Democracy* (Boulder: Westview Press, 1990); John H. McManus, *Market-Driven Journalism: Let the Citizen Beware?* (Thousand Oaks, CA: Sage, 1994); John Soloski, "Economics and Management: The Real Influence of Newspaper Groups," *Newspaper Research Journal,* 1:19-28 (1979); and Herbert I. Schiller, *Culture Inc.: The Corporate Takeover of Public Expression* (New York: Oxford University Press, 1989).

broadcast news is, for historical and organizational reasons, inherently incapable of providing a portrayal of social change or of displaying the operation of power in and between societies. It thus portrays a world which is unchanging and unchangeable.[37]

U.S. communication scholar Celeste Condit concludes that

We can endlessly generate studies that demonstrate that clever readers can take pleasure in reconstructing texts, but this does not certify that mass communication in general functions as a force for positive social change.[38]

And Canadian scholars Marc Raboy and Bernard Dagenais argue that

As all social institutions, media thrive on stability and are threatened by change. But ... media thrive on "crisis" and are threatened by "normalcy."

The tendency is, therefore, for media to seek out crisis where it does not exist, and to obscure the actual forces of change that threaten media privilege along with entrenched social privilege in general. Paradoxically, this means that media will tend to pay even more attention to a fabricated crisis than to one that can stake a material claim to reality. For social actors, provoking a crisis thus becomes a form of empowerment or social control.[39]

Of course, some media critics acknowledge that news content may, on some occasions, promote the goals or interests of social movements; or that audiences may interpret media messages in a manner that is contrary to the "preferred reading" (which is defined as content that supports the interests of political and economic elites); or that people may use that information to protest against the dominant culture or elite groups. However, the overwhelming focus of critical scholarship has been on how media ignore or criticize the goals of social movements (especially liberal movements), and how the media serve (unwittingly or not) as "social control agents" for powerful

---

[37]Peter Golding, "The Missing Dimensions — News Media and the Management of Social Change," pp. 63-81 in Elihu Katz and Tamás Szecskö, *Mass Media and Social Change* (Beverly Hills, CA: Sage, 1981), p. 80.

[38]Celeste Condit, "The Rhetorical Limits of Polysemy," *Critical Studies in Mass Communication*, 6:103-122 (1994), p. 116.

[39]Marc Raboy and Bernard Dagenais, "Introduction: Media and the Politics of Crisis," pp. 1-15 in Marc Raboy and Bernard Dagenais (eds.), *Media, Crisis and Democracy: Mass Communication and the Disruption of Social Order* (London: Sage, 1992), pp. 3-4.

elites and the institutions they control. Corporate and global media are almost always portrayed as organizations that work to the disadvantage of all except a small group of political and economic elites. Critics believe they can do little to help the cause of social movements. As Gamson puts it:

> Qualifications and nuances notwithstanding, the overall role of media discourse is clear: it often obstructs and only rarely and unevenly contributes to the development of collective action (i.e., social movement) frames. [parenthetical added][40]

These and other critics argue that mass media hinder social change largely because their content tends to have a conservative bias. Political scientist Michael Parenti writes that mass media favor

> management over labor, corporations over corporate critics, affluent whites over inner-city poor, officialdom over protesters, the two-party monopoly over leftist third parties, privatization and free market "reforms" over public sector development, U.S. dominance of the Third World over revolutionary or populist social change, nation-security policy over critics of that policy, and conservative commentators and columnists like Rush Limbaugh and George Will over progressive or populist ones like Jim Hightower and Ralph Nader (not to mention radical ones).[41]

More formally, Golding argues that news is ideological. This is not a conspiracy. Rather, the news is ideological because news organizations must make money and they depend upon elites for the news. News reinforces dominant values and social institutions, which themselves often discriminate against various groups. In short, mass media are seen by most critics as playing more of a social control than a social change function.

In this respect, Disney has been a major target of critics, who argue that much of its programming perpetuates gender, age and racial stereotypes that hinder social progress. Indeed, many of its movies portray women as the weaker sex — as being in need of men who will save them (e.g., *A Bug's Life*). *The Lion King* and many other Disney movies also are criticized for perpetuating aristocratic, patriarchal values. Furthermore, the Disney company is frequently accused of being aloof and unresponsive to criticisms about its programming.

---

[40]William A. Gamson, "Constructing Social Protest," pp. 228-244 in Steven M. Buechler and F. Kurt Cylke, Jr., *Social Movements: Perspectives and Issues* (Mountain View, CA: Mayfield Publishing, 1997), p. 242.

[41]Michael Parenti, "Methods of Media Manipulation," pp. 27-31 in Carl Jensen (ed.), *20 Years of Censored News* (New York: Seven Stories Press, 1997), pp. 27-28.

One group of media theorists was angered when Disney refused to allow them to use the name of their company in their book title.[42]

More generally, critics argue that TV entertainment is inherently oppressive because it makes people forget about the inhumanity of capitalism and the "ruling social order." Some time ago, neo-Marxist theorists Theodore Adorno and Max Horkeimer wrote that

> to be pleased means to say Yes, ... Pleasure always means not to think about anything, to forget suffering even where it is shown. Basically it is helplessness, it is flight; not, as is asserted, flight from a wretched reality, but from the last remaining thought of resistance.[43]

Finally, it should be noted that most contemporary critics acknowledge that social control is never fully achieved — that many disadvantaged and "oppressed" groups fight for social change. However, in the final analysis, these critics see corporate mass media as institutions that help maintain the authority, power and privilege of political and economic elites.

Media Imperialism

International communications scholar Chin-Chuan Lee defines "media imperialism" as consisting of four major elements: television program exportation to foreign countries; foreign ownership and control of media outlets; the transfer of the dominant broadcasting norms and media commercialism; and the invasion of capitalist worldviews and infringement upon the indigenous ways of life in the adopting societies. The United States, he points out, is clearly the leading supplier of global television programs.[44]

Many critics believe the ideas and values promoted in global media are destroying indigenous cultures, especially those not founded on capitalism. This is because the content of global media provides strong support for corporate capitalism and representative democracy. According to Professor Lee:

---

[42]Disney has the legal authority to do this because it owns the trademark to the name. For what it's worth, I also called, wrote and faxed Disney's vice president for community relations to get a response to these criticisms, but I received no reply.

[43]Theodore Adorno and Max Horkeimer, "The Culture Industry: Enlightenment as Mass Deception," pp. 349-383 in James Curran, Michael Gurevitch and Janet Woollacott, *Mass Communication and Society* (Beverly Hills, CA: Sage, 1977), p. 36.

[44]Chin-Chuan Lee, *Media Imperialism Reconsidered* (Beverly Hills, CA: Sage, 1980), p. 176.

The strong presence of sleek foreign media products may take away opportunities that could otherwise be accorded to native artists, writers, and performers. ... Traditional arts and culture (both elite culture and folk culture) may have been on the decline as a result of the social change process. ... It is feared that foreign media have distorted the shared symbolic meaning of society and culture in terms of (1) creating mass frustration, (2) strengthening a "conspicuous consumption" pattern, and (3) fostering a "false consciousness."[45]

To the extent that media promote nonindigenous Western values, critics believe local customs, traditions and authority are threatened. Less developed nations in Africa, South America and Asia are believed to be most vulnerable to Western media. According to Chilean literary critic Ariel Dorfman and former sociologist Armand Mattelart, the threat that The Walt Disney Company represents

derives not so much from their embodiment of the "American Way of Life," as that of the "American Dream of Life." It is the manner in which the U.S. dreams and redeems itself, and then imposes that dream upon others for its own salvation, which poses the danger for the dependent countries. It forces us Latin Americans to see ourselves as they see us.[46]

Ironically, although many Third World nations are very critical of Hollywood, many still broadcast a lot of its programming, partly because it's too expensive to generate original programming. But even Europe, with its own highly developed media systems, feels threatened by American global media. According to European media scholars Kim Christian Schrøder and Michael Skovmand:

It is impossible to discuss transnational media cultures without facing the spectre of Americanisation, as it is still widely believed that if the European countries do not react forcefully and mobilize their rich and diverse cultural potential, we shall be committing spiritual suicide in a flood of Donald Duck Americanisation.[47]

---

[45]The extended quote is from Lee, *Media Imperialism Reconsidered,* p. 178.

[46]Ariel Dorfman and Armand Mattelart, *How To Read Donald Duck: Imperialist Ideology in the Disney Comic* (New York: International General, 1975), p. 95.

[47]Kim Christian Schrøder and Michael Skovmand, "Introduction," pp. 1-14 in Michael Skovmand and Kim Christian Schrøder, *Media Cultures: Reappraising Transnational Media* (London: Routledge, 1992), pp. 5-6.

It also should be pointed out that many neo-Marxist scholars prefer the term *cultural imperialism* to *media imperialism*, because they see most institutions, not just media, as playing a role in reinforcing the Western status quo. Other critics, however, do not like the term imperialism because it implies force or a conspiracy. Instead, they prefer the term *hegemony*, which is usually defined as ideological domination of nonelite groups through control of cultural forms and institutions. But whatever term is used, there is widespread agreement even among mainstream social scientists that Western media are "Westernizing" the world. International communication scholar William Hachten writes:

> Whether this trend toward fewer, bigger, and more like-minded media of global communication is good or bad usually depends on the critic's personal tastes and ideology. But the internationalization of mass communication is proceeding in response to the needs and economic opportunities of a shrinking world. The transnational media are doing more than seizing the chance for greater profits from new markets, albeit those factors are obviously important. Whether viewed as another example of Western "media imperialism" or as a significant contribution to global understanding and integration, the international media are becoming increasingly cosmopolitan, speaking English, and catering to an internationally minded audience concerned about world affairs.[48]

Alienating Workers

Critics accuse global and corporate media of alienating workers. This also may be seen as having an adverse impact on diversity, because media workers may feel less motivated to work and do a good job. But having satisfied, self-fulfilled employees may also be an end in itself.

The logic behind the alienation thesis can be traced in part to the writings of Adam Smith and Karl Marx. They argued that the division of labor associated with large-scale organization created work that is alienating because it involves breaking down complex tasks into a number of simpler, more discrete steps or tasks — tasks that can often be performed by machines and unskilled labor. Routinization of the production process, they argued, makes work more mundane and monotonous.

Although many jobs at corporate media organizations do not involve factory-like motions, corporate media are still believed to be alienating because they (1) have a more complex set of rules and regulations, which critics say

[48]William A. Hachten, *The World News Prism,* 4th ed. (Ames: Iowa State University Press, 1996), p. 86.

gives workers less autonomy, and (2) place less emphasis on cultivating close, interpersonal relationships among employees and bosses. In short, corporate media organizations are "cold" bureaucratic environments that are less concerned about their employees.

PROPOSED SOLUTIONS

Critics have offered a number of different solutions to the problem of global and corporate media. Mass communication scholar Garrett W. Ray summarizes some of them.[49] They include (1) strengthening and enforcing antitrust laws; (2) limiting the number of media outlets that a person or organization can own; (3) restricting ownership across various kinds of media; (4) providing government and private monies to encourage and support noncommercial media; and (5) providing tax incentives to independent media.

Golding suggests that third-world nations should explore more alliances to create and support media systems that offer programming and content alternatives to global media.[50] More radically, some scholars, such as Dennis Mazzocco, have argued that private ownership should be abolished and media be placed under ownership of public, nonprofit foundations.[51] Others have taken this even a step farther and argue that capitalism itself needs to be abandoned.

Lee points out that the crucial difference between neo-Marxist and non-Marxist critics is the difference between revolution and evolution. "Revolution cannot be limited to the media realm alone; it is a redefinition of the relationship between man and society, media and politics." Mainstream critics reject such ideas, and instead advocate a limited approach, one that involves increasing people's understanding of media through the schools, encouraging companies to focus on nonprofit goals, and creating councils that serve as a clearinghouse for people who have complaints against the media.

Although most critical scholars are extremely guarded and pessimistic about the impact of media globalization, some hold out hope that real change is possible. Herman and McChesney write:

---

[49]Garrett W. Ray, "Concentration of Mass Media Ownership," pp. 189-205 in Wm. David Sloan and Emily Erickson Hoff (eds.), *Contemporary Media Issues* (Northport, AL: Vision Press, 1998).

[50]Golding, "Global Village or Cultural Pillage?"

[51]Dennis W. Mazzocco, *Networks of Power: Corporate TV's Threat to Democracy* (Boston: South End Press, 1994).

For the short and medium term we expect both the global market and global commercial media to strengthen their positions worldwide ... . But beyond that the future is very unclear and remains the subject of human political control. ... The global market system has not ushered in a liberal democratic utopia and history is not at an end; quite the reverse, as economic polarization, ethnic strife, and a market-based paralysis of democracy hold forth possibilities of rapid and substantial social, political and economic upheaval. If it is to change, and in a positive way, it is important that people who are dissatisfied with the status quo should not be overcome and rendered truly powerless by a sense of hopelessness and cynicism. As Noam Chomsky said, "If you act like there is no possibility for change, you guarantee that there will be no change."[52]

In sum, many scholars predict that during the 21st century corporate and global media will continue to represent a threat to diversity in the marketplace of ideas, and to good journalism and democratic principles. But are they right?

---

[52]Edward S. Herman and Robert W. McChesney, *The Global Media: The New Missionaries of Corporate Capitalism* (London: Cassell, 1997), p. 205.

Chapter 14

WILL THE CRITICS'
PREDICTIONS COME TRUE?

The guest professor was distinguished looking, which added all the more to his credibility. He had just finished an intellectually challenging lecture on the political economy of the mass media — a neo-Marxist term for describing how corporate or global media are destroying the diversity of ideas, good journalism and democratic principles. Most of the graduate students and faculty in the room were impressed. Except for one.

"Professor, do you think the diversity of ideas in the field of mass communication research has increased or decreased during the last 30 years or so?" Like a cat bumped off a ledge, the seasoned professor landed squarely on his feet. His response drew laughter and admiration from those in the room, but it didn't answer the question.

"But do you think the diversity of ideas in our field has increased or decreased?" Once again the professor dodged the question, drawing more chuckles and admiring glances. "But you still haven't answered the question, professor," the persistent inquirer said. "All things considered, is the field of mass communication more or less diverse in terms of theories, ideas and perspectives today than it was 30 years ago?"

"I guess in some ways it's more diverse and some ways less," the professor said, clearly uncomfortable with the question. He went on for another five minutes. This time the room was silent.[1]

CRITICIZING THE CRITICS

This professor avoided answering the question because he knew the correct answer would punch a hole in his neo-Marxist theory of mass media. His theory like other neo-Marxist theories assume that corporate media, especially

---

[1]The incident described in the introduction to this chapter occurred in the mid-1990s.

267

global media, are incapable of producing content could enhance diversity in the marketplace of ideas — especially content that is critical of powerful institutions, values and capitalism. Why? Because, according to the critics, corporate media are more concerned about profits than people or product quality. The profit motive restricts freedom of expression.

But the historical evidence does not provide strong support for this perspective. In fact, there is little question that the number of ideas and theories about the mass media — especially critical ideas — has grown explosively during the 20th century, particularly in the last 30 years. The professor himself (a person highly critical of the status quo) is evidence of this diversity. For more systematic evidence, one only need spend an hour or two at the library or a large bookstore. Thirty years ago only a handful of scholarly journals in the field of communication were devoted solely to critical scholarship. Today there are more than a dozen, and many mainstream journals now welcome such research. Furthermore, neo-Marxist scholars publish thousands of books every year — so many that now there are a dozen or so publishers around the world that specialize in neo-Marxist, cultural studies and postmodern scholarship. In fact, many academics believe that kind of scholarship is becoming the dominant theoretical approach in the field of communication. As Hamid Mowlana, a internationally recognized authority on global communications, put it:

> The first survey of the state of international communication between 1850 and 1960, which I undertook over two decades ago ... [showed] little work in such areas as cultural analysis, the political economy of communication, discourse analysis, and comparative studies. ... A quarter century later, one is overwhelmed by the amount and extent of research output in international communication with diverse areas of inquiry and highly specialized streams of research.[2]

The fact that neo-Marxist scholarship flourishes in a capitalist system poses significant problems for global media critics. First, there is the problem of explaining how Western political systems can tolerate such critical scholarship,

---

[2]Hamid Mowlana, *Global Communication in Transition: The End of Diversity?* (Thousand Oaks, CA: Sage, 1996), pp. 212-213. Later, he follows it up with the statement: "We should not be deceived by an illusion of the diversity of the subject matter and the vastness of the literature. We need to concentrate on promoting the diversity of cultural views and our ability to make the field more interesting and challenging by exploring new avenues and voices of knowledge." With this comment, he appears to be arguing that diversity is increasing in relative terms but that even more critical research is needed.

much of which accuses capitalists of committing great crimes against people and society. Second, there is the problem of explaining how diversity can decrease in the public sector when it is increasing in the academy. The latter problem is particularly difficult for critics because critical writings and documentaries are increasingly finding their way into mainstream bookstores and libraries.

The failure to recognize and account for the expanding diversity of ideas in our world today is, I believe, the most significant shortcoming in critical models of corporate and global media. But there are other shortcomings, too. The critics have failed to back up many of their claims with sound empirical research; explain social changes that have often benefited groups that challenge tradition or the capitalist system (e.g., women, labor and civil rights organizations); and resolve what economists call the "approved contradiction" — or the illogical notion that professional managers can emphasize profits more than capitalists even though the managers do not benefit as directly from the profits.

The purpose of this chapter is to examine these problems. Before we begin, though, I caution the reader that these shortcomings do not mean all aspects of critical models are wrong. For example, the critics are quite correct when they point out that corporate media, like all mainstream media, produce content and programming that reinforces dominant institutions and value systems. All media serve a master. Whether you refer to this social control function as "media imperialism," "media hegemony" or simply "maintenance of the status quo," the fact remains that mass media content clearly helps to promote social order. Thousands of studies support this proposition, as well as the historical review presented in the first half of this book.

Critical models, I want to emphasize, have contributed a great deal to our understanding of media and society. But the main problem with those models is that they generally have overstated the social control part of the equation and understated the social change component. Let's begin with the diversity issue, and then turn to the other three criticisms.

THE EXPANDING WORLD OF IDEAS

As pointed out in the last chapter, an assumption underlying most theories of democracy is that voters need access to a broad range of ideas and opinions on the issues of the day. Therefore, to resolve the diversity debate, it is necessary to ask: Where do ideas come from?[3]

---

[3]The theory of diversity offered here is based on sociological research and theory

From people, of course. But to be more specific, ideas come from social interaction — that is, from people and organizations communicating with each other, often when they are trying to solve problems.

Think about the last time you tried to solve a problem. It may have been related to work, school, family or even play. It doesn't matter. What does matter is that when you think about the problem, many ideas typically race through your mind. Some simple. Some complex. Some make sense. Some don't. Where did they come from?

Well, some probably came from talking with others. You may have consulted with a spouse, friend, co-worker, boss or even a professor. Or you may have tried to resolve the problem on your own. You may have drawn on your own experiences. Or you may have sought out books, newspaper stories or magazine articles. But even if you relied on yourself, your ideas still had their origins in social interaction, because the experiences you've had and the materials you read are all shaped and produced through social interaction.

Now, if ideas are generated through social interaction, then it stands to reason that if social interaction increases, the number of ideas will increase as well. In other words, if you increase the number of individuals and groups in a society or organization, then isn't it reasonable to argue that the number of ideas will increase? The answer, of course, is "yes." And this theory of ideas can be reformulated in a more precise and mathematical way.

A Structural Theory of Ideas

Recall, if you will, the "quadratic theory of social conflict" presented in the Introduction to this book. The same model may be applied to the production of ideas. If you have two people, you have one potential case or set of ideas at any one point in time. Now let's add one more person to the setting. The number of cases or sets increases to three, because you have three pairs of relationships. When you add a fourth, the potential cases or sets increase to six, and so on.

Mathematically, as you add more people to the setting, the number of ideas increases quadratically, as shown in Figure 14.1. The mathematical equation for this model is quite simple: $[n \times (n-1)]/2$, where n equals the number of social actors. For example, if one has 10 social actors in an organization, the potential for social conflict is $[10 \times (10-1)]/2$, or 90 divided by 2, which equals 45. Without even knowing anything about the psychology of

that extends back to the 19th century. For an extended discussion, see David Pearce Demers, *The Menace of the Corporate Newspaper: Fact or Fiction?* (Ames: Iowa State University Press, 1996).

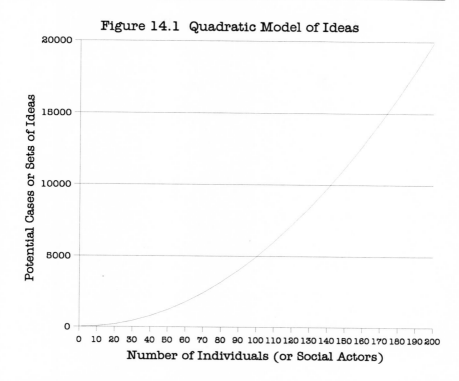

Figure 14.1 Quadratic Model of Ideas

the people involved, you can predict that the potential for new ideas will increase as the number of people increases. In fact, doubling the number of people from three to six actually quintuples the potential for ideas (from 3 to 15).

This model is not a precise measure of the growth of ideas in the real world. For one thing, it doesn't take into account the fact that some people will not interact with each other, some of whom are motivated by choice and others by lack of access. Also, the absolute level of interaction between individuals will decline as the number of individuals increases, so an S-shaped curve would be more realistic for larger social systems. On the other hand, the model underestimates social interaction because it does not account for group interaction, where social actors may serve as agents for social organizations. This, theoretically, would increase the number of ideas.

But, all things being equal, as interaction increases, so does the number of ideas, in absolute as well as relative terms. As noted in the Introduction, there are more "structural opportunities" for people to come into contact to generate ideas.

The "quadratic theory of ideas" presented here explains in part why larger organizations have a greater capacity to adapt to changing conditions. They simply generate more ideas, which increases the probability of finding solutions to problems. Furthermore, if a social system or group encourages people to come up with different ideas, then the number of ideas could be expected to increase even more. And, if these ideas can be recorded in written or electronic form, they can accumulate over time, building an even larger reservoir of ideas and knowledge.

Diversity in the Academy

It's easier to see now why the diversity of ideas has increased so much in the field of mass communication. During the last 30 years or so, the number of mass communication scholars and organizations representing them has grown dramatically (from a handful just before World War II to more than 40,000 worldwide). Fifty years ago you could count on one hand the number of theories and hypotheses about mass communication processes and effects. Today there are literally thousands, covering everything from cognitive processes to institutional and global effects. Some have interesting names: Spiral of Silence, Cultivation Theory, Agenda-Setting Hypothesis, Knowledge-Gap Hypothesis, Priming (cognitive and social), Framing, Mass Media Systems Theory, Discourse Theory, Uses and Gratifications, Media Dependency Theory and Critical Theory.[4]

The growth of these and many other theories in large part stems from an increase in the number of scholars and professional groups representing them, as well as an increase in the number of communications students, who, of course, provide many new ideas. But, as noted above, an increase in the number of social actors is not the only factor. Another is the actual value placed on ideas and diversity themselves. As noted in earlier chapters, historically many religious groups and political rulers discouraged the development of ideas, partly because they were often a threat to their power. Today, however, universities encourage scholars to come up with new ideas and to challenge old ones, and often reward those who do with tenure and pay increases. In fact, professors who don't come up with new ideas will have a difficult time getting

---

[4]Research by W. James Potter, Roger Cooper and Michel Dupagne, "The Three Paradigms of Mass Media Research in Mainstream Communication Journals," *Communication Theory*, 3:317-335 (1993), suggests mainstream social science research continues to dominate in the field of communication. However, neo-Marxist and cultural scholarship makes up about a third of the total amount of research published in major communication journals.

published. The academy places a high value on new ideas, debate and criticism, and these values in turn help promote the development of new ideas and theories.

A third factor enhancing the development of ideas is simply the ability to record them. In other words, there are a lot more ideas and theories around today than in the past because we have the ability to record them in writing and electronic form. Technology, especially electronic, is speeding up the process through which ideas are generated and disseminated. Interestingly, one consequence of the ability to transmit knowledge in writing or in electronic form has been a devaluation of "respect for elders." In ancient times and in traditional cultures, older people were respected in part because they were like walking libraries — they had knowledge (memories) about events that affected the local community. Today, we are more likely to turn to experts, books and libraries for such information, and respect is based less on age than on advanced learning and knowledge. That's one of the reasons polls show that professors and physicians have two of the most prestigious jobs in the system.

Although the diversity of ideas has clearly increased substantially in the academy, there are limits even in the academy. As philosopher of science Thomas S. Kuhn pointed out, scholars who propose radical ideas — outside of the mainstream of science — often have difficulty getting published and are marginalized by other scholars. There are numerous examples of this in the history of natural and social sciences, including Albert Einstein's special theory of relativity. But my point is not that diversity in the academy is tolerated in an absolute sense, because it is not. Rather, diversity is increasing in relative terms, and it is increasing faster than at any time in history.

Diversity in the "Real" World

Now let's apply this theory of diversity to the world outside of the academy, by asking and answering three key questions.

First, have the number of people and groups in the world increased? Of course. The population has grown rapidly over the past century. But just as important has been growth in the number of groups and organizations. Urban, industrial countries are layered with a myriad number of economic, political and social groups. This includes families, places of work, professional organizations, peer groups, neighborhood groups, community groups, churches, political organizations and social organizations. Most people who live in industrial societies belong to many different formal and informal organizations, which also compounds the development of new ideas.

Second, do most societies or nations around the world today encourage ideas? Although many traditional societies and religious groups still discourage ideas — especially those that challenge traditional authorities — it is widely accepted that most urban, industrial societies today are much more tolerant of new ideas, even critical ones, than they were in the past. In fact, new ideas are often encouraged, especially in business. Interestingly, the tolerance in most industrial societies means that even many traditional and nontraditional subcultures can thrive within them. The Amish — a traditional religious group that shuns modern life — is a good example in the United States. Although widely despised, neo-Nazi groups also continue to survive and are not outlawed in most Western countries.

Third, have the number of media and technologies expanded around the world? Incredibly so. The number of mass media and the different forms of communication, such as the telephone, computer, and combinations of the two, accelerate interpersonal and mass communication, feeding the "idea fire" even more. In contrast, 500 years ago there were no media. People had limited contact with each other, which limited ideas. The knowledge they needed to get through everyday life was obtained through experience and contact with others around them.

Diversity in Rural and Urban Areas

The notion that the universe of ideas is expanding as societies grow and become more structurally complex also can be illustrated through a comparison of rural and urban areas within a country or between countries.[5]

Rural areas or communities have small populations and a small number of social, economic and political groups. This "social structure" tends to limit social conflict as well as ideas, especially those critical of the system. If you have ever lived in a small town, you know it usually is not very tolerant of a diversity of ideas, especially liberal ideas. Small towns with universities are sometimes the exception because diversity (of ideas) is highly valued in the academy. Nevertheless, small towns generally embrace more traditional ideas and beliefs, which are not great platforms for radicals or those who wish to challenge the status quo.

One consequence of this relative lack of diversity is that the local weekly or community newspaper usually contains very little news that is critical of

---

[5]The finding that mass media in small communities tend to eschew conflict is documented in a number of studies, including Morris Janowitz, *Community Press in an Urban Setting*, 2nd ed. (Chicago: University of Chicago Press, 1967 [1952]); Phillip J. Tichenor, George A. Donohue and Clarice N. Olien, *Community Conflict and the Press* (Beverly Hills, CA: Sage, 1980); and Arthur J. Vidich and Joseph Bensman, *Small Town in Mass Society* (Princeton, NJ: Princeton University Press, 1968).

people or social institutions. Instead, they are usually filled with "booster" news — social and political news that tends to project a view of the community as harmonious and wholesome. Of course, this does not mean there is no conflict in small towns. There can be and usually is a lot of interpersonal conflict (conflict between individuals) in small towns — proportionately, often just as much as in large cities. However, in relative terms there is a lot less social conflict in small towns (conflict between groups), because they simply have a fewer number of organized groups than larger communities.

In contrast, urban or metropolitan communities are characterized by a large number of social groups, many of which compete for limited social, political and economic resources. In most large cities around the world, you usually can find political groups representing both the extreme right (fascists) and left (communists), as well as the mainstream political parties (such as Democrats and Republicans in the United States). Groups representing the interests of women, minorities, gays, laborers and environmentalists also are in abundant supply in larger systems.

As a consequence of this structural diversity, the news media in metropolitan communities are filled with stories that reflect the conflict, debate and criticism generated in large part by these groups. Although these stories and editorials are often viewed as threatening to the social order, they often play a significant role in contributing to social order because they introduce alternative ideas or innovations that enable organizations and institutions to adapt to changing conditions. As noted earlier in this book, giving challenging groups the right to voice their grievances also is a way of controlling them, because they feel they can make a difference (even if that isn't the case).

The Critics' Response

In response to these arguments, critics often argue that even if the number of ideas is increasing, those ideas are narrowly restricted to the needs of political and economic elites. In other words, the critics see most ideas as serving capitalist goals and ideals.

It is difficult to dispute the fact that many ideas today are generated for the benefit of someone's pocketbook. Most people in the United States live and work in privately owned organizations whose goal is to make a profit from the sale of goods and services in the market. Many needs for information and knowledge are actually derived from such connections to the social system. Moreover, there is no disputing the fact that mainstream corporate media are highly responsive to political and economic centers of power and promote values generally consistent with capitalist ideals and elite interests. Indeed, in absolute terms, corporate and global media may be faulted for failing to challenge some of the more repressive features of Western society, such as ignoring the civil rights movement before the 1950s.

However, the fact that most ideas today generally support existing institutions, values and ways of thinking does not mean there are fewer ideas critical of the status quo, or that people have less access today to them than ever before. If you go into a major bookstore chain, you will find scores of neo-Marxist, cultural studies and postmodern books and reading materials. In fact, some of them, especially in sociology, political science and mass communication, are bestsellers. And check out the lesbian/gay section, the feminist section and the environmental section. If you can't find the time to go to the store, then get online and type in the terms Marxism or postmodernism. Using the search engine Alta Vista, in August 1999 I generated 37,640 references for Marxism and 11,501 for postmodernism. Nineteen months later, in March 2001, I did the search again and produced 158,975 references for Marxism and 562,266 references for postmodernism. In December 2006, I did the search again and found an astonishing 3.9 million references for Marxism and 2.5 million for postmodernism.

Of course, critics will respond that just because there is ample material about Marxism on the Internet doesn't mean that material has an impact. Sure, most people aren't interested in reading that stuff, and, yes, Marxists do not have the same access to resources as major corporations. But the point being made here is that people have more opportunities to access content that is critical of capitalism and mass media than ever before. The information environment now contains millions of new sources that didn't exist a decade ago. Diversity is expanding in relative as well as absolute terms.

WHERE'S THE EMPIRICAL BEEF?

Empirical research provides strong support for the proposition that corporate media, like all forms of media, produce content that contributes to social order. However, the research does not support the notion that corporate media are producing content that is less critical of the status quo than their entrepreneurial counterparts, as is implied by many of the corporate media critics. To the contrary, the empirical evidence overwhelmingly supports the notion that corporate media produce content more critical of dominant institutions and value systems.

Supporting the Status Quo

There is no disputing claims that mainstream media content generally supports dominant institutions, value systems and elite groups. For example, research shows that the flow of information around the world tends to go from economically and politically powerful countries to poor countries. Western mass media, especially media from the United States, Britain and France, have a disproportionate influence in this regard. Research, including my own, also suggests that corporate media are more profitable, because they benefit from economies of scale and have more human and capital resources. They are structurally organized to maximize profits.

A great deal of research provides support for the notion that Western media and global media in particular promote dominant Western values and institutions.[6] Many studies show that mass media rely heavily on bureaucratic, especially governmental, institutions for the news, and they eschew alternative, unorthodox points of view and promote values generally consistent with capitalist ideas and elite interests. One consequence of this is that social problems are usually framed from the perspective of those in power. Agenda-setting studies show that media play an important role in transmitting the political and economic priorities of elites to the masses.

---

[6]David Pearce Demers, *The Menace of the Corporate Newspaper: Fact or Fiction?* (Ames: Iowa State University Press, 1996), pp. 109-114. Evidence backing up the proposition that mass media support the dominant power groups and value systems can be found in numerous studies, including Karen E. Altman, "Consuming Ideology: The Better Homes in America Campaign," *Critical Studies in Mass Communication,* 7:286-307 (1990); J. Herbert Altschull, *Agents of Power* (New York: Longman, 1984); W. Lance Bennett, *News: The Politics of Illusion,* 2nd ed. (New York: Longman, 1988); Robert Cirino, *Power to Persuade* (New York: Bantam Books, 1974); Stanley Cohen and Jock Young (eds.), *The Manufacture of News* (London: Constable, 1981); Edward Jay Epstein, *News From Nowhere* (New York: Random House, 1973); Stuart Ewin, *Captains of Consciousness: Advertising and the Social Roots of the Consumer Culture* (New York: McGraw Hill, 1976); Mark Fishman, *Manufacturing the News* (Austin: University of Texas Press, 1980); Edward S. Herman and Noam Chomsky, *Manufacturing Consent: The Political Economy of the Mass Media* (New York: Pantheon, 1988); Doris A. Graber, *Mass Media and American Politics,* 3rd ed. (Washington, DC: Congressional Quarterly Press, 1989); Herbert J. Gans, *Deciding What's News* (New York: Vintage, 1979); Todd Gitlin, *The Whole World Is Watching* (Berkeley: University of California Press, 1980); Harvey Molotch and Marilyn Lester, "Accidental News: The Great Oil Spill as Local Occurrence and National Event," *American Journal of Sociology,* 81:235-260 (1975); David L. Paletz and Robert M. Entman, *Media Power Politics* (New York: The Free Press, 1981); David L. Paletz, Peggy Reichert and Barbara McIntyre, "How the Media Support Local Government Authority," *Public Opinion Quarterly,* 35:80-92 (1971); Fred Powledge, *The Engineering of Restraint* (Washington, DC: Public Affairs Press, 1971); Leon Sigal, *Reporters and Officials* (Lexington, MA: Heath, 1973); Lawrence C. Soley, "Pundits in Print: 'Experts' and Their Use in Newspaper Stories," *Newspaper Research Journal,* 15(2):65-75 (1994); and Phillip J. Tichenor, George A. Donohue and Clarice N. Olien, *Community Conflict and the Press* (Beverly Hills, CA: Sage, 1980).

Challenging groups also seek to use the media to influence public and elite opinion, but they are often marginalized by elites and, thus, are perceived by the media to be less credible and newsworthy. A number of studies have shown that labor unions receive less favorable news coverage than big business when labor disputes break out. Similarly, Vietnam War protestors were almost always portrayed as spoiled brats who needed old-fashioned discipline. Groups that are perceived as being outside of the mainstream also tend to get less favorable coverage in the news. Contrary to the watchdog metaphor, studies show that most journalists identify very strongly with the governmental news sources they cover. And international news tends to have a strong pro-Western bias.

Studies of television programs indicate that institutionalized groups, such as the police, are usually portrayed humanely and sympathetically, whereas other characters are portrayed in negative ways. Media avoid discussing class conflict issues, and media owners clearly have strong business ties to other powerful governmental agencies and corporations. In short, as a general rule, the greater the power of a group or organization, the greater its ability to get favorable coverage in the mainstream media.

However, this proposition doesn't mean that media coverage becomes less critical of the power structure or that diversity of ideas decreases as media become more corporatized, or structurally complex. In fact, the empirical evidence shows just the opposite.

Lack of Empirical Evidence

To support their case that corporate structure is have an adverse impact on diversity or content, critics rely almost exclusively on case studies or anecdotes, such as the ones in the last chapter about ABC and CBS. Although these incidents appear to provide support for their argument, the problem with using case studies and anecdotes is that they may not be representative of the entire population of media. Comparative research (cross-sectional or historical) and probability research, which are much stronger methods for assessing the impact of corporate structure, are simply lacking. As international communications researchers Lars Willnat, Zhou He and Hao Xiaoming point out:

> [T]he theory of cultural imperialism ... assumes that Western cultural products have deleterious effects on indigenous cultures because of their one-way flow from the West and the undesirable, foreign values

embodied in those products. This approach, though rhetorically powerful and political attractive, has gathered only limited empirical support.[7]

Indeed, Willnat and his colleagues point out that cross-sectional studies, including their own research, show that audiences in developing countries often interpret Western television programs differently from their counterparts in the West and read new meanings into the messages. Consumption of foreign media also does not necessarily lead to a favorable foreign cultural orientation. Moreover, after reviewing the empirical literature on "cultural imperialism," mass communication researcher Michael B. Salwen, concluded that

> we can readily discard the broad claim that exposure to Western media alone will cause foreign peoples to shed their cultural identities and values and adopt Western values. At the very least, factors inherent within cultures, such as gender roles, account for different responses to foreign media messages ... . Indeed, some of the empirical studies suggest active resistance to foreign media messages in some instances. ... Finally, the empirical studies suggest not only negative effects but positive ones as well, such as the "liberation" of women in male-dominated cultures ... and increased cultural exchange ... .[8]

One of the most comprehensive surveys of the empirical literature before 2000, which was conducted by mass communication scholars Michael Elasmar and John Hunter, concluded:

> Based on the concept that foreign TV programs embody a tool of cultural imperialism, we had expected our meta-analysis to reveal that foreign television programs have strong effects on the domestic audience members who view them. The results summarized above reveal that this is not the case. At most, foreign TV exposure may have a very weak impact upon audience members. This result contradicts the assertions of Herbert Schiller and his colleagues, who have long warned against the dangers of cultural imperialism.[9]

---

[7]Lars Willnat, Zhou Hje and Hao Xiaoming, "Foreign Media Exposure and Perceptions of Americans in Hong Kong, Shenzhen, and Singapore," *Journalism & Mass Communication Quarterly*, 74:738-756 (1998), pp. 738-739.

[8]Michael B. Salwen, "Cultural Imperialism: A Media Effects Approach," *Critical Studies in Mass Communication*, 8:29-38 (1991), p. 36.

[9]Michel Elasmar and John Hunter, "The Impact of Foreign TV on a Domestic Audience: A Meta-Analysis," pp. 47-69 in *Communication Yearbook, Vol. 20* (Thousand Oaks, CA: Sage, 1997), p. 64.

Salwen concedes that repeated exposure to Western media messages over long periods of time may "subtly alter cultural values." Indeed, Elasmar and Hunter found that exposure to foreign TV leads people in foreign countries to purchase more foreign products, to hold values similar to those in the country producing the foreign message, and to acquire beliefs about the country originating the message. A survey of Filipino high school students by international mass communication researchers Alex S. Tan, Gerdean K. Tan and Alma S. Tan also found that American television programs have a small effect in terms of eroding traditional Filipino values.[10] Alex Tan argues that Western entertainment programming offers images of a "better life" to which the poor in developing countries may aspire. Thus, to say that Western media content has no effect is misleading. However, the impact of those media may be declining.

In 2007, Oxford University Press published British sociologist Jeremy Tunstall's latest book, *The Media Were American*, which argues that U.S. and Western global media are losing their impact because of the growth of indigenous and national media in many non-Western countries around the world. The book follows up on his 1977 book, *The Media Are American*, which argued that U.S. media dominated the global scene in the mid-20th century. However, his new book argues that the United States lost much of its dominance over the last 40 years.

> Instead of sole American control of the world news flow, we now see a world media structure comprised of interlocking national, regional, and cultural systems. ... China and India ... and ... the ... rise of the mass media in the Muslim world. ... Reconsidering the very notion of "global media," the book posits a reemergence of stronger national cultures and national media systems.[11]

In the book's Introduction, Tunstall points out that

> Most people around the world prefer to be entertained by people who look the same, talk the same, joke the same, behave the same, play the same games, and have the same beliefs (and worldview) as themselves.

---

[10]Alexis S. Tan, Gerdean K. Tan and Alma S. Tan, "American TV in the Philippines: A Test of Cultural Impact," *Journalism Quarterly, 64*:65-72, 144 (1987).

[11]Jeremy Tunstall, *The Media Were American: U.S. Mass Media in Decline* (Oxford: Oxford University Press, 2008). The quoted material is from the back cover of the book, which provided the best summary. Copies of the book were distributed to reviewers early in 2007.

They also overwhelmingly prefer their own national news, politics, weather, and football and other sports.

Many people have argued that the media have become globalized and Americanized. This book points to the resilience and (probably) increasing strength of national culture, national sentiment, and national media — especially in the Asian and other countries where most of the world's people happen to live. ...

A global or world level of media certainly does exist. But world media, or American media, play a much smaller role than national media.[12]

Tunstall's book is perhaps the most important historical, empirical study of global media ever produced. The only major shortcoming is that the book does not provide a theory to explain the changes that are taking place, a topic that will be explored in the next four chapters of this book.

Critics of corporate media also have failed to produce sound empirical evidence to support their claims that corporate media are greedier or that maximizing profits leads to a lower-quality product or threatens democracy. There is no novelty in the argument that profit-making is an important goal of corporate and global media organizations, as it is an important goal wherever media are supported by private sources of capital. Thus, the key questions are not whether corporate or global media are profit-oriented, but whether they, as a unique form of social organization, place more emphasis on profits than entrepreneurial or not-for-profit media and whether the content of corporate media has an adverse impact on democratic processes or good journalism. In other words, to understand the impact that global media are having, researchers need to conduct comparative studies, which means studying changes over time (historical research) or comparing the differences between groups (corporate vs. entrepreneurial media).

But critics rarely conduct comparative studies or study entrepreneurial media.[13] Consequently, they have a self-generated illusion that profit-making is the only goal or the most important goal of corporate and global media. In addition, critics have never been able to provide convincing evidence that corporatization or globalization of media systems inhibit social change or produce more highly dissatisfied employees. In fact, most critical models are unable to account for social change.

---

[12]Ibid, p. xiv.

[13]One exception is Mowlana's study, discussed earlier in this chapter, which showed that diversity of research on international communication increased dramatically in the quarter century.

What Comparative Research Shows

In contrast, empirical research strongly suggests that some media (e.g., newspapers) become more critical of the status quo as they acquire the characteristics of the corporate form of organization. For example, one comprehensive review of the literature in the mid-1990s found that only three of 18 studies which examined the impact of ownership on editorial vigor supported the position of the corporate critics. Eight found that corporate newspapers were more vigorous editorially than independent newspapers and seven had mixed findings or no differences.[14] Prior to this study, journalism professor Gerald Stone had already concluded from his review of the literature that there is

> no consistent documentation that group ownership of newspapers is inherently bad. The chief changes likely to occur with chain ownership are related to economic considerations, primarily: Chains have a distinct economic advantage derived from their experience and expertise in management, marketing and use of the economies of scale. Evidence is that this financial planning sophistication can make newspapers more profitable businesses without debasing the journalistic product.[15]

My own research on U.S. daily newspapers during the 1990s and early 2000s supports Stone's conclusions. In those studies I surveyed editors, reporters and publishers through national probability surveys.[16] Drawing on Max Weber's writings (see Chapter 4), I measured corporate structure as a continuous variable composed of 12 individual items, including structural complexity (number of employees/journalists/news beats; number of promotions a reporter needs to become the publisher); rules and procedures (does newspaper have written code of ethics and employee handbook); ownership structure (chain ownership, public ownership, family ownership, legal incorporation); staff expertise (college degree required to be reporter); and emphasis placed on rationality (efficiency) as an organizational goal. My surveys also measured the amount of emphasis that the organization places on profits, product quality, and a host of other organizational goals.

---

[14]My summary of the 18 studies is contained in David Pearce Demers, *The Menace of the Corporate Newspaper: Fact or Fiction?* (Ames: Iowa State University Press, 1996), p. 234-236.

[15]Gerald Stone, *Examining Newspapers: What Research Reveals About America's Newspapers* (Newbury Park, CA: Sage, 1987), pp. 103-104.

[16]See footnote 286 for a full list of citations.

My research has consistently found that newspapers place less emphasis on profits and more emphasis on product quality as they become corporatized.[17] More important, my data also show that newspapers become more vigorous editorially as they become more corporatized. The greater the "corporatization," the greater the number and proportion of editorials and letters to the editor that are critical of "mainstream" authorities, institutions and values. A study I conducted of news sources also supports the argument that corporate media are more critical of dominant institutions and value systems. I hypothesized that mainstream news sources in communities served by highly corporatized newspapers would perceive news coverage in those papers to be more critical of them and their policies than sources in communities served by less corporatized newspapers. A national probability survey of mayors and police chiefs in 200 U.S. communities supported the hypothesis. The more corporatized the newspaper, the more the mainstream sources perceived that newspaper to be critical of them and their policies and the more biased and less fair they perceived that newspaper's coverage.

---

[17]David Pearce Demers, *The Menace of the Corporate Newspaper: Fact or Fiction?* (Ames: Iowa State University Press, 1996); David Demers, "Corporate Newspaper Structure, Social Control and Social Change," pp. 375-398 in David Demers and K. Viswanath (eds.), *Mass Media, Social Control and Social Change: A Macrosocial Perspective* (Ames: Iowa State University Press, 1999); David Demers, "Corporate Newspaper Bashing: Is It Justified?" *Newspaper Research Journal* (in press); David Demers, "Structural Pluralism, Corporate Newspaper Structure and News Source Perceptions: Another Test of the Editor Vigor Hypothesis," *Journalism & Mass Communication Quarterly,* 75:572-592 (1998); David Pearce Demers, "Corporate Newspaper Structure, Profits and Organizational Goals," *The Journal of Media Economics,* 9(2):1-23 (1996); David Demers, "Revisiting Corporate Newspaper Structure and Profit-Making," *Journal of Media Economics,* 11(2):19-35 (1998); David Pearce Demers, "Corporate Newspaper Structure, Editorial Page Vigor and Social Change. *Journalism & Mass Communication Quarterly,* 73:857-877 (1996); David Pearce Demers, "Use of Polls in Reporting Changes Slightly Since 1978," *Journalism Quarterly,* 64:839-842 (1987); David Pearce Demers, "Corporate Structure and Emphasis on Profits and Product Quality at U.S. Daily Newspapers," *Journalism Quarterly,* 68:15-26 (1991); David Pearce Demers, "Effect of Corporate Structure on Autonomy of Top Editors at U.S. Dailies," *Journalism Quarterly,* 70:499-508 (1993); David Pearce Demers, "The Relative Constancy Hypothesis, Structural Pluralism and National Advertising Expenditures," *Journal of Media Economics,* 7(4):31-48 (1994); David Pearce Demers, "Structural Pluralism, Intermedia Competition and the Growth of the Corporate Newspaper in the United States," *Journalism Monographs, Vol. 145* (June 1994); David Pearce Demers, "Does Personal Experience in a Community Increase or Decrease Newspaper Reading?" *Journalism Quarterly,* 73:304-318 (1996); and David Pearce Demers and Daniel B. Wackman, "Effect of Chain Ownership on Newspaper Management Goals," *Newspaper Research Journal,* 9(2):59-68 (1988).

The finding that corporate newspapers are more editorially vigorous also has found support in four more recent studies by mass communication scholars. In 2005, Timothy Ball concluded that the findings on quality and corporate structure can be extended to not-for-profit public television stations. The more structurally complex a public television station, the more emphasis it places on producing a high-quality product and the more resources it has to produce high-quality programming.[18] In 2006, Masahiro Yamamoto found that larger (corporate) newspapers were far more likely than their smaller entrepreneurial counterparts to write editorials supporting gay rights and gay marriage (i.e., to support liberal values that are still outside of the mainstream values in America).[19]

Linda De Lisle conducted a nonprobability survey in 2006 and found that editorials published in newspapers in more pluralistic communities (i.e., in "corporate" newspapers) provided a greater diversity of ideas when it came to the issue of breaching dams along the Snake River in Washington state than newspapers in less complex communities.[20] In Fall 2006, Tae-hyun Kim conducted a national probability survey and found that structurally complex newspapers were much more editorially vigorous when it came to writing editorials about global warming. In other words, they published more editorials about global warming and the position in those editorials was more critical of the power structure (i.e., more critical of President George Bush's administration) and more supportive of the environmental movement.[21]

This research coincides with other studies which show that journalists from corporate newspapers are more likely than those at entrepreneurial newspapers to emphasize an active, interpretive, investigative and critical role for the news media. Mass communication researcher George Gladney reported that editors at large circulation newspapers — which is an acceptable proxy measure of corporate structure — were more likely than those at small newspapers to rate "editorial courage" and "editorial independence" as primary indicators of

[18]Timothy Clark Ball, "The Public Broadcasting System: A Survey of Organizational Structure, Quality Programming and Organizational Goals," unpublished Ph.D. dissertation (Washington State University, June 2004).

[19]Masahiro Yamamoto, "Corporate Newspaper Structure and Same-Sex Marriage: An Empirical Test of the Editorial Page Vigor Hypothesis," unpublished master's thesis (Washington State University, August 2006).

[20]Linda De Lisle, "Structural Pluralism and Editorial Page Representation," unpublished master's thesis (Washington State University, May 2006). The correlation was .39.

[21]The zero-correlation was .47. Tae-hyun Kim, "Corporate Newspaper Structure, Global Warming and the Editorial Vigor Hypothesis," unpublished Ph.D. dissertation (Washington State University, July 2007).

newspaper excellence.[22] Media scholar Roya Akhavan-Majid and her colleagues concluded that editors of chain-owned newspapers are more likely than their independent counterparts to emphasize an active, interpretive, investigative and critical role for the press, and support for these values increased as the size of the chain increased.[23] Newspaper researcher Randall Beam found that newspapers which employ a strong market-oriented management style (a characteristic of corporate structure) are more likely than those that employ a weak market-oriented style to endorse an adversarial role for journalists and to profess a commitment to publishing an excellent journalistic product and public affairs content.[24]

The criticism that corporate and global organizations treat employees unfairly also isn't well documented.[25] Although job satisfaction among print journalists has declined since the 1970s — a trend that may reflect increasing uneasiness about the future of the industry and diminishing opportunities for advancement in news organizations — my surveys show that journalists at corporate newspapers continue to be much more satisfied and that editors at corporate newspapers actually have more, not less, autonomy.[26] The journalists at corporate newspapers are more satisfied because they pay their employees higher salaries and generally give them more autonomy. The increased autonomy is partly a function of the division of labor and role specialization. As the organization grows and managers are managing more people, they have less direct control over any particular employee's daily work. At corporate newspapers, the owners and publishers actually play a smaller and smaller role in day-to-day decisions regarding news content, and editorial editors play a

---

[22]George A. Gladney, "Newspaper Excellence: How Editors of Small and Large Papers Judge Quality," *Newspaper Research Journal*, 11(2):58-72 (1990).

[23]Roya Akhavan-Majid, Anita Rife and Sheila Gopinath, "Chain Ownership and Editorial Independence: A Case Study of Gannett Newspapers," *Journalism Quarterly*, 68:59-66 (1991).

[24]Randall A. Beam, "The Impact of Group Ownership Variables on Organizational Professionalism at Daily Newspapers," *Journalism Quarterly*, 70:907-918 (1993).

[25]Research on job satisfaction can be found in David H. Weaver and G. Cleveland Wilhoit, *The American Journalists: A Portrait of U.S. News People and Their Work* (Bloomington: Indiana University Press, 1986) and G. Cleveland Wilhoit and David Weaver, "U.S. Journalists at Work, 1971-1992," paper presented to the Association for Education in Journalism and Mass Communication (Atlanta, August 1994).

[26]Support for the claim that journalists are more satisfied with their jobs can be found in David Pearce Demers, "Effect of Organizational Size on Job Satisfaction of Top Editors at U.S. Dailies," *Journalism Quarterly*, 71:914-925 (1994) and David Pearce Demers, "Autonomy, Satisfaction High Among Corporate News Staffs," *Newspaper Research Journal*, 16(2), 91-111 (1995).

greater role. Also, role specialization enables some journalists to become "experts" in various areas, which in turn reduces even further the ability of their manager to control their work.

Research also shows that corporate organizations promote women and minorities more quickly than entrepreneurial organizations. Disney, for example, pays benefits to same-sex partners, which has irked some conservative religious organizations. And even though corporate newspapers may be staffed with editors who have fewer ties to the local community, there is no evidence to support claims that it leads to a breakdown in social order in the community. In fact, corporate newspapers, which appear to place more emphasis on nonlocal news, may help integrate local communities into larger, more complex or global social systems. This, in turn, can help these communities adapt to political, economic and social change.[27]

Unfortunately, critics of corporate and global media systems routinely ignore and rarely cite research that contradicts their ideas. In this regard, their epistemology more closely resembles a religious doctrine than science. Some even argue that reason and logic are the only criteria that should be used to validate ideas or theories, but as is shown subsequently, even there they have failed to address some theoretical problems associated with the critical model.[28]

WHAT ABOUT SOCIAL CHANGE?

One of the hallmarks of modern society — if not its identifying feature — is social change. If we conceptually define social change as the difference between current and antecedent conditions in the social structure (which I define as including not only the enduring patterns of social relationships but also values, norms, laws and social goals, which serve to establish and maintain

---

[27]Technically, my research cannot be applied to other media systems or to other countries. There are many difficulties in studying communication processes across media industries and at a global level. However, my research does call into question some key aspects of critical models. For example, although Frank A. Munsey, the U.S. newspaper owner who built a chain of newspapers during the early 1900s, profited substantially from his newspaper transactions, he also published *Munsey's Magazine*, a mass-circulation muckraking publication that crusaded against corruption and social injustice. Mass communication historians Jean Folkerts and Dwight Teeter also point out that when Munsey merged newspapers, he often strengthened them. Most of his $20 million fortune, by the way, was willed to New York's Metropolitan Museum of Art. See Jean Folkerts and Dwight L. Teeter, Jr., *Voices of a Nation: A History of the Media in the United States.* (New York: Macmillan, 1989).

[28]I, too, place primacy on reason and logic when developing theories of mass media. But I believe that empirical research and observation can help sort good ideas from bad.

such relationships), then most scholars would agree that many social changes have taken place in the United States during the last century. But none of the critical models adequately accounts for social change and the role of mass media.

As noted in the last chapter, the critics assume that as media become more corporatized, the more they promote the interests of their owners and other corporate and business elites. Corporate or global media are expected to have less capacity to publish information that challenges or questions dominant ideas and institutions. Of course, many critics acknowledge that news content may, on some occasions, promote the goals or interests of social movements; or that audiences may interpret media messages in a manner that is contrary to the "preferred reading" (which is defined as content that supports the interests of political and economic elites); or that people may use that information to protest against the dominant culture or elite groups. Scott Robert Olson, for example, writes about indigenous cultures in Africa and Asia that seek to "maintain or create an identity" in a global media world.

> The films and television programs of the global mass media, seeking to use identity to produce consumers, send out the following hail: "Here is your identity! To be yourself, consume these products!" Nationalist media have another message: "Agree to this or be destroyed." But audiences haggle back: "I see my identity there in your media, all right, but it's for me to say what it means and how I'll use it."
>
> They meet in the middle. Identity becomes both imported and projected, and that makes it more fluid than it has ever been in the past. ... The ongoing question for groups wishing to resist imported media ... is how to direct those oppositional readings in ways that abet the indigenous culture, directing identity into useful mutation ... .[29]

However, the overwhelming focus of critical scholarship has been on how corporate mass media ignore or criticize the interests and goals of indigenous peoples and social movements (mostly liberal social movements), and how the media serve (unwittingly or not) as "social control agents" for powerful elites and the institutions they control. Indeed, corporate and global media are almost always portrayed as organizations that work to the disadvantage of all except a small group of political and economic elites. Even when investigative news

---

[29]Scott Robert Olson, "Contaminations and Hybrids: Indigenous Identify and Resistance to Global Media," *Studies in Media & Information Literacy Education,* 2(2) (2002), paragraphs 38-39, available online at <www.utpress.utoronto.ca/journal/ejournals/simile>, accessed February 23, 2007.

reporting uncovers wrongdoing and the political system makes statutory changes that benefit the disadvantaged, critics typically see this as an anomaly that has virtually little or no impact on changing power structures, even in the long run.

Here, for example, is how Olson ends his article.

> Identities are contaminant and contaminated. In a world of global media, the future of every national identity is a hybrid ... The global media tell the stories we've heard before and want to hear again. In doing so, the foreign becomes a part of us. We are contaminated. We are hybrids.

The assumption clearly is that global media have done something bad; they have "contaminated" us, even when we reject their messages and seek to build our own identities. The writings of media studies scholar James Lull also exhibit ambiguity over the relationship between people and corporate media.

> Social change, the defining characteristic of world history, unmistakably demonstrates that ideology is negotiated and contested, not imposed and assumed. Individual persons, social groups, nations, and cultures should not be considered victims of dominant social forces. We must conclude that the media/cultural imperialism thesis ... is not wrong but incomplete. Furthermore, the more complex theory of ideological and cultural hegemony — wherein institutional forces are said to converge on behalf of the vested interests of society's political-economic elite — is also ultimately unsatisfying. ...
>
> The other side of the coin is popular resistance to dominant ideology and culture. But, just as social institutions including mass media cannot completely control their audiences, the autonomy and power of individuals and subjugated groups is also limited. *For this reason I do not want to argue completely against the essential line of reasoning that underlies theories of imperialism or hegemony.*[30] (Emphasis added)

Thus, the argument here is that the media are still agents of control and individuals are capable of contesting or resisting that control.

---

[30]James Lull, *Media, Communication Culture: A Global Approach* (New York: Columbia University Press, 1995), pp. 166-167. Over the past 30 years it appears that critical theorists have become less critical

Mass Media as Agents of Reform

A better way to conceptualize the role and function of mass media to is see them as both agents of reform. One would be hard-pressed to argue that media are radical agents of change. The only possible exception to that rule, as noted in earlier chapters, is the American Revolution, when the "patriot" press played a key role in mobilizing and informing the colonists. But empirical research on mass media clearly supports the idea that mass media can play a reformist role, and one that benefits not just elites but the poor and other disadvantaged groups. In fact, the reformist role helps explain, in turn, the stability and durability of capitalism as an economic institution.[31]

As noted in the previous chapters of this book, mainstream mass media and corporate media in particular have played an important role in legitimating and sometimes facilitating (though rarely initiating) the goals of many social movements, which in turn have led to a number of social changes. The most notable example of this occurred at the turn of the century, with the rise of the so-called "muckrakers," who were responding to the Progressive Movement. Media in Western nations also have played a role in legitimating decisions from the courts and government that expanded rights and opportunities for women, minorities, the working class, environmentalists, homosexuals, and the poor.

---

[31]For a review of the literature on social change, see David Pearce Demers, *The Menace of the Corporate Newspaper: Fact or Fiction?* (Ames: Iowa State University Press, 1996), pp. 109-114. For a discussion of social changes that have taken place in the United States during the 20th century, see L. W. Banner, *Women in Modern America: A Brief History,* 2nd ed. (Orlando, FL: Harcourt Brace Jovanovich, 1984); R. Blauner, "The Ambiguities of Racial Change," pp. 54-64 in M. L. Andersen and P. H. Collins (eds), *Race, Class, and Gender* (Belmont, CA: Wadsworth, 1992); Celeste M. Condit, "Hegemony in a Mass-Mediated Society: Concordance about Reproductive Technologies," *Critical Studies in Mass Communication,* 11:205-230 (1994); J. R. Howard, *The Cutting Edge: Social Movements and Social Change in America* (Philadelphia: J. B. Lippincott, 1974); R. H. Lauer (ed.), *Social Movements and Social Change* (Carbondale: Southern Illinois University Press, 1976); D. McAdam, J. D. McCarthy, and N. Z. Mayer, "Social Movements," pp. 695-737 in N. J. Smelser (ed.), *Handbook of Sociology* (Newbury Park, CA: Sage, 1988). For additional evidence of the media's role in social change see Donald L. Barlett and James B. Steele, *America: What Went Wrong?* (Kansas City: Andrew and McMeel, 1992); Leonard Downie, Jr., *The New Muckrakers* (New York: Mentor, 1976); Mark Neuzil and William Kovarik, *Mass Media and Environmental Conflict: America's Green Crusades* (Thousand Oaks, CA: Sage, 1996); David L. Protess, Fay Lomax Cook, Jack C. Doppelt, James S. Ettema, Margaret T. Gordon, Donna R. Leff and Peter Miller, *The Journalism of Outrage: Investigative Reporting and Agenda-Building in America* (New York: Guilford Press, 1991); and Leonard Sellers, *Investigative Reporting: Methods and Barriers* (Ph.D. Diss., Stanford, 1977).

Such changes certainly have not eliminated inequalities, discrimination or injustices, but they have significantly altered the power structure in most Western countries during the 20th century.[32]

Although journalists tend to support the dominant system of values, research shows that they generally are more liberal than elites, as well as the general public, on a wide variety of social and political issues.[33] These findings suggest that media have the capacity at times to produce content that is critical of dominant groups and beneficial to disadvantaged groups. Polls and historical research show that conservatives are more critical than liberals of investigative reporting and that journalists often are sensitive to the concerns of minorities and consumers groups, are critical of business, and believe that private business is profiting at the expense of Third World countries.[34] One analysis of U.S. network television news coverage of Latin America also failed to produce evidence of a conservative, status-quo bias.[35] Media reports also helped to legitimize rural protest groups in Minnesota, whose goal was to block construction of a power line that would serve a large, Midwestern metropolitan area.[36] Studies often find that media coverage influences governmental policy at the national level[37] as well as the local.[38] And a recent study found that, contrary to the expectations of the researcher, media coverage of separate protest marches in Washington sponsored by gay and lesbian organizations and

---

[32]Herbert Gans, *Popular and High Culture* (New York: Basic Books, 1999). Gans argues that elite or high culture is on the decline in American society.

[33]John W. C. Johnstone, Edward J. Slawski, and William W. Bowman, *The News People: A Sociological Portrait of American Journalists and Their Work* (Urbana, IL: University of Illinois Press, 1976); David Shaw, "Public and Press — Two Viewpoints," *Los Angeles Times* (August 11, 1985); and David H. Weaver and G. Cleveland Wilhoit, *The American Journalist: A Portrait of U.S. News People and Their Work* (Bloomington, IN: Indiana University Press, 1986).

[34]S. Robert Lichter and Stanley Rothman, "Media and Business Elites, " *Public Opinion Quarterly,* 4:42-6 (1981).

[35]W. Q. Morales, "Revolutions, Earthquakes, and Latin America: The Networks Look at Allende's Chile and Somoza's Nicaragua," pp. 79-116 in W. C. Adams (ed.), *Television Coverage of International Affairs* (Norwood, NJ: Ablex, 1982).

[36]The state supreme court eventually allowed construction of the power line, after which the media coverage of the protest groups took on a more negative tone. See Olien, Donohue and Tichenor, "Media and Stages of Social Conflict."

[37]For review, see David L. Altheide, *Media Power* (Beverly Hills, CA: Sage, 1985). Also see Wayne Wanta, Mary Ann Stephenson, Judy VanSlyke Turk and Maxwell E. McCombs, "How President's State of Union Talk Influenced News Media Agendas," *Journalism Quarterly,* 66:537-41 (1989).

[38]David Pritchard, "Homicide and Bargained Justice: The Agenda-Setting Effect of Crime News on Prosecutors," *Public Opinion Quarterly,* 50:143-59 (1986).

pro-choice groups were much more favorable than unfavorable to each of those challenging groups.[39]

Although media need a consistent, inexpensive supply of news and depend heavily on political and economic elites for the news,[40] it is also important to point out that elites depend heavily on the media to achieve their goals. It is widely agreed, for example, that a state or national politician cannot be elected today without effective media coverage. Candidates rely less and less on the political party machine and more and more on direct coverage in media to get elected. This dependence, in turn, has lessened to some extent the power of the traditional political parties.

Although ownership of newspapers is becoming more centralized (i.e., reduction in number of owners), to date there is little evidence showing that this has led to a reduction in message diversity[41] or that other media sectors, like magazines and broadcast television stations, are experiencing the same trends.[42] In fact, some studies have found that media in larger, more pluralistic communities cover a broader range of topics and contain more news.[43] A systems perspective is that current declines in newspaper circulation and national network television penetration reflect increasing differentiation of the social structure and that such differentiation nevertheless can, under some circumstances, promote increased criticism of established institutions and greater diversity in media content.[44] For example, even though research shows that small, community newspapers often omit news that is critical of

---

[39]J. R. Ballinger, "Media Coverage of Social Protest: An Examination of Media Hegemony," paper presented to the Association for Education in Journalism and Mass Communication, Kansas City, MO. (August 1993).

[40]See, e.g., Fishman, *Manufacturing the News,* and Tuchman, *Making News.*

[41]See, e.g., Benjamin Compaine, "The Expanding Base of Media Competition, *Journal of Communication,* 35(3):81-96 (1985) and Maxwell McCombs, "Effect of Monopoly in Cleveland on Diversity of Newspaper Content, *Journalism Quarterly,* 64:740-4,792 (1987).

[42]Compaine, Sterling, Guback and Noble, *Who Owns the Media.* See chapter on magazine industry, which actually grew during the 1970s. D. Waterman, "A New Look at Media Chains and Groups: 1977-1989," *Journal of Broadcasting & Electronic Media,* 35:167-78 (1991).

[43]W. R. Davie and J. Lee, "Television News Technology: Do More Sources Mean Less Diversity?" *Journal of Broadcasting & Electronic Media,* 37:453-64 (1993), and Donohue, Olien, and Tichenor, "Reporting Conflict by Pluralism, Newspaper Type and Ownership."

[44]David Pearce Demers, "Corporate Newspaper Structure and Editorial Page Vigor," paper presented to the International Communication Association (Albuquerque, NM, May 1995) and David Pearce Demers, "Effects of Competition and Structural Pluralism on Centralization of Ownership in the U.S. Newspaper Industry," paper presented to the Association for Education in Journalism (Minneapolis, August 1990).

established institutions and elites, media in more pluralistic communities are much more likely to publish news that is critical of elites or conflict-oriented.[45]

Another study showed that veteran reporters at mainstream newspapers can write stories that challenge components of the dominant ideology.[46] Studying Canadian press coverage of disarmament, peace and security issues, another reported that commentaries, columns and op-ed pieces often challenged the dominant view of bureaucrats.[47] And a study of the press in India suggests that the news media have the potential to challenge the status quo.[48] The researcher found that such challenges may not be direct or comprehensive, but some kinds of news stories may represent a challenge indirectly by contributing, for example, to public awareness of problems with the status quo, which in turn can promote discontent and support for social change.

Research also shows that alternative media often challenge dominant ideologies and contribute to mobilizing and promoting social movements or causes. Challenging the arguments of the "routines theorists,"[49] one participant observation study found that reporters at an alternative radio station could create oppositional news using conventional routines and reportorial techniques.[50] A historical review reported that alternative media have helped to promote the American revolution, abolitionism, and equality for women, minorities, and gay rights groups.[51] And even though one study discussed earlier found that the mainstream mass media marginalize anarchist groups, the study also found that the alternative press idolized them.[52]

Although social control is one of the major functions of media, it does not explain the origins and nature of media themselves.[53] As noted earlier, a basic

---

[45]Donohue, Olien and Tichenor, "Reporting Conflict by Pluralism, Newspaper Type and Ownership," and Tichenor, Donohue and Olien, *Community Conflict and the Press.*

[46]M. Meyers, "Reporters and Beats: The Making of Oppositional News," *Critical Studies in Mass Communication, 9:*75-90 (1992).

[47]P. Bruck, "Strategies for Peace, Strategies for News Research," *Journal of Communication, 39(*1):108-29 (1989).

[48]Hemant Shah, "News and the "Self-Production of Society," *Journalism Monographs, Vol. 144* (April 1994).

[49]See e.g., Epstein, *News From Nowhere;* Gitlin, *The Whole World Is Watching;* Schudson, "The Politics of Narrative Form"; and Sigel, *Reporters and Officials.*

[50]N. Eliasoph, "Routines and the Making of Oppositional News," *Critical Studies in Mass Communication, 5:*313-34 (1988).

[51]John Downing, "Alternative Media and the Boston Tea Party, " pp. 180-191 in John Downing, Ali Mohammadi and Annabelle Sreberny-Mohammadi (eds.), *Questioning the Media* (Newbury Park: Sage, 1990).

[52]McLeod and Hertog, "The Manufacture of 'Public Opinion' by Reporters."

[53]Following Durkheim, a distinction is made here between the functions and causes.

proposition in media system theory is that the structure of a social system sets parameters or constraints on the number and type of media in that system, as well as media content.[54] Specifically, Tichenor, Donohue and Olien point out that homogeneous, traditional societies or communities have a limited number of mass media sources, and those sources tend to represent the interests and concerns of a homogeneous, undifferentiated audience. But, as the level of structural pluralism increases, demand for specialized sources of information and news increases, and social actors respond by increasing the number and diversity of print and electronic media. The rapid proliferation of newsletters, cable systems, highly specialized academic journals and fax machines are examples of how social actors have responded to increasing pluralism. Pluralism also is a strong predictor of the amount and percentage of news space allocated to public affairs issues[55] and to the number and variety of media in a community.[56]

Research on the ideological effects of the media indicates that the media may have dysfunctional consequences for some groups, but this is not always the case and, furthermore, media consumers are not easily manipulated. Hartmann and Husband found that English children's use of mass media leads to distorted perceptions of immigrants.[57] But two other studies conducted in the United States have reached opposite conclusions. One, which was conducted during the 1960s, reported that the greater the number of mass media messages white Southerners attended to, the less likely they were to have strict segregationist attitudes.[58] Although this relationship was not particularly strong, it did hold up when controlling for education. Mass media, the researchers argued, often subvert traditional, patrimonial ways and usher in modern attitudes that promote social change. Researchers behind the *Great American Values Test* concluded that a specially designed 30-minute television program broadcast in 1979 also was able to increase anti-racist beliefs and the

---

[54]See, e.g., Tichenor, Donohue, and Olien, *Community Conflict and the Press.*

[55]G. A. Donohue, C. N. Olien, P. J. Tichenor and D. P. Demers, "Community Structure, News Judgments and Newspaper Content," paper presented at the annual meeting of the Association for Education in Journalism and Mass Communication (Minneapolis, August 1990).

[56]Demers, "Structural Pluralism, Intermedia Competition, and the Growth of the Corporate Newspaper in the United States."

[57]Paul Hartmann and Charles Husband, "The Mass Media and Racial Conflict," pp. 288-302 in Stanley Cohen and Jock Young (eds.), *The Manufacture of News* (London: Constable, 1981).

[58]D. R. Matthews and J. W. Protho, *Negroes and the New Southern Politics* (New York: Harcourt, Brace & World, 1966), p. 344.

importance of equality itself as a basic social value.[59] The researchers also found that people who have a high dependency on television changed their values more and contributed more money to groups that promote anti-racism and equality than people with low dependence on television.

Cultivation analysis also shows that television exaggerates the amount of crime and violence in society and that such content is cognitively translated into increased support for authoritarian measures by police and the state.[60] Gerbner and his colleagues argue that television "is the central cultural arm of American society" whose primary function is "to spread and stabilize social patterns, to cultivate not change but resistance to change."[61] Some re-analysis of the original cultivation data, however, fails to support the theory,[62] and cross-cultural research suggests that cultivation effects may depend on a variety of factors.[63] In contrast to some critical theories of media, a large body of research also indicates that media often impact public policy. Researchers at Northwestern University, for instance, found that investigative stories on police brutality "produced swift and fundamental revisions of regulations regarding police

---

[59]Sandra J. Ball-Rokeach, Melvin Rokeach and Joel W. Grube, *The Great American Values Test: Influencing Behavior and Belief Through Television* (New York: Free Press, 1984) and Sandra J. Ball-Rokeach, Melvin Rokeach and Joel W. Grube, "Changing and Stabilizing Political Behavior and Beliefs," pp. 280-90 in Sandra J. Ball-Rokeach and Muriel G. Cantor (eds.), *Media Audience and Social Structure* (Newbury Park, CA: Sage, 1986).

[60]George Gerbner and Larry Gross, "Living With Television: The Violence Profile," *Journal of Communication*, 26(2):173-99 (1976) and George Gerbner, Larry Gross, Michael Morgan and Nancy Signorielli, "Growing Up With Television: The Cultivation Perspective," pp. 17-41 in Jennings Bryant and Dolf Zillman (eds.), *Media Effects: Advances in Theory and Research* (Hillsdale, NJ: Lawrence Erlbaum Associates, 1994). From the perspective of the individual, the distorted image of crime conveyed on television is generally dysfunctional; it leads to the development of irrational beliefs, or a "mean world syndrome." However, from the perspective of those in power, such "mean world" beliefs may be very functional for supporting authoritarian actions.

[61]Gerbner and Gross, "Living With Television," p. 175.

[62]Paul M. Hirsch, "The 'Scary World' of the Nonviewer and Other Anomalies: A Reanalysis of Gerbner et al.'s Findings on Cultivation Analysis, Part I," *Communication Research*, 7:403-56 (1980); Paul M. Hirsch, "On Not Learning From One's Own Mistakes: A Reanalysis of Gerbner et al.'s Findings on Cultivation Analysis, Part II," *Communication Research*, 8:3-37 (1981); and M. Hughes, "The Fruits of Cultivation Analysis: A Re-Examination of Some Effects of Television Watching," *Public Opinion Quarterly*, 44:287-302 (1980).

[63]Gerbner, Gross, Morgan and Signorielli, "Growing Up With Television."

misconduct."[64] Another study found that media coverage of murder cases influences the way prosecutors handle cases.[65]

Another study suggests that television may actually promote beliefs that oppose economic inequalities.[66] The data, obtained from personal interviews with a probability sample of U.S. adults in 1986, show that people who benefit most from the system — men, whites, conservatives, and those who have high incomes, education and occupational prestige — are most likely to favor economic inequalities. However, the study found no support for the media hypotheses. In fact, the data suggest that television viewing reduces support for beliefs that promote economic inequality, even when controlling for all of the other factors.

Sociologist William Gamson's peer group study also suggests that people often use media to challenge and criticize established authorities. He challenges both the radical view that working people are incorporated by the dominant ideology and the mainstream social science view that working people are uninterested in politics and unable to engage in well-reasoned discussions. Using data collected in peer group sessions with 188 "working people," he concludes that "(a) people are not so passive, (b) people are not so dumb, and (c) people negotiate with media messages in complicated ways that vary from issue to issue."[67]

Mainstream corporate media may also help promote the causes of social movements. I devote the next section to this topic.

Media and Social Movements

Although investigative journalism is often cited as a source of social change, it is not the most significant source in modern society. Social movements, many sociologists would argue, are much more important. Without social movements, today's world would be much different.[68]

---

[64]David L. Protess, Fay Lomax Cook, Jack C. Doppelt, James S. Ettema, Margaret T. Gordon, Donna R. Leff, and Peter Miller, *The Journalism of Outrage: Investigative Reporting and Agenda-Building in America* (New York: Guilford Press, 1991).

[65]Pritchard, "Homicide and Bargained Justice."

[66]David Pearce Demers, "Media Use and Beliefs About Economic Equality: An Empirical Test of the Dominant Ideology Thesis," presented to the Midwest Association for Public Opinion Research (Chicago, November 1993).

[67]William A. Gamson, *Talking Politics* (Cambridge, MA: Cambridge University Press, 1992), p. 4.

[68]For a discussion of social changes that have taken place in the United States during the 20th century, see L. W. Banner, *Women in Modern America: A Brief History,* 2nd ed. (Orlando, FL: Harcourt Brace Jovanovich, 1984); R. Blauner, "The Ambiguities of Racial

Consider, for instance, what it was like to be a woman before the late 20th century. Nowhere in the world did women have the right to vote. They had limited access to a college education — many schools would not accept women. But even if a woman had a college education, she didn't have access to the best jobs in the public or private (corporate) world. Teaching school was her best bet.

Or consider what is was like to be an African American living in pre-Vietnam War America. African Americans could not eat in many restaurants. They had to sit at the back of the bus. They could not drink out of water fountains reserved for whites. Their children could not attend the best schools. They were denied access to good jobs. And, in some areas of the Deep South, they lived in fear for their lives.

Today, there is little question that opportunities and social conditions for women, African Americans and many other historically oppressed groups have improved in the United States and most Western countries. Women are guaranteed the right to vote. Minorities and women have better access to jobs and education. Factory laborers are no longer required to work 16 hours a day. Pollutants and emissions from factories and motor vehicles are much more highly regulated. People now have access to contraceptives. The elderly have social security and health care. The stigma associated with being homosexual has lessened considerably, and some corporations (such as Disney) and governments have extended employment benefits to same-sex partners.

To be sure, these changes and the passage of time have not eradicated discrimination, inequality, income disparities, disregard for the environment, unwanted births, lack of access to opportunity, poor health care and poverty. Sociocultural patterns are deeply embedded, and elites and the institutions they control nearly always resist change, because it usually means a loss of political, social and economic power. But elite resistance to challenges from less advantaged groups is not always effective in preventing social change that benefits those groups. As the preceding examples show, social movements often have played a pivotal role in altering, however subtly, the balance of power between traditional elite groups and the masses. That's one reason why U.S. civil rights leader Jesse Jackson says he remains upbeat and optimistic —

Change," pp. 54-64 in M. L. Andersen and P. H. Collins (eds), *Race, Class, and Gender* (Belmont, CA: Wadsworth, 1992); Celeste M. Condit, "Hegemony in a Mass-Mediated Society: Concordance about Reproductive Technologies," *Critical Studies in Mass Communication,* 11:205-230 (1994); J. R. Howard, *The Cutting Edge: Social Movements and Social Change in America* (Philadelphia: J. B. Lippincott, 1974); R. H. Lauer (ed.), *Social Movements and Social Change* (Carbondale: Southern Illinois University Press, 1976); D. McAdam, J. D. McCarthy, and N. Z. Mayer, "Social Movements," pp. 695-737 in N. J. Smelser (ed.), *Handbook of Sociology* (Newbury Park, CA: Sage, 1988).

despite past and current problems, the civil rights movement, in his view, has won significant battles since the 1960s.[69]

To be sure, social science research clearly demonstrates that all social systems have ideological and coercive means of social control, and that the content of mainstream mass media generally supports those ideologies and those in power. We know that all modern social movements need the mass media to achieve their goals in a representative democracy. Media play an important role in legitimating (or delegitimating) the goals of social movements and accelerating (or decelerating) public attention to the social problems movements identify.

We also know, thanks to media researcher David L. Protess and his colleagues at Northwestern University, that investigative reporting is most likely to promote change when journalists and policy makers actively collaborate to set policy-making agendas prior to story publication.[70] However, we don't know a whole lot more about the conditions when mass media may help promote or hinder social change, partly because, I contend, this topic generally has been ignored by critics of corporate and global media.

Nevertheless, despite the shortage of research, several statements can be made. One is that, historically, mass media have tended to ignore social movements until they gain power. Although the civil rights and women's movements were founded in the 19th century, they did not garner significant favorable media coverage until the 1950s and 1960s. This coincides with a substantial growth in the size and power of those movements. The same thing happened to the environmental movement. Not until 1962, with the publication of Rachael Carson's *Silent Spring*, which drew attention to the problems of pollution, did mainstream media begin giving substantial coverage to environmental issues.

However, since then, mainstream media — especially media in large, pluralistic cities — have published or aired many stories that have lent support to the goals of these movements, and news coverage has been much more favorable.[71] Television entertainment programming in the United States also has

---

[69]Jesse Jackson's remarks were made in a speech he gave July 30, 1997, at the annual meeting of the Association for Education in Journalism and Mass Communication, Chicago.

[70]David L. Protess, Fay Lomax Cook, Jack C. Doppelt, James S. Ettema, Margaret T. Gordon, Donna R. Leff, and Peter Miller, *The Journalism of Outrage: Investigative Reporting and Agenda-Building in America* (New York: Guilford Press, 1991), p. 246.

[71]For additional evidence of the media's role in social change see Donald L. Barlett and James B. Steele, *America: What Went Wrong?* (Kansas City: Andrew and McMeel, 1992); Leonard Downie, Jr., *The New Muckrakers* (New York: Mentor, 1976); Mark Neuzil

become more favorable to women and those with alternative lifestyles. Today, even same-sex relationships are getting some positive portrayals (e.g., the former ABC comedy *Ellen*).

Overall, then, it is clear that mainstream mass media, which include global media, are no agents of radical change. But throughout the 20th century, corporate media have published many stories that have helped promote or legitimize social reforms. As Herbert Gans sums it up:

> News is not so much conservative or liberal as it is reformist; indeed, the enduring values are very much like the values of the Progressive movement of the early twentieth century. The resemblance is often uncanny, as in the common advocacy of honest, meritocratic, and anti-bureaucratic government, and in the shared antipathy to political machines and demagogues, particularly the populist bent.[72]

And comparing the media to legal systems, sociologist Jeffrey Alexander observes:

> In distinguishing the news media from the law, the significant point is the media's flexibility. By daily exposing and reformulating itself vis-à-vis changing values, group formations, and objective economic and political conditions, the media allows "public opinion" to be organized responsively on a mass basis. By performing this function of information-conduit and normative-organizer, the news media provides the normative dimension of society with the greatest flexibility in dealing with social strains.[73]

Indeed, relative to most other social institutions in society — including the church, government, the legal system and schools — the news media are more responsive to alternative groups and ideas. This helps social systems adapt and change. From a systems perspective, news media in Western societies and

and William Kovarik, *Mass Media and Environmental Conflict: America's Green Crusades* (Thousand Oaks, CA: Sage, 1996); David L. Protess, Fay Lomax Cook, Jack C. Doppelt, James S. Ettema, Margaret T. Gordon, Donna R. Leff and Peter Miller, *The Journalism of Outrage: Investigative Reporting and Agenda-Building in America* (New York: Guilford Press, 1991); and Leonard Sellers, *Investigative Reporting: Methods and Barriers* (Ph.D. Diss., Stanford, 1977).

[72]Herbert J. Gans, *Deciding What's News* (New York: Vintage, 1979), pp. 68-69.

[73]Jeffrey Alexander, "The Mass News Media in Systemic, Historical and Comparative Perspective," pp. 17-51 in Elihu Katz and Tomás Szecskö (eds.), *Mass Media and Social Change* (Beverly Hills, CA: Sage, 1981).

global media in particular may be likened from time to time to a tempered social reformer, drawing attention to various problems in society or the world (e.g., sexism in the military, discrimination in the workforce, police brutality and corruption).

WHAT ABOUT THE "APPROVED CONTRADICTION?"

Another serious shortcoming of the critical perspective is that it has failed to resolve what economist John Kenneth Galbraith calls the "approved contradiction."[74] Basically, the question is this: How can organizations managed and controlled on a daily basis by professional managers rather than the owners (i.e., corporate organizations) be expected to maximize rewards for others (owners) but not themselves?

The notion that professional managers seek to maximize profits for the owners contradicts some basic economic assumptions about human behavior. If one assumes that humans usually seek to maximize their benefits and minimize their costs (as do the critics of corporate media owners), then managers cannot be expected to maximize profits for the owners, because most of their rewards come through a fixed salary and not profits. Although a minimum level of profitability is necessary to prevent the board of directors from removing top management, managers are likely to pursue some of their own interests, which are not always related to the bottom line. They include organization growth and increased emphasis on quality.

More formally, the "managerial revolution" holds that as organizations become more corporatized, power and control over day-to-day operations shifts from the owners to the professional managers.[75] (See next chapter for more details.) The shift occurs in large part because increasing complexity in organizational structure forces the owners to rely more and more heavily on highly skilled experts and technocrats for key decisions. A study I conducted

---

[74]John Kenneth Galbraith, *The New Industrial State*, 3rd ed. (New York: Mentor, 1978), pp. 107-108.

[75]The managerial revolution is discussed in a number of works, including Daniel Bell, *The Coming of the Post-Industrial Society* (New York: Basic Books, 1976 [1973]); Adolf A. Berle, Jr. and Gardiner C. Means, *The Modern Corporation and Private Property* (New York: Macmillan, 1932); James Burnham, *The Managerial Revolution* (New York: John Day, 1941); and John Kenneth Galbraith, *The New Industrial State*, 3rd ed. (New York: Mentor, 1978). Also see David Demers and Debra Merskin, "Corporate Newspaper Structure and Control of Editorial Content: An Empirical Test of the Managerial Revolution Hypothesis," paper presented at the annual meeting of the Association for Education in Journalism and Mass Communication, Chicago (July/August 1997).

supports this "power shift." U.S. daily newspaper owners and publishers play less and less of a role in day-to-day decisions about editorial matters as the newspaper exhibits the characteristics of the corporate form of organization, which gives editors a more prominent role.[76]

This shift in power does not mean that the owners or their representatives (board of directors) have no say in the operation. However, their authority over day-to-day decision making is greatly weakened. Increasingly, the experts — the journalists and other managers — make the decisions, and the owners become increasingly dependent upon their knowledge and advice. At the entrepreneurial media organization, on the other hand, the owner is usually involved in daily editorial decisions and maintains direct control over managers in all areas.

This shift in power also does not mean that managers or editors at corporate media are not concerned with profits. They are, because profit-making is crucial for the survival of any business. However, corporate organizations place less importance on profit-making because most managers do not benefit directly or as directly from profits, as most of their income is derived from a fixed salary. Instead, managers place much more importance on maximizing growth of the organization, which, research shows, does contribute directly to higher salaries and greater power. Also, managers place greater importance on product quality and other nonprofit goals because, as professionals, they place a higher value on intrinsic rewards (e.g., peer recognition) as opposed to just extrinsic rewards (salary). "Doing a good job," in fact, is canonized in many codes of ethics that serve journalists and other professional managers.

Some critics charge that managers at corporate media have an MBA mentality. Undoubtedly this is true, as MBAs have the requisite knowledge and training to operate a complex business organization. But the increased concern with profits is more apparent than real. Profit-making is much more likely to be a topic of conversation at a corporate media organization because that organization is more likely to be publicly owned and all managers are expected to play a key role in watching the bottom line. The local publisher or general manager (who is not the owner) needs the assistance of other managers in making the organization profitable. In contrast, profit-making is less likely to be a topic of discussion at entrepreneurial media, because those organizations

---

[76]David Demers, "Who Controls the Editorial Content at Corporate News Organizations? An Empirical Test of the Managerial Revolution Hypothesis," *World Futures: The Journal of General Evolution*, 57:103-123 (2001).

are family owned or privately owned, and the owners rarely want to reveal their income to the community or their employees.

Some critics also argue that corporate media that pay professional managers higher salaries or stock bonuses pursue profits more vigorously. However, in 2001, I analyzed compensation data collected by *Business Week* and found that corporate pay for top media executives has no relation to either shareholder return or profitability. Rather, it's total sales that counts: The bigger the company, the more it pays, regardless of profitability or shareholder return. In fact, for every one percent increase in sales, the pay of top media executives increases by one-half percent. These findings, I concluded,

> fail to support executives' arguments that job performance drives their paycheck. They also fail to support the position of corporate media critics, who argue that corporations which pay more are greedier and place more emphasis on profits than on nonprofit goals (e.g., producing a higher quality news and entertainment product).
>
> But the findings will come as no surprise to many postindustrial theorists, who have argued ... that managers seek not only to serve the owners but also themselves. The managerial revolution has not eliminated the profit motive, to be sure. All businesses seek profits. But the managerial revolution has decreased the power of the owners (i.e., non-management stockholders) relative to the managers. The golden parachute is a visible example of this power shift. And short-term profit maximization is not always in the best interests of the top managers. ...
>
> [P]rofessional managers often place more importance on maximizing growth of the organization. To be sure, growth may benefit owners in the long-run. But managers often stand to gain a great deal in the short run. Growth helps fend off hostile takeovers, explain low profits, increase managerial power, make stockholders more dependent upon management, and, of course, increase managerial pay. Indeed, this study shows that growth is the surest way to increase top executive pay.[77]

[77]David Demers, "Media Executive Pay: It's Size, Not Performance, that Counts," *Global Media News,* 1(1):3-6 (1999), p. 6.

Chapter 15

WHO WILL CONTROL MEDIA OF THE FUTURE?

T ime Inc.'s CEO J. Richard Munro and board of directors were faced with a dilemma. As part of a long-term strategy to give the company a global presence, they had made an offer to merge with a major film and cable television company. However, two weeks before the deal was expected to go through, another media company made an offer to buy out Time Inc. The offer was sweet — the buyer will pay $200 per share, or nearly twice the value of Time Inc.'s stock six months earlier. Stockholders clearly will support the sale. And the deal will make Munro and the board of directors extremely rich.

But they rejected the deal, withdrew the merger offer, and spent $15 billion to buy the film and cable television company outright. What?

That's exactly what Munro and board of directors did in the Summer of 1989. Time Inc. spent so much money to purchase Warner Brothers that Paramount Communications could no longer afford to purchase Time Inc. It had too much debt. As it turned out, Munro and the executives at Time Inc. still made a pile of money, as did the executives and stockholders at Warner Brothers. But Time Inc. stockholders didn't fair too well. The value of their stock fell to $70 a share. And for the next eight years the shares didn't gain much in value.

On the surface, it doesn't seem to make sense. Why would the top executives of a major corporation turn down an offer that would have had everyone at that corporation, including themselves, laughing all the way to the bank? The answer, according to Munro, is that they wanted to preserve the journalistic history that Henry Luce, co-founder of *Time* magazine, had created.

"This is my legacy," Munro, 58, told a *Fortune* magazine reporter. "I did not work here 33 years to bust the company up." He and other Time Inc. executives owned a lot of company stock and could have gotten extremely rich on the Paramount offer. And had Time stockholders been given a chance to vote on the Paramount buy-out, there is no question that they would have approved it.

But Munro and others in top management did not give the stockholders a chance to vote on the measure. The acquisition was imposed upon the stockholders.

CHAPTER OVERVIEW

Since the turn of the century, a number of scholars have argued that control of corporate organizations in modern societies has been shifting from the owners, or capitalists, to professional managers and highly skilled technocrats.[1] This proposition, also known as the managerial revolution hypothesis, occupies a prominent place in postindustrial theories of society, which contend that knowledge, rather than capital, is becoming the key source of power in society.[2]

The notion that power may be shifting in corporate organizations has significant consequences for media managers, scholars and public policy makers. Corporate and global news media organizations are often accused of placing more emphasis on profits than on quality journalism, restricting journalists' autonomy, alienating employees, destroying community solidarity, supporting the interests of big business over those of the public, and, perhaps most serious of all, failing to provide a diversity of ideas crucial for creating or maintaining a political democracy. But if power in the modern corporate news organization is shifting from the owners to the managers and the technocrats (e.g., editors), and if managers pursue not just profits but others goals, such as

---

[1]For purposes of empirical research, corporate control is usually defined as "the power to determine the broad policies guiding the corporation, although it does not necessarily imply active leadership or specific influence on the day-to-day operations of the enterprise." See Robert J. Larner, *Management Control in the Large Corporation* (Cambridge, MA: Dunellen, 1970), p. 2. For a similar definition, see Neil Fligstein and Peter Brantley, "Bank Control, Owner Control, or Organizational Dynamics: Who Controls the Large Modern Corporation," *American Journal of Sociology*, 98:280-330 (1992). These definitions are much too limiting, however, as professional managers often control the day-to-day decision making in most corporations.

[2]Some of the scholars who have presented arguments in support of the managerial revolution hypothesis: Daniel Bell, *The Coming of the Post-Industrial Society* (New York: Basic Books, 1976); Adolf A. Berle, Jr. and Gardiner C. Means, *The Modern Corporation and Private Property* (New York: Macmillan, 1932); James Burnham, *The Managerial Revolution* (New York: John Day, 1941); Ralf Dahrendorf, *Class and Class Conflict in Industrial Society* (Stanford, CA: Stanford University Press, 1959 [1957 German version]); John Kenneth Galbraith, *The New Industrial State* (New York: Mentor, 1971); and Talcott Parsons, "A Revised Analytical Approach to the Theory of Social Stratification," in Richard Bendix and Seymour Martin Lipset (eds.), *Class, Status, and Power* (Glencoe, IL: Free Press, 1953).

maximizing growth of the organization or producing a high-quality product, then these criticisms may be invalid.

The purpose of this chapter is to explore the impact of the managerial revolution on mass media industries. Research generally supports the idea that most stockholders play a relatively limited or no role in day-to-day operations at most large corporations. However, social scientists still disagree on the question of whether power is really shifting from owners to managers. My own research on U.S. daily newspapers clearly shows that power has shifted, that owners and publishers play less of a role in controlling news content, and that newspapers place less emphasis on profits as an organizational goal and more on product quality as they become more corporatized.

A Brief History of the Managerial Revolution Thesis

The origins of the managerial revolution hypothesis are not fully known. Ironically, though, some of the seeds appear to have been planted by Adam Smith and Karl Marx, neither of whom likely would have viewed it with much favor.

Smith originated the idea that manager-controlled firms place less emphasis on maximizing profits than owner-controlled firms — a proposition that still occupies a prominent position in contemporary research programs. Owner-managers could be expected to keep an eye on the bottom line because their pocketbook was directly affected. But this same diligence could not be expected for joint-stock companies that were controlled by non-owning managers, because

> The directors of such companies ... being the managers ... of other people's money than of their own ... cannot ... be expected ... (to) watch over it with the same anxious vigilance with which the partners in a private copartnery frequently watch over their own. ... Negligence and profusion, therefore, must always prevail, more or less, in the management of the affairs of such a company.[3]

As noted earlier, Marx is partly responsible for the idea that, as businesses grow and capital becomes more concentrated, ownership becomes more, not less, dispersed. Concentration of capital leads to an increase, not decrease, in the number of owners, because, over time, capital is divided among family members, often through inheritance, and earmarked for new ventures.

---

[3]Adam Smith, *An Inquiry Into the Nature and Causes of the Wealth of Nations* (Chicago: William Benton, Encyclopedia Britannica, Inc., 1952 [1776]), p. 324.

Although ownership tends to become diffused and decentralized as a firm grows, Marx countered that this process is slow and is more than offset by centralization of capital, which he defined as the combining of capitals already formed — that is, a reduction in the number of competitive firms in a particular sector of industry through merger, bankruptcy or acquisition.

Although Smith underestimated the staying power of the corporate form of organization and Marx overestimated the revolutionary potential of the workers, their ideas nonetheless stimulated other thinkers. In the late 1800s, social democratic theoretician Eduard Bernstein argued that the corporate form of organization led to the splitting up of property into "armies of shareholders" who represented a new "power." The shareholder, he argued, expropriates the capitalist class, transforming it "from a proprietor to a simple administrator."

The writings of the sociologist Max Weber at the turn of the century also may be interpreted as anticipating more formal arguments of later writers, even though he personally disagreed with the idea that managers were gaining power over capitalists. The appropriation of managerial functions from the owners, he argued, does not mean the separation of control from ownership. Rather, it means the separation of the managerial function from ownership. Nevertheless, Weber's writings are somewhat ambiguous. Elsewhere, he observed that bureaucrats, or the technical experts of government, often attempt to control the flow of information to both policy makers and the public.

> The question is always who controls the existing bureaucratic machinery. And such control is possible only in a very limited degree to persons who are not technical specialists. Generally speaking, the trained permanent official is more likely to get his way in the long run than his nominal superior, the Cabinet minister, who is not a specialist.[4]

The first comprehensive analysis of the notion that the proprietors or owners of the means of production were ceding power did not appear until the early 1930s. In *The Modern Corporation and Private Property*, Adolf A. Berle and Gardiner C. Means, an economist and a lawyer, argued that "ownership of wealth without appreciable control and control of wealth without appreciable ownership appear to be the logical outcome of corporate development."[5] The trend toward separation of ownership from management, they argued, occurs because the capital required to operate and own large corporations is often

---

[4]Max Weber, *The Theory of Social and Economic Organization*, trans. A. M. Henderson and Talcott Parsons (New York: The Free Press, 1964 [1947]), p. 338.

[5]Adolf A. Berle, Jr. and Gardiner C. Means, *The Modern Corporation and Private Property* (New York: Macmillan, 1932).

beyond the resources of any single individual or company. As companies grow, they need to draw upon more and more sources of capital, which over time diminishes the percentage of shares owned by any single individual or entity. Berle and Means believed managers, unlike the owners, would be guided by a broader social conscience and professional values, rather than a selfish profit motive.

James Burnham

In the early 1940s, sociologist James Burnham argued that the trend toward separation of management from ownership was leading to the rise of a new class that would replace the capitalists.[6] Growth of business means more than just increasing scale; it also means increasing technical complexity, and this in turn means that the owners must depend more and more on experts and highly skilled managers to run the new means of production. Organizational skills and technical knowledge are the bases of managerial power. However, in contrast to Berle and Means, Burnham believed managers would act in their own self-interest, not necessarily in the public interest.

During the 1940s, economist Joseph Schumpeter made similar arguments.[7] He contended that highly skilled managers and technical specialists, not the capitalists, were the creative force behind the innovative process in modern capitalism. In early capitalism, the capitalist was the entrepreneur, the innovator. Capitalists are driven by profits. But as organizations grow, this role becomes more specialized and routinized and is delegated to highly educated and trained specialists. Because entrepreneurs in modern organizations are not usually the direct beneficiaries of profit, according to Schumpeter, they are driven not by profits but by social status.

By the 1950s many theorists treated the managerial revolution as an empirical fact rather than a hypothesis or theory. Sociologists Talcott Parsons and Ralph Dahrendorf both believed that class relations were being replaced by an occupational system based on individual achievement, in which status was determined by functional importance. In fact, public opinion polls showed then and now that physicians and professors are two of the most prestigious positions in society.

---

[6]James Burnham, *The Managerial Revolution* (New York: John Day, 1941).
[7]Joseph A. Schumpeter, *The Theory of Economic Development* (Cambridge, MA: Harvard University Press, 1949).

During the 1960s and 1970s, economist John Kenneth Galbraith and sociologist Daniel Bell continued this line of thinking, incorporating the managerial revolution hypothesis into larger, more comprehensive theories of social change. Galbraith argues that the "decisive power in modern industrial society is exercised not by capital but by organization, not by the capitalist but by the industrial bureaucrat."[8] One consequence of the shift in power, he says, is less emphasis on profit maximization as an organizational goal. Hence, it would be irrational to argue that those in control (i.e., managers) will maximize profits for others (i.e., stockholders).

J. K. Galbraith

As noted briefly in Chapter 14, Galbraith calls the belief that managers are more profit-maximizing the "approved contradiction." In other words, how can corporate organizations be more profit-oriented when they are more likely to be controlled by professional managers and technocrats, who do not benefit directly or as directly from the profits as the owners? As Galbraith puts it:

> [I]t is now agreed that the modern large corporation is, quite typically, controlled by its management. The managerial revolution — the assumption of power by top management — is conceded. So long as earnings are above a certain minimum, it would also be widely agreed that such management has little to fear from the stockholders. Yet it is for these stockholders, remote, powerless and unknown, that management seeks to maximize profits. Management does not go out ruthlessly to reward itself — a sound management is expected to exercise restraint. Already at this stage, in the accepted view of the corporation, profit maximization involves a substantial contradiction. Those in charge forgo personal reward to enhance it for others.

More important to managers than maximizing profits, Galbraith argues, is prevention of loss, because low earnings or losses make a company vulnerable to outside influence or control. All businesses must earn a minimum level of profit, Galbraith argues, but professional managers place greater emphasis on organizational growth, planning, knowledge, autonomy and expertise, because these factors are recognized as the basis of power in the organization and are essential for long-term survival of the organization (and their jobs).

---

[8]John Kenneth Galbraith, *The New Industrial State,* 3rd ed. (New York: Mentor, 1978), pp. 107-108.

Applying this logic to the Time Warner incident, one might postulate that Munro and other executives were attempting to secure their jobs for the long term, as well as build an even bigger media empire. After all, that's where all the fun is. Top-level managers like money, to be sure. But most professionals also like their work. They derive a sense of power from it and a sense of identity. In addition, the decision to buy Warner did not entail a great deal of risk to the top-level executives, because they didn't have to spend their own money. So, even if the managers received most of their income from profits through stock options or other incentives, one would still argue that they, in contrast to nonmanagerial owners, would place more emphasis on nonprofit goals. For professional managers, work is a calling, not just a job.

Bell's *The Coming of the Post-Industrial Society* contends that theoretical (or scientific) knowledge, rather than capital or practical knowledge, is the primary source of innovation and social organization in a postindustrial society.[9] In the economy, this change is reflected in the decline of manufacturing and goods and the rise of service industries, especially health, education, social welfare services and professional/technical services (research, evaluation, computers, systems analysis). A postmodern society is an information society. Education rather than heritage or social position is the key means of advancement, and rewards are based less on inheritance or property than on education and skill (i.e., a meritocracy). Bell contends that these structural changes foster a new class structure — one based on the supremacy of professional, managerial, scientific and technical occupations (the knowledge or intellectual class) — that gradually replaces the bourgeoisie as the ruling class.

In sum, the managerial revolution is being fueled by at least three factors or trends: the death of major entrepreneurial capitalists or stockholders, whose concentrated economic power is dispersed over time as it is divided among heirs; organizational growth, which forces companies to draw capital from more and more sources, diluting the proportion of ownership of any single owner; and increasing complexity in the division of labor and market competition, which forces owners to rely more and more on the expertise of highly skilled professional managers and technical experts to manage day-to-day operations of the organization. A fourth trend also may be added to the list: the growth of pension, insurance, mutual and trust funds, which invest heavily in corporate stocks and are managed by professional investors, not the owners. Over time, these factors are expected to promote the growth of a professional-technical class that will replace capitalists as the new ruling class.

But does the research support the managerial revolution hypothesis?

---

[9]Daniel Bell, *The Coming of the Post-Industrial Society* (New York: Basic Books, 1976).

Empirical Research on the Managerial Revolution Thesis

The empirical research can be divided into two major categories or approaches. One attempts to answer the question: Is ownership becoming more diversified as organizations and the economic system have grown? The research here is primarily descriptive and focuses on how much stock is controlled by families or individuals and the extent to which they are involved in top management.

The second line of research attempts to answer the question: Even if ownership is becoming more diversified as organizations grow and become more structurally complex, are those organizations still serving the interests of the owners above managers or other groups? Research on this question involves explanatory analysis and examines the relationship between organizational structure and organizational outcomes (i.e., profit maximization, job loss, product quality).

All of the research that has specifically tested the managerial revolution hypothesis except one have been conducted on nonmedia corporations. The media study involved a national probability survey of daily newspapers and is addressed in depth following this review.

Is Ownership Becoming More Diversified?

Research on this question strongly suggests that owners play less and less a role in the day-to-day operations as organizations grow, that the proportion of manager-controlled firms has increased, and that most large companies are manager-controlled rather than owner-controlled. These findings are generally applicable to mass media industries as well.

Using data compiled from Standard's Corporation Records, Moody's manuals, *The New York Times* and *The Wall Street Journal*, Berle and Means concluded that families or groups of business associates owned more than half of the outstanding voting stock in only 11 percent of the top 200 largest nonfinancial corporations. Using 10 percent stock ownership as the minimum criterion for family control, they classified 44 percent of the top 200 largest nonfinancial corporations as management controlled.

In 1937, the Securities and Exchange Commission, using more reliable and comprehensive data, reported that minority ownership control existed in the vast majority of the nation's largest corporations. However, Robert Aaron Gordon challenged the government study, pointing to a number of shortcomings and concluding that probably fewer than a third of the companies were controlled by families or small groups of individuals.[10] A study by *Fortune* magazine in the 1960s also concluded that 71 percent of the 500 largest industrial corporations were controlled by management.[11]

Using a methodology similar to Berle and Means, Robert J. Larner concluded that only three percent of the largest 200 nonfinancial corporations were controlled by families in 1963.[12] At the same time, 84 percent of the companies were controlled by managers, nearly double what Berle and Means had found. The remaining 13 percent were partially controlled.

However, a year later Philip H. Burch challenged Larner's and Berle and Means' findings, arguing that they had used a too restrictive definition of control.[13] Burch argues that control should include not only some measure of stock ownership but also membership in top management or on the board of directors. Using this broader definition, he found that about 36 percent of the top 300 public and private industrial corporations were probably family controlled in 1965. However, Burch also found that the proportion of family-controlled firms had declined about three to five percent a year since 1938, when they controlled about 50 percent of all large companies. These data support Larner's and Berle and Means' argument that family or individual control declines as a company grows.

Do Managers Serve Themselves or Owners?

The second line of research has focused to a large extent on Smith's 200-year-old hypothesis, which posited that managers are less likely to serve the interests of the owners than themselves. Often this has involved examining whether managerial-controlled firms or large corporations are less profitable or place less emphasis on profits. Noneconomic researchers have also examined the impact on organizational goals and practices, with the expectation that managers will place greater value on organizational growth, product quality and innovation. Findings are mixed.

Several studies are interpreted as supporting the managerial revolution thesis. Joseph Monsen and his colleagues examined the impact of ownership

---

[10]Robert Aaron Gordon, *Business Leadership in the Large Corporation* (Berkeley: University of California Press, 1961 [1945]).

[11]Robert Sheehan, "There's Plenty of Privacy Left in Private Enterprise," *Fortune* (July 15, 1966).

[12]Robert J. Larner, *Management Control in the Large Corporation* (Cambridge, MA: Dunellen, 1970).

[13]Philip H. Burch, *The Managerial Revolution Reassessed* (Lexington, MA: D.C. Heath and Company, 1972).

structure on the level of profitability for the 500 largest industrial firms.[14] They found that over a 12-year period the net income to net worth ratio (return on owner's equity) for owner-controlled firms was 12.8 percent, compared with 7.3 percent for manager-controlled firms.

John Palmer also found that manager-controlled firms operating in markets with a high degree of monopoly power report significantly lower profit rates than owner-controlled firms, but no major differences emerged between firms in moderate or low monopoly markets.[15] The reasoning here is that managers can pursue goals other than maximum profits only in the absence of competition, which acts as a constraint on all types of organizational structure. Larner found that manager-controlled firms have slightly lower profit rates.

In contrast, other studies have found no differences or that manager-controlled firms are more profitable. Neil Fligstein and Peter Brantley, for example, found that manager-controlled firms actually outperformed family- or bank-controlled firms in terms of profits. However, they argue that ownership overall has little effect on the economic actions undertaken by large firms; rather, the key determinants are existing power relations within the firm, the concept of control that dominates the firm's actions and the action of competitors.[16]

Several other studies also have found that management control exerts no important influence on profit rates. David R. James and Michael Soref studied the relationship between dismissal of corporate chiefs and five measures of managerial/owner control and found that corporate heads are retained or fired on the basis of profit performance, not ownership structure.[17]

One major problem with these studies, however, is that they tend to focus on the largest 100 to 500 corporations. These corporations are not representative of all businesses, and the restricted variance reduces the ability to detect differences between more-or-less corporatized organizations. In contrast,

---

[14]Joseph R. Monsen, Jr., John S. Chiu and David E. Cooley, "The Effect of Separation of Ownership and Control on the Performance of the Large Firm," *Quarterly Journal of Economics*, 82:435-451 (1968).

[15]John Palmer, "The Profit-Performance Effect of the Separation of Ownership from Control in Large U.S. Industrial Corporations," *Bell Journal of Economics and Management Science*, 4:299-303 (1973).

[16]Neil Fligstein and Peter Brantley, "Bank Control, Owner Control, or Organizational Dynamics: Who Controls the Large Modern Corporation," *American Journal of Sociology*, 98:280-330 (1992).

[17]David R. James and Michael Soref, "Profit Constraints on Managerial Autonomy: Managerial Theory and the Unmaking of the Corporate President," *American Sociological Review*, 46:1-18 (February 1981).

newspapers are the ideal mass medium for testing the managerial hypothesis, because they range greatly in size and complexity.

Research on Newspapers

Breaking with previous theorists, I have argued that a positive correlation between managerial-control and high profit rates is compatible with the managerial revolution thesis. This would be expected, because the corporate form of organization is structurally organized to maximize profits. However, the corporate organization places less emphasis on profits as an organizational goal because professional managers pursue goals other than profits.

These hypotheses are supported by my national probability samples of daily newspapers in the United States.[18] In several studies, I have found that corporate newspapers are more profitable than smaller, less "corporatized" ones. I argue that corporate newspapers are more profitable because they benefit from economies of scale and superior management and human

---

[18]My research on the corporate newspaper is reported in the following sources: David Pearce Demers, *The Menace of the Corporate Newspaper: Fact or Fiction?* (Ames: Iowa State University Press, 1996); David Demers, "Corporate Newspaper Structure, Social Control and Social Change," pp. 375-398 in David Demers and K. Viswanath (eds.), *Mass Media, Social Control and Social Change: A Macrosocial Perspective* (Ames: Iowa State University Press, 1999); David Demers, "Corporate Newspaper Bashing: Is It Justified?" *Newspaper Research Journal* (in press); David Demers, "Structural Pluralism, Corporate Newspaper Structure and News Source Perceptions: Another Test of the Editor Vigor Hypothesis," *Journalism & Mass Communication Quarterly*, 75:572-592 (1998); David Pearce Demers, "Corporate Newspaper Structure, Profits and Organizational Goals," *The Journal of Media Economics*, 9(2):1-23 (1996); David Demers, "Revisiting Corporate Newspaper Structure and Profit-Making," *Journal of Media Economics*, 11(2):19-35 (1998); David Pearce Demers, "Corporate Newspaper Structure, Editorial Page Vigor and Social Change. *Journalism & Mass Communication Quarterly*, 73:857-877 (1996); David Pearce Demers, "Use of Polls in Reporting Changes Slightly Since 1978," *Journalism Quarterly*, 64:839-842 (1987); David Pearce Demers, "Corporate Structure and Emphasis on Profits and Product Quality at U.S. Daily Newspapers," *Journalism Quarterly*, 68:15-26 (1991); David Pearce Demers, "Effect of Corporate Structure on Autonomy of Top Editors at U.S. Dailies," *Journalism Quarterly*, 70:499-508 (1993); David Pearce Demers, "The Relative Constancy Hypothesis, Structural Pluralism and National Advertising Expenditures," *Journal of Media Economics*, 7(4):31-48 (1994); David Pearce Demers, "Structural Pluralism, Intermedia Competition and the Growth of the Corporate Newspaper in the United States," *Journalism Monographs*, Vol. 145 (June 1994); David Pearce Demers, "Does Personal Experience in a Community Increase or Decrease Newspaper Reading?" *Journalism Quarterly*, 73:304-318 (1996); and David Pearce Demers and Daniel B. Wackman, "Effect of Chain Ownership on Newspaper Management Goals," *Newspaper Research Journal*, 9(2):59-68 (1988).

resources. However, corporate newspapers also very clearly place less emphasis on profits as an organizational goal and more emphasis on other, nonprofit goals — such as product quality, maximizing growth of the organization, using the latest technology, worker autonomy and being innovative — because they are controlled by professional managers and technocrats, not the owners.

As mentioned earlier, my research also shows that journalists at corporate newspapers are more satisfied with their jobs because they have more autonomy, status and prestige than journalists at noncorporate or entrepreneurial newspapers. And, more importantly, I found that as organizations become more corporatized, editorials and letters to the editor published in them become more, not less, critical of mainstream groups and ideas. In addition, established news sources (mayors and police chiefs) in communities served by corporate newspapers also believe that those newspapers are more critical of their policies and city hall. I trace the growth and development of the corporate newspaper to the economic and social division of labor in society (i.e., structural pluralism or social differentiation), and I argue that the corporate form of organization helps to explain many of the social changes that have taken place, especially in the last century.

Despite these findings, a fundamental question remains: Can these changes be generalized to other industries as well? The newspaper industry is widely believed to operate in markets where there is little direct competition, which is not characteristic of most markets. Thus, these findings may not be representative of businesses as a whole. At the same time, however, the empirical research by economists and sociologists also cannot be generalized to the entire population of businesses, because virtually all of it is based on national data for only the largest corporations — populations of firms have rarely been studied.

In another study, I attempted to circumvent these problems by examining changes in source attributions in news stories over time. The assumption underlying this approach is that media content reflects in a crude way the power structure of a society. If this power-reflection proposition is correct, then one could postulate that changes in the power structure should be reflected in the sources that journalists use to report on the news. More specifically, I hypothesized that during the 20th century attributions of capitalists declined, whereas attributions of scientists, technicians, researchers and others whose roles involve the production of theoretical knowledge increased. A content analysis of source attributions on the front page of *The New York Times* over a 90-year period during the 20th century supported this hypothesis. Attributions of capitalists declined from 8.8 percent in 1903 to 4.0 percent in 1993. In contrast, attributions of technocrats increased, going from 2.7 percent to 10.5 percent. Although illustrative, the findings from this study should be interpreted cautiously, as they assume that attributions are a measure of the power structure in a society.

Finally — and perhaps most importantly — in 1996 I conducted a national survey of U.S. daily newspapers and asked publishers, owners and editors what role they play in making decisions about editorial and news content. This is the only study to directly test the managerial revolution hypothesis in the media industry.

The logic behind my theory of corporate management control is not complex. Basically, it posits that owners and publishers lose control over the editorial content because of increasing role specialization.

More specifically, as the scale and size of an organization increases, roles generally become more specialized and the division of labor expands. These structural forces increase the productive capacity of the organization and reduce costs; however, they also increase the complexity of the decision-making process. A highly complex organization depends heavily on a highly educated and skilled workforce to achieve its goals. At newspapers, this means that editors and other newsroom experts, not the owners and publishers, have the requisite knowledge and skills to make such decisions. Owners (whether proprietors or absentee stockholders) and other top-level managers (publishers) depend heavily on experts and highly skilled managers to run the organization. And the owners' and publishers' roles also become more specialized; that is, they tend to focus more on budgetary matters and long-term planning rather than on day-to-day matters.

I hypothesized that the more a newspaper exhibits the characteristics of the corporate form of organization the less role owners (proprietors and stockholders) and publishers will play in making decisions that affect editorial content (i.e., what to cover, what to publish on the front page, whether to publish a controversial story, and what positions to take in editorials); and the greater the role editors and reporters will play in making decisions that affect editorial content. The data were collected through a national probability mail survey of top-ranking managers at daily newspapers in the United States.

The data supported the first hypothesis, which expected that owners and publishers would play less of a role in making decisions about editorial content as a newspaper becomes more corporatized. Fewer than one percent of the owners at highly corporatized newspapers said they played a major role in editorial decision making (i.e., major is defined as values five, six or seven on the 7-point scale), compared with 11.3 percent of the owners at newspapers scoring low on the corporate index measure. Similarly, only 17.5 percent of the publishers at highly corporatized newspapers say they play a major role in editorial decision making, versus 38.4 percent of publishers at the least corporatized newspapers. In short, the higher a newspaper scores on the corporate index, the less role owners and publishers play in controlling news content.

The data also generally support the second hypothesis, which expected that editors and reporters would play a larger role in controlling news content as corporate structure increases. This finding applies to managing editors, editorial editors and reporters. The only exception was top editors, for whom corporate structure does not make a difference, because most top editors at all newspapers play a major role in controlling editorial content. But managing editors at highly corporatized newspapers are much more likely than their counterparts at the other papers to say they play a role in controlling content (94.6 percent vs. 84.0 percent and 89.7 percent, respectively). Even more dramatic, nearly half of the reporters at highly corporatized newspapers (47 percent) say they play a major role in deciding what stories to cover, compared with only about a fourth (28.8 percent) of those at the least corporatized newspapers.

Finally, nearly 9 of 10 editorial editors at highly corporatized newspapers say they play a major role in deciding what positions to take in editorials. Additional analysis showed that the relationship between the role variables and corporate structure remained about the same when controlling for respondent's job function (i.e., editor, publisher, owner, reporter, managing editor) and for demographic characteristics (education, age, gender, income).

MANAGERS AND MEDIA OF THE FUTURE

At a minimum these studies and the social scientific literature in general suggests that arguments that dismiss outright the notion that managerial and technocratic occupations are gaining power relative to capitalists are premature. At a maximum, the literature suggests that a major transition of power has taken place. I believe the latter is closer to the truth, and if it is, this transfer of power has at least two major implications for media managers, scholars and policy makers.

First, the managerial revolution casts doubt on arguments that the growth of the corporate form of organization in mass media industries is leading to greater emphasis on profits at the expense of product quality or a diversity of ideas. Instead, the managerial revolution hypothesis suggests that professional managers and editors are placing greater emphasis on information diversity, product quality and other nonprofit goals.

Second, if a transition of power is taking place, then corporate media would be expected to have a greater capacity to promote social change. This does not mean that hegemonic models are wrong; rather, they just overstate the social control consequences of the mass media and understate the media's capacity to promote social change. The growth of corporate media, in fact, may help to explain many of the social changes during the last century or so that have benefited disadvantaged groups (e.g., increasing rights for consumers, women, environmentalists and minorities). This topic is addressed in more depth in the next chapter, which examines how the news media cover the news and whose interests they promote.

Chapter 16

WHOSE INTERESTS WILL
MEDIA OF THE FUTURE SERVE?

Sometimes — no matter what you do — you can't please anyone.

Just ask CNN correspondent Peter Arnett, who was one of the few Western journalists allowed to cover the 1991 Gulf War from inside Iraq. Iraqi officials didn't trust him, so they censored parts of the news reports he filed from Baghdad. But his reports didn't please U.S. officials either — especially the reports about civilian casualties, the bombing of an alleged baby formula factory, and his interview with Saddam Hussein. For example:

- Gen. H. Norman Schwarzkopf told Barbara Walters that Arnett's reports of the civilian deaths made the United States look like it was "lying to the American people when we (American military) told them we were deliberately trying not to target civilian targets."
- American military officials argued that the baby formula factory was actually a biological-weapons facility, but Arnett's reports strongly implied this was not the case.
- Arnett's interview with Saddam, *The New York Times* reported, "gave the Iraqi ruler an opportunity to restate his certainty of victory, to suggest that he might use unconventional weapons if forced and to express gratitude to 'noble souls' in the West who have been demonstrating against the war."
- Sen. Alan Simpson called Arnett an Iraqi "sympathizer."
- A coalition of right-wing groups called him a "traitor" and "an unpaid propagandist" for Saddam Hussein.

Ironically, though, after the war, left-wing mass communication scholars around the world charged CNN and other global news media of reporting the conflict with a pro-Western bias — not an Iraqi one! They argued that global media coverage helped legitimate and justify the West's attacks on Iraq. In fact, polls showed that the U.S. public opinion became much more supportive of President George Bush and his policies after the shooting started. So, in the end,

319

the only organization
apparently pleased with
Arnett's coverage was CNN,
whose audience ratings
soared during the war and
helped boost the network
into one of the world's top
television news networks.

In response to his critics,
Arnett says he was just
doing his job. "Why
shouldn't we show what
bombs do when they hit a

U.S. planes fly over burning oil fields
during the 1991 Gulf War

country?" he asked an audience at the University of California in San Diego.
Many journalists agreed. Arnett was simply reporting events as objectively as
possible, they argued. But if his reports were objective, then why did they
generate so much criticism?

CHAPTER OVERVIEW

Can news really be objective? Can news from global media corporations be
objective now or in the future? Is there really any difference between the way
global media and nation-based media cover events like the 2003 Iraq War? And
whose interests are corporate and global media serving?

The purpose of this chapter is to answer these questions. We'll focus first
on the ethics of objectivity, which is one of the most important principles
guiding Western journalists today. Next we'll examine the impact that the
mainstream bias has on news coverage. And finally we'll examine the effects
terrorism and threats to the environment (e.g., global warming) will have on the
future of the ethic of objectivity as a guiding principle for journalists.

THE ETHIC OF OBJECTIVITY

Although definitions vary,[1] three major ideas or tenets underlie most
conceptions of objectivity: Journalists should keep their personal opinions and
the opinions of their newspapers out of their news stories; All sides to a story

---

[1]For details, see Steven R. Knowlton and Karen L. Freeman (eds.), *Fair & Balanced:
A History of Journalistic Objectivity* (Northport, AL: Vision Press, 2005).

should be covered and reported; and All sides to a story should be given an equal amount of coverage.

The origins of objectivity are often traced to the 1830s and the so-called penny press in the United States, which sold newspapers for a penny apiece and became the first "mass" medium.[2] But it took nearly a century for the concept to gain widespread acceptance. And despite another century of practice, the notion that the news media are objective is under greater assault today than at any time in history.

On one side are the conservatives, who vociferously argue that mainstream media, including global media, have a liberal bias. In their book, *And That's The Way It Is(n't): A Reference Guide to Media Bias,* L. Brent Bozell III and Brent H. Baker argue that

> America's most influential media outlets report the news through a liberal prism. With reprints, excerpts and summaries of more than 40 studies conducted over the past decade, (this book) provides the most thorough analysis ever compiled proving the liberal political slant in the national press.[3]

On the other side are the liberals, who — you guessed it — accuse the media of having a conservative bias. As media critics Jeff Cohen and Norman Solomon put it:

> One of the most enduring myths about the mainstream news media is that they are "liberal." The myth flourishes to the extent that people don't ask pointed questions: If the new media are liberal, why have national dailies and news weeklies regularly lauded those aspects of President Clinton's program that they view as "centrist" or "moderate," while questioning those viewed as liberal?[4]

---

[2]Dan Schiller, "An Historical Approach to Objectivity and Professionalism in American News Reporting," *Journal of Communication,* 29(4):46-57 (1979). Some authors argue that objectivity has a much longer history, but the term wasn't used in a professional publication until 1911. For more details, see Knowlton and Freeman, *Fair & Balanced,* and Susan Thompson, *The Penny Press: The Origins of Modern News Media, 1833-1861* (Northport, AL: Vision Press, 2004).

[3]L. Brent Bozell III and Brent H. Baker (eds.), *And That's The Way It Is(n't): A Reference Guide to Media Bias* (Alexandria, VA: Media Research Center, 1990), quoted material is from the book's back cover.

[4]Jeff Cohen and Norman Solomon, *Through the Media Looking Glass: Decoding Bias and Blather in the News* (Monroe, ME: Common Courage Press, 1995), p. 22.

Of course, the third perspective comes from the journalists themselves, who argue that the news is neither liberal nor conservative. "We don't take sides," they often say. "We are neutral, objective, and nonideological. Indeed, our professional ethic of objectivity holds that we must be unbiased observers of the world. We are supposed to keep our personal opinions to ourselves, cover all sides of the story, and give roughly equal weight to all sides. Opinions are properly expressed only on the editorial and op-ed pages, or in news analyses."[5]

Although journalists readily concede that "pure" objectivity is impossible to achieve, they nonetheless are committed to following a number of news-gathering rules — such as attributing information to sources and quoting different sides to a controversy — that allegedly produce "objective," unbiased news accounts. As former ABC News President James Hagerty put it:

> We're trying to be objective ... we are reporters! We get interpretations from other people and present them. If anyone on this network is expressing his own opinion — well, if I catch him [sic] I won't permit it.[6]

So who's right?

The conservatives, the liberals or the journalists?

None of them, as I shall argue in this chapter.

The news does contain a bias, to be sure. But when viewed from afar, it is neither extremely liberal nor conservative. It is *mainstream*, centrist, or middle of the road. In fact, that's why they often are called "mainstream media." Media now and in the future will continue to present a mainstream bias — a bias that will rely heavily upon mainstream Western elites for news, but a bias that, in relative terms, contains a greater variety of perspectives than alternative approaches.

---

[5]Journalists often argue that they try to be "fair" rather than "objective," the former arising in part from problems in trying to define the latter. Presumably this means that one does not have to give all sides equal weight in a story, as would be required under the ethic of objectivity. However, journalists have never satisfactorily defined fairness and how it differs from objectivity. A better explanation is that "fairness" is used to help deflect criticism when equal weight is not given to all sides in a story. For more on this topic, see, e.g., The Freedom Forum Media Studies Center, "The Fairness Factor," *Media Studies Journal*, 6(4), (Fall 1992).

[6]Former ABC News President James Hagerty, quoted in Edith Efron, "Do the Networks Know What They Are Doing?" pp. 133-149 in David J. Leroy and Christopher H. Sterling (eds.), *Mass News: Practices, Controversies and Alternatives* (Englewood Cliffs, NJ: Prentice-Hall, 1973), p. 134.

THE MAINSTREAM BIAS

The mainstream bias means that Western news media rarely give positive news coverage to extremist groups on either the left or right. For example, communists and others on the "far left" rarely get sympathetic press coverage in daily newspapers or on national television. But the same holds for neo-Fascists and others on the "far right." Virtually all of the coverage given to these groups — in commentaries as well as straight "hard news" stories — is negative or critical. The only notable exception is when one of the extremist groups is denied freedom of speech, in which case the news coverage focuses on the free-speech issue rather than on the ideological goals of the groups. This has happened on several occasions to the neo-Nazi groups in the United States. However, the goals of those groups are strongly condemned and criticized by the mainstream news sources cited in the news stories.

So what is the mainstream ideology? In the United States, it is embodied in the Democratic and Republican parties. In England, it is the Conservative and Labor parties. And throughout much of Europe, it is the Social Democrats. These are the groups that get preferential coverage in the news and generally the most positive coverage. To be sure, there is a lot of critical news directed at mainstream parties — especially when they criticize each other. When that occurs, the mainstream news media usually cover both mainstream sides of a dispute.

However, news media rarely seek the opinions of groups that are considered to be outside of the mainstream. In fact, the more extreme the group, the less the coverage it will receive and the less favorable the coverage will be. Conversely, as a rule, the more the group's goals fall within mainstream values and norms, the more coverage it tends to get and the more favorable that coverage.

Bias in a U.S. Presidential Election

A good way to illustrate the mainstream bias is to examine a U.S. presidential election. All presidential races include more candidates than just those in the Democratic and Republican parties. In 1996, for example, 21 people ran for president (albeit not all names were on all 50 state ballots).

To be purely objective, a reporter ideally should give each candidate in a presidential election equal coverage — that is, each should receive the same amount of space, the same placement and the same balance of views. This ideal is sometimes possible when there is only one Democratic and one Republican candidate, because both are from the political mainstream. However, because presidential elections also include candidates from nonmainstream parties, the coverage has never come close to the ideal of objectivity. Some candidates receive more coverage than others.

For example, in 1996 the media gave much less coverage to Green Party candidate Ralph Nader, Libertarian candidate Harry Browne, and Socialist Workers Party candidate James Harris. The vast bulk of the coverage went to Bill Clinton and Robert Dole. Ross Perot received less coverage than Clinton or Dole but more coverage than the other nonmainstream candidates. Why? Because his views were closer to the mainstream than most of the other candidates, he had a relatively large following (more political power than the other nonmainstream candidates), and he was a curious anomaly (a billionaire running for office).

Now, you may ask, why do the "alternative" candidates get so little coverage? Through the years, I've asked many journalists this question. And the answer is almost always the same. Because, they respond, the alternative candidates have no chance of winning and because the public wants to hear about the mainstream candidates. The public does not want to hear the views of socialist or Green Party candidates, they add.

There is, no doubt, some truth to this. Most of the alternative candidates have no chance of winning, and the public generally is less interested in their views. But this doesn't change the fact that — and most journalists will concede this — the election coverage is not objective. The alternative candidates are "marginalized," meaning that they are assumed not to be viable candidates.

Mainstream Bias in Other News Stories

The mainstream bias is more difficult to see in other stories, especially in those that are not controversial. But it is there.

For example, the very day I am writing the copy you are now reading, the (Spokane, Washington) *Spokesman-Review* published a story titled, "White separatists to be featured at survivalist expo." The story outlined how leaders of neo-Nazi, right-wing Christian separatist, anti-black and anti-Semitic groups would be speaking at the Spokane Convention Center. But the focus of the story was not on what the speakers would say — as it might have been for Republican and Democratic speakers. Rather, the focus was on how the views of these groups were contrary to the dominant values of the community. None of the extremist leaders was interviewed, but there was a generous sampling of critics' views.

"From a legal standpoint, there's nothing we can do to block this kind of event," one city official is quoted as saying. "Do we condone it? Do we want it to be there? The answer is, 'Hell no!'" Says another city official: "Like civil libertarians, I am concerned with ... (respecting) ... First Amendment freedoms.

But as the human rights specialist, I will continue to speak against supremacy and hatred, and I encourage citizens who want to live in a respectful community to do the same."

With this example I am not trying to defend the position of right-wing groups — in my opinion, their views are repugnant and based on ignorance. However, in terms of analyzing the media coverage, this example illustrates quite clearly how the media marginalize extremist groups and, in the process, provide support for dominant groups and community values. Stories about terrorism do the same thing (more on this later in the chapter).

Another front-page story in the same *Spokesman-Review* edition extolled the virtues of a Russian human rights champion who was tormented in prison during the Soviet days of "totalitarian repression." The moral lesson: Communism is bad.

Another story details one of the possible motives why a deputy sheriff charged with murder may have shot his wife. Adultery, which violates virtually all mainstream religious groups' codes of morality, can lead people astray. Still another story in the newspaper noted that a new diabetic drug could reduce the need for insulin. This story reinforced social norms and values about the importance of scientific research and helped the U.S. Food and Drug Administration get the word out to the public.

I must emphasize again that I am not passing personal judgment on these stories or the values promoted in them. In fact, I believe many of them are noble and worthy of coverage. However, my point is that the news is not objective in any absolute sense, despite what journalists may claim. At the same time, the news is not nearly so conservative as the liberals would have us believe nor as liberal as the conservatives would have us believe. Rather, in all cultures, news in the mass media generally promotes the dominant values of that culture and the powerful social institutions. And, at election time, the mainstream bias helps to guarantee that changes in national leadership do not come quickly or radically.

By the way, if you want to understand why some people believe the news media are too liberal or too conservative, simply ask them for their political orientation. As a rule of thumb, the more conservative the orientation, the more likely they are to see the media as liberal. The more liberal the orientation, the more likely they are to see the media as conservative.

So much for objectivity.[7]

---

[7]Having pointed out that news is not objective in any absolute sense, I now face the problem of relativism — if there is no objectivity, then is every news account of an event equivalent and is there no truth? The answer is "no," and I will pull myself out of the quagmire of relativism by building a case for what I call "relative objectivity." Basically,

Origins of the Mainstream Bias

The mainstream bias is not the product of a conspiracy on the part of journalists, film producers or elites in Western countries. Media in all social systems reflect the general concerns and interests of those in positions of power. If they didn't, they would have a difficult time surviving.

Imagine, for instance, what would happen if a news organization published a story that was sympathetic to extremist views, such as those of the neo-Nazis. Community and mainstream political groups would be outraged. Many advertisers would pull their ads, and many readers would drop their subscriptions. In other words, the dependence that media have on profits to survive is also a mechanism for keeping the media "in line" — and it helps uphold and protect the status quo.

The mainstream bias is the product of a number of complex legal, cultural, social and economic constraints that media face to survive in the marketplace. These forces did not just emerge yesterday. They go back to the origins of mass media themselves.

The first newspapers in England and the United States faced major legal constraints, as the first part of this book pointed out. If they published content that was critical of the authorities, the newspaper could be shut down and the publisher prosecuted. In fact, the first newspaper in the United States was shut down after the publication of its first issue in 1690, because it published stories about an attempt to bribe Native Americans to turn them against the colonists and a scandal involving the French king and his daughter-in-law.

Legal constraints, which include libel law (content that harms a person's reputation), continue to play an important role in regulating what people can say. However, they are only a small part of the picture. Cultural and social factors also play a key role.

When John Campbell began publishing a newspaper in the American colonies in 1704, he was well aware that he had to stay within certain moral and ethical boundaries — not just to please the British authorities but to please community leaders as well. At that time, a story about women's rights or sexual relations, for example, would have offended many clergymen and sparked much criticism of the newspaper. Most mainstream media, in fact, did not support women's right to vote until after 1916, when President Woodrow Wilson declared his support for the 19th Amendment. And Wilson's change of

---

this is the idea that contemporary Western-style journalism incorporates more points of view than one can get from communist or totalitarian media, which of course limit expression to the groups in power.

heart, no doubt, was influenced at least in part by the fact that Australia and New Zealand had already given women the right to vote.

Although times have changed and stories about women's rights and sex are much more common today, media are still bound by cultural values and the interests of those in power. Women and minorities in most Western countries still struggle to find legitimacy in mainstream media, and they have yet to achieve equality in the workplace. And the media rely heavily on political and economic elites — not the general public — for news, which means the news tends to legitimize the institutions these elites run.

The dependence that media have on elites for news can be traced to the development of news beats. Prior to the 1830s, the content of most newspapers was composed of national or international affairs. The accounts were usually lifted from newspapers in other countries or from official government documents. Local news stories, when they appeared, were often gleaned from other local newspapers, private letters, correspondence and, occasionally, personal contacts with governmental officials. Newspapers were directed largely to elite audiences, which included government officials, politicians and business people. Most newspapers were highly partisan in character, and many were supported by political parties. Although colorful, such papers had limited appeal — generally to members of their political party.

This changed dramatically with the emergence of the penny press in the 1830s. The penny papers focused not just on economic and governmental news but on social news, which included reporting the affairs of the local police, courts and community groups. These papers were very popular. Circulation and advertising revenues grew rapidly. To maintain a continuous flow of news copy, newspapers created "beats." These beats were anchored in the centers of power in a community, which included governmental sources (police, courts, city hall), businesses (Wall Street), community groups (religious, social) and, eventually, lifestyle beats (sports, food, women's pages).

It was through the penny press that the ethic of objectivity in reporting began to emerge. Gradually throughout the 19th century newspapers began to shed their partisanship in favor of a more neutral stance. This appealed to more readers, which in turn boosted advertising sales and revenues. Whereas the ethic of objectivity did mean that newspapers were now printing more than one opinion when covering a controversial issue, it did not mean that newspapers were objective in some absolute sense. They still obtained news and information from the powerful elites, and those outside the mainstream power groups were still marginalized.

In short, the mainstreaming effects of the news media are not a product of a conspiracy; rather, they are the product of organizational routines and constraints on the news operation. Through a unique set of historical circumstances, media linked themselves to the centers of power, and the outcome was also beneficial for the media. By cooperating with the media, elites helped to legitimate the role of the media in covering news. And the profit motive ensures that media will not stray too far beyond the interests of elites. It is inconceivable, for example, to imagine stories that would attack representative democracy as a political system or capitalism as an economic system. Any Western media organization taking such a stand quickly would find itself without readers and advertisers. And news media of the future will be subject to the same constraints.

Is the Mainstream Bias Good or Bad?

Of course, the answer to this question depends on whether you're a member of a mainstream party or not. During the 1992 presidential election, Dr. Lenora B. Fulani, the only black female candidate in the race, asked reporters why they were not covering her campaign. "Because you didn't raise much money and because you don't have a chance of winning," they told her. Her response: "How can I raise money and win if you don't give coverage to my campaign?"

Catch-22.

Needless to say, news coverage that focuses primarily on mainstream candidates has the consequence of legitimizing those candidates and helping them maintain their advantage in the election. Once again, I must point out that I am not passing judgment on this fact — I am simply pointing it out. Many journalists and elites would defend the current practice of giving less coverage to alternative candidates. They would argue that the country might fall into the hands of some radical element if all alternative candidates were given as much and as favorable coverage as mainstream candidates. Perhaps. But the point remains that the coverage is not objective — it supports a mainstream view of the world, and that has consequences for the distribution of power in societies. Specifically, the mainstream bias helps to maintain the status quo.

IMPACT OF THE MAINSTREAM BIAS

The news coverage of presidential elections highlights one of the major values promoted in the news — moderatism. In other words, excess or extremism in politics should be avoided.

Sociologist Herbert J. Gans has identified seven other enduring values in the news: ethnocentrism, altruistic democracy, responsible capitalism, small-town pastoralism, individualism, (social) order and national leadership.[8] Although he was writing about U.S. media, these values actually can be applied to news media in most Western and many other nations around the world (including global news media corporations), and to most forms of entertainment programming on television, at the movies and on radio (more on this below).

By ethnocentrism, Gans means that the news media value their own nation above all others. This ethnocentrism is most explicit, he says, in foreign news, "which judges other countries by the extent to which they live up to or imitate American practices and values ... ." War news and humanitarian efforts provide the clearest expression of this principle. Recent examples include coverage of the ethnic conflict in Yugoslavia, the 1991 Gulf War and the 2003 Iraq War. Western media coverage helped legitimate intervention by NATO, the United States and other Western countries.

The value of altruistic democracy is highlighted in stories about corruption, conflict, protest and bureaucratic malfunctioning. The news implies that politics should be based on the public interest.

The value of responsible capitalism means that the news has an optimistic faith in capitalism, the good life and competition, and that unreasonable profits and gross exploitation of workers is wrong. Stories about corporate investors who violate federal laws reinforce this value.

Small-town pastoralism refers to the love-affair that most Americans and Westerners have with the idea of small-town life, and to the problems posed by industrialization: urban crime, increasing social conflict and urban decay. British author Peter Mayle's books about rural French life, such as *A Year in Provence*, strongly support this value.

Individualism promotes the idea of freedom of the individual both within and against the system. People are expected to participate in society and act in the public interest but on their own terms.

Although it is often argued that the United States places much more value on individualism than other countries — and there may be some truth to this — the idea of individuality itself was not born in the United States. Individualism is largely a product of modernization, or more specifically, social differentiation and the division of labor. Traditional societies and groups do not give individuals much freedom or autonomy. The "collective" takes precedence over the individual. There is very little tolerance for alternative lifestyles. However, as cities grew and industrialism spread, the number and variety of

---

[8]Herbert J. Gans, "Deciding What's News," *Columbia Journalism Review* (January/February 1979), pp. 40-45.

groups (occupational, social, political) also increased. This means that people in urban areas or modern societies have more options and opportunities. Of course, one of the adverse consequences of greater freedom and autonomy (i.e., individuality) is that many people feel estranged from the community. Sociologists argue that this is one reason for higher crime and suicide rates.

Gans also argues that strong leadership is highly valued, because it is the way through which order and moral values are maintained. In all countries around the world, news media provide substantial coverage of their leaders.

As noted earlier in this book, the news also reinforces the value of order and social cohesion. Whenever a major disorder occurs, such as a riot or protest, the first thing the media call for is calm. Violence is never the way to solve problems. One must always work peaceably for change, even if the system is highly repressive. Well, almost always. There are some interesting historical exceptions to this rule.

For example, in the United States, accounts of the American Revolution are almost always written in a way to justify the use of force and violence against England (see discussion of the Sons of Liberty later in this chapter). Of course, history books would be quite different today if the British had won. But it is fairly safe to say that today virtually no group in America — except the police and armed forces — could use violence and obtain positive news coverage, no matter how overwhelming the repression they face.

Mainstream Bias in Entertainment Programming

We have spent most of this chapter talking about the mainstream bias in Western news media reports. And for good reason. News media play a major role in shaping or influencing public policy. Politicians, bureaucrats, corporate executives and special interest groups depend heavily on news to achieve their goals. But the mainstream bias also exists in Western entertainment programming, and the impact of entertainment programming should not be underestimated, as people spend much more time with it than with the news.

Finding examples of entertainment programming that support mainstream values and institutions is not difficult. Take, for instance, law and order. One of the most significant themes of Western television and movie programs is that "crime doesn't pay." Despite all of the gratuitous violence in such programming, most television and movie programming clearly does not encourage people to engage in criminal activity. Lawbreakers are almost always caught, killed or punished. And those that get away usually have noble motives or are up against a corrupt system.

Through the latter half of the 20th century, mass communication scholar George Gerbner argued, quite correctly I believe, that these tales of morality define the boundaries of acceptable behavior, reinforce laws that punish lawbreakers, and provide support for authoritarian police practices and laws. Although Gerbner's social control model makes a lot of sense, some critics believe television violence produces anti-social behavior, including criminal behavior. Social science research over the past four decades has shown that violent programming increases the probability of aggressive behavior in small children. But the question of whether violent programming can contribute to adult criminal behavior is still unanswered.[9]

Entertainment programming also reinforces many other values that contribute to social order and mainstream views. For example, television programming and movies frequently extol the virtues of a good education and a successful career, but the self-absorbed "filthy" rich and those who turn their backs on materialism (the ascetics) both tend to be marginalized or are portrayed as kooks. Education is also highly revered, because it is seen as the ticket to success in the capitalist job market.

Most Western mass media do not support a particular religious institution, because their societies and communities have a variety of religious groups. But they all place a great deal of importance on the idea that religion is important for social cohesion and stability. Generally, it's also good to be religious, but both fanatics (members of cult groups) and religion-hating atheists are usually portrayed as bad.

Although many television comedies, particularly in the United States, portray characters in nontraditional family situations, the emphasis is almost always on love, friendship, honesty, sincerity and treating others well. And then there is love, perhaps the most commonly found theme in media next to violence. Western media idealize the notion of romance and love, and who could conceive of a more powerful aphrodisiac for social control?

The Mainstream Bias and Social Change

So what does the mainstream bias mean in terms of understanding the role and function of mass media in the future?

Because mass media are creations of Western culture, are profit-seeking organizations and are dependent upon powerful governmental and corporate sources for news, the content of that media will continue to generate strong support for Western values and institutions, such as responsible capitalism and representative democracy. Alternative economic and political systems or ideas

---

[9]Douglas A. Gentile (ed.), *Media Violence and Children: A Complete Guide for Parents and Professionals* (Westport, CT: Praeger, 2003).

still will be marginalized. This helps to explain in part why global media coverage of the 1991 Gulf War, the NATO bombing of Yugoslavia, and the 2003 Iraq War contained a pro-Western bias.

However, because media are becoming increasingly global in orientation and the audiences are transcending national boundaries, the content of global media also will be less nation-centric. When an international dispute emerges, global media cannot afford to alienate audiences in different countries. This helps to explain why U.S. officials were so upset about Arnett's coverage from inside Iraq. And it also explains why Reuter's changed its policy on coverage of terrorism.

Reuter's, Terrorism and Objectivity

The Sons of Liberty.[10]

U.S. historians could have called them America's first terrorists. After all, they used violence to achieve political goals before and during the War of Independence. They tarred and feathered British civilians and destroyed their property. They forced some British tax collectors to resign from their positions. They also were behind the famous Boston Tea Party.

Historian Todd Alan Kreamer points out that the British clearly viewed the Sons of Liberty as a terrorist organization. But American history books today do not characterize that group as a terrorist organization for one simple reason: America won the war. To the victors go the spoils, including the power to define reality. So, today, the Sons of Liberty are known as patriots, or freedom fighters, not terrorists.

The line between terrorist and patriot (or freedom fighter) is thin but not invisible to mass media scholars who study propaganda, culture and language. They know that U.S. government politicians and spokespersons often use highly emotive words to characterize their enemies and their friends. "Terrorist" and "freedom fighter" are two of the most popular. Media research shows that journalists routinely and unquestioningly use such terms in news stories, even outside of directly quoted material.

---

[10]This essay was originally published in *Global Media News*. See David Demers, "When Is a Terrorist a Terrorist? Reuters Policy Exposes Parochialism in U.S. Media," *Global Media News*, 4(1):1, 11 (Winter 2002). Sources include Todd Alan Kreamer, *The Early America Review*, Vol. 1, No. 2 (Fall 1996, a copy of the article is posted at <www.earlyamerica.com/review/ fall96/index.html>); Kim Campbell, "When Is 'Terrorist' a Subjective Term?", *The Christian Science Monitor* (September 27, 2001), p. 16; Peter Wrothington, "War: Winning Is Everthing," *The Toronto Sun* (September 29, 2001), p. 26.

But once in a while a news organization steps out of the mainstream. That happened on September 25, 2001, when Reuter's news service announced that it would no longer use the word "terrorist" or "freedom fighter" in news stories unless those terms were attributed to a source. In essence, the news agency called into question the power of political elites such as George Bush to define reality. Media rarely do that, especially after an event as horrific as the September 11 attack.

Nancy Bobrowitz, who is senior vice president for Reuters' corporate communications, said Reuters has had, for several decades, a policy against using what it calls "emotive" terms without attribution. However, the policy apparently was not formalized until Reuters head Stephen Jukes sent out a memo to his staff in September saying "one man's terrorist is another man's freedom fighter."

Reuters' Web site added that, "As part of a long-standing policy to avoid the use of emotive words, we do not use 'terrorist' and 'freedom fighter' unless they are in a direct quote or are otherwise attributed to a third party. We do not characterize the subjects of news stories but instead report actions, identity and background so that readers can make their own decisions based on facts."

Bobrowitz said Reuters must adhere to such a policy in part because Reuters has a "global audience." She said objectivity is important to gain the confidence and respect of readers around the world. A month later, the BBC World News Service agreed and instituted a similar policy.

None of the major U.S. news organizations, however, has followed Reuters' lead. In fact, so far Reuters' decision has generated more criticism than support from U.S. journalists and their organizations. "Journalism should be about telling the truth, and when you don't call this (September 11) a terrorist attack, you're not telling the truth," Rich Noyes, director of media analysis at the conservative Media Research Center, told the *Christian Science Monitor*.

To support their case, some Reuters critics cite *New York Times* columnist William Safire's definition of terrorism. Safire wrote that the term "terrorist" has its roots in the Latin "terrere," which means "to frighten." "The most precise word to describe a person who murders even one innocent civilian to send a political message is terrorist," Safire added.

This is a reasonable definition. But if one accepts it, critics point out, then U.S. history must be re-written.

The Sons of Liberty would be just the beginning. In the late 19th and early 20th centuries, the list of other "terrorist actions" would include the forced annexation of Hawaii, police violence against labor union workers, state tolerance of lynchings of African Americans, the CIA-backed coup in Chile in 1973, the My Lai massacre in Vietnam, and military invasions in Carribean countries.

Of course, critics would also point out that the quintessential terrorist act was the dropping of atomic bombs on Nagasaki and Hiroshima, because they directly or indirectly contributed to the deaths of thousands of innocent civilians. Proponents of dropping the bomb justify these deaths as unfortunate casualties of war. They blame the Japanese.

But, as critics point out, historically, the ultimate arbiter of what is defined as an act of terror is who wins the war or the conflict. The inability of U.S. media to see this principle stems largely from the structural constraints they face. They serve American elites and institutions, and they ultimately must respond to their concerns. If they don't, then those institutions will de-legitimize journalists and the media.

But global media face a different set of constraints, and if U.S. media expect to compete in the global market, then they undoubtedly will have to shed some of their ethnocentrism.

THE FUTURE OF OBJECTIVITY

Although the ethic of objectivity produces a bias that favors mainstream values and institutions and, thus, is anything but "objective" in an absolute sense, the ethic is likely to remain the most important value guiding news gathering well into the 21st century. That is because in relative terms the ethic of objectivity does produce a journalism that incorporates more points of view or opinion than other approaches.

Recall, that, during the 19th century, most newspapers in Europe and the Americas were highly partisan, usually siding with and sometimes being financially supported by political parties. Many contemporary critics of journalism wish for that kind of press again — one that allegedly contained a robust debate. But, as might be expected from a partisan press, the stories and columns in those publications were often vitriolic, inaccurate and self-serving. Not only that, they also excluded the other point of view. You only got one side of the story. Moreover, most people didn't get more than one side to a story because they just read their own political party's paper. They didn't read the other party's paper, and this, of course, had the effect of limiting the debate.

But the ethic of objectivity changed that. Increasingly newspapers became less partisan and restricted opinion and commentary to special pages. News stories now contained not just one point of view, but two or more views. Of course, to a certain extent, this took some of the bite out of the partisanship. But, at the same time, it improved the accuracy of the news accounts and, more importantly, brought the story to a broader range of people. Now people who were members of different parties could read the same publication and get the views of not only the leaders of their parties but also the opposition. Paradoxically, then, the ethic of objectivity actually broadened the debate on public issues and this is its great strength.

Chapter 17

SEVEN TRENDS FOR MASS MEDIA
IN THE 21ST CENTURY

In the second edition of his book *The Media Monopoly*, former journalist and retired professor Ben H. Bagdikian predicted in 1987 that "if mergers and acquisitions by large corporations continue at the present rate, one massive firm will be in virtual control of all major media by the 1990s." He added that, "Given the complexities of social and economic trends, that is not inevitable." In the fifth edition of the book, published in 1997, Bagdikian qualified that observation a bit more, changing the last clause from "that is not inevitable" to "it is unlikely to result in one owner."[1] Good thing, because the century ended eight years ago and the U.S. media industry is still a long way off from one single owner.

Although ownership in many media segments has become more concentrated, Bagdikian's prediction underscores how risky the crystal ball business can be — and he only had to project a decade into the future. By training, most scholars are cautious and avoid making predictions because they are afraid a mistake will haunt them. Certainly it would be foolhardy to try to predict what will happen in the years to come to any of the major global media corporations. Although most organizations and people resist change, no one can say for certain what will happen to specific media organizations.

However, the inability to make sound predictions about specific organizations doesn't mean that social science research cannot provide some insights into trends that will affect mass media industries and mass communication processes in general. I believe it can, and in this chapter I share with you my vision of media in the 21st century. Of course, those trends assume that nuclear war, environmental degradation or a natural disaster won't destroy our world. They also assume that the world will continue to become more

---

[1]Bagdikian's quote is from Ben H. Bagdikian, *The Media Monopoly*, 2nd ed. (Boston: Beacon Press, 1987), p. 3. The quote from the fifth edition is also on page 3.

Gypsies fortune-telling in 1552

structurally (or socially) differentiated — a topic I have touched on earlier in this book but one which now needs further elaboration.[2]

TREND #1 — STRUCTURAL DIFFERENTIATION

One of the most visible and important changes taking place in most societies today — and this trend is likely to continue in the 21st century — is increasing structural (or social) differentiation.[3] In other words, the number and variety of groups and organizations in societies around the world are increasing, and many organizations are themselves becoming more structurally complex (i.e., the number of departments, units and/or specialized roles are increasing).

---

[2]This chapter was extracted from a book I wrote titled, *Global Media: Menace or Messiah?* (Cresskill, NJ: Hampton Press, 1999). It has been updated here.

[3]An extensive discussion of and additional references about structural differentiation and structural pluralism are contained in Chapters 3-6 in David Pearce Demers, *The Menace of the Corporate Newspaper: Fact or Fiction?* (Ames: Iowa State University Press, 1996).

Another term often used interchangeably with differentiation is the division of labor. It is important to point out, however, that structural differentiation involves growth not only in the economic sector (businesses) but also in most aspects of social (nonbusiness) life. Thus, the number of service, recreational, philanthropic and nonprofit groups also is increasing and diversifying.

Structural differentiation has important consequences for media systems. As social systems or societies become more differentiated, needs for information and knowledge also increase. This, in turn, helps promote growth in the number and variety of media. In fact, historically, the emergence and growth of all forms of mass media, including global media, are directly related to the growing demands for information brought on by urbanization and industrialization, which are two visible indicators of structural differentiation.

Urbanization increases the need for information because it requires collective cooperation to deal with a broad number of social needs and problems, including food distribution, shelter, crime, poverty, waste disposal, public health, pollution and land control. Political elites — who have most of the power for dealing with such problems — depend heavily upon the mass media for information to help them make policy decisions. They also depend upon news reports to help generate support from other elites and the public for the decisions they make. Media coverage helps legitimize such actions, while at the same time conveying the notion that the citizenry in general plays a major role in the decision-making process (even if it doesn't). Urban residents also rely more heavily on newspapers and other mass media than residents of rural or undifferentiated societies, because they depend more heavily upon other individuals and organizations for everyday needs (food, clothing, shelter and public services, such as water and police protection).

Industrialization under capitalism also requires that people work together, but now the purpose is to produce products and services for sale in a market that ultimately earns a profit for the business firms. Manufacturers need access to large, heterogeneous markets, and one efficient method for reaching such markets is through advertising. The dramatic growth of the newspaper in the 19th century is directly related to the growth of advertising in the private sector, with the penny press emerging in the 1830s as the first mass media to offer access to mass markets. News about markets, politics and natural disasters also is crucial for business. Business managers must constantly monitor their economic and political environments to adapt to changing conditions and to lobby for change when necessary.

Increasing urbanization and industrialization, growth in population and the world economy, and expansion of technology also will promote increasing specialization in the business world. Many businesses will become more structurally complex, offering more differentiated products and services. This means creating and marketing goods and services that target specialized markets, consumers and audiences. Market segmentation, target marketing and niche marketing will continue to be the buzzwords of the business world. Professional organizations also will continue to grow and specialize in response to an increasingly differentiated and segmented workforce. It means the "professionalization of everyone," as one sociologist once remarked.[4]

But the economy isn't the only area that is becoming more structurally differentiated. Most aspects of social life are differentiating as well. This includes governmental agencies and institutions around the world, which will be offering more and more services to more and more people. School systems, especially colleges and universities, will be offering more and more programs in specialized areas. Distance learning via the Internet will become much more common. But even public schools for precollege youth and children will offer an increasing diversity of courses and curricula. People also will have a greater choice of recreational and leisure activities or services (e.g., sports, hobbies, travel, clubs). And, despite a continuing trend toward secularism around the world, many new religious groups will emerge. Scientific rationality will not bring an end to beliefs in the supernatural. In fact, religious, mystic or cult groups will flourish. And many of these religious groups will be highly critical of materialism, capitalism and science.

As alluded to in Chapter 13, professors in the social sciences and the humanities and journalists also will become more and more critical of capitalism, Western ideas and the notion of scientific progress. Many will continue to argue that differentiation is creating a fragmented society, one in which social order is breaking down. Although most societies are clearly more differentiated now than in the past and the social sciences have not been very successful in finding solutions to many social problems, such as crime and drug abuse, there is little evidence to suggest that most societies are breaking apart or that most people's faith in science is waning. Advances in the natural sciences and technology will continue to make daily life easier and advances in the medical sciences will continue to extend the lifespans of most people around the world. In fact, most societies or nations will be more stable than at any time in history, even though there will be a greater number of groups pursuing fewer resources than ever before.

---

[4]Harold L. Wilensky, "The Professionalization of Everyone?" *American Journal of Sociology*, 70:137-58 (1964). Wilensky actually argued that most groups would not achieve full professional status, but they would borrow from professional and bureaucratic models.

But an important question remains: If many societies are differentiating and the diversity of ideas is increasing, then what is holding them together? Part of the "glue" comes from the division of labor, which generates needs for information and knowledge and increases interdependence between people.

Division of Labor and Needs for Information

To see how the division of labor contributes to social order, let's compare life in small organizations or in small, relatively undifferentiated societies or groups to that in large organizations or societies. In small organizations or societies, nearly all of the activities crucial for the existence of these groups can be accomplished through interpersonal communication. The social and economic division of labor is limited. Group solidarity and homogeneity in shared sentiments and values tend to be high. Social conflict is minimal, and competition between social actors for scarce resources is limited.

However, as a group or social system grows, competition for scarce resources and social conflict typically increase. This often threatens the stability and existence of these groups. Historically, for example, when a society grew beyond the resources in its environment, its leaders often sought more territory or the society broke up into smaller groups that moved into new territories. Civil war or colonization (exploitation of another society) also solved the problem, even though many people suffered. However, the division of labor is another solution to the problem of scarce resources, because it usually leads to increased efficiency and productivity. As Adam Smith pointed out, when tasks are divided into discrete steps, an organization can produce a lot more goods and services at a fraction of the time and cost.

The historical trend toward the division of labor is certainly not automatic or unilinear. Many cultures, even today, resist such trends. The division of labor also requires greater cooperation among the specialized units and roles to accomplish a goal. As groups and organizations grow and become more structurally differentiated, interpersonal communication as the sole basis for social organization becomes inadequate. The primary reason is that it is inefficient. In large organizations, for instance, it is impossible for even one individual to communicate personally with all others on a regular basis.

More generally, as the number of social actors in a group or organization increases, the amount of interpersonal contact between any single social actor and all others declines. But even if interpersonal communication on a grand scale were possible, it could not, by itself, deal with the problems of coordination and control that accompany increases in the division of the labor and role specialization. For the division of labor to expand, various tasks, functions and jobs generally must be routinized, formalized and standardized.

As a rule, these three elements become more crucial as the organization grows in size. But, in any case, to accomplish these tasks efficiently, organizations and social systems usually need to develop formalized sources and media of communication.

The types of sources and media employed will vary depending upon the level of analysis. For example, within organizations, such sources and media include, but are not limited to, the development of formalized goals and policy statements, written rules and procedures, job descriptions, interdepartmental memos and letters, bulletin boards, newsletters and e-mail. Within industry segments, specialized media, such as magazines and newsletters, emerge to help organizations cope with management problems and changes in the industry. And within communities or social systems as a whole (e.g., nations), mass media, including newspapers, television and radio, provide information about system-wide problems and issues that cut across organizational boundaries and groups. Such media are also important for connecting consumers to producers via advertising.

Today, the growth of large-scale global media and the Internet is driven primarily in response to the growth of worldwide markets and the need for information that integrates the structurally diverse businesses and organizations. Although the types of media and content may vary considerably within and between the three levels mentioned above, in all cases they perform at least one similar function: They link social actors to one another, reducing social distance and enabling them to accomplish their goals more effectively and efficiently.

Thus, in complex societies, people and groups increasingly depend upon each other and the media to achieve their goals. Specialization breeds dependence. And dependence generally contributes to social order and integration. This principle is captured in the popular phrase, "You scratch my back, and I'll scratch yours." The city dweller depends on the farmer for food; the farmer depends on city dwellers to purchase his/her products. The university depends on students for tuition income; the student depends on the university for learning; the business community depends on universities to train future workers; and so on. This interdependence does not guarantee harmony and cooperation, but it can create structural conditions that generally promote social integration.

Paradoxically, although differentiation often produces a much greater diversity of perspectives and ideas, there is also much greater tolerance of others. Large, complex cities, for example, are often safe havens for alternative lifestyles and perspectives. Sit on a street corner in any major city in the world and you'll see what I mean. Large complex systems also can tolerate more social conflict because they have more structural mechanisms for dealing with such conflict (e.g., court systems, moderators, labor boards, administrative judges, public hearings).

Because there is a greater diversity of perspectives in pluralistic systems, shared values also tend to become more general. But agreement on all values is not necessary for people to accomplish their individual goals. And people around the world will continue to share some common values, such as the sanctity of human life, human rights, love, friendship and honesty.

Global Capitalism and the Nation-State

As we travel through the 21st century, more and more countries will embrace a capitalist or a free-market model. Planned economies, such as those under communist states, are difficult to maintain. The problem is that they are unable to efficiently produce and distribute goods and services. The market is much more efficient, even if it continues to be highly inequitable. Huge income inequities between nations and groups continue, but market-driven economics continue to raise the absolute standard of living for most people around the world. This helps to cool down disaffected groups.

Although capitalism appears to have triumphed at a global level, this doesn't mean the economy operates on truly free-market principles or that there is no criticism of capitalism. More appropriately, the world economy has elements of socialism and capitalism. Capitalism cannot solve many of the world's problems, such as poverty, crime and poor health care. So the state (governments) must fill in. Social welfare will continue to consume larger portions of the economic pie.

As postindustrial theorists have predicted, the trend toward a service and information-based economy will continue. But Karl Marx's ghost will continue to haunt Wall Street via the transnational corporation. Although neo-Marxists interpret this as a tightening of the capitalist noose, John Kenneth Galbraith points out that oligopolies reduce risk and enable large companies to pour more resources into research and development. Also, because companies are controlled by managers rather than the stockholders, they place more emphasis on nonprofit goals, such as organizational growth and product or service quality. They can do this partly because they have market power and don't have to worry as much about making a profit. From time to time, governments will step in and enforce antitrust laws.

The nation-state as a geopolitical unit will not disappear any time soon, despite the recent trends in the European Union and many predictions to the contrary. Government bureaucrats and political elites resist change, and increasing concern for multiculturalism and cultural sovereignty will temper moves to do away with the state. However, there is little question that over time economic globalization will siphon off some of the power of the nation-state. The United Nations or some entity like it will increase in power and influence. This is especially true as the world consumes its resources and pollutes the environment. In fact, a threat to the world's environment may very well prove to be more instrumental in global integration than economic interdependence.

In sum, the most significant trend affecting global media and mass communication now and in the future is structural differentiation. Structural differentiation helps explain a number of changes in media industries, including increasing competition and loss of readership and audiences for generalized media (e.g., daily newspapers and broadcast television). Structural differentiation also enables scholars to make more specific predictions about the mass media industries, a topic to which we now turn.

TREND #2 — MEDIA GROWTH AND DIFFERENTIATION

Over the next couple of decades and probably longer, there is little question that the number and size of global media organizations will continue to increase. This growth is partly a function of increasing globalization of other nonmedia companies, which are looking for efficient ways to advertise their products around the world. Global media will deliver consumers to them.

Some scholars have argued that the amount of dollars spent on advertising will decrease as ownership in many industries becomes more concentrated. However, there is no evidence to suggest that advertising revenues in general are declining — in fact, they are increasing — nor is there evidence to suggest that the number of new businesses or the number of units within existing businesses will decline. In fact, most corporations, including global media, will tend to become more structurally differentiated over time. Global media companies, in particular, will offer a multitude of news, information and entertainment services to billions of people around the world. China and Asia will offer the biggest growth potential.

But this growth will not be limited to the big players. The Internet and the technologies that follow for linking people into cyberspace also will create new business opportunities in information services and other areas. This will increase pressures for decentralization of economic power in many industries. With the Internet, small companies and sole proprietors can offer highly specialized information services that larger companies will shun.

Although no one can predict what will happen to global media corporations like Time Warner and Disney, it is a safe bet that many more mergers and acquisitions will take place in the years to come. Economies of scale will be a driving force. New markets and growth in the world's population also will stimulate growth in the size of media organizations. And to reduce risk, global media increasingly will engage in more joint ventures. In some cases, this will diminish competition, but competition in the world and within most countries will continue to increase.

Although media critics and social scientists will continue to raise concerns about concentration and centralization of power in the media industry, few efforts to regulate media industries will be successful. That's because media proponents can easily fight off such efforts by raising concerns about governmental control over media systems. But even more important, proponents of global media will point out that the marketplace now has many new media organizations and alternative sources of information, news and entertainment programming that enhance competition. They will be right.

As global media organizations grow and expand, the number and variety of information and entertainment services, especially teleservices (television or online video), they offer will continue to grow and become more specialized. There will be channels for every professional and recreational interest imaginable. Not all of these services will be successful. And, despite fears of increasing social fragmentation, some media services and programs will appeal to large segments of the world population (e.g., business and political news). But the trend definitely will be toward identifying groups and markets with specialized needs for information and entertainment programming. Market segmentation and target marketing will continue to be the key to success for most media organizations.

TREND #3 — BIGGER MEDIA BUT PROPORTIONATELY LESS POWERFUL

Although global media corporations will grow and reach more people, paradoxically their ability to control the information and entertainment marketplaces will decline. In metaphorical terms, the pie and its slices are getting larger, but each slice is proportionately smaller than the slice in the previous pie (e.g., the previous point in time). In comparative terms, no single company or program will be able to dominate the global market to the degree that the state-run or private television broadcast networks did in Western countries during the 1950s and 1960s. As British scholar Jeremy Tunstall points out in compelling detail (see Chapter 14), there will be too many choices. Consumers and audiences will have access to thousands of new information and entertainment services, many of which will emerge in the industrializing nations.

To be sure, global media news organizations like CNN will continue to reach hundreds of millions and probably billions of people, and their audiences will expand. But needs for information will continue to become more specialized, and many alternative news channels and outlets will emerge within nations to serve those specialized needs. In fact, the trend toward specialized information and entertainment services will continue to grow exponentially, thanks to the Internet and new technologies. Anyone with a computer terminal can create a news, information or entertainment service — and not necessarily for profit; it may just be for fun or entertainment.

Contrary to the predictions of the neo-Marxists, the Internet and the World Wide Web (or whatever we call those technologies in the future) will continue to help decentralize control over information. One current example comes from the music world, where artists are now bypassing the recording companies and marketing their music directly to consumers, who can directly download digitally recorded songs. YouTube.com also is serving as an outlet for independent filmmakers and no doubt copycat companies will spring up offering content that competes with the major Hollywood studios. And a great deal of evidence is piling up showing that the news media are losing some of their mediating power to the Internet, which enables individuals to circumvent the media in the search for news, information and knowledge. Some of the mass media's power also will be checked by bloggers, who, serving as an self-anointed Fifth Estate, will continue to watch over abuse of power in the media themselves.

Of course, large-scale media companies will continue to have a competitive advantage, even in many specialized areas, because they have the capital and resources to produce the kinds of products and services that meet the needs of an increasingly globalized and market-driven world economy. Global media corporations will continue to rake in the lion's share of revenues. However, specialized media services will continue to grow and expand because they will provide services that cannot be easily or profitably offered by global media organizations. Larger companies prefer large, undifferentiated audiences that offer the highest level of profit. But convergence of technologies will make it more difficult for them to control the market.

TREND #4 — CONVERGENCE OF TECHNOLOGIES

For the near future, mass media will continue to deliver their services directly to consumers in a variety of ways — through cables, satellites, over the air and telephone lines. However, as technology advances, the trend will be toward convergence on the Internet (and its "offspring"), which offers video, audio and print media services all in one package.

This tendency toward convergence will blur the boundaries between traditional print and electronic media, especially news media, even further. Although traditional forms of media, such as printed newspapers and magazines, will continue to exist, the online versions will be less expensive to produce and distribute and will offer multimedia formats (e.g., film clips, live reports) — something the printed copy cannot do. News media companies that currently own both print and electronic news services are best positioned to adapt to changes in technology in the 21st century.

Convergence on the Internet also will increase competition. Conventional forms of delivery (cable TV, over the air television, radio, print news media) won't die out immediately. But the media delivery market will become much more diversified, and growth in the traditional forms of delivery eventually will slow or decline, especially in those cases where an electronic version saves the consumer money. The newspaper is particularly vulnerable over the long run, because printing and delivering a hard copy can consume more than 25 percent of the total expenditures. Convergence also will decentralize control even more over information and ideas.

Although convergence of technology on the Internet will blur the lines between print and electronic media, it is important to point out that increasing access to information on the Internet will not kill off the news-gathering business. News media organizations will continue to have a privileged status in Western countries because of the ethic of (relative) objectivity. In other words, traditional news media organizations offer a more objective account of the world relative to the news sources they cover. Moreover, despite all of the criticism of news media, polls show that more than two-thirds of the public trust the reports they get in the news media, and the public will continue to depend very heavily on news media for news and information.

TREND #5 — INCREASING DIVERSITY OF IDEAS

Critics of corporate and global media organizations have made many predictions and claims that growth in size of media organizations is leading to less diversity and greater homogeneity in the news, information and entertainment programming people consume. Although case studies of certain media organizations and media industries (e.g., newspaper industry) may support such claims, when national or global media systems are examined, their predictions do not hold up very well. The trend clearly has been toward an increase in the number and variety of media outlets, as well as an increase in the diversity of content and programming they produce.

The case for increasing diversity is presented in Chapter 14. Let me just add here that the causes of this increase are largely a function of structural differentiation. Interestingly, as global media grow, so will the criticism of them. In fact, the number of critical books, articles, documentaries and web sites will explode over the next couple of decades. Much of this criticism will be based on isolated events or anecdotes, which are true. Global media are no angels. They are profit-seeking corporations that sometimes make decisions that are self-serving and harmful to disadvantaged groups and alternative ideas.

However, as Chapter 14 tried to show, much of this anecdotal evidence is not representative of the bigger picture. Probability surveys and historical research show that corporate media do publish content that is more critical of traditional value systems and dominant institutions, and news sources perceive those media as being more critical of them. Ironically, though, probability research is unlikely to have much impact on critical scholars. As philosopher of science Thomas S. Kuhn pointed out, scientific paradigms are difficult to change.[5] This is especially true in the social sciences, where there is continued disagreement even about basic issues of logic and research. Nevertheless, the appeal of increasing structural differentiation is that people have greater access to more perspectives, ideas and theories than ever before. This diversity, I believe, can only promote better debate and research.

TREND #6 — SPREAD OF WESTERN VALUES

Because global media are creations of Western political and economic systems and need profits to survive, global media will continue to produce news content and entertainment programming that generally promote Western values, such as responsible capitalism, racial and gender equality, representative democracy, a diversity of ideas, religious tolerance and — yes — materialism and consumerism. This doesn't mean these values are automatically or uniformly adopted by non-Western peoples. As noted in Chapter 14, local cultures often interpret Western media messages in ways different from the culture that produced them.

However, despite exceptions to the rule and variances within cultures, there is little question that Western values are spreading and will continue to threaten traditional cultures and ways of doing things. Even highly isolated tribal cultures (e.g., Amazon basin) will find it increasingly difficult to insulate themselves from Western materialism and popular culture. And the comforts and conveniences of modern capitalism, once tasted, are rarely given up (just

---

[5]Thomas S. Kuhn, *The Structure of Scientific Revolutions,* 3rd ed. (Chicago: The University of Chicago Press, 1996).

ask the neo-Marxist scholars, who themselves draw down comfortable salaries at major universities around the world).

But traditional media effects models have not done a good job explaining how Western values are transmitted and adopted. Those models hypothesize that foreigners who consume greater amounts of Western media content are more likely to adopt the values embedded in those messages. To be sure, empirical research provides some support for this proposition, and it would be illogical to argue that repeated exposure to such messages over long periods never has any effects. But it is erroneous to assume that cognitive changes of this sort play the key role in spreading Western values, or that most indigenous citizens need to adopt such values as a prerequisite for social change. In most social systems at most times in history, most people (ordinary citizens) have little power to change things. This is true even in today's so-called "representative democracies." Most power resides with political and economic elites, who make most of the decisions that affect most people. So, although changing the opinions of the typical citizen may help promote change, it is not a necessary condition. Changing the values of elites is much more important.

Historically, perhaps the best example of this is Peter the Great — the Russian Czar who associated with Westerners at an early age and later borrowed many Western technologies and practices to modernize the Russian government and military. Similarly, today the role of Peter is played by young foreign students who are educated at Western universities. Partly through personal experience and partly through exposure to mass media in the host countries, many acquire a "Western view," or at least an understanding of it. It is important to point out again that these experiences and exposure to Western mass media do not lead to wholesale adoption of Western values. Like Peter the Great, foreign visitors like some of the things they see in the West and dislike others. They do not accept everything at face value, but when they return to their own countries, they share many of these Western ideas and practices with others and sometimes they adopt them (if there are no structural barriers to doing this, as is often the case in communist economic systems). But, taken as a whole, a Western education tends to promote better understanding and appreciation for the Western view — an observation also supported by the fact that many foreigners educated in the West often stay and get jobs in Western countries.

This "elite cognitive model" does a much better job at explaining how Western values are disseminated around the world. However, the impact of this social psychological theory should not be overestimated. Historically, in fact, one might argue that coercion has spread Western values much more thoroughly than indigenous acceptance. In modern times, colonialism was the economic tool for doing this. Great Britain, France, Spain and the United States, among other countries, colonized (and often brutalized) many indigenous peoples around the world. Yet, despite much resistence to the colonizers, when the colonizers pulled out their influence did not end there. Rather, many elements of Western culture and values were embedded in those countries' legal, social and economic systems. Most of the empires are now gone, but the structural ties and influence of the Western countries are still there, and the content of global media continues to help maintain and support those structures.

A good example of this was the 1997 Asian economic crisis. Western economists placed most of the blame for the crisis squarely on the Asian countries and their allegedly anti-free-market practices (i.e., high protective tariffs, vertical integration of industries, nepotistic business practices, bribery, lack of competition). But as a condition for helping to bail out those Asian countries, the International Monetary Fund and Western countries did not ask elites or ordinary citizens to change their personal values about capitalism. Rather, the IMF and Western countries simply required those countries to change some aspects of the structure of their economic and political systems. In essence, the West was saying: "Implement our market reforms, or we won't give you economic aid."

Thus, the imposition of Western culture came not through changes in psychology but through (imposed) changes in the social structure, and global media like CNN helped play a supporting role. Their news reports relied heavily on Western economic and political elite sources. Acting as a guard dog for Western values, the news reports helped reinforce and legitimate the Western diagnosis of the illness as well as the prescription for a cure. Although many of the Asian countries continue to resist taking the medicine (i.e., they have been slow to implement reforms), the long-term prognosis for such resistance is not good in a global competitive world. In short, the spread of Western values, especially capitalism, may be structurally imposed, and countries that fail to adopt such practices may find themselves alienated politically and economically (e.g., North Korea).

The argument that Western values are structurally imposed rather than culturally adopted can be seen as an extension of the work of three British sociologists who analyzed the Marxian claim that a capitalist ideology explains the stability and permanence of capitalism. Nicholas Abercrombie, Stephen Hill and Bryan S. Turner studied the subordinate and dominant classes in feudalism, early capitalism and late capitalism and concluded that in all three periods those classes had very different belief systems.[6] The ruling classes

---

[6]Nicholas Abercrombie, Stephen Hill and Bryan S. Turner, *The Dominant Ideology*

subscribed to the ideas that supported the prevailing economic and political institutions, but, contrary to the Marxian model, the subordinate classes did not.

Abercrombie, Hill and Turner argue that capitalism persists not because subordinate classes tacitly accept the dominant ideology, but because they are controlled by the "dull compulsion" of economic relationships, the integrative effects of the division of labor and the coercive nature of law and politics. Although Abercrombie, Hill and Turner reject the idea that ideology incorporates the lower classes, they argue that ideology does have significant effects on the dominant class. "What has been important for the stability of capitalism is the coherence of the dominant class itself, and ideology has played a major role in securing this," Hill writes.[7]

But the impact of structural constraints and the extent to which global media influence traditional cultures also should not be overstated. Western culture and ideas are never fully incorporated. Traditional cultures do not easily pass into history. More accurately, they become overlaid with another sheet of structural and value complexity. The paradox of Western culture also is that many alternative groups and unorthodox cultures are able to survive and thrive in structurally differentiated societies. As mentioned earlier in the book, part of the reason is increased tolerance and sometimes acceptance for such groups. Representative democracies also place a high value on the diversity of ideas, which itself will help protect certain aspects of traditional culture and life.

Of course, the spread of Western ideas, however slow and incomplete, will not necessarily be perceived as harmful even by ordinary citizens in Western or indigenous cultures. In fact, for those who value responsible capitalism, racial and gender equality, representative democracy, a diversity of ideas and religious tolerance, global media will be more liberating than disabling. In contrast, for those who dislike commercialism, materialism, consumerism and commodification, global media will be despised. But in either case, there is little doubt that over the long term Western values and ways of doing things will threaten traditional cultures, as the history of modernization has shown.

Although the content of global media may help liberate some people and integrate many areas of the world, this doesn't mean global media content will automatically lead to less social conflict. In fact, global media have the potential

---

Thesis (London: Allen & Unwin, 1980).

[7]Stephen Hill, "The Dominant Ideology Thesis after a Decade, pp. 1-37 in Nicholas Abercrombie, Stephen Hill and Bryan S. Turner (eds.), *Dominant Ideologies* (London: Unwin Hyman, 1990), p. 2.

to increase conflict, I believe, between some Western and Muslim cultures. Predictions are difficult here, to be sure. It is safe to say that most Muslim countries will continue to limit imports of Western media products and services. But time probably is not on their side. Muslim media systems are, at this point, unable to compete on a global level, and some forms of technology (satellite transmission, cellular phones, fax machines) are making it more difficult for governments to control information within their borders.

Perhaps even more important is the economic dependence (i.e., oil revenues) that many Muslim countries have on the Western world. That dependence is likely to contain some of the conflict between cultures for the near future, at least. But should oil supplies dry up or Western demand for Middle East oil drop substantially, then Western control over global information may do little to ease the conflict. At this point, the safest prediction is that the ideas and values promoted in global media, as they permeate other cultures, will be altered to fit the needs of the host culture. Again, this should not be interpreted as a case of full-fledged hegemony, but rather as another level of complexity.

In short, the spread of Western values is facilitated by both ideology and social structure. In this respect, I am turning both the critical/cultural theorists and the traditional media effects scholars "on their heads."

TREND #7 — INCREASING KNOWLEDGE GAPS

One likely consequence of the growth of global media systems will be increasing gaps in knowledge between nations and between individuals within nations. For critics and others who value democracy and seek to reduce disparities in knowledge between peoples, this trend can be interpreted as having adverse consequences for developing countries.

The knowledge-gap hypothesis was proposed in 1970 by University of Minnesota media sociologists Phillip J. Tichenor, George A. Donohue and Clarice N. Olien, who argued that

> As the infusion of mass media information into a social system increases, segments of the population with higher socioeconomic status tend to acquire this information at a faster rate than the lower status segments, so that the gap in knowledge between these segments tends to increase rather than decrease.[8]

---

[8]Phillip J. Tichenor, George A. Donohue and Clarice N. Olien, "Mass Media Flow and Differential Growth in Knowledge," *Public Opinion Quarterly, 34*:159-170 (1970).

This hypothesis can be applied to individuals, groups or to nations. From a worldwide perspective, the argument is that the "information rich" countries (e.g., France, Great Britain, Japan, United States) are gaining more power and influence over the "information poor" countries (e.g., African and Latin American countries). And the logic is straightforward: People high in terms of socioeconomic status (education, income, occupation) have more resources to obtain and understand information.

The "Minnesota Team" tested their theory using longitudinal public opinion data on sending an astronaut to the moon and cigarette smoking. Prior to World War II, for example, most people, regardless of status, didn't believe it was possible to send a spaceship to the moon. However, as technology advanced and media began publishing reports that space travel was possible, the gaps in knowledge between high-status and low-status individuals widened. That's because high-status people were reading more and talking about science more than low-status people. Similarly, as media began publishing more information linking cigarette smoking to cancer, high-status individuals acquired this information at a faster rate than low-status individuals.

Mass communication scholars Cecilie Gaziano, Kasisomayajula Viswanath and John R. Finnegan Jr., who have reviewed the literature on the knowledge-gap hypothesis, generally find support for it.[9] But aside from making information more readily available, there is little agreement on what can be done to reduce gaps. Even then, the problem isn't solved.

Take, for instance, the popular children's television show *Sesame Street*, which originated in the United States and is broadcast in many countries around the world. When first proposed in the 1960s, the goal was to help disadvantaged children living in inner-city areas catch up intellectually to their peers from the more affluent suburbs (e.g., to correct a knowledge gap). By the way, that's one of the reasons the show is filmed on a television set modeled after an urban neighborhood. Studies showed that the program boosted the verbal and math test scores of children from disadvantaged backgrounds. However, the program boosted scores for children from advantaged backgrounds even more. In fact, the knowledge gaps got even bigger. Why? Because parents of high SES children were giving their children more

---

[9]Cecilie Gaziano, "The Knowledge Gap: An Analytical Review of Media Effects," *Communication Research*, 10:447-486 (1983), Cecilie Gaziano, "Forecast 2000: Widening Knowledge Gaps," *Journalism & Mass Communication Quarterly*, 74:237-264 (1997), and Kasisomayajula Viswanath and John R. Finnegan Jr., "The Knowledge Gap Hypothesis: Twenty-Five Years Later," pp. 187-227 in B. R. Burleson (ed.), *Communication Yearbook, Vol. 19* (Thousand Oaks, CA: Sage).

encouragement to watch the program and spending more time with them during the programming.

Because Sesame Street produces greater gaps in knowledge, should the program be discontinued? Similarly, should global news and information programming be halted because it produces knowledge gaps? Many people see this as throwing the baby out with bath water. Limiting information or access to it is clearly not the answer. And developing countries are caught in a bind, as mass communication Professor Chin-Chuan Lee points out:

> For how long can the Third World reject modern communication technologies and their potential benefits? It is undesirable for them, on the one hand, not to enjoy the benefits of technology; continued resistance may widen the gap between them and the richer countries. It is more undesirable, on the other hand, that they have to tolerate a continued or heightened Western media hegemony and the concomitant cultural dependence. How to resolve this paradox while formulating a sound communication policy will undoubtedly be a blend of art and science.[10]

Although there is no easy solution to the knowledge-gap problem, a good starting point, I would argue, is the "new communication strategy" adopted in 1989 by United Nations Educational, Scientific and Cultural Organization. That strategy, adopted by a consensus of its member states, has three major objectives: to encourage the free flow of information at both national and international levels; to promote a wider and more balanced dissemination of information, without any obstacle to freedom of expression; and to strengthen the communication capacities of the developing countries, in particular through the International Programme for the Development of Communication. In 1997, UNESCO Director-General Federico Mayor added that

> There can be no doubt that the future of the new democracies will depend in part on the development and strengthening of free, independent and pluralist media in both the public and private sectors, since the spread of knowledge and values is impossible without freedom of communication. The importance of this principle ... is undeniable: free communication enables ordinary citizens to express themselves and make their voices heard and, as a result, to influence the events that shape their daily lives.[11]

---

[10]Chin-Chuan Lee, *Media Imperialism Reconsidered* (Beverly Hills, CA: Sage, 1980), p. 200.

[11]Federico Mayor, "Preface," pp. 5-6 in *World Communication Report: The Media and the Challenge of the New Technologies* (Paris: UNESCO Publishing, 1997).

A Final Comment

Many scholars are worried about the future of mass media. In fact, many seem to be infected with what I call the "Chicken Little Syndrome" — the sky is always falling. They get a lot of attention, by the way, for trying to find the worst in media systems. And, admittedly, there is a lot to be found. It bothers me, for example, that most journalists are unaware of the extent to which their reports help justify and support political and economic systems that are often unjust and unfair. The same applies to producers of entertainment programming. I wish the journalists and media producers could see how the content they produce socially constructs problems and reality. That awareness still wouldn't guarantee change in the system, because media are structurally dependent on advertisers, sources and consumers.

However, I cannot buy into the argument so often expressed in much of the writings that come from scholars that the mass media are destroying good journalism and democratic principles. Well, the sky has been falling for more than century, and who today would argue that the information environment is less diverse and more repressive than it was when Hearst and Pulitzer battled for domination in New York City. To the contrary, diversity in terms of ideas — especially ideas critical of capitalism and the wealthy — is flourishing, and I believe mainstream media systems are more responsive to the needs and problems of disadvantaged and alternative groups today than ever before. I think a more constructive approach is to increase the search for ways to make media systems even more responsive. I hope this book has made a small contribution toward that goal.

INDEX

N

Q-R

S